BATTLES OVER FREE TRADE

CONTENTS OF THE EDITION

VOLUME 1
General Introduction
By Mark Duckenfield

The Advent of Free Trade, 1776–1846
Edited by Gordon Bannerman and Cheryl Schonhardt-Bailey

VOLUME 2
The Consolidation of Free Trade, 1847–1878
Edited by Gordon Bannerman and Anthony Howe

VOLUME 3
The Challenge of Economic Nationalism, 1879–1939
Edited by Anthony Howe and Mark Duckenfield

VOLUME 4
The Emergence of Multilateral Trade, 1940–2006
Edited by Mark Duckenfield

Index

BATTLES OVER FREE TRADE

General Editor: Mark Duckenfield

Volume 4
The Emergence of Multilateral Trade, 1940–2006

EDITED BY
Mark Duckenfield

LONDON AND NEW YORK

First published 2008 by Pickering & Chatto (Publishers) Limited

Published 2016 by Routledge
2 Park Square, Milton Park, Abingdon, Oxfordshire OX14 4RN
711 Third Avenue, New York, NY 10017, USA

First issued in paperback 2015

Routledge is an imprint of the Taylor & Francis Group, an informa business

Copyright © Taylor & Francis 2008
Copyright © Editorial material Mark Duckenfield

All rights reserved, including those of translation into foreign languages. No part of this book may be reprinted or reproduced or utilised in any form or by any electronic, mechanical, or other means, now known or hereafter invented, including photocopying and recording, or in any information storage or retrieval system, without permission in writing from the publishers.

Notice:
Product or corporate names may be trademarks or registered trademarks, and are used only for identification and explanation without intent to infringe.

BRITISH LIBRARY CATALOGUING IN PUBLICATION DATA

Battles over free trade: Anglo-American experiences with international trade, 1776–2006
1. Free trade – History
I. Duckenfield, Mark
382.7'1'09

ISBN-13: 978-1-138-66052-6 (pbk)
ISBN-13: 978-1-1387-5035-7 (hbk)
ISBN-13: 978-1-85196-935-7 (set)

Typeset by Pickering & Chatto (Publishers) Limited

CONTENTS

Introduction	ix
The International Trade Organization	1
'Editorial: Trade Agreements', *Journal of the National Union of Manufacturers* (1946)	5
Letter from National Union of Manufacturers to Sir Stafford Cripps (President of the Board of Trade), 21 October 1946	8
'Chapter V. Retaliation and Other Indirect Consequences', Board of Trade Economic Group Report on Long-Term Problems and Consequences of Failure to Approve ITO, 8 July 1947	10
Confidential Note on a Meeting with the FBI on 20 February (1947)	18
'Confidential Note of a Meeting Held at the Board of Trade on the 25th February 1947, Between the National Union of Manufacturers and the Board of Trade'	23
Jacob Viner, 'Conflicts of Principle in Drafting a Trade Charter', *Foreign Affairs* (1947)	27
Clair Wilcox, 'The London Draft of a Charter for an International Trade Organization', *American Economic Review* (1947)	42
Memorandum on Imperial Preference, Loans from the United States and Tariff Negotiations between the United States and United Kingdom, 14 October 1947	54
E. J. Elliot (Federation of British Industries) to E. A. Cohen (Board of Trade), 1 April 1948	57
R. J. Shackle (Board of Trade) to E. J. Elliot (Federation of British Industries), 8 April 1948	58
'Resolution on the Havana Charter', First Draft, 10 May 1948	59
The European Economic Community	63
Notes for Prime Minister Winston Churchill in Preparation for Meeting with Jean Monnet regarding United Kingdom Association with the European Coal and Steel Community, 25 May 1954	67

Memorandum for Prime Minster Anthony Eden on Meeting of the Ministerial Committee Meeting on Relations with the ECSC, 4 July 1956   69

'Record of Conversation between the Secretary of State [Foreign Secretary Selwyn Lloyd] and the Netherlands Ambassador on July 15, 1960'   71

'Press Conference by President de Gaulle, Paris, 14th January 1963'   74

Remarks, made by President Charles de Gaulle at his Fifteenth Press Conference, 16 May, 1967   78

Sir Con O'Neill (Head of UK Delegation to the European Communities), 'Valedictory Despatch', 3 May 1965   81

'Record of a Meeting Between the Prime Minister [Harold Wilson], and the Foreign Secretary [George Brown] and the Acting Vice-President [Albert Coppé] and Other Members of the High Authority of the European Coal and Steel Community, on 8th March 1967'   88

Memorandum for Non-Cabinet Ministers, 'Ten Reasons Why Britain Should Join the Common Market', December 1970   96

'Record of Conversation between the Chancellor of the Duchy of Lancaster [Sir Geoffrey Rippon] and the Portuguese Foreign Minister [Dr Rui Patricio]', 8 March 1972   98

'Cassis' Decision, Judgement of the European Court of Justice, 20 February 1979   104

German Beer Purity Law Decision, Judgement of the European Court of Justice, 12 March 1987   110

The Association of South East Asian Nations   125

Statement of S. Rajaratnam (Minister for Foreign Affairs of Singapore) at the ASEAN Conference, 8 August 1967   129

Statement of Adam Malik (Minister of Foreign Affairs of Indonesia) at the ASEAN Conference, 8 August 1967   132

Priority Telegram from UK Embassy in Bangkok regarding Declaration Establishing the ASEAN, 8 August 1967   134

Restricted Telegram from UK Embassy in Moscow regarding Soviet Response to South-East Asian Regional Cooperation, 14 August 1967   136

Confidential Summary on the Association of South-East Asian Nations from Giles Bullard (British Embassy in Bangkok) to George Brown (Foreign Secretary), 15 August 1967   138

Telegram from British Embassy in Manila on the Philippines and ASEAN, 30 October 1967   142

Report of British Embassy in Bangkok on EEC Visit to Thailand, 13 September 1973   143

Memorandum on EEC/ASEAN Relations, 2 October 1975   147
'Address by Mr Lee Kwan Yew, Prime Minister of Singapore, at the Opening Session of the ASEAN Summit, Bali, on 23 February 1976'   149
'Treaty of Amity and Cooperation in Southeast Asia', 24 February 1976   152
Confidential Memorandum, 'ASEAN Summit: A Thai View', 2 March 1976   157
Cooperation Agreement between the EEC and ASEAN, 7 March 1980   159
Background Brief, 'ASEAN's Changing Priorities', June 1992   165

The North American Free Trade Agreement   169
    The Second Clinton-Bush-Perot Presidential Debate, 15 October 1992   173
    The Third Clinton-Bush-Perot Presidential Debate, 19 October 1992   177
    House of Commons Debates, Official Record (Canada) (1993)   187
    'NAFTA Debate: Gore vs. Perot', on Larry King Show, , 9 November 1993   203
    'Canada Prepared if NAFTA Fails; Movement Afoot to Arrange Bilateral Deal with Mexico', *Globe and Mail* (Toronto), 13 November 1993   244
    'NAFTA Backers Must Speak Now', *Crain's Detroit Business*, 15 November 1993   246
    'The National Interest: House Members Have Clear Obligation to Free Trade', *Houston Chronicle*, 16 November 1993   247
    Dennis Wharton, 'H'wood: Muy Bueno, eh? Valenti Sees Doors Opening as House Passes NAFTA Treaty', *Daily Variety*, 18 November 1993   248
    'NAFTA All Clear in Mexico', *Record* (Canada), 23 November 1993   250
    Jonathan Ferguson, 'NAFTA: Canada's Concerns', *Toronto Star*, 30 November 1993   252
    'U.A.W. Wants Trade Payoff in Jobs', *New York Times*, 1 January 1994   256

The World Trade Organization   259
    Cordell Hull, Statement on Tariffs and an International Tariff Congress, *Congressional Record*, 8 July 1916   263
    Senate Debate on the World Trade Organization (Uruguay Round Agreements Act), *Congressional Record*, 30 November 1994   267
    Scott Sunde, 'Chaos Closes Downtown', *Seattle Post-Intelligencer*, 1 December 1999   282
    'Remarks by the President to Farmers, Students from the Seattle-Tacoma Area Who Study Trade, and Area Officials', Seattle, 1 December 1999   286

Kerry Murakami, 'Geneva Sounded WTO Warning That Went Unheeded in Seattle', *Seattle Post-Intelligencer*, 10 March 2000   293

Doha Ministerial Declaration, 14 November 2001   296

Statement by President George W. Bush Announcing Temporary Safeguards for the US Steel Industry, 5 March 2002   310

Gordon Brown, UK Statement to the International Monetary and Financial Committee, 17 September 2006   312

Copyrights and Permissions   319

Index   323

INTRODUCTION

The most striking feature of the post-war international system was the wide-scale creation of influential multilateral institutions for the management of political and economic disputes. After the Second World War, the organization of the world trading system, and, indeed, the world economy more generally, moved decisively from a system of bilateral arrangements and exclusive economic blocs to one centred on multilateral institutions and inclusive regional organizations. In the immediate aftermath of the Second World War, the United States took the opportunity of its position of international strength to lead the effort to construct liberal economic institutions for the management of the world economy. A unique alignment of ideas and interests facilitated the launching of this project, although the major institution that was proposed for mediating international trade negotiations and disputes, the International Trade Organization (ITO), foundered on the rocks of domestic opposition in the United States Congress. The 'temporary' General Agreement on Tariffs and Trade (GATT) provided the framework for international trade negotiations for the next fifty years, until it was replaced by the World Trade Organization (WTO) in 1995.

Ideas

Classical economic solutions to economic problems were widely discredited by the Great Depression and the subsequent collapse in world commerce. The war also discredited nationalism, militarism and autarkic solutions to economic problems. Ideas of economic cooperation continued, but not in the exclusive, vindictive form that characterized the embryonic Allied economic cartel discussed at the 1916 Allied Economic Conference in Paris or the German-dominated ideas of Friedrich Naumann's *Mitteleuropa* and Walter Funk's 'New Economic Order'. Simultaneously, the wartime destruction created a demand for economic rebuilding and coordination, especially in Western Europe. Many of the mechanisms for economic planning developed during the Second World War were redirected towards rebuilding devastated economies. On the Continent, the system of controls imposed by the Germans in the interests of their wartime economy was turned to the objectives of economic reconstruction. American

Marshall Plan aid, with its requirement of cooperative rebuilding plans and economic planning institutions, also facilitated the development of European-level institutions for economic cooperation.[1]

In the years after the war, many countries created systems of Keynesian-style demand management.[2] The extensive state intervention that had characterized wartime economies was perpetuated in the post-war environment, and even extended in the countries where parties of the left came into power. In the United Kingdom, the victory of the Labour Party in the 1945 general election ushered in a period of rapid growth in the welfare state. State intervention in the economy remained a dominant theme, as the nationalization of the Bank of England along with the steel and coal industries suggested. In the realm of international trade, imperial preference remained the dominant – but not unchallenged – policy.

In the United States, many policymakers in the Democratic Administrations of Franklin Roosevelt and Harry Truman were proponents of free trade. Foremost among them was Secretary of State Cordell Hull, who as a Congressman and later Senator from Tennessee had been a fierce opponent of the Smoot-Hawley tariff and an advocate for a multilateral international trading authority as early as 1916.[3] However, the New Dealers had other ideological commitments as well. While they accepted, and promoted, the market economy, they rejected traditional laissez-faire economic policies and 'pure' theories of free trade, placing their reliance on a Keynesian welfare state rather than the unfettered market economy. This predisposition to look at the state's role as economic manager was transposed to the international level in the creation of 'embedded liberalism' in institutions like the International Monetary Fund (IMF) for the management of money, the World Bank for promoting reconstruction and development, and the GATT for international commerce.[4] The post-war Republican Party in the United States, while arguing for the virtues of the free market, domestically remained enamoured with protection as a trade policy for many years after the Second World War. Republican Congressional opposition blocked the ratification of the ITO and Republican representatives and senators frequently targeted the GATT for criticism. The combination of international protection and domestic laissez-faire was always an uncomfortable intellectual alliance within the Republican Party. While the Republicans remained wary of transferring sovereignty to international institutions, they gradually brought their trade policies in line with their domestic economic agenda of low taxes and a rolling back of the welfare state, although Patrick Buchanan a harked back to these traditional Republican policies in his challenge to President George H. W. Bush in the 1992 Republican primaries under the protectionist banner of 'A Call to Economic Arms'.

The Cold War with the Soviet Union provided a geopolitical rationale for increased economic cooperation and the corresponding development of multilateral organizations. The American system of regional military alliances, of which the North Atlantic Treaty Organization was the most prominent, was supplemented by American encouragement for regional economic arrangements in addition to the GATT. Against the backdrop of their ideological and political struggle with the Soviet Union, the United States and its allies sought to develop their own economies and demonstrate capitalist institutions' ability to provide material benefits to their populations. In trade policy, this manifested itself in the American encouragement of cooperative negotiations within a multilateral framework.

American allies also sought cooperation with each other in order to limit their reliance on the United States. Proponents of the European Common Market argued that negotiating a common trade policy in the GATT would strengthen the hand of all European countries in talks with the United States and other countries. The loss of sovereignty that would result from surrendering control over customs negotiations would be more than compensated for by an improvement in the terms of international trade agreements. Small and medium-sized economies, who could either be ignored or pressured by the United States, could combine their political and economic power and reap the gains of their combined and expanded influence.

The linkage between security and trade extended beyond the United States' alliance system, regional institutions and the GATT. On the other side of the Iron Curtain, the Soviet Union organized its military allies into the Warsaw Pact and coordinated their economic activity through the Council for Mutual Economic Assistance (COMECON).[5] The end of the Cold War and the disintegration of the Soviet Union appeared to end the ideological struggle between the capitalist world and the socialist bloc. The abject failure of the Soviet statist model as a political and economic enterprise was contrasted with the high levels of prosperity and democratic rights prevailing in Western Europe and the United States.

Most former Soviet satellites in Eastern Europe implemented programmes of 'shock therapy' to rapidly reduce the role of the state and convert their economies to market-based systems. While the conversion to the market was rapid, integration with Western Europe proceeded at a slower pace for the former Communist societies. While previously neutral, and wealthy, countries such as Austria, Finland and Sweden quickly joined the European Union; the poorer countries to the east had to wait until 2004 – fifteen years after the fall of the Berlin Wall – before they had brought a sufficient range of their domestic economic policies into compliance with European Union standards to become members. In the meantime, twelve of the fifteen members of the European Union had deepened the Single Market programme with the creation of a single currency, the euro, managed by a powerful European Central Bank.

The United States' position as the sole superpower and its economic renaissance in the 1990s contributed to the creation of the so-called Washington Consensus, a series of neo-liberal policy prescriptions for developing economies favouring open markets, stable macroeconomic policies and institutions.[6] Not only East European countries, but many in Latin America and Africa, liberalized their economies, reduced tariffs, cut subsidies and began a process of fiscal retrenchment and consolidation. However, as the 1990s progressed, the initial enthusiasm for the market began to wane and many groups came to see the market more as a threat than an opportunity. Environmental groups saw unrestricted development as a threat to the world's ecological balance. Labour groups saw globalization both as a strategy of exploiting impoverished workers in the developing world and as a means of undermining wages and employment in the developed economies. Many officials in the developing world believed that neo-liberal policies were designed to favour capital-rich countries at their expense; they were also quick to note that even the new WTO continued to tolerate high levels of protection in product areas where developing countries might have an advantage – such as agriculture and textiles. As a result, the intellectual support for the WTO has increasingly come into question.

Interests

The exposure of domestic economies to international market forces has always created winners and losers. Both groups have historically sought to garner political support in their societies for their economic interests – groups that believed rising levels of international trade would benefit them lobbied for openness, groups threatened by import competition mobilized in support of protectionist policies. The post-war environment was no different, although domestic institutions served to alleviate many of the problems of economic adjustment. The creation of extensive welfare states and the pursuit of Keynesian policies allowed countries to pursue relatively liberal external policies with a domestic economic cushion.

The unusually dominant economic position of the United States after the Second World War provided American business and labour with the opportunity to press their competitive advantage in the post-war period. American industries, especially those that utilized mass-production manufacturing, were the most efficient and technologically advanced producers in the world. American financial institutions, multinationals and the trade unions representing their workforces were active supporters of a liberalized trading regime. Not coincidentally, all three groups were key members of the New Deal coalition. Non-tradable businesses and the few American industries that in that period faced international competition were less enthusiastic with the creation of the

IMF and the proposed ITO. These groups tended to support the Republican Party and were instrumental in the successful opposition to the ITO.

British industry in the immediate post-war period continued to cling to the policies of imperial preference that were solidified in Ottawa in 1932. Long-standing trading relationships with the British Empire and Dominions gave them the prospects of revitalized imperial trade. Many in the Empire and the Dominions shared this view and sought to continue the pre-war trading pattern of British manufactured exports being exchanged for raw materials and foodstuffs from the rest of the Empire. However, British dependence on the United States for loans placed the United Kingdom in a vulnerable position. American financial assistance came with strings attached, and the United States was intent on prying apart imperial preference and opening the British Empire up to American exporters. The United States was also able to provide economic inducements to important members of the Commonwealth, particularly Australia and Canada, to reduce their dependence on the British market and provide additional access to the immense American market.

In Europe, the process of rebuilding and American aid provided the dollars Western European countries required to purchase capital equipment and rebuild their devastated economies. Extensive Marshall Plan aid also served multiple purposes. In the first instance, it provided European countries with the loans and credits necessary to purchase goods and materials from the United States that were used to build factories and invest in the reconstruction of the European economy. Second, it provided an external means of stimulating American exports, thus providing jobs to American workers. Third, the American requirement that European participants develop common, cooperative economic policies to avoid redundancy and wasted assistance encouraged regional political cooperation and deeper economic integration.

European economic cooperation and the expansion of the single market provided larger 'domestic' markets for European producers, exposing them to increased competition and providing larger markets to exploit. The heightened competition led to improved efficiency and accelerated adjustment of European producers to new economic realities. While Britain remained outside the Common Market, its producers were relatively sheltered, but limited to the British market. Consequently, throughout the 1960s and early 1970s British industries lagged behind their increasingly efficient competitors on the Continent.

With the decline of the Commonwealth as an attractive market for British products and the rapid growth and economic success of the Common Market, British business came to see advantages in deepening economic linkages with the rest of Europe. Labour unions were less enthusiastic about membership in the European Economic Community (EEC), seeing the increased competition as a threat to jobs in a time of economic uncertainty. As the 1973 oil embargo pushed the British economy into recession and triggered an economic crisis, the Trades Union Congress campaigned against British membership of the EEC during the 1975 referendum campaign.

In East Asia, the military and political hegemony of the United States brought much of the region under American economic influence. The countries of the region – particularly Japan – tended to focus their economic activities on exporting to the American market. This created the opportunity for export-led growth, but also led to a high degree of dependence on American consumers. The success of Asian industrialization began to generate economic tensions with the United States in the 1970s and 1980s as Japanese, Taiwanese and South Korean producers threatened long-standing American producers in industries as diverse as automobiles and electronics.

The erosion of the United States' manufacturing industries in the post-war period accelerated in the 1970s and 1980s as intense competition from Asia took its toll on American producers. Major American industries such as steel and automobiles saw factories closed, workers laid off and market share reduced. Nationally, the number and share of manufacturing workers in the labour force steadily declined until it was under 13 per cent in 2007. As job losses mounted and employment became less secure, the American labour movement abandoned its traditional attachment to free trade and began to actively oppose new trade agreements. Textile firms and their unions were the first to press for protection in the 1970s, but they were soon followed by auto workers and other unions. Despite being supported by a Democratic President, the North American Free Trade Agreement (NAFTA) crystallized the union opposition to trade agreements. However, President Bill Clinton was able to soften the economic consequences of NAFTA for labour with programmes for worker retraining and adjustment assistance for specific industries thought to be especially vulnerable. Clinton's support for both labour and international trade liberalization did not forestall increasingly aggressive labour opposition to trade agreements, including extensive resistance to the ongoing negotiations of the WTO.[7]

However, many American businesses had diversified their production facilities and relied less on their American plants than overseas factories for their profits. Their foreign subsidiaries needed to export back into the United States, so internationally-oriented business had a strong interest in preserving an open trading system. American firms also had extensive investments in branding as well as research and development with the resulting patents and licence agreements. Business support for the WTO extended beyond simply promoting market access to include support for a convention on trade-related intellectual property to protect their trademarks, licences and patents.

Institutions

The reconstruction of the international economic system after the Second World War was designed to restore normal trade relations and provide a framework for cooperative adjustment to changing terms of trade. Policymakers were well aware that the pre-war trading system, relying as it did on bilateral agreements and domestic support for free trade, had proved extremely fragile in times of economic stress. In contrast to the limited and short-lived negotiations and agreements of the interwar period, post-war planners sought to create durable multilateral institutions that would be resilient in the face of an economic slowdown and avoid a repeat of the economic chaos and depression that had characterized the interwar period. The institutions created, such as the IMF, World Bank and GATT, were designed to encourage liberal economic activities, but still allow for numerous exceptions and exemptions from the general principles in times of economic distress or sudden changes in the terms of trade. The GATT and IMF encouraged gradual adjustment to economic shocks and a shared burden between countries under economic pressure. Temporary limits on imports and exports were allowed to countries experiencing current account difficulties or in times of economic dislocation. Limitations on foreign exchange convertibility and procedures for limited devaluations in consultation with other IMF and GATT members were also sanctioned for countries in difficult economic straits.

Domestic institutional developments in the major western democracies proved supportive of the combination of liberal economic policies and economic management proposed for international institutions. The new American welfare state, with its panoply of institutions covering broad swathes of economic activity, had created a strong central government equipped with extensive means for influencing the economy. The institutions of the New Deal were designed to insulate the domestic economy from international market forces as well as the extreme vagaries of the business cycle. The market economy continued to function, but its rougher edges were smoothed over to make for a kinder, gentler economic system.

In the United Kingdom similar, but more extensive, developments were underway. The Labour Party's victory in the 1945 elections made way for the nationalization of the commanding heights of finance and industry and a major expansion in the welfare state. The Bank of England, coal and steel, energy, utilities and railroads were all nationalized under Labour. The National Health Service was created, pensions and unemployment insurance expanded. Government management of the economy became the norm. While the Conservative Party made a limited effort to privatize the steel industry after their return to power in 1951, this went against the tide of prevailing sentiment, and for the most part they endorsed the welfare state and committed themselves to a programme of economic stewardship.[8] This focus on domestic welfare and full employment carried over into Britain's international economic policy where the UK government negotiated features of both the IMF and ITO that allowed members to prioritize the conditions of their domestic economy over international obligations.

Having succeeded in negotiating a degree of autonomy for their domestic economy and just having taken control of many key industries, Britain focused on its domestic conditions and relied upon the British Empire and Commonwealth for overseas markets. Joining either the European Coal and Steel Community or the European Economic Community and pooling sovereignty over economic questions ran counter to the ongoing movement towards concentrating power over the macroeconomy in the hands of British policymakers. Only when the limitations of the Commonwealth as a market became clear and when economic policies were otherwise inadequate for stimulating the desired levels of growth did Britain turn to the EEC.

In the late 1940s and early 1950s, the countries of Western Europe began a process of deeper economic integration and cooperation.[9] The institutions they developed pooled sovereignty over a range of policies, most importantly the creation of a customs union and the setting of common external tariffs. This highly successful experiment in regionalism has proven to be the deepest and most far-reaching series of multilateral institutions in existence.[10] European institutions now cover an extensive range of policy areas from trade to the environment, transport, agriculture and competition policy. The Single Europe Act and the legal concept of mutual recognition removed most visible barriers to trade by the end of 1992.[11] The evolution of European institutions not only promoted free trade within Europe, but also served as an impetus to reduction in trade barriers in the GATT. Concerns about the creation of a 'Fortress Europe' proved unfounded, as qualified-majority-voting rules for European policymaking decision empowered groups and member states favouring liberalization. These decision-making rules enabled pro-liberalization countries to outvote protectionist members in the setting of European Union negotiating strategies.[12] The Maastricht Treaty, signed in 1991, paved the way for the launching of the single currency and the monetary integration of eleven European Union members in 1999. By 2008, the number of European Union members participating in the single currency had grown to fifteen.

The United States had long remained aloof from regional trading arrangements, preferring to allow other countries to utilize them in order to preserve existing preferences with traditional trading partners or develop deeper trading relations within a subset of countries when broader international solutions were not feasible. However, in the late 1980s, the Americans began to see advantages in both unilateral trade sanctions as well as bilateral regional agreements in addition to their preference for multilateral negotiations under the auspices of the GATT. With the Uruguay Round effectively stalled in the mid-1980s, the United States entered into free trade agreements first with Canada (1988) and then Mexico (1994) in NAFTA. While NAFTA has been the centrepiece of the United States' multiple-track trading policy, it has also sought a variety of regional agreements and pushed for the approval and then the expansion of the WTO.[13]

The American decision to pursue unilateral trade action against countries who the Americans deemed to be violating trade rules provided an impetus for many developing countries and Japan to seek a further international codification and adjudication of trade disputes.[14] The creation of the WTO expanded the role of the supranational institution over domestic policies – including not only tariffs and quantitative restrictions, but also including other perceived impediments to trade which have included environmental regulations, labour restrictions and concerns about production methods. The WTO's dispute resolution mechanism is more powerful than was the case under the GATT, but this potential intrusion into the domestic politics of countries has caused consternation among environmentalists, trade unionists and other activists. They see the WTO has an institution that promotes trade liberalization for corporations, rather than one sensitive to workers' rights and the environment. Issues of governance in the modern WTO – and the IMF, World Bank and other international institutions – centre around transparency, access and the influence of powerful groups and countries over the decision-making process. The ongoing Doha Round has done little to resolve these concerns.[15]

Text Selection

Texts included in this volume were selected to highlight changing ideas about how to manage the world trading system, the position and activities of interest groups and the extent of domestic political debates over trade. Government documents including draft copies of treaties, Cabinet minutes and memoranda, briefing notes and judicial opinions are all presented. Public statements by politicians are used to show what appeals to politicians with different opinions about the future course of trade policy made to the public, positions that on occasion might differ from private discussions among policymakers. In the case of internal government papers, the documents demonstrate the different issues and groups that decision-makers were concerned about. For instance, British officials linked concerns about the consequences for imperial preference of the proposed ITO with the question of how supporting the ITO would improve the prospects of a loan from the United States.[16] Government communications with other governments and interest groups also reflect the concerns of officials about the impact of different trade policies on close political partners and key domestic industries.

The treaties and court decisions lay out the legal basis and legal reasoning behind important developments in trade and highlight the increasing legalization of trade issues – especially in the European Union.

Industry sources are also used as a means of revealing the preferences of different business and labour groups towards trade policy. Many times this depended on the various policy options available to business at any point in time. British industry in late 1940s still clung to the belief that economic prosperity could be restored through adherence to imperial preference. These illusions had dissipated by the time that Britain sought entry into the EEC in the 1960s and early 1970s. Likewise, many American industries favoured NAFTA – both before and after Bill Clinton negotiated a series of environmental and labour protocols designed to support the employment prospects of American workers threatened with having their jobs outsourced. Trade unions in the United States were much less supportive of NAFTA, and many remained opponents of international trade agreements, including the WTO.

Articles from journals of opinion such as *Foreign Affairs* and academic journals such as the *American Economic Review* are likewise presented to give an account of the intellectual debates of the day. They reveal the degree to which orthodox prescriptions of free trade could be marginalized both politically and intellectually at the same time that policymakers sought practical means to open foreign markets, reduce domestic tariffs and encourage international cooperation in the years after the end of the Second World War. These articles serve to provide an idea of how concepts of 'embedded liberalism' contributed to the creation of an international network of institutions designed to support and accommodate national economic planning with an international component equally devoted to economic stability.[17]

Media sources are used extensively in all the cases presented. Mass media sources, in particular, are included for the NAFTA and WTO to demonstrate the increased role of television in public debates over trade policy. The selections from two of the 1992 presidential debates provide clear distinctions in the trade policy positions of the three major candidates, but also provide an insight into the level of brevity and superficiality with which modern presidential debates cover major substantive issues. Somewhat contradictory was the subsequent hour-long televized debate on NAFTA between Ross Perot and Vice President Al Gore on 'The Larry King Show'. Not only did the debate focus exclusively and in depth on one specific issue, but it also aroused an extraordinary level of public interest. The debate not only provided the nightly television interview show with its highest ratings in its thirty-year history, but also gave the network, CNN, its highest ratings on a public event to date.

The ability of differences of political opinion over trade policy to inspire such fervent interest extended beyond NAFTA. Opposition to the WTO from trade unionists, environmentalists, students and anti-globalization activists has spilled over into the streets on more than one occasion. However, they received the most public attention at the 1999 WTO ministerial conference in Seattle. The various selections from the local Seattle press presented in this volume show that battles over trade policy are not simply metaphorical, but literal.

Notes
1. K. Tribe, *Strategies of Economic Order: German Economic Discourse, 1750–1950* (Cambridge: Cambridge University Press, 1995).
2. P. Hall, (ed.), *The Political Power of Economic Ideas: Keynesianism Across Nations* (Princeton, NJ: Princeton University Press, 1989).
3. See Cordell Hull, 'Economic Policies of the Government', *Congressional Record*, 16 February 1931, in Volume 3 of this edition, pp. 296–9; and Cordell Hull, Statement on Tariffs and an International Tariff Congress, *Congressional Record*, 8 July 1916, below, pp. 263–6.
4. J. G. Ruggie, 'International Regimes, Transactions and Change: Embedded Liberalism in the Postwar Economic Order', *International Organization*, 36:2 (1982), pp. 379–415.
5. J. Gowa, *Allies, Adversaries and International Trade* (Princeton, NJ: Princeton University Press, 1994).
6. J. Williamson, *Latin American Adjustment: How Much Has Happened?* (Washington, DC: Institute for International Economics, 1990), ch. 2.
7. J. Frieden, *Global Capitalism: Its Fall and Rise in the Twentieth Century* (London: W. W. Norton & Company, 2006).
8. A. Shonfield, *Modern Capitalism* (London: Oxford University Press, 1966).
9. A. Moravcsik, *The Choice for Europe* (Ithaca, NY: Cornell University Press, 1998).
10. W. Wallace, 'Regionalism in Europe: Model or Exception?', in L. Fawcett and A. Hurrell (eds), *Regionalism in World Politics* (Oxford: Oxford University Press, 1995), pp. 201–27.
11. See 'Cassis' Decision, Judgement of the European Court of Justice, 20 February 1979, below, pp. 104–9.
12. B. Hanson, 'What Happened to Fortress Europe?: Trade Policy Liberalization in the European Union', *International Organization*, 52:1 (1998), pp. 55–86.
13. D. W. Drezner, *U.S. Trade Strategy: Free Versus Fair* (New York: Council of Foreign Relations, 2006), pp. 89–91.
14. A. Brown, *Reluctant Partners: A History of Multilateral Trade Cooperation, 1850–2000* (Ann Arbor, MI: University of Michigan Press, 2003), pp. 152–4.
15. J. Stiglitz, *Globalization and its Discontents* (London: Penguin Books, 2002), pp. 224–9.
16. See Memorandum on Imperial Preference, 14 October 1947, below, pp. 54–6.
17. Ruggie, 'International Regimes, Transactions and Change'; C. Kindleberger, *The World in Depression, 1929–1939* (1973; Berkeley, CA: University of California Press, 1986).

Dedicated to

Crisanto Ampel Duckenfield-Carcamo,

with all my love

THE INTERNATIONAL TRADE ORGANIZATION

During and after the Second World War, American and British policymakers sought to lay the foundations for a post-war economic system that avoided the pitfalls of high unemployment and economic depression that had characterized the interwar period. They sought to create a system that would contain and ameliorate these economic problems while simultaneously allowing for post-war reconstruction and encouraging international engagement and exchange. Both the United States and Britain feared that after the war countries would again resort to protectionist trade measures and beggar-thy-neighbour monetary policies. Their joint solution was a series of interlinked international institutions that would contribute to the stable management of the world economy.

The Allied countries had a general interest in restoring the international terms of exchange, and monetary negotiations were the first to be completed, taking place in Bretton Woods, New Hampshire, in 1944. The Bretton Woods institutions that covered international monetary affairs – the International Monetary Fund (IMF) – and post-war development – the World Bank – were originally intended to function alongside a multilateral trade institution – the International Trade Organization (ITO). However, trade proved to be a more intractable issue for the Allies than monetary cooperation. In return for lend-lease assistance in 1942, the United States had extracted a British concession to eliminate imperial preference and reduce tariffs after the war.[1] However, the British were reluctant to turn this commitment in principle into practical reality and further wartime trade negotiations made little progress. Talks between the United States and the United Kingdom were intermittent and a preliminary agreement was not reached until 1945.

The proposed ITO was not designed to be an entity overseeing a system of international free trade; rather it was designed to allow for a large degree of national intervention in the interests of full employment and economic stabilization. Rather than doctrinal commitments to a barrierless trading environment the ITO put forth an institutional mechanism filled with exemptions designed to ensure that the broader principles could be pursued.

For example, while existing imperial preference arrangements were recognized and exempted from the general principle of most-favoured-nation status enunciated in the ITO articles, the agreement prohibited their further expansion. The tariff negotiation framework also provided for reducing preferential margins as part of the scheduled tariff talks.[2] Importantly, the ITO allowed for the creation of regional customs and free trade areas outside the general rules of the agreement. All of these arrangements were included in the (supposedly) temporary General Agreement on Tariffs and Trade (GATT) negotiated at Geneva in 1947.

The ITO also allowed countries experiencing balance of payments difficulties and/or low monetary reserve levels an exemption from rules on tariffs and quantitative restrictions in order to maintain domestic economic stability. The 'scarce currency clause' of the International Monetary Fund (IMF) was likewise reflected in the ITO's sanction of discrimination against imports from scarce currency countries (i.e., the United States). Because of these monetary arrangements and in order to prevent the creation of counter-productive trade or monetary policies, it was agreed that ITO members should also either be members of the IMF or have a special agreement with the IMF to regulate their monetary and trade relations with IMF members. The balance of payments exemptions were so substantial as to allow a country to arrange its monetary policies so as to enable it to continue to take advantage of quotas and tariffs in the name of domestic full employment.[3]

British industry welcomed the ITO's acknowledgement of imperial preference's place in the international trading system and the National Union of Manufacturers urged Whitehall's economic diplomats not to exchange access to the markets of the British Empire for too low a price. Their mid-century argument that 'British industry knows that the British Empire is for every country in the world the most desirable market, and the right to enter it is worth a fair and reasonable price'[4] foreshadows the fin-de-siècle statements of American politicians ranging from Ross Perot to Al Gore and Bill Clinton.

While British industry expressed confidence in the future capacity of the Empire's economy, British officials worried that if they did approve the ITO, American retaliation could seriously peel off many of the preferential economic arrangements that Britain enjoyed. Latin America was conceded as an American sphere-of-dominance with no discussion. British officials felt that American military dominance, economic power and political influence in East Asia – especially in Japan, China and Indonesia – could easily be leveraged to create an American economic zone to Britain's detriment. Even nearby and traditionally British markets in the Mediterranean such as Italy, Greece and Turkey were seen as vulnerable to American economic enticement. This was especially true as financial necessity had compelled Britain to cut off military and financial aid to Greece and Turkey and turn responsibility for the support of their governments from Soviet pressure to the United States. Deeper trade ties, British officials felt, would soon follow the expansion of Greece and Turkey's security relationships with the United States.[5]

The American debate in the mid-1940s over international trade was hardly settled. As Joseph Viner commented, 'there are few free traders in the present-day world, no one pays any attention to their views, and no person in authority anywhere advocates free trade'.[6] While protectionists of the Smoot-Hawley stripe were not a dominant force, protection remained influential in the Congress and retained a dominant hold on the ideology and policy of the Republican Party. Even within the Executive Branch the more domestically-oriented Cabinet departments of Commerce and Agriculture supported the provision of quotas in international commercial and commodity agreements.

The Truman administration had negotiated the ITO and GATT under the Reciprocal Trade Agreements Act that allowed the president to negotiate trade agreements and then submit them for an unamendable vote in both houses of Congress. This procedure was designed to avoid the tendency of a log-rolling Congress to increase tariffs as had happened under the Smoot-Hawley Act. President Harry Truman's Democratic Party lost control of the Congress to the Republicans in the 1946 elections and Truman's trade negotiating authority expired at the end of 1947. Faced with a protectionist Congress controlled by the opposition party, Truman was unable to obtain ratification of the ITO in 1948.

Even after the Democrats regained control of Congress after the 1948 elections, American business refused to support the ITO. The ITO Charter negotiated at Havana preserved imperial preference – at least temporarily – and allowed for the continuation of quotas and limits on foreign direct investment, arrangements that pleased the British and infuriated international business in the United States. America's international businesses and exporters opposed the ITO as providing insufficient protection for American investment, failing to do away with colonial preferences and generally being riddled with so many exemptions as to make a mockery of its pretension of trade liberalization.[7] Confronted with opposition from the very businesses that were supposed to benefit the most from international engagement and facing continued Congressional reluctance, Truman allowed the agreement to languish. When the Democrats suffered further electoral setbacks in the 1950 elections, Truman withdrew the ITO Charter from Congressional consideration in December 1950.[8]

With the United States no longer promoting the ITO, the British also declined to ratify the agreement and the ITO was stillborn. However, like a phoenix from the ashes of the ITO, the GATT emerged as the fundamental framework for the international trade regime in the post-war era. The GATT negotiations in Geneva were designed as an interim trade measure that would ultimately be folded into the ITO. Embodying many of the principles but lacking the binding institutional arrangements of the ITO, the GATT proved to be both more flexible and more resilient. While it was never submitted for Congressional approval in the United States and remained the target of much scorn on the part of Republican legislators, the GATT provided a multilateral framework for reducing tariffs through the principles of reciprocity, most-favoured-nation status and equal treatment of national and foreign firms.[9] Characterized by long negotiating periods lasting years, the GATT went through eight rounds before the creation of the World Trade Organization after the 1986–94 Uruguay Round.

Notes

1. W. K. Hancock and M. M. Gowing, *The British War Economy* (London: His Majesty's Stationery Office, 1949), pp. 246–7.
2. Jacob Viner, 'Conflicts of Principle in Drafting a Trade Charter', *Foreign Affairs* (1947), below, pp. 27–41, on p. 30.
3. Ibid., below, pp. 33–4.
4. See 'Editorial: Trade Agreements', *Journal of the National Union of Manufacturers* (1946), below, pp. 5–7, on p. 6.
5. See 'Chapter V. Retaliation and Other Indirect Consequences', Board of Trade Economic Group Report, 8 July 1947, below, pp. 10–17.
6. Viner, 'Conflicts of Principle in Drafting a Trade Charter', below, p. 28.
7. W. Diebold, *The End of the ITO* (Princeton, NJ: Princeton University, 1952), p. 9.
8. R. Gardner, *Sterling–Dollar Diplomacy in Current Perspective* (New York: Columbia University Press, 1980), pp. 375–82.
9. A. Brown, *Reluctant Partners: A History of Multilateral Trade Cooperation, 1850–2000* (Ann Arbor, MI: University of Michigan Press, 2003), p. 88.

THE INTERNATIONAL TRADE ORGANIZATION

'Editorial: Trade Agreements', *Journal of the National Union of Manufacturers* (June 1946), pp. 686–7.

EDITORIAL

TRADE AGREEMENTS

There is no subject, with the possible exception of Nationalization, which is exercising the minds of British Industrialists interested in export trade to a greater degree than that of the decisions which may be reached at the forthcoming Conference on Trade and Employment. It is impossible to exaggerate the importance to British industry of this Conference which is designed to be the forerunner of a comprehensive International Conference to be convened under the auspices of the Economic and Social Council of the United Nations. Its results will set the pattern for world trade for years to come. Very wisely, the British Government is in this instance consulting industry more widely than probably on any other subject. As Members will be aware, the National Union has already placed its views before the Board of Trade.

The preliminary Conference, when it meets, will be faced with the colossal task of arriving at a fair basis of tariffs and conditions for some fourteen countries. The difficulties are enormously increased by the fact that it is proposed to tackle the problem at a time when conditions in Europe, and indeed throughout the world, are in such a fluid state that it is well-high impossible to calculate what will be the relative competitive position of the various countries during the coming years. It is the duty of the National Union, with the help of its Affiliated Associations, to tender to the Government the best advice it can in these very difficult conditions, and this is being done. The National Union is content to leave to the expert negotiators the maze and mass of possible permutations and combinations which can possibly arise in seeking to fix in detail the tariffs of so many countries within the pages of one agreement. But behind all this bargaining there are the broad questions of policy which will determine the basis on which any agreements that may be reached will be negotiated, and with these matters the National Union is gravely concerned.

British Strength

It must be admitted that economically we are not yet in the best shape and that we still need time for recuperation. But the indisposition is nothing more than temporary exhaustion resulting from strenuous effort. There is no disease, organic or malignant. Therefore it is to be hoped that our representatives will sit down at the conference table in no mood of inferiority or as suppliants.

British industry knows that the British Empire is for every country in the world the most desirable market, and that the right to enter it is worth a fair and reasonable price. British industry, too, is conscious of its own returning strength and its ability, if allowed the full exercise of its native initiative and inventiveness without crippling taxation to compete on level terms where quality and ingenuity count. We are aware that we have under the British flag every raw material that our industry can need, and happily there is a growing consciousness of what proper development of the vast resource of the Empire could mean. Their development is not viewed merely from the angle of Britain as the workshop of the Empire; the extent to which the development of secondary industries overseas has been speeded up to meet the needs of war is fully realized and understood, and it will need to be accorded its full value at the Conference table.

Empire Influence

This aspect of the matter leads naturally to the problem of Empire Preference. Empire Preference has always been, and still is, cherished as a major item of the National Union's policy. It is true that in the Anglo-American Trade Agreement of 1938 there was, with Dominion concurrence, some modification of the Preferences laid down in 1932 at Ottawa, and it may well be that in the light of all the circumstances which arise there may have to be some further slight change. But the National Union, in common with other bodies, will not hesitate to urge upon the Government in the strongest possible manner that any change in this connection can only be justified by some very substantial return which can be shown to be without any shadow of doubt of equal value to those engaged in industry. It has to be remembered also that a vast amount of employment for our workers is involved in this question. As the Prime Minister stated in the House of Commons on the 7th December, 1945, we are only ready to agree 'that the existing system of Preference within the British Commonwealth and the Empire will be contracted, provided there is adequate compensation in the form of improvement in trading conditions between Commonwealth and Empire countries and the rest of the world.' British manufacturers are further comforted by the fact that any such change in Imperial Preference can only be brought about by consent of all the signatories to the Ottawa Agreements and that the views of the Commonwealth countries will have been ventilated at the talks which the Government will have had with the Dominions in advance of the Conference.

Family Unity

Some of our friends in other countries may find it a little difficult to understand us in this regard. The British Commonwealth and Empire is very much the family. We have, and shall have, our differences, but no one in this world should be in any doubt after the evidence from 1914 to the present day that once injury to the family as a whole is threatened there arises a unity which overrides all sectional interests.

Britain's representatives, when they come to the conference table, will know what the Empire thinks and will be further fortified by the knowledge that their case does not rest on the views of Whitehall and the dictates of diplomacy alone, but embodies the considered wishes of British industry. They will have a strong hand to play, and that there will be hard bargaining at the Conference is beyond doubt. But no one minds hard bargaining as long as it is just.

Letter from National Union of Manufacturers, Sir Leonard Browett (Director) and Sir Patrick Hannon (President), to Sir Stafford Cripps (President of the Board of Trade), 21 October 1946, PRO, BT 11/3242, no. 31.

NATIONAL UNION OF MANUFACTURERS

DIRECTOR: 6 HOLBORN VIADUCT
SIR LEONARD BROWETT
SECRETARY: LONDON E.C.1
LT. COL. V.I. ROBINS

21st October, 1946.

The Rt. Hon. Sir Stafford Cripps, M.P.,
President of the Board of Trade,
Millbank,
LONDON. S.W.1.
Sir,

    With the Committee now meeting in preparation for the International Conference on Trade and Employment to be held next year, the National Union of Manufacturers desire to re-affirm their belief that the economic recovery and future prosperity of the British Commonwealth and Empire depends upon the maintenance of the policy of Imperial Preference.

    The National Union feel that the existence of the British Commonwealth and Empire is the greatest factor at the present time in preserving the stability and peace of the world and they would strongly deprecate any weakening of Imperial Preference, not only because of its great material advantages, but also because of its enormous influence in maintaining and strengthening the links between the Empire countries.

    Any weakening of Imperial Preference is calculated to inflict considerable injury on the producers in the Dominions and Colonies and, furthermore, the exporting industries of this country would be likely to suffer great losses in our Empire markets if they are deprived of that certain outlet for our goods which has been of such inestimable value during the inter-war years and which has meant that more than half of our exports of manufactured goods has found its markets within the Commonwealth and Empire.

    The National Union are doing everything possible to further the Government's policy of full employment for our people and for the recovery of our balance of trade, and believe that this policy depends for its success in no small degree upon Imperial Preference.

Therefore, the National Union earnestly ask that in the forthcoming International negotiations, His Majesty's Government in the United Kingdom will not allow the policy of Imperial Preference to be undermined.

We are, Sir,
Your obedient Servants,

President   Director

'Chapter V. Retaliation and Other Indirect Consequences', Board of Trade Economic Group Report on Long-Term Problems and Consequences of Failure to Approve ITO, 8 July 1947, PRO, BT 11/3544, pp. 69–74.

CHAPTER V.

RETALIATION AND OTHER INDIRECT CONSEQUENCES

1. In considering the desirability of making preferential arrangements with individual countries or groups of countries, we have so far been concerned mainly with the possible <u>direct</u> gains to British trade. But even more important may be the indirect consequences of such a policy. Closer trading relations with one set of countries might conceivably result merely in an increase in trade with these countries which does not reduce the trade of the rest of the world. But it will almost certainly, in practice, reduce the trade of other countries as well. In discussing possible preferential arrangements with the Western European countries, we have already taken account of the effect on the Dominions of our granting preferences to Denmark and Holland. But we have not considered the reaction of, for example, Sweden, Switzerland, Italy, Czechoslovakia and the United States to a loss of part of their export trade to British exporters. Nor have we considered the reaction of foreign as distinct from Empire, suppliers of Britain who might be hit if we granted preferential treatment in our market to their competitors.
2. Most countries, other than the United States, that found their exports curtailed in this way would have to restrict their imports, and they might be forced in self-defence to make their own preferential arrangements with other sets of countries; all of which would reduce, directly or indirectly, the demand for British exports.
3. The United States is in a different position. Only a very large reduction in her experts would reduce her <u>power</u> to import, but the making of preferential arrangements between Britain and other countries might nevertheless provoke American retaliation that would have a serious affect on British trade.

<u>The circumstances in which the U.S. might retaliate</u>

    4. It is very difficult to decide in what circumstances the United States would in fact retaliate.
    It may be argued that, as we are postulating a world in which I.T.O., has broken down, the United States would already be 'doing her worst'. But it

is not unrealistic to imagine a world in which, although I.T.O. had broken down, the United States and the United Kingdom were both pursuing a restrained policy in international trade, either by tacit or by written agreement. Neither country would be making new preferential arrangements; the United States would be pursuing a moderate tariff policy, and a loans policy which did not discriminate unduly against British exports to the borrowing countries.

If, in these circumstances, the U.K., decided to make new preferential arrangements with, say, a number of Western European countries, what would be the reaction of the United States?

5. United States opinion has hitherto been strongly opposed to preferential arrangements and discrimination of all kinds. But it is possible that she might not retaliate if it could be shown that such arrangements led merely to an increase in trade between, say, Britain and Western Europe and did not reduce the demand for American experts.

The U.S. administration has already admitted that such arrangements are possible
   (a) in proposing the scarce currency clause of the International Monetary Fund, and
   (b) in agreeing to the clause in I.T.O., which allows discrimination when this will enable trade to be done that would otherwise not have been done.

[...]

6. Even where there was obvious discrimination by, say European countries in favour of British and against American goods, we might still argue that the demand for American goods as a whole was not being reduced, because the world as a whole would, in some way, always contrive to spend in America all the dollars that America was making available by importing, lending and gifts. And if, further, preferential arrangements between Britain and Western Europe could be represented as part of an American sponsored scheme, such as the 'Marshall Plan', aimed primarily at the economic recovery of Europe, which would eventually make it possible for Europe as a whole to import more from the United States, then it is possible that America might accept such preferential arrangements without retaliation.

7. But even if it could be demonstrated that these arrangements did not harm America on a whole, the argument would not necessarily convince individual American exporters whose interest were damaged; and they might not convince the general American public, or Congress.

The danger of American retaliation is thus a very real one and it is necessary to examine the possible forms it might take and the consequences for British trade.

8. <u>The possible forms of retaliation by the United States</u>

Two possible forms of retaliation may be distinguished.

(a) In the first place, the United States might try to break up the arrangements made by Britain with other countries.

For example the United States could easily dispense with imports from Denmark and Be-Ne-Lux, which in 1938 totalled 77 million dollars, although as the exports from those countries to the United States are only a small part of their total exports (Denmark 2%, Holland 4% and Belgium 7%) a U.S. embargo on them might not offset their gaining in our market. Alternatively, since U.S. exports of manufactured goods to these areas form so small a proportion of total U.S. trade, which is small in relation to total U.S. national income, the United Stated could off-set by export subsidy the effect of even a substantial tariff preference afforded the United Kingdom in these countries; and though, no doubt, this could be circumvented by the introduction of import quotas, the administrative complexities of this would certainly reduce the benefits of the bargain to Denmark and Be-Ne-Lux. Lastly Denmark, Holland and Belgium are all dependent on U.S.A. loans.

9. If we attempted to intensify preferential arrangements within the Empire, the United States' power to prevent this would be much greater than in the case of Be-Ne-Lux and Denmark. Many Empire countries depend very much more on the United States than on the British market.

Canadian exports for example before the war, depended even more on the American market than on the British; and a threat by the United States to reduce her imports from Canada might well pursuade her to abandon any schemes for an extension of Imperial Preferences. Canada is also, of course, greatly dependent on the U.K. market and she might find it difficult to finance her imports from the U.S. without triangular trade through the U.K. but it must not be forgotten that Canada's gold output (165 million dollars in 1938) was more than enough to finance her adverse visible trade balance with the U.S. (145 million dollars in 1938).

10. South Africa too, is greatly dependent on her gold exports, which pay for the great bulk of her imports. (In 1938 her visible imports were 468 million dollars, her gold output 426 million dollars). Any threat by America to stop buying gold might well pursuade South Africa (and possibly Southern Rhodesia) to stay out of any schemes for extending Imperial Preference. It is perhaps unlikely that the United States, by far the largest holder of gold reserves in the world, would be prepared to stop buying gold, since this

would involve dissolution of the International Monetary Fund, and might lead to the general abandonment of the use of gold for settling international debts; but she might try to procure a reduction in the price of gold. The 'gold scare' of 1937 provides an illustration of how such action might affect the gold producing countries. Circumstances might arise in which a refusal to raise the price of gold might be equally effective (gold is one of the few commodities whose dollar price has not risen since before the war; its production has thus become less profitable, and its power to purchase imports reduced). South Africa, as a large gold producer, is, therefore, very vulnerable to pressure by the United States.

The same is true, to a lesser extent, of the British Empire as a whole. Canada, Australia, Rhodesia and the Gold Coast are all large gold producers. The Empire as a whole produced in 1938 over 700 million dollars worth of gold, more than enough to cover the total visible adverse balance of trade of the Empire with the U.S.

11. Apart from Canada and the gold producing countries, many other Empire countries are greatly dependent on the U.S. market. This is especially true of British Malaya; the United States is by far the biggest market for her tin and rubber.

    It is, therefore, by no means impossible that American pressure would prevent any intensification of Imperial Preference; and it might even, as we have seen, prevent the establishment of preferential arrangements between the U.K. and the Western European countries.

12. [...] Let us suppose, however, that American pressure would not be sufficient to prevent developments of this type. It is then necessary to balance the resulting gains to British trade against the losses resulting from American retaliation.

13. In the first place, the United States could restrict her imports of United Kingdom goods, which amounted in 1938 to over 100 million dollars. The loss of a substantial part of this market would itself offset a considerable part of the possible gain from forming preferential arrangements with, say, Be-Ne-Lux and Denmark.

14. In the second place, the United States might restrict imports from countries with which we had made preferential arrangements. We have already discussed the possible embargo on U.S. imports from Be-Ne-Lux and Denmark. If we were to intensify Imperial Preference, the U.S. might impose higher barriers to the importation of, say, Canadian products, Dominion wool, Malayan rubber, or reduce the price of South African gold. We have already seen that, for many important Empire countries, especially Canada, South Africa and Malaya, the loss of a substantial part of their American markets would seriously impair their power to import; and as they take a large part of their imports from us,

our exports would clearly suffer. Those three countries alone took imports from us in 1938 valued at 380 million dollars.

15. In the third place, the United States might well attempt to secure for herself British markets in third countries, if we pursued a commercial policy that roused her hostility. This she might do in various ways – by herself giving preferences or favourable loans to countries that agreed to import more from the United States and less from Britain; or by threatening to restrict her imports from countries that depend greatly on the U.S. markets, unless they would favour American goods at the expense of British.

16. A policy of this sort would stand a very good chance of success in

   (a) the tropical countries of Latin America, which depend to an overwhelming extent on the U.S. Market;
   (b) the Far Eastern countries, especially
   　(i) The Philippines, which depends on the U.S. Market for four-fifths of its exports;
   　(ii) the Dutch East Indies, which depend greatly on the U.S. markets for rubber and tin (it is assumed that Indonesia will be independent of Holland);
   　(iii) Japan, Korea, Formosa, which are under U.S. military control;
   　(iv) China, which, besides depending greatly on the American and Japanese markets, is likely to be dependent on American loans.

   (Were Malaya not a part of the Colonial Empire, she would also figure in this group of countries, because of her dependence on the American market).

The United States might also be able to force her exports, at our expense, in

   (c) countries being financially assisted by the U.S., especially Turkey, Greece, and Italy, all of which are in any case more dependent on the U.S. than on the British market.

She might even be able to persuaded

   (d) Canada and
   (e) South Africa, for the reasons explained above, not merely to refrain from extending Imperial Preference, but actually to reduce, or possibly to abolish, the preferences afforded to U.K. goods, at least in certain lines.

17. All these countries, together with the U.S. herself, make a formidable list of markets in which we might lose export trade in the event of retaliation by the U.S. In 1938 their imports from the U.K. amounted to nearly 650 million dollars (roughly one quarter of our total exports) as follows:–

	Imports from U.K. 1938 (million dollars)
(a) Tropical America*	83
(b) Far Eastern Countries	67
(c) Turkey, Greece, Italy	67
(d) Canada (including Newfoundland)	126
(e) South Africa	203
(f) U.S.	118
	644

* All Latin America, except Argentina, Uruguay and Bolivia, all of which depend more on the U.K. than on the U.S. market.

18. The potential loss of export markets in those countries is considerably greater than the possible gains resulting from preferential arrangements with Western European countries. It is also greater than the potential gain of American markets in the empire. Empire countries, excluding South Africa and Canada (including Newfoundland) imported only 267 million dollars worth from the U.S. in 1938.

19. The possibility of retaliation by the U.S., would, therefore, have to be very carefully considered before we embarked on a policy of making, or extending, preferential arrangements with other countries. The losses caused by such retaliation might well exceed the gains from preferential arrangements. This is because of the great power of the U.S. to affect the trade, or to influence the trade policy, of other countries – a power that results from
    (a) the dependence of many countries on U.S. purchases:–
        (i) U.S. imports of merchandise, which amounted to three-quarters of U.K. imports in 1937, are now as great as our own; with a reasonable level of employment in the U.S., this is likely to remain true in the future.
        (ii) Her policy can determine the fate of gold producing countries.
        (iii) Her tourists spend much more abroad than those of any other country.
    (b) The ability of the U.S. to give financial assistance, and to supply the goods.
    (c) The General political power of the U.S.

Many of our most important markets, too, come within a possible American sphere of influence; South Africa was by far our biggest customer before the war, Canada our fourth largest, the U.S. fifth.

20. On the other hand, our power of winning markets from the U.S. by making preferential arrangements is not very great. The countries where our bargaining power is greatest (such as Australia, New Zealand, Eire, India, the Colonial Empire, Denmark) already took a large fraction of their manufactured imports from Britain before the war, and comparatively little from

the U.S.* In the countries where there are large markets to win from the U.S. (such as Central America and the Far East) our bargaining power is small.

Imports in 1938 from

	U.S.	U.K.		
	(million dollars)			
Australia	82	224	i.e.	3 times as great
New Zealand	26	106		4
Eire	23	102		4
India, Burma, Ceylon	47	225		5
British Malaya	10	59		6
African Colonies	17	86		6
Denmark	29	123		4

(British Malaya is included here because she is part of the 'Controlled' Empire).

CONCLUSION

21. The making of preferential arrangements between British and a group of other countries may have certain unfavourable effects which must be set against the direct gains to British Trade. These unfavourable consequences are:-

    (i) The loss of importing power by third countries, adversely effected by the arrangements.

    (ii) Retaliation by countries, especially the U.S., whose hostility is aroused by the arrangements.

    (iii) Possibly a deterioration in general standards of commercial policy throughout the world. If, even in the absence of I.T.O, a large number of important trading countries were following moderate policies not widely divergent from the principles of I.T.O., a new departure in British policy might usher in a new phase of tighter restrictions on trade, preferential blocs, bilateral bargaining, etc., which would tend to restrict world trade and British trade.

22. When contemplating preferential arrangements with a group of countries taking say, one-tenth of our exports (such as France, Be-Ne-Lux and Denmark before the war), it must be borne in mind that, even if our exports to those countries could be doubled (an optimistic assumption), the whole gain would be offset by a consequent fall, for the reasons given above, of only one-ninth in our exports to the rest of the world.

23. We might, of course, consider a scheme for initiating, or intensifying, preferential arrangements with a much larger group of countries, say a group that has hitherto taken one-half of our exports. If America is excluded from the group, it is most unlikely that we could include a larger number of countries than this. In this case the reaction of the U.S. might well be violent. If, for

example, the arrangements covered the British Empire (excluding Canada and South Africa), Scandanavia, Be-Ne-Lux and France – which between them took about half our exports before the war – nearly ⅔ths of the United States' export markets would be adversely affected. Assuming that the U.S. failed to break down such an arrangement, she would no doubt make her own arrangements with a large part of the rest of the world, and our trade in those areas might suffer severely. In these circumstances, a doubling of our total exports of manufactures would involve perhaps a trebling of our trade to the countries with which we had made new preferential arrangements – many of them countries which were already, before the war, taking the bulk of their manufactured imports from this country.

24. It would seem, therefore, that large scale preferential arrangements would be of doubtful value unless either,

    (a) we could be certain that the danger of American retaliation was remote; or

    (b) the U.S. was already 'doing her worst', and the arrangements were regarded as a defensive measure to prevent the share of American exports from increasing in the countries concerned; in this case, we should probably have to revise drastically our ideas about the possibility of expanding British exports and so of regaining our pre-war standard of living.

Confidential Note on a Meeting with the FBI on 20 February (1947) attended by Mr Helmore (Secretary for Overseas Trade), Mr Holmes, Mr Summerscale, Mr Cohen, Miss Fisher and Mr Marquand, PRO, BT 11/3254.

MEETING WITH THE F.B.I. ON 20TH FEBRUARY

The Secretary for Overseas Trade, Mr. Helmore and Mr. Holmes attended a meeting at the F.B.I. on the 20th February for a general discussion about the Second Session of the Preparatory Committee in Geneva and Commonwealth talks in London. Mr. Summerscale, Mr. Cohen and Miss Fisher were also present. Mr. Marquand outlined briefly the work of the First Session of the Preparatory Committee and referred to the work of the Drafting Committee then sitting in New York. The meeting then proceeded to consider certain particular questions which were of interest to the F.B.I.

(1) Full Employment.

The F.B.I. considered that the employment obligations in the Draft Charter attached to the Report of the First Session of the Preparatory Committee were not sufficiently definite. Mr. Helmore said that the Charter set out certain objectives: domestic action to maintain full employment was left to the particular countries concerned; but the ultimate responsibility for international action to avoid a World slump rested with the Economic and Social Council of the United Nations, in conjunction with various specialised agencies, such as the I.T.O. when it was set up, F.A.O., the I.M.F. and the International Bank. Mr. Helmore pointed out that as a result of the discussions at Church House the impairment clause now applied to the whole of the Charter, including the chapter on full employment, and not only to the section on commercial policy.

(2) Development

The F.B.I. were concerned lest the Charter gave too much freedom to the under-developed countries at the expense of the more industrialised countries. Mr. Marquand said that there were virtually two schools of thought among the members of the Preparatory Committee. It has been feared that unless some compromise was reached there would be no hope of obtaining agreement to the Charter. Safeguards for the industrialised countries had been written into the Charter. It was perhaps not without significance that at the end of the proceedings the Indian Delegation had considered that the safeguards were so numerous that the value of the Charter to the under-developed countries was doubtful.

(3) The danger of reversion by the U.S.A. to a High Tariff Policy after 3 years

The F.B.I. felt that there was some danger of the U.S.A. withdrawing from the I.T.O. after 3 years and reverting to a high tariff policy after preference had been abandoned or reduced which could not then be re-imposed. Mr. Helmore said that although under the Reciprocal Trade Agreements Act agreements must be denounceable after 3 years, it did not follow that, in fact, action would be taken to denounce them. Indeed, it was the general custom to make Commercial Treaties valid for 3 years and thereafter liable to termination with 6 months notice although in practice Treaties frequently remained valid for many years after this period. The U.K./U.S.A. Trade Agreement of 1938 was an example. Mr. Helmore also said that the time limit of 3 years applied to the whole Charter and that if the U.S. withdrew from the I.T.O. or revoked the Agreement on Tariffs the U.K. would not then be bound by any agreement.

(4) Meaning of Preferences exclusively in force between negotiating countries

The F.B.I. asked what was the significance of Article 14 (2) (c). It was explained that this clause had been written in to meet one or two special cases of cross-border preference systems, e.g. the one in operation between Chile and Brazil.

(5) The Importance of the Preferential System

The F.B.I. asked whether effective reduction in the U.S. Tariff could be made within the limits of the 50% reduction allowed under the Reciprocal Trade Agreements Act. Mr. Helmore pointed out that the U.S. Administration had power to make reductions of 50% on the Tariffs at present in force which, in many cases, already represented substantial reductions on pre-war rates. He went on to say that the value of the maximum reduction of 50% depended entirely on the commodity in question. The reduction on preferences was only being contemplated as part of a bargain. If sufficient return were not forthcoming on the items of importance to the U.K., substantial reductions in preferences would not be made. There followed a discussion on the interpretation of the 'automatic' reduction of preferences. Mr. Helmore said that, however the clause was phrased, the intention was that this rule should operate as follows:– If the m.f.n. rate were 6 and the preferential rate were 3, if the m.f.n. rate were reduced to 5, thus reducing the preferential margin to 2, compensation would be sought from the country agreeing to the reduction in the margin of preference. In answer to a question Mr. Helmore said that the intention was to generalise the Tariff concession provisions to non-members of the I.T.O. If and when such countries joined the I.T.O. the benefits they had already received under this provisional generalisation of tariffs concessions would be taken into account.

(6) <u>Consultation with Industry.</u>

The F.B.I. remarked that in the U.S.A. lists of commodities on which foreign countries were requesting reductions were published. It was understood that in Australia also steps were being taken to publish lists of commodities which might be in question in the negotiations. The F.B.I. asked whether, although it was not the common practice to do so, the Board of Trade would consider publishing similar lists in connection with the negotiations in Geneva. Mr. Helmore said that it was not the intention to publish lists of items in this way. Arrangements were being made to consult industries generally about reductions, but it was not the intention that they should be asked to comment on specific requests which had been received. Mr. Marchant of the F.B.I. asked whether it followed that if industries had not so far been consulted their products were not in danger. Mr. Helmore said that the majority of requests from other countries on the U.K. tariff had not so far been received. Mr. Holmes pointed out that in the negotiations some of these requests would be turned down out of hand and that in such cases it was not necessary to consult industries. Moreover, time was so short that it would, in any case, be physically impossible to discuss with industries the detailed requests as they were received. Mr. Marquand explained the arrangements which were being made for a committee of industrial representatives, which would sit in London during the progress of the negotiations at Geneva, and would be consulted on particular points as they arose. Mr. Marchant pressed for a more exact definition of the functions of this Committee. He wished to have it clearly stated that representatives of individual industries would be called in ad hoc to deal with problems of their individual industries as these came up during the Tariff negotiations and he said that it was extremely important that if this was the intention industries should get notice of the questions which were to be discussed, and for this reason he thought that publication of lists of requests was desirable. No assurance was given to the F.B.I. in these terms, but it was said that industries should be consulted about items of major importance during the course of the negotiations at Geneva.

(7) State Trading (Article 33)

Some doubt was expressed about Article 33. Mr. Holmes said that the final form of the Article would probably not be decided by the Drafting Committee in New York. It was doubtful whether the Report of the Drafting Committee would be publicly available, but this matter was still being considered. Mr. Helmore said that Article 33 was obviously designed for the Russians if they should decide to join the I.T.O. but that no detailed consideration had been given to it so far because the Russians had not been present at the First Session of the Preparatory Committee. Major Watling of the F.B.I. stated that in his view the Article would be of more value if it consisted of the first sentence only.

(8) Best date for preference

The view expressed by one member of the F.B.I. was that a uniform base date should be adopted in the negotiations and that this should be a date before the signing of the Atlantic Charter. Mr. Helmore replied that it was not possible to obtain unanimity on the base date, but although different dates would be used those would, of course, be taken into account in the course of the negotiations.

(9) High and Low Tariffs

The view was expressed by one member of the F.B.I., although it was not generally acceptable to his colleagues, that a rate of 30% represented a low tariff. Mr. Helmore said it was not possible to determine in the abstract what were high or low tariff rates, since the effect of a rate varied greatly according to the commodity in question.

(10) Benefits and disadvantages of the negotiations as supplied to individual industries.

Sir Edger Jones of the F.B.I. asked for an assurance that any loss of preference which a particular industry suffered in one country would be made up by corresponding benefits for the same industry elsewhere. He deprecated the suggestion that some industries should gain at the expense of others. Mr. Helmore said that while an effort would be made to spread the advantages and the disadvantages over as wide an area as possible, regard must be had principally to the overall advantage of the country.

(11) Escape Clause

The question was asked whether the escape clause was not sufficiently wide to allow the whole effects of the Charter to be nullified. Mr. Helmore said that there was this danger, but that without an escape clause of this kind it would not have been possible to secure agreement over as wide an area as that represented by the Report of the first session of the Preparatory Committee.

(12) Date of operation of the new Tariff Rates

The F.B.I. asked whether the new rates were to come into force at once and what effect this would have on the U.K. balance of payments. Mr. Helmore said that the intention was that the rates should come into effect as soon as possible, but pointed out that the Charter allowed for the imposition of restrictions to safeguard the balance of payments and that under this Article the U.K. would certainly have to impose restrictions for some time to come because of its shortage of hard currency.

(13) Position of the Philippines

Mr. Helmore said that by the recent Agreement between the U.S. and Philippines, preferences granted by each country to the other would be eliminated gradually over a period of years. The Philippines were not members of the Preparatory Committee and any reduction in the Philippines rates would have to be negotiated direct with the Philippines outside the context of the present negotiations.

(14) The Relation between Exchange Manipulation and Trade

A member of the F.B.I. thought that the I.T.O. was taking too little account of the damage which could be done to trade by currency manipulation. Mr. Marquand said that while this matter was largely one for the International Monetary Fund, Article 29 of the draft Charter of the I.T.O. provided that if a member of the I.T.O. was not a member of the I.M.F. he must give a special undertaking about exchange which, in effect, was the same as a relevant part of the I.M.F. Agreement.

The view was expressed by one member of the F.B.I. that the dates of operation of the I.T.O. and I.M.F. Agreement should be synchronized.

'Confidential Note of a Meeting Held at the Board of Trade on the 25th February 1947, Between the National Union of Manufacturers and Mr. Marquand, Mr. Helmore, Mr. Holmes, Mr. Summerscale, Miss Fisher and Mr. Sydenham-Clarke of the Board of Trade', PRO, BT 11/3242.

CONFIDENTIAL

NOTE OF A MEETING HELD AT THE BOARD OF TRADE ON THE 25th FEBRUARY, 1947, BETWEEN THE NATIONAL UNION OF MANUFACTURERS AND MR. MARQUAND, MR. HELMORE, MR. HOLMES, MR. SUMMERSCALE, MISS FISHER AND MR. SYDENHAM-CLARKE OF THE BOARD OF TRADE.

1. Imperial Preference (Article 24).

Sir Patrick Hannon asked the Board to consider the possible reduction in employment in the United Kingdom which might follow from the modification or elimination of Imperial Preference and emphasised that this country should, at all costs, try to avoid a repetition of the slump of the early '30s. Mr. Marquand said that it might contribute to full employment in this country if in return for reduction in preferential margins, foreign countries reduced their tariffs; it might often be difficult to forecast accurately the ultimate effect on trade of the alteration of a tariff. Mr. Helmore agreed and described the plan by which it was hoped that United Kingdom industries particularly concerned in the reduction of preference margins could be contacted during the negotiations and given an opportunity to state their views before the negotiators finally committed themselves to important concessions. He emphasised that the principal aim of the United Kingdom Delegation at the negotiations would be to get the United States of America to reduce their tariffs as much as possible and to increase United Kingdom exports to the United States. He would, therefore, insist on a substantial reduction in U.S. tariffs before agreeing to reductions in margins of preference.

2. Tariff Negotiations.

Mr. Marquand said that we proposed to conduct detailed negotiations on specific tariff items. He agreed that these negotiations were bound to prove complicated and to take a long time but he said that this seemed to be the only practical method of obtaining all-round reductions in tariffs. It would not be feasible to try to bring about a reduction of all tariffs by a formula. In answer to a question Mr. Helmore explained that although the U.S. Reciprocal Trades Agreement Act expired in 1948, any tariff agreements made before then as a result of these discussions would nevertheless remain in force for at least three years from the date of agreement and would continue in force indefinitely unless action was taken to terminate them.

3. Economic Development.

Mr. Marquand said that the new chapter on industrial development had been brought into the proposed Charter by way of a compromise. Without some clauses of this kind it would have been impossible to get any general agreement, from the under-developed countries. Sir Leonard Browett said that the N.U.M. appreciated the argument in favour of the development of under-industrialised countries but said that we must beware of the possible adverse effects on our export trade. He said that everything depended on the tempo of industrialisation in the countries in question; if they developed their industries reasonably slowly the resulting increase in their purchasing power might well be of great benefit to us, but we should not encourage them to develop their young industries too fast. Sir Patrick said that the N.U.M. were satisfied with the Board's attitude in this matter.

4. Escape Clause (Article 34).

Sir Patrick stated emphatically that in the opinion of the N.U.M. this Clause is too sweeping and should not be allowed to appear in the Charter at all, since it would invite those who found themselves harmed by some of the provisions of the Charter to escape from their obligations. Mr. Helmore said that when the inclusion of an 'escape clause' was originally suggested the U.K. Delegation had challenged its wide scope but had met with little support. They had agreed to its being brought into the Charter as a result of considerable pressure, particularly from the United States delegates, who had pointed out that similar 'escape clauses' were normally included in their bilateral trade agreements. Moreover, the escape clause might act as a spur to prevent excessive caution in negotiating concessions, since delegates who knew that they had this escape clause behind them would feel that if, owing to miscalculation, they granted too extensive a concession, there were means of rectifying the mistake. It was pointed out that the clause could only be invoked by Government action and that it would not be easy to abuse it by too frequent use, since a good many conditions had to be complied with before it could be invoked.

5. State Trading.

Mr. Marquand confirmed that the state trading clauses had been drafted in the first place with the Russians chiefly in mind. Since the Russians had not been represented at the First Session of the Preparatory Committee the clauses had not so far been considered in any detail by the Preparatory Committee. It was hoped that the Russians would eventually join the I.T.O.

6. Customs Union (Article 38).

Sir Leonard Browett asked what was the policy of His Majesty's Government towards customs unions between other countries. He said that we should not forget the possible harmful effects on us of foreign customs unions and suggested that we might start customs unions with and between our own Colonies. Mr. Helmore said that His Majesty's Government was not, generally speaking, opposed to customs unions provided that they were complete; that is to say, provided that there were no customs barrier whatever between the two countries concerned and consequently no preferential import system.

7. Marks of Origin.

Mr. Dorizzi said that the N.U.M. feels strongly that the present regulations on marks of origin should be maintained to the full and that it was most important that buyers should always know the origin of goods. We should guard against attempts to mislead buyers by making up articles and wrappings in such a way that they are very similar to those of other countries; further, the mark 'Made in England' had often proved to be of enormous value to this country in its foreign trade. The point was noted and it was agreed to bear it in mind in considering the part of the Charter concerned with marks of origin. Mr. Helmore said that we would let the N.U.M. see the draft of the proposed article before we finally agreed to it.

8. Tied Loans.

Sir Leonard said that tied loans were equally effective as tariffs as a barrier to world trade. Mr. Helmore confirmed that this important matter was well in mind.

9. Shipping.

Sir Leonard Browett said that although the N.U.M. were not directly concerned, he would be glad to know what arrangements were being made about shipping, which was, of course, of fundamental importance to world trade.

Mr. Holmes said that the Charter of the International Trade Organisation was deliberately being confined to goods. Services, including shipping, were being excluded, not because their importance was not recognised but because it was thought that they would best be handled by other means.

Jacob Viner, 'Conflicts of Principle in Drafting a Trade Charter',
Foreign Affairs, 25:4 (June 1947), pp. 612–28.

CONFLICTS OF PRINCIPLE IN DRAFTING A TRADE CHARTER

By Jacob Viner

IN September 1946, our Department of State presented a 'Suggested Charter' for an International Trade Organization of the United Nations. A Preparatory Committee of the United Nations Conference on Trade and Employment, on which 17 countries (Soviet Russia abstaining) were represented, met in London in October and November 1946, discussed this Suggested Charter, and issued a new draft and a covering Report. The Charter was further revised at Lake Success. A second meeting of the Preparatory Committee is in process at Geneva at the time of writing, and the countries represented are negotiating reciprocal reductions of tariffs as well as working on the text of the Charter. The process of reciprocal negotiation of tariff reductions is later to be extended to the countries not represented at the London and Geneva meetings of the Preparatory Committee. In the fall of 1947 a full International Conference on Trade and Employment is scheduled to take place, when a definitive draft of the Charter is to be submitted to the member governments of the United Nations.

It is my purpose here to examine the issues of principle dealt with in the Charter as revised at London and in those American suggestions which at London were left for later consideration. The proposed Charter covers a great deal of ground, and it is possible to raise questions of principle with respect to most of its provisions. Attention will be confined here, however, to what seem to be five of the most important issues. These can be briefly formulated in five questions: (1) What level of trade barriers should be the goal for the postwar period? (2) Should trade barriers be, in general, non-discriminatory as between foreign countries? (3) Are ordinary tariffs preferable to, or less objectionable than, quantitative import restrictions such as import quotas? (4) Can international commitments with respect to the form and extent of trade barriers be made consistent with comprehensive national economic planning? (5) Can an international trade code be devised which can effectively bridge the gap between free-market economies and state-trading economies and will be acceptable to both?

II

Only the traditional free trader can deal with the problem of the desirable level of trade barriers as a clear-cut question of principle. He wants the reciprocal reduction of trade barriers carried as far as governments can be persuaded to carry it, even to the point of total elimination of tariffs, subject to a few debatable exceptions such as protection of infant industries and those which are strategically important. The free trader objects to trade barriers both as obstacles to international specialization of production in accordance with comparative national advantages for production, and as sources of international friction. But there are few free traders in the present-day world, no one pays any attention to their views, and no person in authority anywhere advocates free trade. The practical issue turns on whether existing trade barriers should be reduced, and, if so, how much; and on these points there is perhaps nearly as much division of opinion within countries as between countries. Despite the fact that the international negotiations were launched by the United States Government and undoubtedly would collapse if this country were to lose interest in them, intransigent American protectionism is at least as serious an obstacle to the successful realization of the American trade proposals as the protectionism of other countries, and it would be difficult to overestimate the extent to which the particular pattern which the American proposals have taken is the result of the fortuitous – and fortunate – circumstance that Cordell Hull's vision and drive came into action at a strategic moment in our history.

At this stage of the negotiations, a special difficulty arises out of the facts that the proposals were initiated by a Democratic Administration, that they involve reduction of the American tariff by executive action without reference to Congress, that the Republicans in both Houses of Congress voted against the Trade Agreements Act under which the Executive has the authority to negotiate reciprocal reductions in duty, and that the Republicans are now in a majority in both Houses of Congress.

Countries which have lower or younger tariffs than ours feel that they cannot reasonably be asked to make reductions of the same proportions, absolutely or relatively, as those which the United States, with its riches, its competitive ability, and its creditor status, should make. Many of them face formidable reconstruction problems. They are poor, or small, or industrially undeveloped, and they believe they face the prospect of chronic deficits in their balances of payments with the United States.

The State Department has at all stages of the negotiations carefully avoided taking a doctrinal position on the issue of free trade and protection. It has confined itself to advocating lower tariffs, without suggesting at any time that a complete absence of tariffs might be the superior solution. It has committed itself against any reductions in the American tariff which are not accompanied by equivalent reductions of the restrictions which other countries place on imports of American commodities. It has pledged itself to make only 'selective' (as distinguished from 'across-the-board') reductions in American duties, and to take into full account the effect that tariff reduction would have on the competitive capacity of American industries. President Truman and the State Department have given assurances that no reduction of duty will be made which would involve 'serious injury' to any American industry. On American initiative, there was inserted in the draft Charter an escape clause – known as the 'Mexican Clause' because it was first introduced in the Hull Trade Agreement with Mexico – under which a member may withdraw any particular concession on import duties if it brings an increase in imports threatening serious injury to domestic producers. Except possibly on issues turning on the rôle of Congress in the formation and administration of commercial policy, this should suffice for anyone who does not insist that the Smoot-Hawley-Hoover Tariff was the last word in American Statesmanship in this field. Those who really want significant cuts in the American tariff have some warrant, in fact, for fearing lest these reservations result in only homeopathic doses of reduction of the American tariff. The old schoolmen distinguished between that grace which inspires good resolutions and that other grace which provides the will to fulfill them. There is great danger that the American supply of the latter will fall far short of the State Department's supply of the former.

The understanding that no country is to be expected to grant tariff concessions which are not counterbalanced by return concessions is mainly relied upon to overcome the reluctance of other countries to reduce their tariffs. Those countries whose tariffs are already comparatively low are offered the assurance that the freezing of low tariffs or of free entry will be recognized as a concession equivalent to the substantial reduction of high tariffs. Countries industrially undeveloped or with special reconstruction problems can appeal to the International Trade Organization for release from the tariff (and other) obligations they have assumed, and the ITO can grant such release at its discretion, where the obligations are general in character; if the obligations were incurred in negotiations with particular countries, the agreement of the countries substantially affected is required. The process of tariff reduction is thus, in effect, made a matter of bargaining and of ITO administration, rather than of the application of a rigid formula or even of an agreed principle.

On the tariff question, therefore, the Charter evades a conflict of principles by a complete avoidance of doctrine. Chapter II in the covering Report of the London meeting of the Preparatory Committee which deals with this question does, however, indulge in doctrine; it states the case *for* trade barriers and against international specialization, both in the long run and in emergency situations, at some length and *con amore*. If one were to take this chapter seriously one might easily be misled into thinking that the major purpose of the negotiations was to give international sanction to the tariff doctrines of Friedrich List and of Henry Clay. It is not clear, however, what was the intended function of this Report. I am not aware of any evidence that this chapter, or for that matter any other part of the Report, is exercising any influence on the course of the negotiations.

III

Since 1923, the United States has steadily supported the principle of unconditional most-favored-nation treatment of foreign commerce, that is, of equality of treatment of imports and of exports without regard to their source or their destination. Since the beginning of the depression of the 1930's, however, the trend over most of the world has been strongly in the opposite direction – toward bilateralism, or the limitation by countries of the imports which they will permit from any particular other Country to some agreed proportion of their exports to this country. The Charter gives unequivocal support to the equality of treatment principle. Provisions, it is true, is made for exceptions from equality of treatment. But these exceptions are carefully limited and are for the most part applicable only in emergency situations or where their absence would make necessary an abrupt termination of preferential practices of long standing. Existing intra-imperial preferences, including our own, are not outlawed, but new ones are not to be established, and the existing margins of preference are to undergo automatic reduction as a by-product of tariff reduction. The right to discriminate against imports from 'scarce-currency' countries, established by the International Monetary Fund Agreement, is reaffirmed and somewhat strengthened. The International Trade Organization is to have the authority to sanction limited departure from the equality of treatment principle in some other cases, as, for instance, in the case of regional agreements even if they do not completely meet the traditional criteria of 'customs unions.' Even where the Charter does sanction new discrimination it apparently withholds sanction from concerted bilateral arrangements of a discriminatory character for which the customs union provision cannot be invoked, although this could be made much more explicit. In general, ratification of the Charter in its present form would mean greater international sanction of the principle of equality of treatment than has ever existed. This is the one instance where the proposed Charter registers a definite victory of one doctrine over another one having substantial significance.

The case for equality of treatment as the general rule is a strong one. It is the only available rule in this field which is of general applicability, is relatively simple to administer, and distributes its advantages and burdens with some approach to mutuality. Tariff discriminations are invariably resented by the countries which are discriminated against, the three centuries of experience demonstrates that under all circumstances they operate to poison international relations and to make more difficult the task of maintaining international harmony. Any departure from equality of treatment involves a deviation from the weighty economic principle that imports shall come from their lowest-price sources and that exports shall go to the most eager markets. The trade which is forced into bilateral channels, moreover, will ordinarily be not only economically inferior to the multilateral trade which it displaces but also less in volume.

The opposition to the equality of treatment principle, however, continues to be strong, even within the United States, but especially abroad. Adherence to the principle presents an obstacle to rewarding friends or punishing enemies, whether in the economic or in the political field. If universally and automatically applied, its requirement that any tariff reductions made must be extended alike to high-tariff and to low-tariff countries strengthens the reluctance to reduce tariffs. Countries whose exports are lagging in volume behind their imports, or are exchanging for imports on unfavorable price terms, sometimes imagine that by resort to bilateral bargains they can force the countries mainly supplying their imports to accept their goods in larger volume or at better prices. During a world-wide depression, when fear of imports and aggravated dread of balance of payments deficits are endemic, bilateral bargains may cut channels for trade through the morass of emergency trade restrictions, and may thus give scope for some measure of mutually-profitable trade which otherwise would have succumbed both to the loss of monetary buying power and to the reinforcement of the customary tariff walls. It will thus be a major achievement if the American initiative succeeds in reversing the trend toward bilateralism.

Under the Suggested Charter not only will there be no obligation to extend most-favored-nation treatment to non-members of the ITO, but member countries will not be permitted to extend to non-member countries, unless the Organization grants special permission, the concessions which they grant to the other member countries as the result of the tariff-reduction negotiations. A provision of somewhat this character is desirable, since much of the opposition to the unconditional most-favored-nation principle in the past has resulted from the situation which arises when a high-tariff country refuses to make any reductions in its own tariff but automatically shares in the benefits of the tariff reductions which other countries make in their reciprocal bargains. This species of 'free riding' on the unconditional most-favored-nation principle has been a major obstacle to the reduction of trade barriers, and unless it is stopped membership in the International Trade Organization will be deprived of much of its potential attractiveness to low-tariff countries.

IV

Quantitative restrictions on imports, such as import quotas and import licensing, are an ancient institution, but they became important again in times of peace only in the early 1930's with the coming of the depression. As a means of warding off balance of payments deficits by restricting the volume of imports to the amount of foreign exchange available to pay for them, as a means of guaranteeing to domestic producers a minimum share of the domestic market, as concessions in bilateralistic bargains and in barter transactions, they can be more effective, more predictable in some of their effects, and more flexible than ordinary tariff duties. This has won them many friends in a period when all of these considerations have loomed large in public opinion. Quantitative import restrictions, moreover, are an indispensable adjunct of domestic crop-restriction or price-support programs.

The State Department has since 1934 opposed quantitative restrictions on imports as inherently more objectionable in principle than ordinary import duties. The Congress and the Department of Agriculture have not seen eye-to-eye on this question with the State Department, and it has not been the State Department which emerged the victor. Congress has enacted some quota legislation. In a few instances the Department of State, seeking to avoid the introduction of import quotas which otherwise would have become legally or politically inevitable, has induced other countries to apply quotas on exports to the United States. This roundabout way of securing quantitative restriction of imports transfers to the exporting country both the obloquy and the burden of administration of the quotas, and compensates it by abandoning to it the gap between the market prices in the two countries.

Import quotas are open to the objections that as compared to ordinary import duties they lend themselves more readily to violation of the equality of treatment principle, and involve a greater degree of interference with the ordinary processes of the free market. If import quotas are allotted by countries, as is ordinarily the case, there is not much choice except between more or less arbitrary allotment and deliberately discriminatory allotment. There is no formula of allotment of quotas which can assure to each supplying country that share of the import market which would accrue to it if competitive processes in terms of available supply and price were the only determining factors. Global or unallotted import quotas, with imports admitted in order of entry until the maximum is reached, tend to favor neighboring countries and to result in a wasteful concentration of imports at the beginning of each quota period. Import quotas as usually administered result in an excess of the price in the import market over the laid-down cost (including import duties, if any) of the imported commodity, and this excess goes as a windfall profit to the exporters, or to the importers.

To this last objection, import licenses sold in the desired quantity to the highest bidders would not be open and they conform most closely to the equality of treatment principle, but this procedure might offer too much facility for monopolization of the import trade by a few dealers. Import quotas, finally, are more rigid than import duties in the sense that until modified they constitute absolute ceilings for the volume of imports regardless of changes in business conditions. This, however, is partially offset by the fact that import quotas are usually made more subject to administrative discretion than are the levels of import duties, which, as revenue measures, often require legislation and are consequently more frequently revised than are statutory levels of import duty.

The treatment of quantitative restrictions in the redrafted London Charter reflects a cautious balancing of these conflicting economic and political considerations. The Charter proposes that import quotas shall be outlawed in principle, but that they shall be permitted as supplements to domestic crop-restriction or price-support or industrial development programs, as adjuncts of sanctioned intergovernmental commodity agreements, and as means of correcting actual or threatened balance of payments deficits. If any country uses quantitative restrictions on imports to safeguard its balance of payments, the ITO is empowered to investigate, to make recommendations, and to release other countries adversely affected from some of their obligations under the Charter to the member applying the restrictions.

The privilege of applying quantitative import restrictions to correct an adverse balance of payments can readily be abused. Any country can with the greatest of ease adopt monetary or other policies which will produce a balance of payments deficit. Any country which from other motives embarks on a full-employment policy, or on an investment policy, or on a wages policy, or on an inflationary monetary policy has some degree of choice as to the extent to which the necessary burden of economic adjustment shall be internal or, through special import restrictions, shall be made to fall on imports. The redrafted London Charter, in a paragraph added to the original American Suggested Charter, prohibits the International Trade Organization in such cases from recommending 'the withdrawal or the general relaxation of restrictions on the ground that the existing or prospective balance of payment difficulties of the member in question could be avoided by a change in that Member's domestic employment, reconstruction, development or social policies.'

For many countries, including such countries as Great Britain, France, China and India, this is likely to operate in practice to permit them to retain about as many of their existing import quotas and to impose about as many new ones as they please, while enjoying with respect to them a degree of international sanctification which was not available even in the bad days of the 1930's. There is widespread expectation – and perhaps intention – abroad that even in the absence of the generally-anticipated major depression in the United States many countries will have difficulties in paying for the volume of American and other hard-currency-country commodities which their peoples will want to import in the absence of special restrictions. Given the universal lack of confidence in the adequacy of the International Monetary Fund and the International Bank for Reconstruction and Development as sources of replenishment of dollars in short supply, it is probably not reasonable to expect that other countries could be persuaded to accept stronger general provisions against resort to quantitative restrictions than those contained in the revised Charter. The United States, on the other hand, is precluded from making their legitimacy a genuine question of principle, since it is unwilling to abstain from using import quotas itself.

By the terms of the Charter all existing quantitative restrictions of imports which cannot be brought under one of the exceptions referred to above must be eliminated. At the London Conference the issue was raised as to whether the removal of import quotas should not be treated on a parity with the reduction of import duties in the process of negotiation of balanced reduction of trade barriers. The texts of the revised Charter and of the rules adopted at London to govern the negotiations at Geneva for reductions in tariffs seem to indicate an acceptance of the American position that import quotas were inherently an illegitimate form of trade barrier and should be removed without compensation. The Preparatory Committee's covering Report, however, in rather characteristic fashion, blunts the edge of the text of the revised Charter. After stating that it was agreed that quantitative restrictions were to be dealt with by a general rule (that is, of uncompensated elimination) it proceeds as follows:

At the same time it was recognized that, in accordance with the plan for conducting tariff negotiations among the members of the Preparatory Committee, those countries would not be called upon to subscribe to the most-favored-nations and quantitative restrictions provisions until selective tariff negotiations had been completed and vice-versa. It was believed that this circumstance would assure that due weight will be given in the tariff negotiations to the benefits to be derived from the elimination of quantitative restrictions and the general grant of most-favored-nation treatment.

What this seems to mean is that it was understood that no country need subscribe to the Charter nor accept the results reached in the tariff negotiations unless it was satisfied with the two combined, but that in the tariff negotiations proper it will not be permitted to offer removals of specific quotas as compensation for removal or reduction of particular import duties. The way it will work out, presumably, is that if most countries are sufficiently satisfied to subscribe to the Charter after the tariff negotiations have been concluded, the remaining countries will in most cases also subscribe in order not to be excluded from membership in the International Trade Organization. Such procedures inevitably lead to compromise of principles, but practical statesmen have no alternative where action must wait upon consent, and where, in fact, they are far from ready themselves to adhere rigorously to the principles they proclaim. All that the ordinary citizen can reasonably ask is that the weight of the principle shall not be impaired by refusal to acknowledge that it has been compromised, and that if the use of quotas is given added respectability at Geneva, at least the range of quotas in actual operation shall be less.

An unregulated foreign trade is bound to create difficulties for a domestic economy regulated in conformity with a general economic plan adopted in advance. The major difficulties will take the form of balance of payments deficits, of the unavailability of essential imports in the needed volume, or of the unpredictable fluctuation of exports, with consequent scarcities and bottlenecks at home or embarrassing unemployment. The zeal of the United States for the elimination of special and flexible controls over foreign trade is in large part explained by the absence of any prospect that the United States will in the near future devise or accept a significant program for stabilization of employment or for the planning of investment, the confidence prevailing in this country that our competitive position in foreign trade and the exchange position of the American dollar will continue to be strong, and the availability of the cache of gold at Fort Knox to tide us over even a prolonged and substantial adverse balance of payments if perchance it should occur.

Many commentators on the American trade proposals, here and abroad, regard them as part of an American campaign in support of the free-enterprise principle and against the principle of national economic planning. There prevails abroad, moreover, a general apprehension lest the notorious instability of the American economy again manifest itself in a major depression which will spread to other countries if they surrender the right to impose special restrictions on imports from the United States and to make bilateral deals with other more stable countries.

The same issue arose in connection with the negotiation of the Articles of Agreement of the International Monetary Fund. That Agreement sanctions resort to exchange depreciation to remedy a continuing balance of payments deficit, and in addition sanctions the use of control of exchange transactions to restrict imports from any country whose currency has been declared by the Fund to be a 'scarce currency.' The London Charter provides additional sanction for these measures, and extends the range of internationally-approved measures, presumably on the ground that exchange depreciation may prove too slow and otherwise too ineffective a remedy for a balance of payments crisis.

Other countries are not satisfied with these concessions to their fears about the impact on their economies of the boom-and-bust pattern which they attribute to the American economy. It is true that there is already not much in the way of import restriction that they would be precluded from doing by either the Monetary Fund Agreement or the Trade Charter after a sharp reduction in the American intake of foreign commodities had resulted for them in adverse balances of payments with the United States. It may be taken for granted, moreover, that if a major depression occurs in the United States the Monetary Fund and the ITO will evaporate, and with them the international code of trade behavior laid down in their charters. Nevertheless, other countries are pressing for more positive protection against the threat of an American depression. They would like a firm undertaking from the United States that either by preventing a major depression from occurring here or by maintaining a minimum volume of American imports regardless of conditions in the American market it will see to it that it does not spread instability abroad. Failing this, they ask international sanction for long-run bilateral agreements which assure *in advance* a minimum volume of exports for the participating countries.

To sanction bilateralism would be an outright surrender of one of the main objectives of American economic foreign policy since the signing of the Atlantic Charter and the Lend-Lease Master Agreements. To undertake genuine advance commitments to maintain stability of American economic conditions through governmental action would go against the American political grain, especially after the results of the Congressional elections of last autumn. The United States, by offering participation in a large-scale anti-cyclical international investment program designed to promote economic stability in the world at large, might provide other countries with the assurance they crave that an American depression will not disrupt their economic planning. It might do so, moreover, without either sanctioning bilateralism or involving the adoption of a national stabilization program. I am not aware, however, that our Government has given any consideration to this alternative.

Given these limitations on American policy, the American negotiators have been impelled to agree to sanction important deviations from the general rules of outlawry of quantitative restrictions of imports (some of which may in practice be hard to distinguish from bilateralism) if these rules were to be acceptable at all. The net outcome is that pro-forma international acceptance of a substantial proportion of the original American program is on the way to being obtained, but that the existence or threat of balance of payments difficulties will suffice to provide an international sanction for substantial deviation from the pattern of international trade sought by this country.

VI

There remains for consideration the most perplexing question of all in the field of commercial policy: can an international code be devised which is applicable to the trade relations between free-market and state-trading economies or between state-trading countries themselves? Soviet Russia's great political power and growing economic importance make this a significant question. The growth of state trading elsewhere, as in Czechoslovakia and other Russian satellite countries, in Great Britain and in the Argentine, adds to its importance.

The failure of Soviet Russia to accept the invitation to the London Conference led the Conference to postpone consideration of the special article in the Suggested Charter relating to countries which exercise a complete state monopoly of import trade. This article proposed that each such country should undertake to import from other members of the International Trade Organization an agreed amount in the aggregate over a specific period, subject to periodic adjustment. If the minimum agreed upon were low, such an undertaking would be of little consequence. Yet it would be unreasonable and impracticable to expect the state-trading countries to guarantee sizeable purchases in the absence of correspondingly rigid commitments by other countries to make purchases from them. Under the Suggested Charter a country exercising a state monopoly of foreign trade would presumably be precluded, like other countries, from making special bilateral arrangements outside these general multilateral negotiations. It is not clear that acceptance of the Charter would in practice impose any other genuine limitations on the behavior of state monopolies. But this limitation is of itself of great importance and may perhaps largely explain the apparent coldness of Soviet Russia to the original American proposals.

The Suggested Charter contained also two provisions relating to particular state-trading 'enterprises' which the London draft retains without substantial amendment. One of these provisions proposes that in its external purchases and sales such enterprise shall operate in a non-discriminatory manner and that 'to this end such enterprise shall ... be influenced solely by commercial considerations, such as price, quality, marketability, transportation and terms of purchase or sale.' This association of 'non-discriminatory' with 'commercial' behavior is confusing, since there is nothing more 'commercial' than the discriminatory practices of a monopoly operating with a single eye to profits. As an antonym to 'political,' 'commercial' would make sense, but this does not seem to be its intended meaning here. In neither case, however, is there any attempt to make clear what the criterion of violation would be, how it could be objectively determined, and what its consequences would be. The other provision would make subject to international negotiation, in the same manner as tariffs, the maximum margin of protection against imports and the maximum excess of export price over cost of production which the monopoly would be permitted to maintain. It is highly doubtful whether the obvious practical difficulties of application of such a provision could be surmounted, especially where blending of domestic and imported materials and complex processing before sale of the imported materials are involved, as they often would be. This is not intended as a reflection on the craftsmanship of those who drafted these provisions, as there is as yet evident no solution of the problem of framing a code of practice for monopolies in international trade – or in domestic trade, for that matter – which shall be reasonably equitable, administratively workable, and acceptable. The draftsmen, however, should not deceive themselves or the public as to the extent of the contribution which the Charter makes to the solution of this problem.

There is even ground for the fear that the Charter would provide an artificial inducement to some countries to resort to, or to expand, state trading. It offers to state-trading member countries all the advantages of all-around reduction of trade barriers and of abstention from discriminatory practices by free-market countries, while leaving the state-trading countries effectively free, subject to one qualification, from corresponding obligations. There is one, but only one, significant restraint which the American Suggested Charter or the London draft would impose on the foreign-trade operations of state-trading monopolies, namely, the prohibition against overt bilateral deals with other countries, and this prohibition, of course, would apply with at least equal force to free-market countries. The problem of finding a suitable pattern of regulation of international trade for a world in which there exist state-trading countries, I repeat, still awaits solution.

It is not yet clear, however, that the special privileges which state-trading countries would be able to exploit under the Charter would have much economic importance for us. Soviet Russia, even with her enlarged territory, is not a major factor in international trade, and this narrowly limits the degree of monopoly power she can exercise, whether as buyer or seller. Even if a number of small European countries follow Russia's example in operating their foreign trade under state monopolies, it will still not matter much to us economically, so long as they act as national units and not in combination. It would be a more serious threat to us, to other countries, and to the significance of the Charter as a whole, if Great Britain should move much further in the direction of state trading, whether in the special form she is giving it of 'bulk purchasing,' or otherwise. But the most serious threat would arise if Soviet Russia were to incorporate in her foreign-trade monopoly the trade of her satellite countries, and if the number of her satellites were to grow.

The threat in these circumstances would be political as well as economic, given Soviet Russia's autarchic tendencies. The great political virtue of multilateralism, far exceeding in importance its economic virtues, is that it makes it economically possible for most countries, even if small, poor and weak, to live in freedom and with chances of prosperity without having to come to special terms with some Great Power. The greater the area embraced in Russia's economic system, the more difficult it would be economically for the countries adjoining to maintain an independent existence, and therefore the more susceptible they would be to Russian pressures or blandishments. It would be conceivable under these circumstances that the Charter would not effectively hinder a glacier-like advance westward and southward of Russian economic and political hegemony, regardless of whether Russia accepted membership in the International Trade Organization. It may well be that the only way of checking such a movement would be for the United States to offer both Soviet Russia and her neighbors such generous measure of commercial and financial aid as would induce her, and enable her satellites, to participate wholeheartedly in a program of international economic collaboration under which the pressure of sheer national power, economic or political, was reduced to a minimum. At present, however, such a program is neither practical nor desirable, given the tension and the mutual distrust between the United States and Soviet Russia.

VII

It has not been possible here to deal with all of the issues of principle raised by the Charter, still less with the areas of commercial policy with which the Charter does not even attempt to deal, such as, for example, the entire field of trade in services: shipping, banking, insurance, the tourist trade, movies, hydropower and so forth.

One range of problems omitted from the draft Charter calls for special comment at this time. Strong pressure is being exerted on the American Government by American business interests to press for inclusion in the Charter of provisions assuring American capital access to opportunities for direct investment in foreign countries and satisfactory treatment of such investments. There is need for an international investment code, but it should be drafted with the greatest care so as not to weigh the balance too heavily on the side either of creditors or of debtors. At the moment, it would be highly inexpedient, for obvious reasons, if we were to take any step which would provide any basis for charges by our numerous foreign critics that our trade negotiations are only one phase of our general pursuit of economic hegemony in the service of American 'capitalistic-imperialism.' We should take great care lest we are found to be asking other countries to grant legal privileges to American capital which our own laws withhold from foreign capital and business enterprise in this country. It seems wise not to enlarge the scope of the Charter in this manner, and to postpone multilateral negotiations on the problems of international private investment until careful preparation has been made in that field.

In the range of problems with which the Charter does deal, including problems not commented on here, it is generally true that the Charter makes no serious attempt to apply rigorously-formulated principles in a doctrinaire manner, but attempts instead to find a basis for general agreement on movement toward two goals: minimum trade barriers and non-discrimination. The extent of movement is left largely to a process of multilateral bargaining whose outcome cannot be predicted. Where rules of some degree of precision are proposed, they are invariably qualified by exceptions and escape clauses necessary to make them generally acceptable, but easily capable of becoming more important than the rules to which they are attached. Where the clash of principle is particularly sharp, as in the case of state monopolies of foreign trade, the problem is evaded or is postponed. In the process of evolution which the draft Charter has already undergone, there can easily be detected a general tendency toward blurring and relaxing its principles and rules; the effort to strengthen and expand the discretionary authority of the International Trade Organization is presumably intended to provide an offset for this tendency.

Ardent supporters of particular principles may find all this discouraging. But it was probably inevitable from the beginning of the program of negotiation. The pattern of international legislation on complex matters cannot reasonably be expected to be tidier than the patterns with which we are familiar in the field of domestic legislation. No economic principle has universal appeal. No government has objectives single enough and simple enough to enable it to avoid mixing its principles. Rules specific enough to have bite need qualifications and escape clauses if the hard cases are to be provided for. There must be accommodation to established patterns and varying circumstances, and allowance for future contingencies. An inflexible code would be immediately unacceptable. If accepted, it would probably crack under the first severe strain to which it was put. Complete reliance upon *ad hoc* diplomacy, at the other extreme, would in practice be very little removed from complete international anarchy. The Charter which is in process of negotiation seeks a middle way between the code too rigid to withstand strain and the near anarchy which would be likely in the absence of any code. Increasing reliance is being put upon the discretionary authority of the International Trade Organization to reconcile the need for international discipline with the aversion of the member countries to irrevocable commitments and to submission to rigid rules.

The Charter is, therefore, a compromise document. It could no doubt be improved upon, but not at the pleasure of the United States, and not without strong opposition from American sources. If adopted it will bring some, though by no means all, of the degree and type of order in the international trade field which our country needs and the State Department wants. If it is rejected, whether by us or by other important countries, the consequences are clearly indicated: a return to the systematic economic warfare which prevailed in the 1930's, with its political tensions, its economic wastefulness, and its favorable setting for the launching by desperate leaders, on behalf of despairing peoples, of ventures fatal to the world at large as well as to themselves. The International Trade Organization Charter is the only available safeguard against such a development. There are no alternatives. Without our full and active support even this safeguard will not be brought into operation. It is, in fact, by no means certain that our support will suffice. But it is as certain as such things can be that it is in our national interest to support it, and to support it vigorously and unreservedly.

Clair Wilcox, 'The London Draft of a Charter for an International Trade Organization', *American Economic Review*, 37:2 (May 1947), pp. 529–41.

INTERNATIONAL TRADE ORGANIZATION

THE LONDON DRAFT OF A CHARTER FOR AN INTERNATIONAL TRADE ORGANIZATION

By CLAIR WILCOX
Department of State

The London meeting of the Preparatory Committee for an International Conference on Trade and Employment, in October and November, 1946, represents a single step in a long program of international collaboration with respect to trade policy in which the initiative, at every stage, has been taken by the United States. This program had its origin in the Hull Trade Agreements legislation in 1934 and found expression in the Atlantic Charter in 1941, the Mutual Aid Agreements in 1942, and the Bretton Woods Agreements in 1944. In 1945, it motivated the renewal of the Trade Agreements Act, the conclusion of the Anglo-American Financial Agreement, the publication of the *American Proposals for Expansion of World Trade and Employment*, and the issuance to fifteen other countries of invitations to participate in trade agreement negotiations. In 1946, it led to the adoption by the Economic and Social Council of a resolution, introduced by the United States, providing for the calling of an International Conference on Trade and Employment and setting up the Preparatory Committee; to the preparation, circulation, and publication by the United States of the *Suggested Charter for an International Trade Organization*; to the discussion of this draft with the other governments represented on the preparatory committee; and to its adoption by the Preparatory Committee as the basis of the deliberations at its first meeting.

The next steps, in their chronological order, are the public hearings on the tariff list in Washington, beginning on January 13, 1947, the meeting of an Interim Drafting Committee in New York, beginning on January 20, 1947, the public hearings on the draft charter in Washington and other cities, beginning on February 25, 1947, the second meeting of the Preparatory Committee, incorporating the trade agreement negotiations, in Geneva, beginning April 10, 1947, and the International Conference on Trade and Employment sometime in the fall of 1947. The instrument that emerges from this conference will be submitted to the Congress of the United States and to the governments of other countries, and, with their approval, the International Trade Organization should be established sometime in 1948.

At its meeting in London, the Preparatory Committee considered drafts of texts of eighty-nine articles prepared for possible inclusion in a charter of an International Trade Organization. On two of these articles (those dealing with complete state monopolies of import trade and with relations with nonmembers) it deferred action until its second meeting. On eleven articles (dealing primarily with formal and organizational matters and with indirect forms of protection) it referred the texts to the Interim Drafting Committee. On two other articles (dealing with voting in the International Trade Organization and with membership on the executive board of the Organization) it came to no agreement and instructed the Interim Drafting Committee to prepare alternative drafts. On the other seventy-four articles, covering all of the important substantive questions that were before the committee, and most of the detailed provisions with respect to organization, it came to wide agreement. On two of these articles, three delegations recorded reservations and fourteen agreed. On three others, two delegations recorded reservations and fifteen agreed. On each of six others, one delegation reserved its position and sixteen agreed. On the remaining sixty-three articles, agreement was unanimous.

It should be emphasized that the work of the meeting was carried on at the expert level, that the negotiations were preparatory rather than conclusive, and that the positions taken involve no final commitments. It is nonetheless true that the committee has carried the work of drafting a world trade charter to a stage that should make possible its approval without major changes in principle.

At its final session, the committee also approved the reports of six subcommittees, outlining in detail the issues discussed, the views expressed, and the agreements reached on employment, economic development, commercial policy, restrictive business practices, commodity arrangements, and organization. The report of the subcommittee on commercial policy includes a detailed memorandum on 'Procedures for Giving Effect to Certain Provisions of the Proposed I.T.O. Charter by Means of a General Agreement on Tariffs and Trade Among the Members of the Preparatory Committee.' Approval of this memorandum establishes an agreed procedure to be followed in the reciprocal trade negotiations at Geneva this spring. In the meantime, it commits the governments concerned, morally if not legally, to a trade restriction truce.

The problems to which the meeting devoted the major part of its attention, and the problems which were most important from the point of view of the United States, were those arising in the field of commercial policy. Here, the pattern adopted, as suggested in the American proposals, was the enunciation of a general rule, the enumeration of specific exceptions to the general rule, narrowly limited and precisely defined, the establishment of regulations and procedures whereby members of the Organization may avail themselves of these exceptions, and the provisions of penalties that may be imposed in cases of violation. This pattern can best be illustrated by its application to the principal issue that came before the meeting: the desire of many countries to retain a large measure of freedom to impose quantitative restrictions on their trade and the insistence of the United States and certain other delegations that quantitative restrictions should be condemned in principle and that the right to employ them should be strictly limited.

I. *Quantitative Restrictions and Exchange Control*

In the London draft, the general rule with respect to quantitative restrictions is stated as follows: 'no prohibition or restriction, other than duties, taxes, or other charges, whether made effective through quotas, import licenses or other measures, shall be imposed or maintained by any member country, on the importation of any product of any other member country, or on the exportation or sale for export, of any product destined for any other member country.'

Detailed exceptions to this general rule permit the use of (1) transitional export or import prohibitions designed to effect the equitable distribution of products in short supply, the maintenance of wartime price control, and the orderly liquidation of government surpluses and war industries, (2) temporary export restrictions designed to relieve critical shortages of foodstuffs and other essential products, (3) controls required to enforce the observance of standards for the classification and grading of commodities, (4) export or import quotas established under intergovernmental commodity agreements, (5) restrictions designed to confer a monopoly upon a state-trading enterprise, and (6) import quotas on agricultural and fisheries products required to enforce domestic production and marketing restrictions and surplus disposal programs, provided that such quotas do not reduce the share of imports in the domestic market.

Of greater importance is a final exception which permits a member of the Organization to employ import controls as a means of safeguarding its balance of payments. Here the test is the member's need '(1) to stop or to forestall the imminent threat of a serious decline in the level of monetary reserves, or (2) in the case of a member with very low monetary reserves, to achieve a reasonable rate of increase in its reserves.' Under this provision, a member may also 'select imports for restriction on the grounds of essentiality,' but it 'shall avoid all unnecessary damage to the commercial interests of other members' and it shall not carry such restriction 'to the point at which it involves the complete exclusion of imports of any class of goods.'

A member considering the imposition of new restrictions is required to consult with the Organization 'as to the nature of its balance of payments difficulties, the various corrective measures which may be available, and the possible effects of such measures on the economies of other members.' A member maintaining or intensifying existing restrictions may also be required to consult with the Organization at any time with regard to 'alternative methods ... of meeting its balance of payments difficulties.' The International Monetary Fund is to be invited to participate in all such consultations.

Any member may complain that another member is employing quantitative restrictions in a manner inconsistent with the provisions of the charter or unnecessarily damaging to its trade. The Organization will then consider the complaint, in consultation with the International Monetary Fund, and if it is found to be justified, may recommend the withdrawal or modification of the restrictions in question. If the offending member does not comply with its recommendation, the Organization may then release the other members, in whole or in part, from their obligations toward the member in question, permitting them, for instance, to withhold from it the tariff concessions which they have made.

In order to avoid the imposition of such a penalty, a member may request the Organization to give prior approval to restrictions which it desires to maintain or to impose or to a statement of the circumstances under which such restrictions may be imposed. The Organization, after consulting the International Monetary Fund, may grant such approval, specifying the general extent, degree, and duration of the restrictions permitted. Thereafter, no other member may successfully challenge the legitimacy of the restrictions falling within the scope of the approval, but a member may still seek redress for unnecessary stringency in their application to particular products.

Members are required to relax their quantitative restrictions as the difficulties which justified their imposition are improved and to eliminate them entirely when such difficulties disappear. Within two years of its institution, the Organization is required to call into question all restrictions then in use. And finally, whenever the employment of quantitative controls, under the foregoing provisions, is so persistent and widespread as to indicate the existence of general disequilibrium, the Organization, in collaboration with the International Monetary Fund, is directed to 'initiate discussions to consider whether other measures might not be taken, either by those countries whose balances of payments are under pressure or by those countries whose balances of payments are tending to be exceptionally favourable, or by any appropriate intergovernmental agency or agencies, to remove the underlying causes of the disequilibrium.'

In those cases in which the use of quantitative restrictions is permitted, there is a general rule which prohibits discrimination in their administration. The methods of applying this rule, in the order of their desirability, are listed as follows: (1) avoidance of allocation among sources of supply by announcing global quotas or by issuing licenses unrestricted as to source, or (2) announcement of allocations established on the basis of commercial principles through agreement among exporting countries, or, if this is not practicable, by reference to the share supplied in a previous representative period, subject to consultation at the request of the Organization or any of its members. It is further provided that members thus restricting imports shall supply adequate information concerning the administration of their controls.

Exceptions to this general rule permit the discriminatory administration of quantitative restrictions for the following specific purposes: (1) to enable members, until the end of 1951, to assist countries whose economies have been disrupted by war, (2) to enable them to conform to the provisions of intergovernmental commodity agreements, (3) to permit them to use import quotas, insofar as the International Monetary Fund permits them to use exchange controls, to ration scarce currencies, (4) to enable a group of territories with a common quota in the Fund to protect their common monetary reserves, (5) to enable members so to control their exports as to obtain convertible rather than inconvertible currencies, and (6) to enable them to use inconvertible currencies to pay for imports, where this would involve an addition to the volume of imports that would otherwise obtain and where the discrimination either would parallel exchange controls permissible under the Articles of Agreement of the Fund or would have the prior approval both of the Fund and of the I.T.O. Provision is made for the possible elimination of this final exception when general convertibility of currencies has been restored or, at least, by the end of 1951.

If any of these restrictions is applied in a manner which is inconsistent with the exceptions provided or which discriminates unnecessarily against the trade of another, and if the use of such restrictions has not been previously approved, the Organization, after consultation with the Fund, may direct the offending member to modify or remove the discrimination within sixty days.

Since quantitative restrictions and exchange controls may be employed alternatively to affect the flow of trade, it is important that the rules that govern these two devices should be laid down and administered with such consistency that it will be impossible, by resorting to one of these devices, to escape from the rules that govern the other. Accordingly, the London draft provides that members 'will not seek by exchange action to frustrate the purposes of this charter and that they will not seek by trade action to frustrate the purposes of the Articles of Agreement of the International Monetary Fund.' The committee, moreover, took the view that every member of the I.T.O. should be a member of the Fund or, failing this, that a nonmember of the Fund should be required to enter into a special exchange agreement with the I.T.O. and that this agreement should be established and administered in collaboration with the Fund.

The present draft is a complete revision of the American text. But it preserves the general approach and the essential principles of the original proposals and strengthens them in many ways. It eliminates the transition period provided in the earlier version and brings the balance of payments test into play immediately upon the establishment of the Organization. It affords greater flexibility in the exceptions permitted to the rule of nondiscrimination. But, at the same time, it provides more adequate safeguards and more effective supervision through the collaboration of the International Monetary Fund and the I.T.O. On balance, it represents a distinct improvement over the previous draft.

It will doubtless be said, in criticism of the charter, that the general rule condemning quantitative restrictions will be of little value if exceptions are allowed, but these exceptions have been realistically devised to meet the actual conditions that now prevail throughout the world. They were dictated, not by political expediency, but by economic necessity. Without them, the general rules could not be accepted or, if they were accepted, could not be expected to work. Clearly, it would have been unwise to have proposed a rule so rigid that it could not be enforced. As a practical matter, our only choice is between a rule that condemns quantitative restrictions in principle, limits them to exceptional cases, and subjects them to international control and a situation in which any nation, at any time, will enjoy complete freedom to impose quantitative restrictions as extensively and intensively as it may choose. Confronted with such a choice there can be no question as to where our interest lies.

II. *Tariffs and Preferences*

Under the present draft, members of the Organization are committed to enter into reciprocal and mutually advantageous negotiations directed toward the substantial reduction of tariffs and the elimination of preferences. Members who, in the judgment of the Organization, have unjustifiably failed to fulfill this obligation may be denied the benefits of the tariff concessions that are made to others. A new clause, inserted in London, provides that the binding of low tariffs or tariff-free treatment shall be recognized as a concession equivalent in value to the reduction of high tariffs. Otherwise the rules to govern the process of tariff bargaining are identical in substance with those originally proposed by the United States and accepted by the United Kingdom. Prior commitments are not to be permitted to stand in the way of negotiations with respect to preferences. And reductions in tariffs are to operate automatically to reduce or eliminate margins of preference. With quantitative restrictions limited to exceptional cases and brought under international control and with preferences subject to reduction or elimination through the operation of an agreed rule, a firm basis has been established for the negotiation of reciprocal agreements for the binding or reduction of tariff rates.

With respect to discrimination in customs duties, the general rule requires members to accord to one another general unconditional most-favored-nation treatment. Exceptions to this rule permit the maintenance of such preferences as may survive the process of reduction or elimination during tariff negotiations, preferences incidental to the formation of a customs union, and new preferential arrangements that may be approved, in exceptional circumstances, under the provision of the charter, as originally drafted, that permits the conference of the Organization, in special cases, to waive an obligation of a member by a two-thirds vote.

The present draft retains a provision, modeled after the escape clause in the trade agreement with Mexico, which permits members to withdraw or modify tariff concessions they may have made, in the event that imports so increase as to 'cause or threaten serious injury to domestic producers.' A member taking such action is required to consult with the other member affected, but may proceed without its consent. In this case, however, the latter member may, in turn, suspend concessions made to the former member to any extent that the Organization may approve.

The provisions in this section closely follow the original American draft and, up to the present, have evoked little comment in the United States.

III. *Employment*

The United States proposed, in its suggested charter, that each member of the I.T.O. should take action designed to achieve and maintain full employment within its own jurisdiction through measures which are not incompatible with undertakings designed to promote an expanding volume of international trade. Certain of the countries attending the London meeting expressed the view that greater emphasis should be given to the objective of full employment. But none of them proposed the delegation to an international agency of any authority that would enable it to make an affirmative contribution to this end. The only commitment with respect to the maintenance of employment in the London draft corresponds closely to that proposed by the United States. It provides that each member of the I.T.O. 'shall take action designed to achieve and maintain full and productive employment and high and stable levels of effective demand within its own jurisdiction through measures appropriate to its political and economic institutions and compatible with the other purposes of the Organization.'

This provision is likely to be attacked from two sides. Those who read into the objective of full employment a commitment to deficit spending and work relief will object to the very mention of the words. Those who believe that the attainment of this objective is imperative will complain that members are committed not to assure full employment but only to take action that is designed to achieve that goal and that the charter confers upon no international agency the authority to take affirmative action in this field. To the first group it may be said that full employment is defined, in the committee report, in the words of the Employment Act of 1946, as a condition in which useful employment opportunities are available to all those able and willing to work and that the measures that any nation may adopt for the purpose of achieving this condition are for it alone to choose. To the second group it can only be said that the success of domestic measures designed to maintain employment cannot be guaranteed; that thinking with respect to the functions that an international agency might perform in maintaining employment is still in the embryonic stage; and that the delegation to such an agency of any authority in the matter is not within the realm of practical politics. The charter does, however, give formal recognition to the necessary relationship between policies affecting employment and those affecting trade.

The principal issues considered in the discussions on employment arose from the fear expressed by certain countries that participation in a freer trading system might make it more difficult for them to maintain their domestic employment programs. To explain this fear, it was argued that one country, if it were a large factor in world trade, might exercise deflationary pressure on others in one of two ways: first, by buying too little from abroad and investing too little abroad in relation to its exports; and second, by falling into a depression which would involve a serious or abrupt decline in its effective demand for imported goods.

To meet the first situation, it was proposed that each member of the Organization should agree to take action designed to assure that its currently accruing international receipts are fully utilized for international payments or for investment abroad. In the draft that was finally adopted, this proposal does not appear. Instead, it is provided that each member shall agree 'that, in the case of a fundamental disequilibrium in its balance of payments, involving other countries in persistent balance-of-payments difficulties which handicap them in maintaining employment, it will make its full contribution to action designed to correct the maladjustment,' and the accompanying report explains that 'the particular measures that should be adopted [e.g., the stimulation of imports or the removal of special encouragement to exports, an appreciation of the country's exchange rate, an upward revision of its internal cost and price structure, an increase in foreign investment, etc.] should, of course, be left to the government concerned to determine.' As it stands, the article serves the useful purpose of calling to the attention of the members of the Organization the fact that those who expect to sell must be prepared to buy.

To meet the situation created by a serious or abrupt decline in international demand, it was proposed that one member might complain to the Organization that another, by failing to maintain its demand, had prevented the complaining member from maintaining employment and that the Organization might then release this member from its obligations with respect to trade. This proposal was substantially modified in the final draft. Under the terms of a general provision of the charter, if a member considers that any other member has adopted a measure, or that any situation has arisen, which has the effect of nullifying or impairing any object of the charter, including the object of maintaining employment, the members concerned shall enter into consultation with a view to effecting a satisfactory adjustment of the matter. If no adjustment is thus effected the matter may be referred to the Organization, which shall then make an investigation, if necessary consulting with the Economic and Social Council and with other specialized international agencies, to determine what remedial action may be available, and shall recommend such action to the members concerned. In particularly serious cases, the Organization may authorize the suspension of specific obligations assumed under the charter. But no member may suspend such obligations without the permission of the Organization. It is further provided that the Organization shall have regard, in the exercise of this function, 'to the need of members to take action ... to safeguard their economies against deflationary pressure in the event of a serious or abrupt decline in the effective demand of other countries.'

The effect of these provisions is to afford a country a means of obtaining a partial release from its commitments with respect to trade policy in the event that its economy is seriously affected by a depression originating outside its borders. In such a situation, however, it is likely that the country concerned would be in balance-of-payments difficulty. It is therefore doubtful that these provisions afford any prospect of release that was not already available under the balance-of-payments exception in the American draft. It would be illusory, in any case, to hold that liberal trade commitments can be enforced if the world is again plunged into a major depression. Here, again, the charter does no more than recognize the facts of life.

IV. *Economic Development*

One of the purposes of the Organization, as set forth in the suggested charter prepared by the United States, is 'to encourage and assist the industrial and general economic development of member countries, particularly of those still in the early stages of industrial development.' It was the opinion of many of the delegations attending the London meeting that this problem, too, should receive greater emphasis than it was accorded in the American draft. To this end, a long list of proposals was advanced. It was suggested, for instance, that an industrial country with a favorable balance of payments should assume an obligation to provide capital to countries in the process of development; that it should recognize that such capital would have to be provided on a nonremunerative basis; that industrialization and diversification should be accepted as sufficient justification for the imposition of trade restrictions; that these restrictions should be imposed on the basis of decisions made by national tribunals in accordance with such criteria as they might employ; and that industrial countries should recognize the necessity of contracting particular industries as these industries expand elsewhere. None of these proposals was accepted.

The London draft, as finally adopted, contains a new chapter on economic development that was prepared and introduced by the delegation of the United States. Under the terms of this chapter, members agree to promote the continuing development of their respective territories and to co-operate through the Economic and Social Council and through international specialized agencies in plans and programs and in the provision of facilities required for such development. Members exporting these facilities agree to impose no unreasonable impediments to their exportation and members importing them agree to take no unreasonable action injurious to the interests of those who provide them. A proposal that the I.T.O. assume jurisdiction over the function of providing technical assistance to countries in the process of development has been referred to the Economic and Social Council for its opinion.

Here again, however, the principal issue was created by the desire of many countries to promote industrialization by restricting imports. Under the suggested charter, countries were free to subsidize domestic production and to impose or raise tariffs on products that were not covered by trade agreements. But many delegations sought freedom to impose or raise tariffs on other products and to employ import quotas to protect new industries. The final draft does not afford such freedom, but it does establish a procedure through which permission to make a limited use of these restrictions may be obtained. Under this procedure, the I.T.O. will consider the case presented by the applicant and the views of other members whose trade would be substantially affected, in the light of such criteria as to productivity and other factors as it may establish. It may then decide either to drop the case or to proceed. If the product in question has not been covered in a trade agreement, the Organization may, in its discretion, grant the applicant permission, within such limits as it may fix, to impose restrictions that are otherwise proscribed. If the product has been so covered, however, the Organization must sponsor negotiations between the applicant and the members affected and cannot grant such permission unless substantial agreement is achieved.

The United States made this concession in recognition of the insistent pressure for industrialization that is felt in every corner of the globe. It was the only case in which the delegation departed from the principles that were elaborated in the American draft. But it was this compromise that brought the meeting close to unanimous agreement. And the draft, as it stands, establishes a new principle in international affairs: that quantitative restrictions on trade are not to be employed, without international sanction, for the development of infant industries.

V. *Restrictive Business Practices*

On the international cartel problem, the London draft follows the pattern originally proposed by the United States. Its provisions apply to business practices in international trade which 'restrain competition, limit access to markets, or foster monopolistic control,' whether they are engaged in by a single private enterprise or by a group which includes within its membership private enterprises or public enterprises or both. These practices are to be judged by their effects and are to be condemned whenever they interfere with 'the expansion of production and trade and the maintenance in all countries of high levels of real income.' Each member agrees to 'take all possible steps, through legislation or otherwise, to ensure that ... enterprises within its jurisdiction do not engage in practices which have [this] effect.' A member may complain to the I.T.O. that 'specific practices exist which have or are about to have the effect described.' The I.T.O. will then make an investigation, hold hearings, and if it finds that the practices in question have such an effect, may 'request each member concerned to take every possible action to prevent the continuance or recurrence of the practices and, at its discretion, recommend to the members concerned remedial measures to be carried out in accordance with their respective laws and procedures.' Each member agrees 'to take the fullest account of the Organization's findings, requests, and recommendations ... in considering the initiation of action ... to prevent ... the continuation or recurrence of [these] practices,' to report on the action taken and, in cases in which no action is taken, 'to explain to the Organization the reasons therefor and discuss the matter further with the Organization if requested to do so.'

In this case, again, criticism will come from two extremes. It will be said that the chapter goes too far, subjecting domestic business to international control and limiting its freedom to participate in foreign market-sharing schemes. It will be said that the chapter does not go far enough, providing a forum for international discussion instead of outlawing cartels per se. But as far as this country is concerned, the plan does not go beyond the provisions of the antitrust laws. And for most other countries, it involves a greater commitment than anyone had any reason to expect. Certainly a beginning has been made; a principle has been established; specific cases can be called into question; the pressure of world opinion can be brought to bear. Beyond this it is not now practicable to go.

VI. *Commodity Arrangements*

The chapter on intergovernmental commodity arrangements has been completely reorganized and substantially improved. It retains all of the principles and most of the text of the American draft. The circumstances under which governments may enter into agreements regulating the production, export, import, or prices of primary commodities are carefully defined. Such agreements are limited in duration and subject to periodic review. They must assure the availability of adequate supplies. They must 'afford increasing opportunities for satisfying world requirements from sources from which such requirements can be supplied most effectively and economically.' And countries participating in such agreements are required to formulate and adopt a program of economic adjustment designed to make them unnecessary. All commodity arrangements must be open to participation by any member of the Organization. They must afford consuming countries and producing countries an equal voice. And they must be accompanied, at every stage, by full publicity.

This chapter, as many of the others, will draw fire both from the right and from the left. Those who oppose all commodity agreements will say that it compromises with evil; that government cartels should be outlawed along with private cartels. Those who seek the creation of large numbers of such agreements will complain that its restrictive provisions will make them too hard to get. Between these two positions, the chapter occupies a middle ground. It neither prohibits commodity agreements nor promotes them. It attempts to prevent abuses of the sorts that have arisen in the past. It seeks to establish principles that are economically defensible and morally sound. It marks the first approach toward agreement on international policy in this field.

The foregoing review has set forth at length the provisions of the London draft that deal with quantitative restrictions. This has been done because these provisions are central and because they illustrate the pattern which has been followed in the document as a whole. The review has outlined, though less fully, the closely related provisions that have to do with exchange control, tariffs, and preferences, employment, and economic development and the chapters devoted to restrictive business practices and commodity arrangements. It has not covered the provisions that are concerned with subsidies, state trading, and the organization of the I.T.O. On each of these matters the London text adheres closely to the American draft.

The present document undoubtedly contains some passages that are obscure, ambiguous, or inconsistent. In some cases, such defects mark the outcome of a hard-fought compromise. In others, they are the inadvertent product of the collaboration of some two hundred people during six weeks of steady work. But, on the whole, this work was well done. The committee came to a series of agreements that expresses not the lowest common denominator but the highest common denominator of their several views. And they embodied these agreements in a charter which has achieved a better balance, a greater realism, and a finer precision than the draft on which they built.

Memorandum on Imperial Preference, Loans from the United States and Tariff Negotiations between the United States and United Kingdom, 14 October 1947, PRO, PREM 8/490.

SECRETARY OF STATE.

Sir S. Cripps and the President of the Board of Trade intend to speak to you after the Cabinet this afternoon about the latest developments in the preference negotiations with the Americans. An account of these developments is contained in Washington telegrams.

2. You will see that,

    (i) The U.S. Government would only accept our refusal to reduce Colonial preferences by 25% if they themselves withdraw the proposed concession regarding rubber.

    (ii) This is the official American reply to your message to Mr. Marshall and the U.S. representative at Geneva has been instructed to pursue negotiations on this basis.

    (iii) Both Lord Inverchapel and the U.K. Delegation, Geneva, feel strongly that as between the two alternatives of no rubber concession and no reduction of colonial preferences and the inclusion of both, the latter would be greatly to the advantage of the Commonwealth as a whole, from every point of view, both economic and political. The Geneva delegation suggests that the decision taken last week by the Cabinet should be reviewed and it is in connexion with this suggestion that Sir S. Cripps and the President of the Board of Trade wish to talk to you.

3. There are only three possibilities now open to us:

    (a) to insist on the inclusion of the U.S. concession on rubber while continuing to withhold any counter-concession on the U.K. side.

    (b) to accept the elimination of the U.S. rubber concession retaining the colonial preferences unimpaired.

    (c) to reconsider the balance of advantage of the U.S. rubber concession as compared with a concession by the U.K. with respect to colonial preferences. Among such possible concessions it appears that the one already discussed, namely a 25% reduction in all colonial preference margins scheduled in the 1938 agreement is the only one which can be found which, while providing an acceptable quid pro quo for the rubber concession, is relatively innocuous from our own point of view.

4. Course (a) would almost certainly lead to a breakdown. The effect of this on Anglo-American relations in general and on our prospects for obtaining a release of the blocked $400 million of the Loan and of reaching a relatively satisfactory re-negotiation of the German Fusion Agreement (to mention

only two current instances of the highest importance) would be incalculable. It would mean foregoing what we all believe to be an advantageous bargain in itself and of obtaining in return nothing except a guarantee of further violent shocks to our economy which we are in no position to stand. Its effect on Commonwealth relations would be most serious. Each Dominion has now reached a satisfactory stage in its bilateral tariff negotiations with the U.S. A breakdown over Colonial preferences would mean that all these prospective arrangements for the Dominions would be jeopardised, and the U.K. would be held largely responsible.

5. The question therefore arises which of courses (b) and (c) yields the most favourable balance of advantage to the Commonwealth as a whole. On this point all the Departments primarily concerned (Colonial Office, Board of Trade and Commonwealth Relations Office) unanimously agree that economic considerations are in favour of making our concession with respect to colonial preferences and getting the rubber concession in return rather than having neither concession included in the agreement. Lord Inverchapel viewing the question from the angle of Anglo-American relations strongly supports this view. He says 'Agreement on the wider basis would be a sound investment in the good will of the United States Administration, whereas agreement without some reduction of colonial preferences would leave a rankling disappointment.'

6. Apart from these wider considerations which are of critical importance, the case for preferring alternative (c) to alternative (b) is as follows:-

   (i) the proposed reduction in colonial preferences is not a concession by the colonies. It is a concession by the U.K. and would have no economic effect on the colonies, except to the extent that the lowering of preferential margins gives them slightly greater opportunities of buying their requirements in the cheapest market. If we do decide to refuse this concession we could only honestly argue in public that we were acting in the U.K. interest alone and even this argument would be fallacious.

   (ii) The reduction in preference would not affect any plans to form a Customs Union with the colonies.

   (iii) This concession would not take effect even nominally until the U.S. counter concession with respect to rubber had been put into operation; and it would not take effect in practice, that is to say, would not confer any actual benefits on the American exporters until our balance of payments difficulties were at an end and quantitative restrictions on colonial imports lifted, and then only to the extent that our exporters were unable to compete with them even with the help of the surviving margins of preference.

   (iv) The indications are that the Canadians would look on a refusal to include the colonial and rubber concessions as unreasonable on our part. The Canadians themselves suggested it informally at one stage.

(v) It is left open to the colonies to implement the reduction of preferences either by lowering the general rate or by raising the preferential rate against the U.K. In practice they would no doubt look at each case on its merits in the light of the revenue position, and sometimes do one thing and sometimes the other. The proposal therefore involves no sacrifice by the Colonies. The only sacrifice involved is the potential loss by United Kingdom manufacturers of orders in the Colonies over the field of trade affected by the reductions. This loss cannot be exactly stated but it would certainly be less than £1 million a year. On the other hand the benefit to be derived by the Colonial territories concerned from the increased opportunities for the sale of rubber in the United States as a result of the American counter-concession would be very large. It is also impossible to measure this exactly because its extent at a given moment depends on the price of rubber and the level of consumption in the United States, but it could hardly amount to less than some millions of pounds worth of dollars. These dollars would go into the sterling pool, where they would be used for the benefit of the whole of the Commonwealth. The benefit would be greater in volume when the rate of consumption of rubber in the United States was high, but would be more important when this was low since it would be precisely in these circumstances that the world price would be most weakened by continued large production and consumption of synthetic rubber by the United States.

7. In these circumstances I would strongly recommend that the Cabinet decision of last week should be reconsidered and the American proposal for a reduction in colonial preferences conditional upon the satisfactory concession on the American side regarding rubber should be accepted.

(Signed) ROGER MAKINS.
14th October, 1947.

E. J. Elliot (Federation of British Industries) to E. A. Cohen (Board of Trade), 1 April 1948, PRO, BT 11/3254.

FEDERATION OF BRITISH INDUSTRIES
21 Tothill Street, London, S.W.1.
Director-General: SIR NORMAN KIPPING, J.P.   General Secretary: D.L. WALKER, C.B.E.
Telegrams: FOBUSTRY, PARL, LONDON.
Telephone: WHITEHALL 6711.

1st April, 1948.

E.A. Cohen Esq.,
Board of Trade,
Millbank, S.W. 1.

Dear Cohen,

There are one or two points in regard to the situation as arrived at at Havana which I should like to get cleared up, if possible, and I know you will do what you can to help me.

Under the General Agreement on Tariffs and Trade. provision is made for the CONTRACTING PARTIES to meet as a body to deal with complaints and other matters under the Agreement. According to my information the first such meeting has actually been held, at Havana, on February 28th last. At the same time it has also been stated in the Press that the Havana Conference itself appointed on March 16th last an interim commission to operate in the place of I.T.O. until the latter is properly set up. This interim commission has, it was also reported, already met and has appointed an executive committee.

I should be glad if you could give me any information as to what are the actual relations between this 'interim commission' and the body of the CONTRACTING PARTIES referred to above.

It would, of course, be a great convenience to us to have a full copy of the Final Act signed at Havana on March 24th last, which, no doubt, contains the agreed text of the Charter for an International Trade Organisation.

Yours sincerely
E. J. Elliot

R. J. Shackle (Board of Trade) to E. J. Elliot (Federation of British Industries), 8 April 1948, PRO, BT 11/3254.

8th April, 1948.

Dear Elliot,

Your letter of 1st April to Cohen has been passed to me on my return from Havana.

What you say about the meetings of the Contracting Parties to the General Agreement on Tariffs and Trade and of the Interim Commission is quite correct.

The two bodies are separate and of different composition. As to the first, the Contracting Parties to the General Agreement on Tariffs and Trade (published in this country as Cmd. 7258) are the countries which are at present applying it under the Protocol of Provisional Application (printed on page 42 of Cmd. 7258), i.e. Australia, Belgium, Canada, Cuba, France, Luxembourg, the Netherlands, the United Kingdom and the United States.

The Interim Commission consists of each of the countries represented at Havana which supported a resolution setting up the Commission, i.e. all those countries except, Portugal, Switzerland, Turkey, Bolivia, Guatemala and Honduras. The Interim Commission has elected an Executive Committee of 10 to carry out its functions of preparing the ground for the eventual establishment of the International Trade Organisation on this Executive Committee the United Kingdom is represented. The Executive Committee has put in hand a programme of work.

The two bodies happen to have the same Chairman (Mr. Dena Welgrown, Canadian Minister in Berno) and the same Secretariat (Mr. Wyndham White and the Havana Conference Secretariat), and, of course, both are related to the I.T.O. project, but otherwise, as already said, they are independent of each other.

I expect the Havana documents will shortly be published in this country, but cannot give an exact date at the moment.

Yours sincerely,
(R. J. Shuckle)

'Resolution on the Havana Charter', First Draft Prepared by the International Headquarters of the International Chamber of Commerce, 10 May 1948, PRO, BT 11/3721.

INTERNATIONAL CHAMBER OF COMMERCE.

International Headquarters.
38, Cours Albert Ier, Paris, VIII.

Commercial and Financial Relations Document No. 8249 – or
RB. 10.V.1948 lb

SPECIAL COORDINATING COMMITTEE FOR THE I.T.O. CHARTER

Meeting to be held at International Headquarters on June 4th and 5th, 1948, at 10 a.m. and 3 p.m.

RESOLUTION ON THE HAVANA CHARTER

First Draft prepared by International Headquarters in consultation with the Rapporteur of the Committee

Since the Proposals for Expansion of World Trade and Employment were first issued by the United States Government in December, 1945, the International Chamber of Commerce has given active support and cooperation to the efforts of the United Nations to establish an effective Charter for an International Trade Organisation. In three successive reports first to the London and Geneva Sessions of the Preparatory Committee (Brochures 101 and 106) and finally to the Havana Conference itself (Brochure 124), the I.C.C. has constantly emphasised the great need for the world of a code of international behaviour in the field of trade and employment policy and of an organisation to watch over its application. The suggestions and criticisms it has formulated in these reports and through its delegates at the Conferences themselves all bear witness to the vital importance attached by world business to the success of this great venture.

At the same time, the I.C.C. has consistently upheld the view that to be effective the Charter of the International Trade Organisation should, broadly speaking, satisfy the following three conditions:

– It should clearly state the essential principles governing the operation of a world economy based on free markets and should at the same time define succinctly the aims of the new Organisation, limiting them primarily to the creation of conditions favourable to the freest possible development of world trade on a multilateral basis;

– It should make separate provision for a transition period in which, subject to consultation with or approval by the Organisation, clearly defined exceptions to the general principles would be admitted, it being understood that it would be one of the main functions of the Organisation to work towards their gradual elimination as circumstances permitted;

– It should lay the foundations for a detailed code of international economic policy for the post-transition period, with particular emphasis on ways and means of coping with future emergencies by international cooperation.

None of these requirements is met by the Havana Charter. The principles it states are qualified from the outset, and the aims of the Organisation are defined in such general terms as to cover practically the whole field of economic endeavour. What should have been transition period exceptions are not clearly defined as such, and there is a grave danger of their perpetuation as permanent instruments of economic policy. The problem of post-transition emergencies, instead of being squarely faced as belonging primarily to the sphere of international consultation and cooperation, is dealt with in the Charter on a purely national basis.

The discussions leading up to the Havana Charter were overshadowed by three major problems which proved unfortunately to be stumbling blocks in the way of the adoption of a liberal Charter for the promotion of international trade. These problems are: maximum employment and economic stability, the economic development of under-developed areas, and the disequilibrium of balances of payments.

The Havana Charter contributes little of a positive character to their solution. In each case, the fact that the problem exists is simply used as a justification for qualifying the long-term principles and establishing far-reaching exceptions. Instead of pointing the way to a solution of these three great groups of problems within the framework of an increasingly free world economy, the method of approach has been for the most part negative and nationalistic.

Believing as it does that freedom of payments and the greatest possible freedom of trade on a multilateral basis are essential for the improvement of living standards throughout the world, the I.C.C.'s approach to these problems is along entirely different lines.

As regards economic stability, the I.C.C. believes that prosperity as well as depression are world economic phenomena, with national manifestations which may vary from country to country but which are all organically inter-related. It believes that attempts to deal with the problem of economic instability by means of purely national planning of the economic life of each particular country must inevitably result in a break-up of the world economy. Economic instability is an economic problem of international scope and must be dealt with in a manner compatible with the sound operation of a harmonious world economy.

Similarly the I.C.C. has frequently emphasised in its resolutions the importance of promoting the sound economic development of the under-developed areas of the world. It considers that such economic growth is conditioned by the attainment of political security and closely dependent upon the restoration of freer trade and of more abundant capital movements throughout the world. The former requires the abolition of discrimination and of quantitative restrictions and the lowering of tariffs, the latter an undertaking by capital-exporting and capital-importing countries alike to adhere to the principles of an international code of fair treatment which would protect the legitimate interests of both the borrowers and the lenders against arbitrary action and abuses of power.

Finally, while keenly aware of the precarious condition of the balance of payments of many countries in the world, including most of the great trading nations, and acknowledging the need for elastic transition period provisions, the I.C.C. does not believe that the remedy for this great problem should be sought in measures that interfere with the flow of international commerce. It feels that, in drawing up the Charter, too little attention was paid to the positive efforts going on at the same time independently of the Charter and the I.T.O., for instance through the European Recovery Program, to find a practical solution to the international payments problem.

The I.C.C. believes it to be of vital importance that the future policy of the trading nations of the world, great and small alike, should be increasingly positive and international, rather than, as at present, narrowly nationalistic and restrictive, in its approach to the major economic problems of our time. Without a clear international code to govern national policies, nothing effective can be achieved by the mere establishment of international machinery, however elaborate.

Although fully realising the immense difficulties the governments have had to face throughout the long and laborious negotiations culminating in Havana, the I.C.C. feels in duty bound not to conceal its grave misgivings concerning the Havana Charter. It doubts whether the Charter as it now stands is an adequate foundation upon which to build a peaceful and efficient world economy. It therefore welcomes the provision made for a general review of the Charter not later than five years after the establishment of the I.T.O., for it is to be hoped that during that time national apprehensions, due to the post-war emergencies, will grow weaker, and that it will be possible to relax to a great extent existing measures of national economic protection. When the time comes for revision, the I.C.C. will come forward with proposals for strengthening and simplifying the Charter.

In the meantime, the I.C.C. is prepared to collaborate whole-heartedly with the International Trade Organisation, should the Havana Charter be ratified by a sufficient number of governments to enable it to be established. The I.C.C. will in particular make it its duty to continue its own study of those great problems upon the solution of which the future of international economic cooperation so largely depends. The I.C.C. believes that by making available to the I.T.O. the vast aggregate of experience it can call upon in the field of trade, industry and finance, it will contribute, by friendly suggestion and criticism, to making the I.T.O. an effective instrument of economic progress.

THE EUROPEAN ECONOMIC COMMUNITY

From the founding of the European Coal and Steel Community in 1951, British policymakers had to confront a series of difficult choices about what deeper European economic, social and political integration meant for Britain's position in both international politics and the international economy. In the aftermath of the Second World War, the long-term economic and political weakness and unsustainability of the British Empire was not fully apparent to either the British public or the government.

In the early post-war period, the British government continued to use imperial preference to protect British industry and use the Empire and the Commonwealth as a market for British producers. The faith that the British National Union of Manufacturers had placed in the British Empire as a viable economic entity and a secure market for British goods proved ill-founded.[1] As a market, the British Empire proved a disappointment, one that was even more disappointing after decolonization as the hoped-for economic growth in many colonies failed to materialize to the same degree as was occurring in mainland Europe. Preferential trading arrangements with the former colonies and Dominions were not as helpful to British business as had been hoped. While pressure from the United States and the possibility of selling goods in European markets led to a reduction in British tariff levels in the mid-1950s, Britain still exported approximately 50 per cent of its finished products to its colonial empire and missed out on many trading opportunities in the rapidly expanding economies of Continental Europe.

Britain missed repeated opportunities to engage in deeper European economic integration. Having just nationalized the British coal and steel industries in the early post-war period, the British government was not interested in turning management of this crucial sector over to a supranational authority, so the United Kingdom declined to be a founding member of the European Coal and Steel Community. Later, the British only sent observers to the negotiations for the Treaty of Rome which created the European Economic Community (EEC). Britain repeatedly chose to prioritize its domestic economy and relations with the Commonwealth over those with the European Community until the Suez debacle exposed British and French pretensions of still being great powers as a cruel hoax. If Britain's independent ability to influence world affairs was diminished, linking Britain with the EEC promised a route to expanded influence on the world stage.

How precisely such a linkage could be accomplished while maintaining Britain's historical links to the Commonwealth and at the same time not requiring a complete renegotiation of the Treaty of Rome proved a difficult sticking point.[2] British diplomats were very suspicious – and perhaps more than a little envious – of the success of French diplomacy within the European Community both in terms of EEC policies favourable to French economic and political interests and in France's apparent ability to thwart EEC policies that were unwelcome to Paris.[3] Conservative Prime Minister Harold Macmillan sought greater involvement with the EEC, but ran into French resistance. French President Charles de Gaulle was unconvinced that Britain and Macmillan had the same conception of the EEC as France did and he consequently vetoed Britain's application for membership in 1963.

Britain was forced to settle for organizing the European Free Trade Area (EFTA) along with Portugal, Denmark, Switzerland, Austria, Sweden and Norway. As EFTA allowed different external tariffs and free trade in most industrial products, the British felt that it would serve as a useful means of putting pressure on the six EEC countries to negotiate a broader European free trade area.[4] While the Conservatives were largely in favour of joining the EEC in the 1960s and 1970s, the Labour Party was officially opposed, although Prime Minister Harold Wilson's Labour government reapplied for EEC membership, only to see it vetoed again by de Gaulle in 1967.[5] With de Gaulle's death and the election of pro-European Edward Heath to the premiership in Britain, the path was finally cleared for a third attempt at negotiating British entry into the Common Market. This time, the British application was successful and the United Kingdom entered the EEC along with Ireland and Denmark in 1973.

However, British membership was far from settled as the Labour Party, critical of EEC membership to begin with, pledged to renegotiate Britain's accession agreement in order to promote employment and revise the agricultural arrangements accepted by the Heath government. In addition, Labour promised an unprecedented national referendum on British membership in the EEC. The left wing of the Labour Party saw joining a supranational customs union as giving away macroeconomic policy instruments that could be used to shelter vulnerable sectors of the British economy. Labour duly won the October 1974 election in the unusual circumstances of having a pro-European leader, Wilson, standing on an anti-EEC campaign manifesto. Wilson returned as Prime Minister and conducted a brief renegotiation of the terms of British membership in the EEC. The Labour Party and government were deeply divided over the issue of whether or not to remain in the EEC. The divisions were so deep that the government took the extraordinary step of ignoring collective Cabinet responsibility for the decision and allowing Cabinet ministers such as the left-wing Minister for Industry Tony Benn to retain their offices while campaigning against the referendum. This 'free vote' removed the issue of EEC membership from the strict field of party politics and allowed the leaders of all the major parties to support the referendum while not binding their parties to do so. The Labour Party conference went so far as to vote by a margin of 2 to 1 to oppose the referendum, a position promptly ignored by Wilson and most of his Cabinet. Not only did Wilson and the leaders of Conservative and Liberal parties support the referendum, but the major business associations also did so, as did the Trades Union Congress and all the major newspapers. After an intense campaign, nearly two-thirds of the electorate voted to remain in the EEC.[6]

Joining the EEC meant surrendering sovereignty over trade negotiations, agricultural policy and other regulatory policy areas in exchange for British influence over EEC (and later European Union) decisions that would be binding on all the member states. As most of the decisions required unanimity, finding common ground on harmonizing different national regulations proved to be slow, tedious and largely unsuccessful. Throughout the remainder of the 1970s, the agenda of European market integration proceeded slowly, hindered by the multitude of different national regulations and the resistance of individual countries to any regulations that differed substantially from their own pre-existing domestic arrangements. Intriguingly, it was the legalization of European law that helped overcome the impasse.

In the Treaty of Rome and the accession agreements, Britain and the other EEC members had agreed to give the European Court of Justice (ECJ) the power to interpret the treaties and to determine whether EEC institutions or member states were abiding by them. In 1979, while national and European bureaucrats struggled to come up with harmonized product definitions and regulatory arrangements for production in the face of domestic efforts to privilege national rules and producers, a niche alcoholic beverage, Cassis de Dijon, became the liqueur that saved Europe. For many years, Germany had protected the German alcoholic drinks industry by keeping Cassis and other products out of the German marketplace, arguing that they did not fit into any recognized German regulatory categories. In a groundbreaking decision, the ECJ ruled that goods produced legally in one member state could be sold in all other member states, even in the absence of common European rules and when national rules would have prohibited its local production.[7] Subsequent ECJ rulings emphasized the broader applicability of this precedent, striking down the application of Germany's cherished *Reinheitsgebot* – a law that traced its traditional origins to the Bavarian *Reinheitsgebot* of 1516 – to imported beers as a restriction on the free movement of goods within the Community.[8]

The Cassis decision cut the Gordian knot of European-wide regulation by allowing national variation to exist but not impede the sale and movement of goods within the EEC. This proved a major impetus to the development of a single European marketplace. In the absence of European-wide common rules, the Cassis decision prevented regulatory barriers from impeding product flows. New decision-making procedures for the introduction of common European regulations were introduced in the Single Europe Act that allowed EEC regulations to be passed by a super-majority of member states rather than the unanimity rules that had previously prevailed. This allowed a large majority of members to overcome opposition from one or more members to rules that would be common to all members. This allowed for a rapid liberalization of the European marketplace and allowed member states either to remove obnoxious non-tariff barriers that existed in a minority of countries or simply allowed exporters to bypass many foreign production regulations in sending goods to market. The ability to do both hastened the completion of the Single European Market in 1992.

Notes

1. See 'Editorial: Trade Agreements', *Journal of the National Union of Manufacturers* (1946), above, pp. 5–7.
2. See 'Record of a Conversation between the Secretary of State [Foreign Secretary Selwyn Lloyd] and the Netherlands Ambassador on 15 July 1960', below, pp. 71–3.
3. See Sir Con O'Neill (Head of UK Delegation to the European Communities), 'Valedictory Dispatch', 3 May 1965, below, pp. 81–7.
4. A. Moravcsik, *The Choice for Europe* (Ithaca, NY: Cornell University Press, 1998), pp. 164–5.
5. See 'Commonwealth and US Ties Impede our Market Entry', *The Times*, 17 May 1967, p. 13.
6. See 'End of 14 Years' Argument, Mr Wilson Says', *The Times*, 7 June 1975, pp. 1, 2.
7. K. Alter and S. Meunier-Aitsahalia, 'Judicial Politics in the European Community: European Integration and the Pathbreaking *Cassis de Dijon* Decision', *Comparative Political Studies*, 26:4 (1994), pp. 535–61; see 'Cassis' Decision, Judgement of the European Court of Justice, 20 February 1979, below, pp. 104–9.
8. See German Beer Purity Law Decision, Judgement of the European Court of Justice, 12 March 1987, below, pp. 110–24.

THE EUROPEAN ECONOMIC COMMUNITY

Notes for Prime Minister Winston Churchill in Preparation for Meeting with Jean Monnet regarding United Kingdom Association with the European Coal and Steel Community, 25 May 1954, PRO, PREM 11/1340.

PRIME MINISTER

United Kingdom Association with the European

Coal and Steel Community

(C. (54) 173 and 174)

M. Monnet is due to arrive in London about 18th June, for a visit of two or three days, without experts. He will not expect detailed negotiations, but will expect an indication of our policy on closer association with the European Coal and Steel Community.

The Ministerial Committee set up to consider this have agreed (i) that we should refuse to join a common market for either coal or steel, and (ii) that we could take certain steps, short of this, as regards coal. But they have failed to reach agreement on the question whether we should discuss with M. Monnet any reduction in the 25 per cent tariff on steel.

The majority view, of which the Ministers of Supply and Fuel and Power are the protagonists, supported by the Commonwealth Secretary, is that we cannot concede to M. Monnet a common market and a tariff reduction since this would not be acceptable to our industries; and that we should therefore offer to discuss these and other subjects in a Council of Association, to be set up forthwith. The establishment of this body, which M. Monnet contemplated as taking place after major practical measures had been taken, would be our contribution to co-operation with the European Community, and our objective in the negotiations. Tariffs would not be discussed with M. Monnet, except 'to arrange with him the basis on which talks would take place'.

The minority view, put forward by the Board of Trade and supported – though not to the point of downright dissent with the majority – by the Foreign Office and Treasury, is that it is not realistic to talk of economic co-operation from over a 25 per cent tariff wall; that we should therefore agree to tackle this subject at the outset and not defer it for subsequent discussion in a Council of Association; that if we give away in advance our strongest bargaining card – M. Monnet's desire for some kind of association – we shall be in a weak position over any subsequent negotiations; and that membership of an association, with the tariff issues unsolved, would worsen, rather than improve, our relations with the Schuman countries.

The Foreign Office view is that M. Monnet will be most disappointed by, and may reject, a proposal from us that the questions which he put to us in December should be discussed in a Council of Association, instead of with him. If we go only as far as the majority report, he will be deeply disappointed; but it is in his interests as much as ours to dress up the Council of Association as a British contribution, and he could go home with that in his pocket, ostensibly to renew discussions later, though this might be indefinitely delayed.

If we decide to face the tariff issue, there is a Working Party paper, agreed with representatives of the Iron and Steel Board, recommending a 15 per cent reduction, on steel, on political grounds. This would obviously be more satisfactory from M. Monnet's point of view; but it would be difficult, though not perhaps impossible, to convince the industry that it was satisfactory from theirs.

Memorandum for Prime Minster Anthony Eden on Meeting of the Ministerial Committee Meeting on Relations with the ECSC, 4 July 1956, PRO, PREM 11/1340.

President

Prime Minister,

I think you would want the Cabinet to be informed of the tariff reduction proposal, so it would be convenient for the parliamentary consultative point to be mentioned as well.

(The 'tariff reduction' is in present circumstances a rather empty offer, since the tariff on steel imports is completely suspended while we need imports. In return, we would like that the ECSC committees would reduce their tariff – to our benefit if we become steel exporters again.)

PRIME MINISTER

The Ministerial Committee on Relations with the European Coal and Steel Community discussed this morning the line to be taken at the meeting of the Council of Association with the High Authority on July 10. There are two points I should like to mention.

(i) The United Kingdom Steel Tariff

In the Agreement concluded with the European Coal and Steel Community, the United Kingdom and the High Authority undertook to -

'examine restrictions or other factors affecting the normal flow of trade in coal and steel ... such as ... tariffs and other charges on imports and exports, ... dumping and antidumping measures, and export subsidies with a view to making such proposals for their reduction or elimination as may be agreed for the mutual benefit of the Community and the United Kingdom.'

We have played this slowly, but feel that we should make some move now. After discussing the matter with the Iron and Steel Board, who have themselves consulted the steel industry and the unions, we propose that we should offer to the High Authority to reduce our tariff to 15 per cent, with alternative specific duties of a kind designed to impose an additional barrier against dumping. (The present theoretical tariff, allowing for the reductions recently agreed in Geneva, ranges from 15 to 33, but this has been largely suspended on account of the steel shortage here to enable imports to come in duty-free. It will remain suspended after we have made our offer.)

(ii) Common Assembly's Proposal for a Joint Parliamentary Group

The Common Assembly has proposed that a Joint Parliamentary Committee consisting of nine British Parliamentarians and nine members of the

Common Assembly should meet together to examine the annual report of the Council of Association.

My colleagues and I agreed that this suggestion should be turned down for the following reasons:-

(a) The machinery for consultation between British and Community Parliamentarians already exists in the joint meetings of the Common Assembly and Consultative Assembly of the Council of Europe.

(b) In the negotiations with the High Authority on the Agreement of Association we rejected their plan for a Parliamentary link-up on these lines.

(c) The proposal would be unpopular with the steel industry in this country.

(d) The creation of yet another Parliamentary Group would diminish the status of the existing European Assemblies.

If you would like me to mention these proposals at Cabinet tomorrow, I will let Sir Norman Brook have copies of this minute to put round.

Board of Trade, 4th July, 1956.

Horse Guards Avenue,

S.W.I.

'Record of Conversation between the Secretary of State [Foreign Secretary Selwyn Lloyd] and the Netherlands Ambassador on July 15, 1960', PRO, PREM 11/3774, no. 140.

CONFIDENTIAL

THIS DOCUMENT IS THE PROPERTY OF HER BRITANNIC MAJESTY'S GOVERNMENT

M 611/251 *Foreign Office and Whitehall Distribution*

GENERAL AFFAIRS (ECONOMIC)
July 18, 1960
Section 1

RECORD OF CONVERSATION BETWEEN THE SECRETARY OF STATE AND THE NETHERLANDS AMBASSADOR ON JULY 15, 1960

Mr. Selwyn Lloyd to Sir Paul Mason (The Hague)
(No. 140. Confidential) *Foreign Office,*
Sir, *July 18, 1960.*

The Netherlands Ambassador called to see me on the 15th of July at his request in order to make some enquiries about the attitude of Her Majesty's Government towards the proposal that they should accede to Euratom and to the European Coal and Steel Community.

2. Baron Bentinck said that a Ministerial Meeting of the Six was to be held on the 18th of July at which one of the subjects to be discussed was the relationship of the United Kingdom to the two communities. Dr. Luns had been considering what attitude he should adopt and he was anxious to have an up-to-date account of our own views on the subject. Baron Bentinck mentioned in confidence that the Netherlands Government had been making some enquiries about the attitude of their partners in the Community, and it was clear that there were considerable differences of opinion. For example, Signor Grazzi had said that he was opposed to admitting the United Kingdom to the E.E.C. and he therefore saw little point in having her in the other two Communities. The French had taken the line that there was nothing to prevent the United Kingdom from applying for membership of the two communities if she felt able to do so. In

that case, however, she must not insist on the complete renegotiation of the Treaties. The French had added that they were really very doubtful whether the United Kingdom really wanted to come in.

3. I replied that since the meeting of the *ad hoc* committee with the Six Ambassadors we had been examining further the problems which would be involved for us in joining the two Communities. There were of course a number of complicated issues, particularly in the field of defence. I thought there was a need on both sides for further study. We certainly did not wish to force the Six and particularly the French into a position where they might have to say that they did not really want us to join. In any case this question must be looked at in the context of our whole relationship with Western Europe. It was of course clear that we could not simply ask to be allowed to accede to the Treaty of Rome. There was a number of very difficult issues for us arising from our economic relations with the Commonwealth, in particular the problem of free entry into this country, and there were great difficulties about agriculture and horticulture. We must also take account of our commitments to our E.F.T.A. partners. On the other hand, I thought that to some extent opinion on the Continent was evolving in a favourable direction, and from our point of view the tendency towards a confederation, as opposed to a federal solution, which under the lead of General de Gaulle seemed to be gathering strength, was a satisfactory development. I believed that it was very important to avoid another clash such as had occurred in November 1958. I thought that since then our relations with the mainland, particularly France, had been improving and we should continue to do all we could to make the atmosphere better. It might be that the negotiations in the GATT would help to reduce the scope of the tariff problems and in any case we would do our best to bring about more harmonious relations between E.F.T.A. and the E.E.C. Perhaps some association would ultimately prove possible. I was most anxious to show that we were prepared to play our full part as a European nation and this was one reason why it had seemed to me that we should study very carefully the possibility of joining Euratom and the E.C.S.C. I still thought that this idea was worth further examination though neither side was probably yet ready to reach any definite decisions. In the meanwhile if Dr. Luns could encourage his partners to give the matter genuine consideration that would certainly be helpful.

4. As far as the *ad hoc* committee of Sir Roderick Barclay and the Six Ambassadors was concerned, I hoped that it would soon be possible for us to have ready a list of questions which we should like to ask the Six, relating primarily to how they interpreted or operated the Treaties. The Ambassadors would doubtless have to refer these back to their Governments, and if the latter had any questions they would like to put to us they would be very welcome

to do so. It was agreed that it might be desirable to hold a further meeting of the committee at the end of this month. The problem would then be remitted for further study by the Seven Governments and it was not certain whether the committee would have to take the matter up again or whether the discussions should be continued through other channels.

5. Baron Bentinck expressed his appreciation of my explanation of our position, and said he was sure that Dr. Luns would do his best to keep the possibility of our acceding to the two Communities open. He could not of course say what line would be taken by the other members of the Six.

6. I am sending copies of this dispatch to Her Majesty's Representatives at Berne, Bonn, Brussels, Copenhagen, Lisbon, Luxembourg, Oslo, Paris, Rome, Stockholm and Vienna, to the United Kingdom Delegation, O.E.E.C., and the United Kingdom Delegation, E.F.T.A., Geneva.

I am. &c.
SELWYN LLOYD

'Press Conference by President de Gaule, Paris, 14th January 1963', Assembly of the Western European Union, 'The Political Year in Europe', 1963.

17. *Press conference by President de Gaulle, Paris*

14th January 1964
(Extracts)

The Common Market

Question: Could you define explicitly France's position towards Britain's entry into the Common Market and the political evolution of Europe?

Answer: A very clear question, to which I shall endeavour to reply clearly.

I believe that when you talk about economics – and much more so when you practise them – what you say and what you do must conform to realities, because without that you can get into impasses and, sometimes, you even head for ruin.

In this very great affair of the European Economic Community and also in that of eventual adhesion of Great Britain, it is the facts that must first be considered. Feelings, favourable though they might be and are, these feelings cannot be invoked against the real facts of the problem. What are these facts?

The Treaty of Rome was concluded between six continental States, States which are, economically speaking, one may say, of the same nature. Indeed, whether it be a matter of their industrial or agricultural production, their external exchanges, their habits or their commercial clientele, their living or working conditions, there is between them much more resemblance than difference. Moreover, they are adjacent, they inter-penetrate, they prolong each other through their communication. It is therefore a fact to group them and to link them in such a way that what they have to produce, to buy, to sell, to consume – well, they do produce, buy, sell, consume, in preference in their own ensemble. Doing that is conforming to realities.

Moreover, it must be added that from the point of view of their economic development, their social progress, their technical capacity, they are, in short, keeping pace. They are marching in similar fashion. It so happens, too, that there is between them no kind of political grievance, no frontier question, no rivalry in domination or power. On the contrary, they are joined in solidarity, especially and primarily from the aspect of the consciousness they have of defining together an important part of the sources of our civilisation; and also as concerns their security, because they are continentals and have before them one and the same menace from one extremity to the other of their territorial emsemble. Then, finally, they are in solidarity through the fact that not one among them is bound abroad by any particular political or military accord.

Thus it was psychologically and materially possible to make an economic community of the Six, though not without difficulties. When the Treaty of Rome was signed in 1957, it was after long discussions; and when it was concluded, it was necessary – in order to achieve something – that we French put in order our economic, financial, and monetary affairs ... and that was done in 1959. From that moment the community was in principle viable, but then the treaty had to be applied.

However, this treaty, which was precise and complete enough concerning industry, was not at all so on the subject of agriculture. However, for our country this had to be settled. Indeed, it is obvious that the agriculture is an essential element in the whole of our national activity. We cannot conceive, and will not conceive, of a Common Market in which French agriculture would not find outlets in keeping with its production. And we agree, further, that of the Six we are the country on which this necessity is imposed in the most imperative manner.

This is why when, last January, thought was given to the setting in motion of the second phases of the treaty – in other words a practical start in application – we were led to pose the entry of agriculture into the Common Market as a formal condition. This was finally accepted by our partners but very difficult and very complex arrangements were needed – and some rulings are still outstanding. I note in passing that in this vast undertaking it was the governments that took all the decisions, because authority and responsibility are not to be found elsewhere. But I must say that in preparing and untangling these matters, the Commission in Brussels did some very objective and fitting work. Thereupon Great Britain posed her candidature to the Common Market. She did it after having earlier refused to participate in the communities we are now building, as well as after creating a free trade area with six other States, and, finally, after having – I may well say it (the negotiations held at such length on this subject will be recalled) – after having put some pressure on the Six to prevent a real beginning being made in the application of the Common Market. If England asks in turn to enter, but on her own conditions, this poses without doubt to each of the six States, and poses to England, problems of a very great dimension.

England in effect is insular, she is maritime, she is linked through her exchanges, her markets, her supply lines to the most diverse and often the most distant countries; she pursues essentially industrial and commercial activities, and only slight agricultural ones. She has in her doings very marked and very original habits and traditions.

In short, the nature, the structure, the very situation (conjuncture) that are England's differ profoundly from those of the continentals. What is to be done in order that England, as she lives, produces and trades, can be incorporated into the Common Market, as it has been conceived and as it functions? For example, the means by which the people of Great Britain are fed and which are in fact the importation of food-stuffs bought cheaply in the two Americas and in the former dominions, at the same time giving, granting considerable subsidies to English farmers? These means are obviously incompatible with the system which the Six have established quite naturally for themselves.

The system of the Six – this constitutes making a whole of the agriculture produce of the whole Community, in strictly fixing their prices, in prohibiting subsidies, in organising their consumption between all the participants, and in imposing on each other its participants payment to the Community of any saving they would achieve in fetching their food from outside instead of eating what the Common Market has to offer. Once again, what is to be done to bring England, as she is, into this system?

One might sometimes have believed that our English friends, in posing their candidature to the Common Market, were agreeing to transform themselves to the point of applying all the conditions which are accepted and practiced by the Six. But the question, to know whether Great Britain can now place herself like the Continent and with it inside a tariff which is genuinely common, to renounce all Commonwealth preferences, to cease any pretence that her agriculture be privileged, and, more than that, to treat her engagements with other countries of the free trade area as null and void – that question is the whole question.

It cannot be said that it is yet resolved. Will it be so one day? Obviously only England can answer. The question is even further posed since after England other States which are, I repeat, linked to her through the free trade area, for the same reasons as Britain, would like or wish to enter the Common Market.

It must be agreed that first the entry of Great Britain, and then these States, will completely change the whole of the actions, the agreements, the compensation, the rules which have already been established between the Six, because all these States, like Britain, have very important peculiarities. Then it will be another Common Market whose construction ought to be envisaged; but one which would be taken to 11 and then 13 and then perhaps 18 would no longer resemble, without any doubt, the one which the Six built.

Further, this community, increasing in such fashion, would see itself faced with problems of economic relations with all kinds of other States, and first with the United States. It is to be foreseen that the cohesion of its members, who would be very numerous and diverse, would not endure for long, and that ultimately it would appear as a colossal Atlantic community under American dependence and direction, and which would quickly have absorbed the community of Europe.

It is a hypothesis which in the eyes of some can be perfectly justified, but it is not at all what France is doing or wanted to do – and which is a properly European construction.

Yet it is possible that one day England might manage to transform herself sufficiently to become part of the European community, without restriction, without reserve and preference for anything whatsoever; and in this case the Six would open the door to her and France would raise no obstacle, although obviously England's simple participation in the community would considerably change its nature and its volume.

It is possible, too, that England might not yet be so disposed, and it is that which seems to result from the long, long, so long, so long Brussels conversations. But if that is the case, there is nothing there that could be dramatic. First, whatever decision England takes in this matter there is no reason, as far as we are concerned, for the relations we have with her to be changed, and the consideration, the respect which are due to this great State, this great people, will not thereby be in the slightest impaired.

What England has done across the centuries and in the world is recognised as immense. Although there have often been conflicts with France, Britain's glorious participation in the victory which crowned the first world war – we French, we shall always admire it. As for the role England played in the most dramatic and decisive moments of the second world war, no one has the right to forget it.

In truth, the destiny of the free world, and first of all ours and even that of the United States and Russia, depended in a large measure on the resolution, the solidity and the courage of the English people, as Churchill was able to harness them. Even at the present moment no one can contest British capacity and worth.

Moreover, I repeat, if the Brussels negotiations were shortly not to succeed, nothing would prevent the conclusion between the Common Market and Great Britain of an accord of association designed to safeguard exchanges, and nothing would prevent close relations between England and France from being maintained, not the pursuit and development of their direct co-operation in all kinds of fields, and notably the scientific, technical and industrial – as the two countries have just proved by deciding to build together the supersonic aircraft Concorde.

Lastly, it is very possible that Britain's own evolution, and the evolution of the universe, might bring the English little by little towards the Continent, whatever delays the achievement might demand, and for my part, that is what I readily believe, and that is why, in my opinion, it will in any case have been a great honour for the British Prime Minister, for my friend Harold Macmillan, and for his Government, to have discerned in good time, to have had enough political courage to have proclaimed it, and to have led their country the first steps down the path which one day, perhaps, will lead it to moor alongside the Continent.

Remarks, made by President Charles de Gaulle at his Fifteenth Press Conference, 16 May, 1967, French Press and Information Service.

[...]

[T]he Common Market is a sort of prodigy. To introduce into it now new and massive elements, into the midst of those that have been fit together with such difficulty, would obviously be to jeopardize the whole and the details and to raise the problem of an entirely different undertaking. All the more that if the Six have been able to build this famous edifice it is because it concerned a group of continental countries, immediate neighbors to each other, doubtless offering differences of size, but complementary in their economic structure. Moreover, the Six form through their territory a compact geographic and strategic unit. It must be added that despite, perhaps because of their great battles of the past-I am naturally speaking of France and Germany – they now find themselves inclined to support one another mutually rather than to oppose one another. Finally, aware of the potential of their material resources and their human values, all desire either aloud or in whispers that their unit constitute one day an element that might provide a balance to any power in the world.

Compared with the motives that led the Six to organize their unit, we understand for what reasons, why Britain-who is not continental, who remains, because of the Commonwealth and because she is an island, committed far beyond the seas, who is tied to the United States by all kinds of special agreements-did not merge into a Community with set dimensions and strict rules. While this Community was taking shape, Britain therefore first refused to participate in it and even took toward it a hostile attitude as if she saw in it an economic and political threat. Then she tried to negotiate in order to join the Community, but in such conditions that the latter would have been suffocated by this membership. The attempt having failed, the British Government then asserted that it no longer wanted to enter the Community and set about strengthening its ties with the Commonwealth and with other European countries grouped around it in a free-trade area. Yet, apparently now adopting a new state of mind, Britain declares she is ready to subscribe to the Rome Treaty, even though she is asking exceptional and prolonged delays and, as regards her, that basic changes be made in the Treaty's implementation. At the same time, she acknowledges that in order to arrive there, it will be necessary to surmount obstacles that the great perceptiveness and profound experience of her Prime Minister have qualified as formidable.

This is true, for instance, of the agricultural regulations. We know that they tend to have the countries of the Community nourish themselves on what they produce and to compensate, by what is called 'financial levies,' for all the advantages that each could have in importing less expensive produce from elsewhere.

Now, Britain nourishes herself, to a great extent, on food-stuffs bought inexpensively throughout the world and, particularly, in the Commonwealth. If she submits to the rules of the Six, then her balance of payments will be crushed by 'levies' and, on the other hand, she would then be forced to raise the price of her food to the price level adopted by the continental countries, consequently to increase the wages of her workers and, thereby, to sell her goods all the more at a higher price and with more difficulty. It is clear that she cannot do this. But, if she enters the Community without being really subjected to the agricultural system of the Six, this system will thereby collapse, completely upsetting the equilibrium of the Common Market and removing for France one of the main reasons she can have for participating in it.

Another basic difficulty arises from the fact that, among the Six, it is a rule that capital circulates freely to promote expansion, but that in Britain-if she were allowed to enter-it is forbidden for capital to leave so as to limit the balance-of-payments deficit, a deficit that, despite praiseworthy efforts and some recent progress, still remains threatening. How can this problem be solved? For it would be for the British an excessive risk to eliminate the sluice-gates which, in Britain, block the movement of money to the outside and, for the Europeans, it would be unthinkable to take into the organization a partner which, in this respect, would find itself isolated in such a costly regime,

Also, how can it not be seen that the very situation of the pound sterling prevents the Common Market from incorporating Britain. The very fact that the organization of the Six is entirely freeing their mutual trade necessarily implies that the currency of the member countries has a constant relative value and that, if it happened that one of them were disturbed, the Community would ensure its recovery. But this is possible only due to the well-established soundness of the mark, the lira, the florin, the Belgian franc and the French franc. Now, without despairing of seeing the pound hold its own, for a long time we would not be assured that it will succeed ... Monetary parity and solidarity are the essential conditions of the Common Market and assuredly could not be extended to our neighbors across the Channel, unless the pound appears, one day, in a new situation and such that its future value appears assured; unless it also frees itself of the character of reserve currency; unless, finally, the burden of Great Britain's deficitary balances within the sterling area disappear. When and how will this happen?

What is true, at this very moment, from the economic standpoint, would also be true, eventually, from the political standpoint. The idea, the hope which, from the beginning, led the Six continental countries to unite, tended without any doubt toward the formation of a unit which would be European in all respects, and, because of this would become capable not only of carrying its own weight in production and trade, but also of acting one day politically by itself and for itself toward anyone. Considering the special relations that tie the British to America, with the advantage and also the dependence that results for them; considering the existence of the Commonwealth and their preferential relations with it; considering the special commitment that they still have in various parts of the world and which, basically, distinguishes them from the continentals, we see that the policy of the latter, as soon as they have one, would undoubtedly concur, in certain cases, with the policy of the former. But we cannot see how both policies could merge, unless the British assumed again, particularly as regards defense, complete command of themselves, or else if the continentals renounced forever a European Europe.

[...]

In truth, it really seems that the change in the situation of the British in relation to the Six, once we would be ready by common consent to proceed with it, might consist of a choice between three issues.

Either recognize that, as things stand at present, their entry into the Common Market, with all the exceptions that it would not fail to be accompanied by, with the irruption of entirely new facts, new both in nature and in quantity, that would necessarily result from this entry, with the participation of several other States that would certainly be its corollary, would amount to necessitating the building of an entirely new edifice, scrapping nearly all of that which has just been built. What, then, would we end up with if not, perhaps, the creation of a free-trade area of Western Europe, pending that of the Atlantic area, which would deprive our continent of any real personality?

Or, establish, between the Community on the one band, and Britain and some States of the 'little' free-trade area on the other, a system of association, such as the one provided for in the Treaty of Rome and which could, without creating an upheaval, multiply and facilitate the economic relations between the contracting parties.

Or else, lastly, before changing what exists, wait until a certain internal and external evolution, of which Great Britain seems already to be showing signs, is eventually completed, that is to say, until that great people which is endowed with tremendous ability and courage has itself accomplished first and for its part the necessary profound economic and political transformation so that it can join with the Six continental countries. I really believe that this is the desire of many people, who are anxious to see the emergence of a Europe corresponding to its natural dimensions and who have great admiration and true friendship for Britain. If, one day, she were to come to this point, how warmly France would welcome this historic conversion.

Sir Con O'Neill (Head of UK Delegation to the European Communities), 'Valedictory Despatch', 3 May 1965, PRO, PREM 13/306.

THIS DOCUMENT IS THE PROPERTY OF HER BRITANNIC MAJESTY'S GOVERNMENT

M 10831/2 *Foreign Office and Whitehall Distribution*

ECONOMIC AFFAIRS (GENERAL)
3 May, 1965
Section 1

SIR C. O'NEILL'S VALEDICTORY DESPATCH

Sir C. O'Neil to Mr. Stewart. (Received 3 May)

SUMMARY

1. The predominance of French influence in the European Communities is too much taken for granted, and deserves to be more fully described (paragraphs 1–2).
2. The Treaty of Rome suits France well. She has added to the advantages it gave her (paragraph 3) and has delayed or frustrated the Community's internal development where that suited her (paragraph 4).
3. But it is in the Community's external relations that French obstruction is most extensive (paragraphs 5–11).
4. Three special reasons for the effectiveness of French obstruction (paragraph 12).
5. There is not much prospect of this situation changing (paragraph 13); and there are serious limitations on the effectiveness of any action which others might take to change it (paragraphs 14–18).

UKDEL to the European Communities.

(No. 13. Confidential) *Brussels.*
Sir, *29 April, 1965.*

I have considered whether I should address the customary 'valedictory despatch' to you before leaving this post, but have come to the conclusion that, so far as general ideas or reflections are concerned, I really have nothing to add to what I have from time to time written to your predecessors or yourself. I have concluded, however, that it may be useful if my valedictory despatch concentrates instead on a single notable feature of the European Communities, so conspicuous and all-pervasive here in Brussels that we may sometimes, I feel, fail to convey in our reports a sufficient sense of it, because we take it so much for granted. I refer to the predominance of French influence in the Communities and the degree to which it is French policy, and with only one major exception French policy alone, which frustrates the objectives which most third countries seek to achieve in their relations with the Community.

2. I propose therefore in this despatch to draw up a catalogue of the main French achievements in this field. I will then consider whether there is, or is not, anything we can attempt to do, or persuade others to do, about this state of affairs.

3. I referred in my despatch No. 10 of the 13th of April to the fact that the provisions of the Rome Treaty suited French policy well, and to the consequence that the Commission tended by its very function to strengthen the already naturally strong French position within the Community. The provisions relating to the former French dependent territories constitute the most signal example of this. Many others could be cited. I referred in the same despatch to the success with which French planning, skill and ruthlessness have been able to add to the advantage with which France started. The Common Agricultural Policy and the principles of the financial arrangements accompanying it constitute the most far-reaching example in this field. But many others could be cited.

4. French success in delaying or frustrating internal developments in the Community which are unwelcome to her are apt to attract less attention, but the list is an impressive one – far more impressive than that of any other Member State. It includes institutional development; further progress on capital movements; important aspects of establishment and services; export credits to Soviet *bloc* countries; the European patent convention; State aids; State trading monopolies; and the frustration by administrative practices of the advantages her partners should enjoy in her former dependencies. In two important cases in the application of the Common Agricultural Policy, France has simply broken the rules when it suited her to do so: the freeing of trade in some horticultural produce early last year, where she followed Germany; and the regionalisation of cereals markets.

5. But it is in the Community's relations with third countries, bilaterally and multilaterally, that French obstruction is most extensive, and most clear-cut.

6. There are, of course, exceptions. France was ready to grant satisfactory conditions for the association of Greece with the Community. But Greece associated with the Community in the aftermath of the Free Trade Area

negotiations when all member countries, including France, had strong reasons of general policy for demonstrating that the Rome Treaty provided a satisfactory solution for relations with other countries in Europe. To-day France would like to see her three former North African territories associated with the Community (the only instance in the Community's external relations where the French have allowed themselves to appear, in their own terminology, as 'demandeurs'). Finally, it is Italy rather than France who has taken the lead in blocking the efforts of the Mediterranean countries outside the Community to safeguard their exports of fruit and vegetables to the Common Market. But here, the Maghreb countries excepted, France is probably not unhappy to see the Community's economic commitment limited by another member country, leaving France free, as in the case of relations with Israel and Spain, to enjoy the reputation, and bilateral rewards, of the more forthcoming attitude which Italian opposition allows her safely to adopt. To some extent the same is true of relations with Austria. But here the French will see that the Community drives a hard bargain, and one which will not interfere with French economic interests, for instance in the field of agriculture, while serving her political interests by forcing Austria to leave EFTA if she is to achieve a relationship with the Community.

7. Elsewhere, whether in Europe or outside it, it is France who has been responsible for obstructing the aims of third countries. This is so whether we consider the bilateral relations of individual countries or international conferences and commodities.

8. The key role which France played in denying Britain and other European countries their objectives during the negotiations in Brussels in 1961–63 needs no description. It is France alone who prevents Britain joining in talks on the political development of Europe, and indeed who now prevents talks taking place even without Britain. More aid would certainly have been forthcoming for Turkey as part of her association with the Community had France not opposed it. Eastern Europe's trade with the Community stands to suffer through the implementation of the Common Agricultural Policy, and the adoption of co-ordinated policies by the Community in relation to Eastern Europe has been handicapped by France's determination to outbid her partners, for example in the granting of export credits, and to encourage Eastern European countries to look to France in the first place to secure their objectives in their dealing with the Community (of which the tariff concessions unsuccessfully offered by the Community to the Soviet Union last year were an example, since they were offered at French instigation). It is France who is making the difficulties for the Swiss over watches and chemicals and for the Scandinavians over paper, pulp and aluminum in the context of the Kennedy Round negotiations.

9. Outside Europe, the picture is the same. In the Community's relations with Latin America, it is French policy which has led to a deterioration in the prospects for exports to the Community, especially of cereals, coffee and bananas, and it is France's attitude which now prevents any remedy being found. The United States' difficulties over the export of poultry in 1964 derived essentially from the Community's readiness to meet French interests. If the prospects for United States exports of cereals and vegetable oils to Europe have decreased, it is French interests which are responsible (though not in the case of rice). Canada shares Scandinavia's difficulties in paper, pulp and aluminum and those of the United States and the Argentina as well as Australia in cereals. In Africa, it is France alone who stands between Nigeria and an agreement with the Community in line with the GATT New Chapter and Nigeria's tradition of non-discrimination. If there is no great enthusiasm elsewhere in the Community for associating the East African Commonwealth countries, it is nevertheless France who insists, and is likely to continue to insist, on terms which the East Africans will at least be very reluctant to grant and which will damage and their relations with other countries if they grant them. In the contrary sense, when the Egyptian Government denounced American aid, France agreed to supply flour to Egypt – a quarter of the cost being at the charge of her Community partners – at the very moment when the Egyptian Government were inviting Herr Ulbricht to Cairo.

10. The difficulties which countries in Asia face in increasing their earnings from the Community, whether from tropical products or from low-cost industrial products, while by no means wholly attributable to France, are nevertheless attributable to her more than to other member countries. It is France who refuses to agree to Community treatment for Indian textiles worked up in the Netherlands. France's quota restrictions on Asian Commonwealth manufactured products continue to be highly restrictive. Hong Kong suffers especially from French restrictions. And if France is prepared to make concessions to Japan, whether on quotas or more formally in relation to Article XXXV of the GATT, she clearly intends to make them not as part of any Community decision or action, which she is resisting, but in isolation where she has most to gain for herself.

11. Multilaterally, the picture is the same. France is primarily responsible, where she is not alone responsible, for the successive delays in the Kennedy Round, on the industrial as on the agricultural side: *écrêtement* and the long discussions over disparities, the length of the Community's exceptions list, and delay in tabling offers on agriculture. Whether France has any intention of allowing the Community to conclude a worthwhile agreement in Geneva cannot yet be judged. But she has made it clear that if there is to be an agreement, she will expect her partners in addition to all else to come nearer to French views

on the related issues of United States investment, industrial concentration and technological research. Alone of the six E.E.C. countries France has so far declined to sign the GATT New Chapter on the developing countries. Although the Community's attitude in the United Nations Conference on Trade and Development in 1964 was not in all respects subject to co-ordination, France played an important role in opposing a global approach to the problems of the under-developed countries, and maintaining regional preferences. Her attitude to the Common Fisheries Policy of the Community, when it comes up for discussion, will be the least helpful from the point of view of outside countries. France has blocked all useful developments in the Western European Union since agreeing to (in fact proposing, to avoid anything less satisfactory to her) a revival of its meetings at Ministerial level in the summer of 1963. In the international monetary field, France, though not alone, has adopted the most extreme position over world liquidity, and France alone has proposed a return to the gold standard.

12. In setting down this catalogue of French obstruction, I would not wish to be thought to suggest that other member countries of the Community (I have remarked on one important example in the case of Italy) have not tried, sometimes successfully, to defend their national interests in the Community's dealings with third countries. Three things, however, distinguish French obstruction in this field. In the first place, France is more successful, because she is more ruthless, and less sensitive to the criticism of others. Even when one or more of the Five are happy, or not unhappy, to see France take a negative position, they are so precisely because they would not wish to sustain a negative position themselves. Secondly, France has less hard national interest than her partners in a more liberal development of the Community's external relations. The tradition of autarky, however many inroads have been made into it in recent years in practice, seems to hang on in France as an ideal, and France seems to have translated the tradition from her national hexagon to the ideal of a tight-knit Community of six. How false to reality this ideal is can be seen from a glance at the attitude of the other five member countries to the issues set out in paragraphs 7–10 above. But the myth is an important one, because on it alone can a 'European Europe' in the French sense be built. In closing the door to Britain in January 1963, General de Gaulle was at pains to emphasize, quite falsely, the likeness of the Six to each other in this respect and the unlikeness of Britain. Thirdly, France started from a position of bargaining strength in her dealings with the outside world greater than that of any of her partners, because the degree of liberalization which she had achieved when the Treaty entered into force was lower than that of any of the Five. Where the Treaty does not oblige France to move in a more liberal direction under a set timetable, the present

French Government seems to prefer to sell what France has got to give in return for advantages for France alone, and therefore bilaterally.

13. I cannot report that I see any reason to suppose that France's attitude will improve in the foreseeable future. In the foreseeable future France alone of the Six is likely to be generally satisfied with the existing situation, and ready therefore to wait if necessary for opportunities to make it still more satisfactory from her point of view. Alone of the Six she is, on the other hand, prepared to see the Community brought to the brink of collapse in order to safeguard her essential objectives. In these circumstances, it cannot be expected that any of France's five partners in the Community, who regard their interests as being increasingly bound up in its future development, are going to dig in their toes to oppose France. They did not do so in January 1963, and I do not expect that they would do so even if the Kennedy Round were to collapse altogether. The Five will continue in this way as long as the balance of their interests lies in the survival of the Community, and as long as they regard the present situation in France as temporary. Only by changing their assessment on these two counts could they be brought to react more strongly against French influence on the external relations of the Community.

14. Is there therefore any chance of promoting a change in the assessment of the Five regarding either the predominance of their interests within the Community as it now is, or the temporary nature of French obstruction?

15. On the first score, the difficulty from Britain's point of view is that there is little or nothing that we can at present attempt alone to persuade the Five which would not harm Britain herself more than it would influence the Five. It is idle to think in this connection of the effect of world opinion. Hard interests – defence, trade or monetary – must be affected before there will be a change of attitude. And the United States alone are in a position to affect such hard interests acutely in any of the Five. Switzerland and Scandinavia, with their large trading deficits with the Community, are perhaps in a position to exercise greater trade pressure than we – but only in a context and a manner we should not welcome. But these possibilities have only to be stated to bring out the long-term danger of action on these lines. For the United States, the Scandinavian countries and Switzerland, if they are to exert pressure, would be likely to exert it in their own interests, not in ours. Although these might sometimes coincide with ours they woud not always do so. And looking further ahead, such pressures in the sphere of trade might well emerge as the first serious steps to a return to bilateralism in trade relations between the developed countries, which could not be in our long-term interests.

16. Nor does it seem likely that much can be achieved in the direction of convincing the Five that the present French attitude may be more than

temporary. Not even the current tightening up of France's attitude to Community questions and the prospect, universally accepted here, that General de Gaulle will be returned for a further period in December, seem likely to cure the rest of the Community of their ingrained optimism that France's present attitude is merely de Gaulle's attitude, and that once he is gone there will probably be a return to a less nationalistic French approach to the Community's internal and external problems.

17. In time, the difficulties which the Common Agricultural Policy are bound to bring may force France herself to modify her attitude to trade with third countries, or even to the question of admitting new members to the Community. But this prospect is distant, and it could be made still more distant by agreement in the Kennedy Round on arrangements which would help to perpetuate the Community's present agricultural policies. Similarly, France's attitude to the interests of third countries could change if she came to feel a greater degree of isolation and relative weakness in industry, technological research and development. This too may be a distant prospect but it is one which we could bring nearer, particularly by being readier to pool what we have to offer in this field with European countries other than France. For the rest, a change of prospect must await developments in the policies of the Five, particularly Germany; or in United States policy. As for the latter, short of applying aggressive pressure on the Community, there are perhaps some things which the Americans could do piecemeal to help towards an improvement, not least the adoption of a more encouraging attitude to those in The Hague who are trying to keep some of the windows of the Community open. As Community delays over the Kennedy Round repeat themselves during this year, the moment may be approaching when we could with profit discuss these questions more extensively with the American Administration.

18. Meanwhile, I feel no harm could be done in any quarter if the general situation described in this despatch could be made rather better known to the public, in Britain and elsewhere, than at present it is.

19. I am sending copies of this despatch to Her Majesty's Representatives at Bonn, Brussels, The Hague, Luxembourg, Paris, Rome, Washington, United Kingdom Delegation to EFTA and United Kingdom Delegation to OECD.

I have, &c.
C. O'NEILL.

'Record of a Meeting Between the Prime Minister [Harold Wilson], and the Foreign Secretary [George Brown] and the Acting Vice-President [Albert Coppé] and Other Members of the High Authority of the European Coal and Steel Community at the British Embassy, Luxembourg, on 8th March 1967', PRO, PREM 13/1495.

RECORD OF A MEETING BETWEEN THE PRIME MINISTER AND THE FOREIGN SECRETARY AND THE ACTING VICE-PRESIDENT AND OTHER MEMBERS OF THE HIGH AUTHORITY OF THE EUROPEAN COAL AND STEEL COMMUNITY AT THE BRITISH EMBASSY, LUXEMBOURG, ON 8th MARCH, 1967, AT 4 p.m.

Present:

The Right Hon. Harold Wilson, M P
The Right Hon. George Brown, M P
Sir Burke Trend
Sir Con O'Neill
Sir James Marjoribanks
Mr. Dugald Malcolm
Mr. W. A. Nield
Mr. A. N. Halls
Mr. A. M. Palliser
Mr. T. Lloyd-Hughes
Mr. C. M. MacLehose
Mr. D. J. D. Maitland
Mr. N. Statham
Mr. W. K. Reid
Interpreter (Mr. Lederer)
Mr. Albert Coppé
M. Albert Wehrer
Herr Fritz Hellwig
M. Roger Reynaud
M. Edmond P. Wellenstein
Interpreter

Background to the United Kingdom initiative

Mr. Wilson welcomed M. Coppé and the other members of the High Authority. He said that in his tour of European capitals he and the Foreign Secretary had now had the opportunity of meeting all six Heads of Government and had had a short meeting with members of the Commissions of the European Economic Community and EURATOM. Our intention to enter the European Economic Community, provided that our difficulties could be satisfactorily met, involved, as matters now stood, entry to all three European Communities. But there was, of course, the question of timing; it was the intention of the Communities, he understood, that the three Executives should shortly be merged. Of course, we intended to achieve full membership of all three Communities, if our problems could be solved. He would be grateful if he could learn from the members of the High Authority some of the difficulties which they foresaw, and which we should bear in mind in the context of our eventual entry into the ECSC.

Attitude of the High Authority

M. Coppé said he and his colleagues were very happy to have the opportunity of meeting Mr. Wilson and Mr. Brown. Mr. Wilson had referred to the merger of the Executives. He expected this would take place in a few weeks or months. But, of course, it was only a first step towards the more important question of merging the Communities themselves. He would like to call on his colleagues to speak in greater detail upon more specific points. But, in the case both of coal and, to some extent, steel, the development in the ECSC had proceeded somewhat beyond what had been expected under the Treaty. A number of exceptional escape clauses had been applied recently because of the situation in both the coal and steel sectors. The Treaty prohibited subsidies. But in fact every coal mining enterprise had subventions of one kind or another, and recourse had been had to a clause in the Treaty which permitted this sort of development. There had recently been an agreement in the Council of Ministers on subsidies for coking coal. They had been able to agree on how these subsidies would be paid, their maximum extent, and how the money would be found. A system of compensation for coking coal exported within the Community would also be involved. In the steel sector an almost totally harmonised tariff had been achieved. They were trying also to achieve greater discipline in production in this sector.

The problem of British accession to the ECSC did not therefore involve only accession to the Treaty but also acceptance of the way in which the Community had developed. It had not always been easy to get agreement upon the applications of exceptions, but as he had said some exceptions were now in force. The question of coking coal to which he had referred and arrangements for importation of steel from East European countries were examples.

Kennedy Round

M. Coppé said he would ask M. Wehrer to speak about the Kennedy Round, which was a subject of immediate importance on which, in the steel sector, the High Authority were spokesmen for the Community.

M. Wehrer said that the discussions on steel in the Kennedy Round at Geneva were now in a difficult phase. We would remember that the mandate given to the High Authority by the Council of Ministers had led to their taking as their base rate the 14 per cent recognised as the Community's legal tariff when they had obtained a waiver in GATT. They had offered to cut this 14 per cent base rate by 50 per cent, and had said immediately that their final objective was a harmonised tariff involving all large producers and exporters in applying a comparable customs tariff. There had been at the outset much opposition to the position which the Community had adopted. The British Delegation in particular had reminded them of the actual level of the Community's harmonised tariff, which was of the order of 6.8 per cent, and had objected to the use of 14 per cent as a base rate. But, M. Wehrer added, that when the reduction in Community tariffs had been made in 1958, this had been a unilateral decision on their part. Most countries had not offered a counterpart. Only the United Kingdom had responded by making a reduction in its own tariff at that time. If the British Delegation now insisted that further reductions needed to be made beyond the effective level to which the Community tariff had then been reduced, this would produce an impossible situation. The Governments of member countries could not accept 3 per cent or thereabouts (the rate which would be produced by making a further cut of 50 per cent) as the level of their protection when much higher tariffs continued to be applied in other States, and when a tariff of 3 per cent provided no effective protection at all. In consequence, he had hoped that the question of the base tariff had been removed from the area of discussion; the idea upon which the discussions had later concentrated was that of seeing whether there was any basis for harmonisation of tariffs between the major producers. This idea had met with a not unfavourable response from most countries, but the United Kingdom Delegation had insisted on its previous attitude. The American Delegation had then suggested the idea of a target rate and discussions were proceeding upon this basis. But he understood, from the latest reports he had had from Geneva, that there was still resistance on the part of the British Delegation to this idea.

M. Wehrer feared that if it was impossible to arrive at a satisfactory settlement there would be complete failure of the Kennedy Round in the steel sector. He could not say what the repercussions might be elsewhere. He thought that if it was possible to reach agreement upon a common or harmonised tariff, the possible check to the progress of the Kennedy Round might be avoided.

There followed a general discussion during which M. Wehrer made clear that the Community's present effective tariff rate was on average 9 per cent (having been increased from the figure of 6.3 per cent); *M. Coppé* said that what they were aiming at was a figure of around 5 per cent for the Community – and they could not go lower than this; *M. Wehrer* noted that the Community wished to maintain a flexible attitude and their minds were not closed towards making further offers in particular areas; and *Mr. Brown* said that the difficulty was that we had offered a 50 per cent reduction in our own existing rates of tariff, which was what the Kennedy Round foresaw, and we thought it was up to the Community to make further moves. *M. Wehrer* objected that British tariffs were higher than Community tariffs.

M. Coppé said he did not think it was useful to pursue the discussion further (it had been said earlier that it would be desirable to leave the question to the negotiators in the Kennedy Round) but added that he could not see why we wished to place pressure upon the Community to reduce their tariffs further if we ourselves expected shortly to be members of the Community.

Mr. Wilson said that this was certainly a dilemma in that what was desirable from the United Kingdom point of view whilst outside the Community might not exactly coincide with her interests inside. But he attached the highest importance to a successful outcome of the Kennedy Round.

Mr. Brown said that the Kennedy Round must not be impeded by the discussions on our own entry. We believed that it was for the Community to make a further move if there was to be a satisfactory outcome in the steel sector.

Problems of United Kingdom entry

Mr. Wilson enquired what difficulties the Community would see as regards British entry. M. Coppé said that the volume of United Kingdom coal production, all under the control of the National Coal Board, was a real problem. But during the previous negotiations they had thought, and they still thought, that the question could be solved. A similar problem arose in connection with steel nationalisation. 25 million tons of steel produced under one owner also constituted a block of a size which the Community was not used to.

Mr. Wilson pointed out that the nationalised steel industry would only be taking over the largest firms, and that it would be organised into four producing groups; and so far as he knew none of them would be significantly larger than some of the groups in the Community. *M. Coppé* said that if these groups were totally independent of each other then no problem would arise. If they were not independent of each other then there would be a problem, but he believed that the Community would be able to handle it. Special arrangements had been made in the case of Charbonnages de France to avoid any misuse of a dominant position within the Community. He repeated that although there were problems, he was confident they could be dealt with.

Mr. Brown said that the groups in the British nationalised steel industry would not be totally independent of each other, but equally the industry would not be monolithic. *Herr Hellwig* said that under Community doctrine one owner was treated as one unit. The NCB might produce the same amount of coal as the total produced within the Community at the moment. *M. Coppé* and *Herr Hellwig* said that they expected that coal production in the Community would be 170–190 million tons by 1970, and might undergo further reductions after 1970. Herr Hellwig said that he thought that the economic problem presented by the accession of so large a volume of production as that of the United Kingdom would not be any reason for the Community to refuse British membership, but ways and means, including transitional periods, must be found to provide solutions to the market problem.

There was agreement that transitional periods were desirable, not only in the interest of the United Kingdom, but in the interest also of the Community. There followed a brief discussion about stocks in the coal industry and unused capacity in the steel industry.

Mr. Wilson asked what the High Authority's advice would be on the manner of a new application. *M. Coppé* suggested that there was no point in waiting for further developments within the Community; the Community progressed the whole time. Nor could there be any question merely of intensifying or amplifying the activities of the present Council of Association. Common solutions for coal and steel problems were necessary. But he and *Herr Hellwig* agreed with the Prime Minister that the operations of the Council of Association had been of great help and made the possibility of speedy agreement with the Community easier in that each side well knew the problems of the other. Herr Hellwig suggested that the last negotiations did not perhaps offer much help. There had been provisional results in the steel sector, but the shape of our nationalised industry might affect these results; and coal had not been discussed properly in the last negotiations, which had not proceeded beyond the stage of fact-finding when they were suspended. *M. Coppé*, in answer to a question from Sir James Marjoribanks, said that it was his opinion that the negotiations should be kept as short at possible. *Mr. Wilson* said this was fully his intention.

Mr. Wilson enquired whether *pricing policies* had been a problem in the last negotiations. *Herr Hellwig* said that on steel they had not been, but the National Coal Board's system had presented rather more difficulty. But transitional periods could adequately cover any problems. The Community did not exercise any control over retail prices but was based on pithead prices with full publicity being given to freight tariffs. If Britain entered the Community if would be necessary to look at the question of rates for movement by sea; sea transport was not covered at the moment by the Community's freight regulations.

M. Coppé said it was his view that all the problems could be solved once the United Kingdom became a member of the Community. The Treaty of Paris provided powers to deal with most situations. Certainly unanimity was required for the application of exceptions, and thus long discussions were required. But it was fully possible to solve virtually every problem within the framework of the Treaty of Paris and he did not doubt that any problems could be overcome once the United Kingdom had joined the Community.

In answer to a question by Mr. Wilson about *national subsidies* within the the Community M. Coppé said that the French applied a differential system of interest rates. So far there was no harmonisation of monetary policy within the Communities and a cheap loan, with a rate of interest below the normal market rate, could not be objected to by the ECSC if there was no objection to it by the EEC in Brussels.

There was some discussion of the Community's *Guarantee Fund*, which had originally been financed by levies on steel production. *Herr Hellwig* said that it would be open to us to 'buy a share' in the Fund; but he did not think that it would be possible to set off payments under the Community's agricultural policy against any payment involved in 'buying this share'. The ECSC Fund was the property of the coal and steel industry and he did not think it possible to arrange offsets in this way.

Common energy policy

In answer to a question from *Sir Con O'Neill* about the establishment of a common energy policy, *Herr Hellwig* said that this depended upon the establishment of a common import policy. Of course it raised problems going far beyond the ECSC alone. *M. Coppé* said that the Communities were not in favour of protection of the energy market. The High Authority had advocated that there should be no protection at the borders, and this philosophy was now generally accepted within the Communities. Of course there was still internal taxation.

There was some discussion of the relative roles which coal, water, atomic energy, oil and gas would play in a common energy policy. *Herr Hellwig* said that 1970 would be a critical year for decision on coal policy since atomic energy might be commercially economic by that time. *M. Coppé* added that the Community had already decided that it would be incorrect to defend the position of coal producers as if the whole energy future of the Community depended on it.

The meeting finished at 5.20 p.m.

Coppé, Albert (Belgian)

Vice President of the High Authority since 1952 and acting President. Born 1911. Graduated in political and social sciences and a Dr. of Economics of the University of Louvain. A member of the Belgian Catholic Trade Union Party, was elected to Parliament in 1946 and was Belgian Minister of Public Works in 1950 and Minister for Economic Affairs in 1951. Is described as intelligent and vigorous but somewhat volatile. Fluent English speaker was successful as Chairman of the High Authority Delegation at the Council of Association on the last two occasions

Wehrer, Albert (Luxembourger)

Member of the High Authority since 1952 and specially responsible for external relations. Born 1895. Educated at the Universities of Munich, Geneva, Liege and Strasbourg. Graduated in law in 1921 and practised at the Bar from 1921–29. Counsellor in the Ministry of Foreign Affairs in 1926, Chargé dè Affairs at Berlin in 1938, Head of the Luxembourg Military Mission in Berlin 1945, Luxembourg Minister to Bonn in 1949 and to Paris in 1951. Has a working knowledge of English.

Hellwig, Fritz (Germen)

Member of the High Authority since 1959. Specially responsible for marketing. Born 1912. Educated at Universities of Hamburg, Vienna and Berlin. Worked in the German steel industry 1940–43. Prisoner of war in the United States and Britain. A prominent member of the CDU since 1947. Director of the German Institute of Industry from 1951. Elected to the Bundestag in 1951 and later Chairman of its Economic Policy Committee. A dynamic personality with wide political and administrative experience, and wide culture and considerable charm. Speaks very good English.

Reynaud, Roger (French)

Member of the High Authority since 1958. Specially responsible for the preparation of long term objectives and for readaptation schemes for industry. Born in 1916. Inspecteur in the Ministry of Finance in 1954. A member of various Governmental Committees concerned with finance, economic and productivity matters. Although of unprepossessing appearance is in fact a man of considerable wit and charm, widely respected by his colleagues. Speaks no English.

Wellenstein, Edmond P. (Dutch)

Secretary General of the High Authority and Chief Executive of the European Coal and Steel Community. Born 1919. Educated at the Polytechnic College of Delft. During the war was a member of the Resistance movement and imprisoned by the Germans. Travelling Secretary in the United States for the World Student Service Fund in 1945 and from 1946–50 a member of the staff of the Queen's personal Secretariat in The Hague. Joined The Netherlands Ministry of Foreign Affairs in 1950, later Head of the German Section, and Deputy Director of the European Department. Joined the High Authority in 1953 as Secretary of the Market Division. Secretary of the High Authority 1956 and Secretary General since 1960. An outstandingly competent official with a wide knowledge and understanding of Community matters. Has always been helpful to the United Kingdom Delegation. Speaks excellent English.

Memorandum for Non-Cabinet Ministers, 'Ten Reasons Why Britain Should Join the Common Market', December 1970, PRO, PREM 15/62.

TEN REASONS WHY BRITAIN SHOULD JOIN THE COMMON MARKET

1. FOR REAL INDEPENDENCE AND SOVEREIGNTY. Decisions are already being taken in Europe which affect Britain profoundly, and their number and scope will increase. Outside the EEC we have no voice in them. It is time we took our place on the Board of Directors. As members of the Council of Ministers in Brussels, British Ministers responsible to the British Parliament would have their say in controlling the Administration of the European Community and ensuring that Britain's basic interests are safeguarded.

2. FOR A RISING STANDARD OF LIVING. Real wages and the standard of living have risen in Britain since 1958; but they have risen much faster in the EEC. Then, we were better off per head than all the Six except tiny Luxembourg. Today we are worse off than all except Italy. If the present trend continues and we remain outside Community Europe, we shall, by 1980, be even worse off by comparison.

3. FOR A FULLER LIFE. In the EEC countries the average citizen has more paid holidays and higher family allowances than in Britain. We spend less of our gross national product on social welfare and security than any country of the Six. The larger market which a Community of Ten will provide will bring more choice for the housewife, lower prices for many products, more jobs, and better career opportunities. Increased wages will compensate for increases in food prices. The rising standard of living will enable British families increasingly to enjoy the pleasures of holidays abroad.

4. TO IMPROVE OUR FOREIGN EARNINGS. Western Europe (EEC plus EFTA) is our largest and fastest growing market. But we can do better still, if we join. Between 1958 and 1968 our exports to the Six multiplied 2½ times; but intra-Community trade multiplied 4 times. In the EEC, trade barriers will no longer be an obstacle for us. Joining will not affect tariffs against our exports to the USA or the rest of the world. It will mean loss of preferences and exports to the Commonwealth, but this loss will be swallowed up in our increased earnings from exports to Western Europe.

5. FOR ECONOMIC GROWTH. Increased exports demand a growing economy to produce them. Between 1958 and 1968 GNP in Britain rose by

49%; but it rose by 112, in the EEC. Inside an enlarged Community of Ten. Britain should share in this quicker growth. Each 1% improvement in our growth adds some £400 million to our national income.

6. TO DEVELOP OUR INDUSTRY AND TECHNOLOGY. American experience shows that technologically advanced industries must be based on a large home market. Britain's entry into the enlarged Community will provide the best guarantee that British research and British brains will bring about advance and growth in Britain's industry and technology. This will provide real opportunities at home for those who now go abroad in frustration. It will help to stop the brain drain.

7. FOR OUR WAY OF LIFE. The Six sovereign states of the EEC have kept their national character. The Dutch still have their Queen, the Belgians their King, the French are no less French than they were in 1958. Any differences, as regular visitors to Europe know, are those brought about by more prosperity, more leisure, and easier travel. Bound to Europe by two thousand years of shared history and tradition, Britain in Europe can ensure that our qualities and virtues can best make their own contribution to our civilisation.

8. FOR PEACE AND SECURITY. The enlarged Community will strengthen Western Europe's capacity to defend itself and provide the best base for a stable relationship with East Europe. Whereas the Communist nations have in the past concentrated on exploiting the divisions of Western Europe, they are now rapidly strengthening their trading links with the EEC.

9. FOR WORLD PROSPERITY. An enlarged Community of Ten will be the world's largest trading group, handling 40% of the world's external trade. It will also play the largest part in aid to and trade with the developing countries. This is why an ever-increasing number of countries (including Nigeria and the East African Commonwealth countries) have become associated with the EEC or are seeking closer links with it.

10. FOR OUR CHILDREN'S FUTURE. The enlarged EEC will be the most important experiment in democracy in history. The Treaty of Rome is not only for today but for tomorrow. In its first 10 years the Six have succeeded in demolishing not only tariff barriers but misunderstanding, distrust and fear among themselves. But Six is not enough. We owe it to our children that Britain, which has in the past shed so much blood in Europe, should join with courage and vision in the creation of a new partnership. A strong and unified Europe will itself be a Super-Power, capable of harnessing the energies and genius of its people; of talking on equal terms with any nation, and of ensuring a future of peace, prosperity and liberty.

'Record of Conversation between the Chancellor of the Duchy of Lancaster [Sir Geoffrey Rippon] and the Portuguese Foreign Minister [Dr Rui Patricio]', 8 March 1972, PRO, PREM 15/887.

RECORD OF CONVERSATION BETWEEN THE CHANCELLOR OF THE DUCHY OF LANCASTER AND THE PORTUGUESE FOREIGN MINISTER:

CABINET OFFICE, 8 March 1972 at 12 noon

The Rt Hon Geoffrey Rippon QC, MP
His Excellency
Mr D F Muirhead
Mr J A Robinson
Mr G E Clark
Mr M A Pakenham
His Excellency
 Dr Patricio
His Excellency
 The Portuguese Ambassador
His Excellency
 Senhor Guerra
Dr da Silva Lopez
Dr Tomaz Andresen

1 After the opening courtesies Mr Rippon said that his concept of a united Europe stretched from the Iberian Peninsula to Finland. It was not limited to 7, 9 or 10 countries. The aim was to bring together the original EEC and EFTA. Clearly some countries were in a position to join the enlarged Community as full members, while others wished to seek less close arrangements. Our aim was to preserve what had been built up in EFTA. There had been close consultations with our EFTA partners, starting from before the EFTA meeting in Reykjavik, on the progress of the negotiations.

2 Mr Rippon hoped that the Portuguese would feel that the mandate given to the Commission for the negotiations was reasonable. We hoped that it would be possible to conclude the negotiations by July. As there was another EFTA Ministerial meeting at the beginning of May we should have the opportunity to review progress in that forum. As Dr Patricio would know we had urged that the list of sensitive products should be kept to a minimum, but as we were still only an acceding state our influence was limited. We

should however continue to keep in touch with the non-candidates through all the available channels. Mr Rippon added that we too have our own items which are sensitive.

3 <u>Dr Patricio</u> congratulated Mr Rippon on the tremendous success of the United Kingdom's enlargement negotiations which were a triumph for him personally. The Portuguese had reached a turning point in their policy towards Europe. He recalled that in 1959, when EFTA was in the process of being established, it was aimed at all the members of the OEEC. Portugal was not a new-comer to integration schemes as she had participated from the outset in EFTA. She appreciated the recognition among all the Ten, and at the Commission, that Portugal was a special case. But he was very concerned at the way Portugal had been dealt with in practice so far. So many problems of detail had arisen. There appeared to be a contradiction between the general principle of accepting Portugal as a special case and the practice adopted in the negotiations so far both in the industrial and agricultural fields.

4 In the present state of development of the Portuguese economy the dominance of agriculture was giving way to that of industry. This was essential if further economic progress was to be made. Industry already made a greater contribution to the Portuguese GNP than agriculture. This was in a large part the result of their membership of EFTA. If this were put in jeopardy by their negotiations with the EEC, ten years of economic co-operation in EFTA would be lost, and ten years of industrial progress in Portugal would be endangered.

5 This was a problem which concerned textiles above all else. The textile industry was now an important party of the industrial production of Portugal. It employed a great part of the labour force. If the sensitive products régime as proposed by the EEC Commission were adopted by the Community the textile industry would be placed in great danger. Under EFTA Portugal had refrained from competing in certain spheres of industrial development. If she did not now obtain free access to the enlarged Community, and especially to the United Kingdom, or nearly free access, in textiles, this would create a terrible problem for Portugal. Although Mr Rippon had said that Britain was only an acceding state, he felt that British opinion on these matters would carry a great deal of weight.

6 Many of the problems in the Portuguese negotiations were connected with their trade with Britain. Senhor Guerra and Senhor Lopez might add more detail later in the discussion. This was true in agriculture as well as industry. The treatment in the Community and in EFTA was different, and if the present Community treatment dominated it would have serious consequences for the Portuguese economy.

7 For example, the EEC price régime for tomato concentrate would reduce

access to the Community for Portuguese tomato concentrate, to no visible benefit to itself or to the United Kingdom. Similarly there was no free access for cork, which was in the sensitive products list. The Portuguese argument was based on the concept of 'imbalance'. Exports of cork were enormously important for Portugal, but the size of the other side's imports of cork was a comparatively minor factor in their import régime. The same was true of textiles. Their exports of textiles had had a tremendous impact on Portuguese development, quite out of proportion to the impact of these imports on the other side. He recognised that this was a political argument rather than an economic argument, but he felt that it ought to be taken into account by their friends. The Portuguese had stated it many times in Brussels and he asked Mr Rippon to take it into consideration.

8 The Portuguese had also asked in Brussels that something similar to the Annex G régime in EFTA should be applied for the benefit of Portugal. They had asked for an extension of the possibility of introducing new industry protection until the 1980s. Portugal needed this additional opportunity to develop new industries because they were very concerned about the rate of emigration. (It went mostly to France.) As a result of a political decision emigration was completely free in Portugal but this meant that the Government had to put more emphasis on economic development if it was to avoid the depopulation of the country. If the EEC did not give free access to Portuguese goods there was really no possibility of a solution of this problem. Dr Patricio also thought that in the interest of the homogeneous development of Europe the countries in the Community had a strong interest in promoting the economic development of Portugal.

9 <u>Mr Rippon</u> thanked Dr Patricio for this exposition. He thought he was right to point out the difference between a general position of principle, and what happened when negotiators got down to detail. There had however to be a balance of mutual advantage. He thought it worth remembering that what was good for one partner to a negotiation was not necessarily bad for the others. He understood there were to be technical talks with officials of the DTI on the complex problem of textiles. He hoped that as the negotiations continued Portugal would continue to keep in close touch with us.

10 <u>Dr Guerra</u> said that he had been present at the founding discussions for EFTA, and at the setting up of OECD. That Organisation had failed to make arrangements for the proper organisation of investments in Europe. Each country had preferred to follow its own narrow advantage, with the result that 300 million people in Europe counted for little, compared with 200 million in the Soviet Union and the United States.

11 <u>Dr Guerra</u> continued that Portugal had lost one million people in the last ten years, although she had asked her friends to import goods rather than

men. She recognised that not all countries could go at the same speed, and although they wished to have membership of the Community in the long run they were not yet prepared for it. Sir Con O'Neill had recognised the need last autumn to help Portugal and Iceland. Free trade in EFTA had helped Portugal a great deal (her trade had increased fourfold); but the loss of people showed that this was not enough. Portugal would also like to be nearer the centre of decision in Europe, and hoped that her friends would help her to bridge the technological gap. A united Europe should not forget the countries on its periphery. The peripheral countries should not simply be suppliers of manpower. Imports of men created the opposite problem; while the periphery suffered from anaemia, the centre suffered from congestion.

12 <u>Mr Rippon</u> said that in our own negotiations difficulties were caused by the need to have separate negotiations for each of the four acceding states. The problem of the non-candidates negotiations was even more complex, as their interests differed even more. For example Switzerland had the obverse of Portugal's problem on immigration.

13 The main need in his view was for speed, so that all the arrangements could come into effect on 1 January 1973. He had gathered from other countries involved that the negotiations were now going faster after a rather slow start.

14 <u>Senhor Lopez</u> said that the great problem for Portugal was to avoid the imposition of new barriers to her trade. But the Commission's mandate suggested that barriers would be placed on 45% of Portuguese exports to the enlarged Community. There would be barriers in agriculture, which accounted for 21% of her exports, whereas some products had been completely free in EFTA. The main products where this contained dangers for the future were canned fish and tomato paste. The Community duty on canned fish was extremely high. He did not understand why this should be, as the Community was not self-sufficient. He supposed that it arose from the Six's desire to give special treatment to some non-European countries. The best aim of Portugal was to integrate herself in the long run into Europe. Portugal felt that preference should be given to her.

15 <u>Dr Patricio</u> added that the canned fish industry was an important source of employment. <u>Mr Rippon</u> asked whether the arrangements the Community had made with other countries were more satisfactory. <u>Senhor Lopez</u> said that the Mediterranean policy of the Community lay behind the restriction of offers. The EEC did not wish to extend any concessions to other countries in the Mediterranean area. But Portugal, unlike the Magreb countries, wished to integrate itself with the Community.

16 <u>Senhor Lopez</u> said that, as for tomato paste Italy was unable to supply the present needs of the Six; with the entry of the UK the demand would be

even greater. Mr Rippon asked what proportion of Portuguese exports went to the United Kingdom. Senhor Lopez said around 40%. Mr Rippon asked whether the maintenance of existing access was the point at issue. Dr Patricio said that the Community seemed to be proposing restrictions in the interest of non-EFTA countries. Senhor Lopez said that on canned fish and tomato paste the British interest in his view coincided with that of Portugal, as we would wish to get the best product at the lowest possible price. Mr Rippon agreed.

17 Senhor Lopez said that they also sought concessions on wine, and in particular on table wine, but they recognise that their case was not strong as there was no special treatment for wine in EFTA. He could not understand why cork was in the list of sensitive products. The EEC imported 40% of their cork from Portugal, and only supplied 10% of their demand from home production. The Portuguese industry was not going to expand very much, so the position was not too serious provided they were given an adequate growth factor. He said that it was not in the UK's interest to accept the restrictions as Portugal's competitors produced cork of a lesser quality.

18 Senhor Lopez said that textiles was the most important sector where United Kingdom and Portuguese interests did not coincide. It was because growth was possible in this sector in EFTA that the industry had been able to develop. (Two-thirds of the growth of Portuguese exports to EFTA countries came from textiles alone.) Some of the products in the sensitive list were not in fact exported by Portugal to the Community, and hardly to the United Kingdom. There was no reason to have them in the list. Other items were more important. Portugal would like to exclude them too but it was realistic to assume that they would probably remain. Mr Rippon interjected that it would be best to leave the ones which did not matter in the list as the price of excluding those which did.

19 Senhor Lopez said that the Commission seemed sympathetic to the idea of removing the smaller items. If the other more important items remained, the problem centred on the size of the indicative ceiling and the rates of growth to be applied. It was also important to know whether the quota for the Community would be global or whether the old and new Member States would be treated separately. A global quota would be best both for Portugal and for the United Kingdom. In the long run there was a possibility that trade might be diverted away from the United Kingdom when the duties prevailing in the Six came down, thus easing the pressure on the UK market. At present Portugal's exports to the United Kingdom were higher than those of the Six taken together. Thus, if there were separate quotas, high rates of increase would be absolutely essential. A global quota would present fewer problems. The rate of growth would be important. Even in the United

Kingdom market, where she had concentrated her efforts, Portugal's market share was only around 4%.

20 Senhor Lopez said there was another difficult point. The Community proposed to keep in existence after 1980 the 'surveillance souple' system. This meant in fact the possibility of protection forever. It would create a great deal of uncertainty. In his view it was necessary to establish a fixed end to protection now if this was to be avoided.

21 On the import side Portugal had asked for the possibility of introducing protection for new industries up to 1980, which would mean postponing their final tariff cuts until 1988. Taken together with the Annex G items these proposals covered about 20% of Portugal's imports from the EEC, which was much less than the restrictions which the mandate proposed for Portuguese exports. This added to the problem of imbalance.

22 Dr Guerra observed that Ministers of the Six had made the mandate stiffer than the Commission's original proposals. He was afraid they would cause more difficulties after the plenary meetings at the end of March. He hoped the United Kingdom would use her influence on Portugal's behalf.

23 Mr Rippon thanked the Portuguese Delegation for their detailed exposition of their case, and promised to take a personal interest in it. He understood there would be technical discussions on 9 March. He hoped that the Portuguese would seek direct contacts with himself and with officials, either in Brussels or through their Ambassador in London, whenever necessary.

'Cassis' Decision, Judgement of the European Court of Justice, Rewe-Zentral AG v. Bundesmonopolverwaltung für Branntwein, 20 February 1979, European Court of Justice, Case 120/78.

Judgment of the Court of 20 February 1979.

Rewe-Zentral AG v Bundesmonopolverwaltung für Branntwein.

Reference for a preliminary ruling: hessisches Finanzgericht – Germany.

Measures having an effect equivalent to quantitative restrictions.

Case 120/78.

[...]

Summary
1. *Since it is a provision relating specifically to state monopolies of a commercial character, Article 37 of the EEC Treaty is irrelevant with regard to national provisions which do not concern the exercise by a public monopoly of its specific function – namely, its exclusive right – but apply in a general manner to the production and marketing of given products, whether or not the latter are covered by the monopoly in question.*
2. *In the absence of common rules, obstacles to movement within the Community resulting from disparities between the national laws relating to the marketing of a product must be accepted in so far as those provisions may be recognized as being necessary in order to satisfy mandatory requirements relating in particular to the effectiveness of fiscal supervision, the protection of public health, the fairness of commercial transactions and the defence of the consumer.*
3. *The concept of 'measures having an effect equivalent to quantitative restrictions on imports', contained in article 30 of the EEC Treaty, is to be understood to mean that the fixing of a minimum alcohol content for alcoholic beverages intended for human consumption by the legislation of a member state also falls within the prohibition laid down in that provision where the importation of alcoholic beverages lawfully produced and marketed in another member state is concerned.*

Parties

In case 120/78

Reference to the court under Article 177 of the EEC Treaty by the Hessisches Finanzgericht for a preliminary ruling in the action pending before that court between

Rewe-Zentral AG, having its registered office in Cologne,

and

Bundesmonopolverwaltung fur Branntwein (Federal Monopoly Administration for Spirits),

Subject of the Case

On the interpretation of Articles 30 and 37 of the EEC Treaty in relation to Article 100 (3) of the German law on the monopoly in spirits,

Grounds

1. By order of 28 April 1978, which was received at the court on 22 May, the Hessisches Finanzgericht referred two questions to the court under Article 177 of the EEC Treaty for a preliminary ruling on the interpretation of Articles 30 and 37 of the EEC Treaty, for the purpose of assessing the compatibility with Community law of a provision of the German rules relating to the marketing of alcoholic beverages fixing a minimum alcoholic strength for various categories of alcoholic products.

2. It appears from the order making the reference that the plaintiff in the main action intends to import a consignment of 'Cassis de Dijon' originating in France for the purpose of marketing it in the Federal Republic of Germany. The plaintiff applied to the Bundesmonopolverwaltung (Federal Monopoly Administration for Spirits) for authorization to import the product in question and the monopoly administration informed it that because of its insufficient alcoholic strength the said product does not have the characteristics required in order to be marketed within the Federal Republic of Germany.

3. The monopoly administration's attitude is based on Article 100 of the Branntweinmonopolgesetz and on the rules drawn up by the monopoly administration pursuant to that provision, the effect of which is to fix the minimum alcohol content of specified categories of liqueurs and other potable spirits (Verordnung uber den Mindestweingeistgehalt von Trinkbranntweinen of 28 February 1958, Bundesanzeiger no 48 of 11 March 1958).

Those provisions lay down that the marketing of fruit liqueurs, such as 'Cassis de Dijon', is conditional upon a minimum alcohol content of 25%, whereas the alcohol content of the product in question, which is freely marketed as such in France, is between 15 and 20%.

4. The plaintiff takes the view that the fixing by the German rules of a minimum alcohol content leads to the result that well-known spirits products from other member states of the Community cannot be sold in the Federal Republic of Germany and that the said provision therefore constitutes a restriction on the free movement of goods between member states which exceeds the bounds of the trade rules reserved to the latter.

In its view it is a measure having an effect equivalent to a quantitative restriction on imports contrary to Article 30 of the EEC Treaty.

Since, furthermore, it is a measure adopted within the context of the management of the spirits monopoly, the plaintiff considers that there is also an infringement of Article 37, according to which the member states shall progressively adjust any state monopolies of a commercial character so as to ensure that when the transitional period has ended no discrimination regarding the conditions under which goods are procured or marketed exists between nationals of member states.

5. In order to reach a decision on this dispute the Hessisches Finanzgericht has referred two questions to the court, worded as follows:

> 1. Must the concept of measures having an effect equivalent to quantitative restrictions on imports contained in Article 30 of the EEC Treaty be understood as meaning that the fixing of a minimum wine-spirit content for potable spirits laid down in the German Branntweinmonopolgesetz, the result of which is that traditional products of other member states whose wine-spirit content is below the fixed limit cannot be put into circulation in the Federal Republic of Germany, also comes within this concept?
> 2. May the fixing of such a minimum wine-spirit content come within the concept of 'discrimination regarding the conditions under which goods are procured and marketed ... between nationals of member states' contained in Article 37 of the EEC Treaty?

6. The national court is thereby asking for assistance in the matter of interpretation in order to enable it to assess whether the requirement of a minimum alcohol content may be covered either by the prohibition on all measures having an effect equivalent to quantitative restrictions in trade between member states contained in Article 30 of the treaty or by the prohibition on all discrimination regarding the conditions under which goods are procured and marketed between nationals of member states within the meaning of Article 37.

7. It should be noted in this connexion that Article 37 relates specifically to state monopolies of a commercial character.

   That provision is therefore irrelevant with regard to national provisions which do not concern the exercise by a public monopoly of its specific function – namely, its exclusive right – but apply in a general manner to the production and marketing of alcoholic beverages, whether or not the latter are covered by the monopoly in question.

   That being the case, the effect on intra-Community trade of the measure referred to by the national court must be examined solely in relation to the requirements under Article 30, as referred to by the first question.

8. In the absence of common rules relating to the production and marketing of alcohol – a proposal for a regulation submitted to the Council by the Commission on 7 December 1976 (Official Journal c 309, p. 2) not yet having received the Council's approval – it is for the member states to regulate all matters relating to the production and marketing of alcohol and alcoholic beverages on their own territory.

   Obstacles to movement within the Community resulting from disparities between the national laws relating to the marketing of the products in question must be accepted in so far as those provisions may be recognized as being necessary in order to satisfy mandatory requirements relating in particular to the effectiveness of fiscal supervision, the protection of public health, the fairness of commercial transactions and the defence of the consumer.

9. The government of the Federal Republic of Germany, intervening in the proceedings, put forward various arguments which, in its view, justify the application of provisions relating to the minimum alcohol content of alcoholic beverages, adducing considerations relating on the one hand to the protection of public health and on the other to the protection of the consumer against unfair commercial practices.

10. As regards the protection of public health the German government states that the purpose of the fixing of minimum alcohol contents by national legislation is to avoid the proliferation of alcoholic beverages on the national market, in particular alcoholic beverages with a low alcohol content, since, in its view, such products may more easily induce a tolerance towards alcohol than more highly alcoholic beverages.

11. Such considerations are not decisive since the consumer can obtain on the market an extremely wide range of weakly or moderately alcoholic products and furthermore a large proportion of alcoholic beverages with a high alcohol content freely sold on the German market is generally consumed in a diluted form.

12. The German government also claims that the fixing of a lower limit for the alcohol content of certain liqueurs is designed to protect the consumer

against unfair practices on the part of producers and distributors of alcoholic beverages.

This argument is based on the consideration that the lowering of the alcohol content secures a competitive advantage in relation to beverages with a higher alcohol content, since alcohol constitutes by far the most expensive constituent of beverages by reason of the high rate of tax to which it is subject.

Furthermore, according to the German government, to allow alcoholic products into free circulation wherever, as regards their alcohol content, they comply with the rules laid down in the country of production would have the effect of imposing as a common standard within the Community the lowest alcohol content permitted in any of the member states, and even of rendering any requirements in this field inoperative since a lower limit of this nature is foreign to the rules of several member states.

13. As the Commission rightly observed, the fixing of limits in relation to the alcohol content of beverages may lead to the standardization of products placed on the market and of their designations, in the interests of a greater transparency of commercial transactions and offers for sale to the public.

    However, this line of argument cannot be taken so far as to regard the mandatory fixing of minimum alcohol contents as being an essential guarantee of the fairness of commercial transactions, since it is a simple matter to ensure that suitable information is conveyed to the purchaser by requiring the display of an indication of origin and of the alcohol content on the packaging of products.

14. It is clear from the foregoing that the requirements relating to the minimum alcohol content of alcoholic beverages do not serve a purpose which is in the general interest and such as to take precedence over the requirements of the free movement of goods, which constitutes one of the fundamental rules of the Community.

    In practice, the principle effect of requirements of this nature is to promote alcoholic beverages having a high alcohol content by excluding from the national market products of other member states which do not answer that description.

    It therefore appears that the unilateral requirement imposed by the rules of a member state of a minimum alcohol content for the purposes of the sale of alcoholic beverages constitutes an obstacle to trade which is incompatible with the provisions of Article 30 of the Treaty.

    There is therefore no valid reason why, provided that they have been lawfully produced and marketed in one of the member states, alcoholic beverages should not be introduced into any other member state; the sale of such products may not be subject to a legal prohibition on the marketing of beverages with an alcohol content lower than the limit set by the national rules.

15. Consequently, the first question should be answered to the effect that the concept of 'measures having an effect equivalent to quantitative restrictions on imports' contained in Article 30 of the Treaty is to be understood to mean that the fixing of a minimum alcohol content for alcoholic beverages intended for human consumption by the legislation of a member state also falls within the prohibition laid down in that provision where the importation of alcoholic beverages lawfully produced and marketed in another member state is concerned.

Decision on Costs

Costs

16. The costs incurred by the government of the Kingdom of Denmark, the government of the Federal Republic of Germany and the Commission of the European Communities, which have submitted observations to the court, are not recoverable.

Since these proceedings are, in so far as the parties to the main action are concerned, in the nature of a step in the action before the Hessisches Finanzgericht, costs are a matter for that court.

Operative Part

On those grounds,

The court,

In answer to the questions referred to it by the Hessisches Finanzgericht by order of 28 April 1978, hereby rules:

The concept of 'measures having an effect equivalent to quantitative restrictions on imports' contained in Article 30 of the EEC Treaty is to be understood to mean that the fixing of a minimum alcohol content for alcoholic beverages intended for human consumption by the legislation of a member state also falls within the prohibition laid down in that provision where the importation of alcoholic beverages lawfully produced and marketed in another member state is concerned.

German Beer Purity Law Decision, Judgement of the European Court of Justice, Commission of the European Communities v. Federal Republic of Germany, 12 March 1987, European Court of Justice, Case 178/84.

Judgment of the Court of 12 March 1987.

Commission of the European Communities v Federal Republic of Germany.

Failure of a state to fulfil its obligations – purity requirement for beer.

Case 178/84.

[...]

Summary
1. *In the absence of common rules relating to the marketing of the products concerned, obstacles to free movement within the Community resulting from disparities between the national laws must be accepted in so far as such rules, applicable to domestic and to imported products without distinction, may be recognized as being necessary in order to satisfy mandatory requirements relating inter alia to consumer protection. It is also necessary for such rules to be proportionate to the aim in view. If a member state has a choice between various measures to attain the same objective it should choose the means which least restricts the free movement of goods.*
2. *A member state is not entitled – on the grounds of the requirements of consumer protection – to restrict the use of a designation to products satisfying the requirements of its national legislation. Firstly, consumers' conceptions are likely to vary from one member state to another and to evolve in the course of time within a member state, and hence the legislation of that state must not crystallize given consumer habits so as to consolidate an advantage acquired by national industries concerned to comply with them, and, secondly, a generic designation may not be restricted to products manufactured in accordance with the rules in force in that member state.*
3. *Where consumers in a member state attribute specific qualities to a product manufactured from particular raw materials, it is legitimate for the member*

state in question to seek to give consumers the information which will enable them to make their choice in the light of that consideration. But the means used to that end must not prevent the importation of products which have been legally manufactured and marketed in other member states. Whilst a system of mandatory information is permissible, it must not entail negative assessments for imported products manufactured in accordance with processes other than those in use in the importing member state.

4. In view of the uncertainties at the present state of scientific research with regard to food additives and of the absence of harmonization of national law, Articles 30 and 36 of the Treaty do not prevent national legislation from restricting the consumption of additives by subjecting their use to prior authorization granted by a measure of general application for specific additives, in respect of all products, for certain products only or for certain uses.

However, in applying such legislation to imported products containing additives which are authorized in the member state of production but prohibited in the member state of importation, the national authorities must, in view of the principle of proportionality underlying the last sentence of Article 36 of the Treaty, restrict themselves to what is actually necessary to secure the protection of public health. Accordingly the use of a specific additive which is authorized in another member state must be authorized in the case of a product imported from that member state where, in view, on the one hand, of the findings of international scientific research, and in particular of the work of the Community's Scientific Committee for Food, the Codex Alimentarius Committee of the FAO and the World Health Organization, and, on the other hand, of the eating habits prevailing in the importing member state, the additive in question does not present a risk to public health and meets a real need, especially a technical one. The concept of technological need must be assessed in the light of the raw materials utilized and bearing in mind the assessment made by the authorities of the member state where the product was manufactured and the findings of international scientific research.

By virtue of the principle of proportionality, traders must also be able to apply, under a procedure which is easily accessible to them and can be concluded within a reasonable time, for the use of specific additives to be authorized by a measure of general application.

It must be open to traders to challenge before the courts an unjustified failure to grant authorization. Without prejudice to the right of the competent national authorities of the importing member state to ask traders to produce the information in their possession which may be useful for the purpose of assessing the facts, it is for those authorities to demonstrate that the prohibition is justified on grounds relating to the protection of the health of its population.

Parties

In case 178/84

Commission of the European Communities, represented by R. C. Beraud, Principal Legal Adviser, and J. Sack, a member of its legal department, with an address for service in Luxembourg at the office of G. Kremlis, also a member of the Commission's legal department, Jean Monnet Building, Kirchberg,

Applicant,

v

Federal Republic of Germany, represented by M. Seidel, Ministerialrat at the Federal Ministry of Economic Affairs, J. Dietrich, Ministerialrat at the Federal Ministry of Youth, Family Affairs and Health, J. Sedemund, Rechtsanwalt, Cologne, and R. Lukes, Professor of Law in the University of Muenster, acting as agents, with an address for service in Luxembourg at the Office of the Chancellor of the Embassy of the Federal Republic of Germany, 20–22 Avenue E. Reuter,

Defendant,

Concerning the application of the 'Reinheitsgebot' ((purity requirement)) to beers imported from other member states,

The court

Composed of: Lord Mackenzie Stuart, President, Y. Galmot, C. Kakouris, T. F. O'Higgins and F. Schockweiler (Presidents of chambers), G. Bosco, T. Koopmans, O. Due, U. Everling, K. Bahlmann, R. Joliet, J. C. Moitinho de Almeida and G. C. Rodriguez Iglesias, Judges,

Advocate General: Sir Gordon Slynn

Registrar: H. A. Ruehl, Principal Administrator

Having regard to the report for the hearing as supplemented following the hearing on 13 and 14 May 1986,

After hearing the opinion of the Advocate General delivered at the sitting on 18 September 1986,

Gives the following

Judgment

Grounds

1. By an application lodged at the court registry on 6 July 1984, the Commission of the European Communities has brought an action under Article 169 of the EEC Treaty for a declaration that, by prohibiting the marketing of beers lawfully manufactured and marketed in another member state if they do not comply with Articles 9 and 10 of the Biersteuergesetz (law on beer duty) (law of 14 March 1952, Bundesgesetzblatt I, p. 149), the Federal Republic of Germany has failed to fulfil its obligations under Article 30 of the EEC Treaty.
2. Reference is made to the report for the hearing for the facts of the case, the course of the procedure and the arguments of the parties, which are mentioned or discussed hereinafter only in so far as is necessary for the reasoning of the court.

The applicable national law

3. In the course of the proceedings before the court, the German government gave the following account of its legislation on beer, which was not contested by the Commission and is to be accepted for the purposes of these proceedings.
4. As far as the present proceedings are concerned, the Biersteuergesetz comprises, on the one hand, manufacturing rules which apply as such only to breweries in the Federal Republic of Germany and, on the other, rules on the utilization of the designation 'bier' (beer), which apply both to beer brewed in the Federal Republic of Germany and to imported beer.
5. The rules governing the manufacture of beer are set out in Article 9 of the Biersteuergesetz. Article 9 (1) provides that bottom-fermented beers may be manufactured only from malted barley, hops, yeast and water. Article 9 (2) lays down the same requirements with regard to the manufacture of top-fermented beer but authorizes the use of other malts, technically pure cane sugar, beet sugar or invert sugar and glucose and colourants obtained from those sugars. Article 9 (3) states that malt means any cereal artificially germinated. It must be noted in that connection that under Article 17 (4) of the Durchfuehrungsbestimmungen zum Biersteuergesetz (implementing provisions to the Biersteuergesetz) of 14 March 1952 (Bundesgesetzblatt I, p. 153) rice, maize and sorghum are not treated as cereals for the purposes of Article 9 (3) of the Biersteuergesetz. Under Article 9 (7) of the Biersteuergesetz, derogations from the manufacturing rules laid down in Article 9 (1) and (2) may be granted on application in specific cases in respect of the manufacture of special beers, beer intended for export or beer intended for scientific experiments. In addition, under Article 9 (8), Article 9 (1) and (2) do not apply to breweries making beer for consumption on

their premises (hausbrauer). Under Article 18 (1) (1) of the Biersteuergesetz fines may be imposed for contraventions of the manufacturing rules set out in Article 9.

6. The rules on the commercial utilization of the designation 'bier' are set out in Article 10 of the Biersteuergesetz. Under that provision only fermented beverages satisfying the requirements set out in Article 9 (1), (2), (4), (5) and (6) of the Biersteuergesetz may be marketed under the designation 'bier' – standing alone or as part of a compound designation – or under other designations, or with pictorial representations, giving the impression that the beverage in question is beer. Article 10 of the Biersteuergesetz entails merely a partial prohibition on marketing in so far as beverages not manufactured in conformity with the aforementioned manufacturing rules may be sold under other designations, provided that those designations do not offend against the restrictions laid down in that provision. Contraventions of the rules on designation may give rise to a fine under Article 18 (1) (4) of the Biersteuergesetz.

7. Imports into the Federal Republic of Germany of beers containing additives will also be confronted by the absolute prohibition on marketing in Article 11 (1) (2) of the Gesetz ueber den Verkehr mit Lebensmitteln, Tabakerzeugnissen, Kosmetischen mitteln und Sonstigen bedarfsgegenstaenden (law on foodstuffs, tobacco products, cosmetics and other consumer goods), hereinafter referred to as the 'Foodstuffs Law', of 15 August 1974 (Bundesgesetzblatt I, p.*1945).

8. Under the Foodstuffs Law, which is based on considerations of preventive health protection, all additives are in principle prohibited, unless they have been authorized. Article 2 of the law defines additives as 'substances which are intended to be added to foodstuffs in order to alter their characteristics or to give them specific properties or produce specific effects'. It does not cover 'substances which are of natural origin or are chemically identical to natural substances and which, according to general trade usage, are mainly used on account of their nutritional, olfactory or gustatory value or as stimulants, and drinking and table water'.

9. Article 11 (1) (1) of the Foodstuffs Law prohibits the use of unauthorized additives, whether pure or mixed with other substances, for the manufacture or processing by way of trade of foodstuffs intended to be marketed. Article 11 (2) (1) and Article 11 (3) provide that that prohibition does not cover processing aids or enzymes. Article 11 (2) (1) defines processing aids as 'additives which are eliminated from the foodstuff altogether or to such an extent that they ... are present in the product for sale to the consumer ... only as technically unavoidable and technologically insignificant residues in amounts which are negligible from the point of view of health, odour and taste'.

10. Article 11 (1) (2) of the Foodstuffs Law prohibits the marketing by way of trade of products manufactured or processed in contravention of Article 11 (1) (1) or not conforming with a regulation issued pursuant to Article 12 (1). Under Article 12 (1) a ministerial regulation approved by the Bundesrat may authorize the use of certain additives for general use, for use in specific foodstuffs or for specific applications provided that it is compatible with consumer protection from the point of view of technological, nutritional and dietary requirements. The relevant authorizations are set out in the annexes to the Verordnung ueber die Zulassung von Zusatzstoffen zu Lebensmitteln (regulation on the authorization of additives in foodstuffs) of 22 December 1981 (Bundesgesetzblatt I, p.*1633), hereinafter referred to as 'the Regulation on Additives').

11. As a foodstuff, beer is subject to the legislation on additives, but it is governed by special rules. The rules on manufacture in Article 9 of the Biersteuergesetz preclude the use of any substances, including additives, other than those listed therein. As a result, those rules constitute specific provisions on additives within the meaning of Article 1 (3) of the regulation on additives. That paragraph provides that the regulation on additives is to be without prejudice to any contrary provisions prohibiting, restricting or authorizing the use of additives in particular foodstuffs. In this way, additives authorized for general use or for specific uses in the annexes to the Regulation on Additives may not be used in the manufacture of beer. However, that exception applies only to substances which are additives within the meaning of the law on foodstuffs and whose use is not covered by an exception laid down in the Foodstuffs Law itself, which was enacted after the Biersteuergesetz. Consequently, the prohibition on the use of additives in beer does not cover processing aids or enzymes.

12. As a result, Article 11 (1) (2) of the Foodstuffs Law, in conjunction with Article 9 of the Biersteuergesetz, has the effect of prohibiting the importation into the Federal Republic of Germany of beers containing substances covered by the ban on the use of additives laid down by Article 11 (1) (1) of the Foodstuffs Law.

The subject-matter of the proceedings

13. It must first be established whether the proceedings are limited to the prohibition of the marketing under the designation 'bier' of beer manufactured in other member states in accordance with rules inconsistent with Article 9 of the Biersteuergesetz or whether they extend to the ban on the importation of beer containing additives which are authorized in the member state of origin but prohibited in the Federal Republic of Germany.

14. In its letter giving the Federal Republic of Germany formal notice, the Commission's objections were directed against Articles 9 and 10 of the

Biersteuergesetz in so far as they precluded the importation into the Federal Republic of Germany of beers which, although lawfully manufactured in other member states, had not been brewed in conformity with the rules applicable in the Federal Republic of Germany. The Commission took the view that that marketing prohibition could not be justified on grounds of the public interest relating to the protection of consumers or the safeguarding of public health.

15. In its reply to that letter the German government argued that the Reinheitsgebot was vital in order to safeguard public health: if beer was manufactured using only the raw materials listed in Article 9 of the Biersteuergesetz the use of additives could be avoided. In a supplementary letter dated 15 December 1982 to a member of the Commission, the German government repeated that argument and made it clear that the requirement to use only the raw materials listed in Article 9 of the Biersteuergesetz included the prohibition of the use of additives, which was designed to protect public health.

16. In its reasoned opinion the Commission adhered to its point of view. It considered that the fact that beer brewed according to the German tradition of the Reinheitsgebot could be manufactured without additives did not signify generally that there was no technological necessity for the use of additives in beer brewed according to other traditions or using other raw materials. The question of the technological necessity for the use of additives could be decided only in the light of the manufacturing methods employed and in relation to specific additives.

17. In its reply to the reasoned opinion the German government reiterated its arguments relating to preventive health protection which, in its view, justified the provisions in Articles 9 and 10 of the Biersteuergesetz. However, it did not elucidate the exact scope of that legislation or its relationship with the rules on additives.

18. In the statement of the grounds it relies on in its application, the Commission complains of the barriers to imports resulting from the application of the Biersteuergesetz to beers manufactured in other member states from other raw materials or using additives authorized in those states.

19. It was only when it submitted its defence that the German government stated that the rules on the purity of beer were contained in two separate but complementary pieces of legislation, and provided the description of its legislation which is given above.

20. In its reply the Commission set out its separate objections to the rules on designation in Article 10 of the Biersteuergesetz and to the absolute ban on additives in beer. In the Commission's view, the German government's comprehensive description of the applicable law does not fundamentally alter

the facts underlying this case. The Commission stresses that its application is not aimed exclusively at Articles 9 and 10 of the Biersteuergesetz but generally at the prohibition on the marketing of beer from other member states which does not satisfy the manufacturing criteria set out in those provisions. In its opinion, the precise statutory basis for that prohibition is of no importance.

21. In those circumstances there are two reasons why it must be considered that the application is directed both against the prohibition on the marketing under the designation 'bier' of beers manufactured in other member states in accordance with rules not corresponding to those in Article 9 of the Biersteuergesetz, and against the prohibition on the importation of beers containing additives whose use is authorized in the member state of origin but forbidden in the Federal Republic of Germany.

22. In the first place, the Commission identified the substance of the infringement from the outset in so far as from the beginning of the pre-litigation procedure it challenged the prohibition on marketing beer imported into the Federal Republic of Germany from other member states which is not brewed in accordance with the rules in force in the Federal Republic of Germany. It referred to Article 9 of the Biersteuergesetz only in order to specify those rules more precisely. As the German government stated, the scope of Article 9 is not restricted to raw materials but also covers additives. Besides, the arguments developed by the Commission during the pre-litigation procedure to the effect that an absolute ban on additives is inappropriate show that it intended its action to cover that prohibition.

23. In the second place, it must be observed that, from the start of the procedure, the German government itself raised in its defence mainly arguments concerning additives and the protection of public health, which shows that it understood and acknowledged that the subject-matter of the proceedings also covered the absolute ban on the use of additives and makes it clear that it has not been denied the right to a fair hearing in that respect.

The prohibition on the marketing under the designation 'bier' of beers not complying with the requirements of Article 9 of the Biersteuergesetz.

24. It must be noted in the first place that the provision on the manufacture of beer set out in Article 9 of the Biersteuergesetz cannot in itself constitute a measure having an effect equivalent to a quantitative restriction on imports contrary to Article 30 of the EEC Treaty, since it applies only to breweries in the Federal Republic of Germany. Article 9 of the Biersteuergesetz is at issue in this case only in so far as Article 10 of that law, which covers both products imported from other member states and products manufactured in Germany, refers thereto in order to determine the beverages which may be marketed under the designation 'bier'.

25. As far as those rules on designation are concerned, the Commission concedes

that as long as harmonization has not been achieved at Community level the member states have the power in principle to lay down rules governing the manufacture, the composition and the marketing of beverages. It stresses, however, that rules which, like Article 10 of the Biersteuergesetz, prohibit the use of a generic designation for the marketing of products manufactured partly from raw materials, such as rice and maize, other than those whose use is prescribed in the national territory are contrary to community law. In any event, such rules go beyond what is necessary in order to protect the German consumer, since that could be done simply by means of labelling or notices. Those rules therefore constitute an impediment to trade contrary to Article 30 of the EEC Treaty.

26. The German government has first sought to justify its rules on public-health grounds. It maintains that the use of raw materials other than those permitted by Article 9 of the Biersteuergesetz would inevitably entail the use of additives. However, at the hearing the German government conceded that Article 10 of the Biersteuergesetz, which is merely a rule on designation, was exclusively intended to protect consumers. In its view, consumers associate the designation 'bier' with a beverage manufactured from only the raw materials listed in Article 9 of the Biersteuergesetz. Consequently, it is necessary to prevent them from being misled as to the nature of the product by being led to believe that a beverage called 'bier' complies with the Reinheitsgebot when that is not the case. The German government maintains that its rules are not protectionist in aim. It stresses in that regard that the raw materials whose use is specified in Article 9 (1) and (2) of the Biersteuergesetz are not necessarily of national origin. Any trader marketing products satisfying the prescribed rules is free to use the designation 'bier' and those rules can readily be complied with outside the Federal Republic of Germany.

27. According to a consistent line of decisions of the court (above all, the judgment of 11 July 1974 in case 8/74 Procureur du Roi v Dassonville ((1974)) ECR 837) the prohibition of measures having an effect equivalent to quantitative restrictions under Article 30 of the EEC Treaty covers 'all trading rules enacted by member states which are capable of hindering, directly or indirectly, actually or potentially, intra-community trade'.

28. The court has also consistently held (in particular in the judgment of 20 February 1979 in case 120/78 Rewe-Zentral AG v Bundesmonopolverwaltung ((1979)) ECR 649, and the judgment of 10 November 1982 in case 261/81 Walter Rau Lebensmittelwerke v De Smedt ((1982)) ECR 3961) that 'in the absence of common rules relating to the marketing of the products concerned, obstacles to free movement within the Community resulting from disparities between the national laws must be accepted in so far as such rules, applicable to domestic and to imported

products without distinction, may be recognized as being necessary in order to satisfy mandatory requirements relating inter alia to consumer protection. It is also necessary for such rules to be proportionate to the aim in view. If a member state has a choice between various measures to attain the same objective it should choose the means which least restricts the free movement of goods'.
29. It is not contested that the application of Article 10 of the Biersteuergesetz to beers from other member states in whose manufacture raw materials other than malted barley have been lawfully used, in particular rice and maize, is liable to constitute an obstacle to their importation into the Federal Republic of Germany.
30. Accordingly, it must be established whether the application of that provision may be justified by imperative requirements relating to consumer protection.
31. The German government's argument that Article 10 of the Biersteuergesetz is essential in order to protect German consumers because, in their minds, the designation 'bier' is inseparably linked to the beverage manufactured solely from the ingredients laid down in Article 9 of the Biersteuergesetz must be rejected.
32. Firstly, consumers' conceptions which vary from one member state to the other are also likely to evolve in the course of time within a member state. The establishment of the common market is, it should be added, one of the factors that may play a major contributory role in that development. Whereas rules protecting consumers against misleading practices enable such a development to be taken into account, legislation of the kind contained in Article 10 of the Biersteuergesetz prevents it from taking place. As the court has already held in another context (judgment of 27 February 1980 in case 170/78 Commission v United Kingdom ((1980)) ECR 417), the legislation of a member state must not 'crystallize given consumer habits so as to consolidate an advantage acquired by national industries concerned to comply with them'.
33. Secondly, in the other member states of the Community the designations corresponding to the German designation 'bier' are generic designations for a fermented beverage manufactured from malted barley, whether malted barley on its own or with the addition of rice or maize. The same approach is taken in Community law as can be seen from heading no 22.03 of the common customs tariff. The German legislature itself utilizes the designation 'bier' in that way in Article 9 (7) and (8) of the Biersteuergesetz in order to refer to beverages not complying with the manufacturing rules laid down in Article 9 (1) and (2).
34. The German designation 'bier' and its equivalents in the languages of the

other member states of the community may therefore not be restricted to beers manufactured in accordance with the rules in force in the Federal Republic of Germany.

35. It is admittedly legitimate to seek to enable consumers who attribute specific qualities to beers manufactured from particular raw materials to make their choice in the light of that consideration. However, as the court has already emphasized (judgment of 9 December 1981 in case 193/80 Commission v Italy ((1981)) ECR 3019), that possibility may be ensured by means which do not prevent the importation of products which have been lawfully manufactured and marketed in other member states and, in particular, 'by the compulsory affixing of suitable labels giving the nature of the product sold'. By indicating the raw materials utilized in the manufacture of beer 'such a course would enable the consumer to make his choice in full knowledge of the facts and would guarantee transparency in trading and in offers to the public'. It must be added that such a system of mandatory consumer information must not entail negative assessments for beers not complying with the requirements of Article 9 of the Biersteuergesetz.

36. Contrary to the German government's view, such a system of consumer information may operate perfectly well even in the case of a product which, like beer, is not necessarily supplied to consumers in bottles or in cans capable of bearing the appropriate details. That is borne out, once again, by the German legislation itself. Article 26 (1) and (2) of the aforementioned regulation implementing the Biersteuergesetz provides for a system of consumer information in respect of certain beers, even where those beers are sold on draught, when the requisite information must appear on the casks or the beer taps.

37. It follows from the foregoing that by applying the rules on designation in Article 10 of the Biersteuergesetz to beers imported from other member states which were manufactured and marketed lawfully in those states the Federal Republic of Germany has failed to fulfil its obligations under Article 30 of the EEC Treaty.

The absolute ban on the marketing of beers containing additives

38. In the Commission's opinion the absolute ban on the marketing of beers containing additives cannot be justified on public-health grounds. It maintains that the other member states control very strictly the utilization of additives in foodstuffs and do not authorize the use of any given additive until thorough tests have established that it is harmless. In the Commission's view, there should be a presumption that beers manufactured in other member states which contain additives authorized there represent no danger to public health. The Commission argues that if the Federal Republic of Germany wishes to oppose the importation of such beers then it bears the onus of proving that such beers

are a danger to public health. The Commission considers that in this case that burden of proof has not been discharged. In any event, the rules on additives applying to beer in the Federal Republic of Germany are disproportionate in so far as they completely preclude the use of additives whereas the rules for other beverages, such as soft drinks, are much more flexible.

39. For its part, the German government considers that in view of the dangers resulting from the utilization of additives whose long-term effects are not yet known and in particular of the risks resulting from the accumulation of additives in the organism and their interaction with other substances, such as alcohol, it is necessary to minimize the quantity of additives ingested. Since beer is a foodstuff of which large quantities are consumed in Germany, the German government considers that it is particularly desirable to prohibit the use of any additive in its manufacture, especially in so far as the use of additives is not technologically necessary and can be avoided if only the ingredients laid down in the Biersteuergesetz are used. In those circumstances, the German rules on additives in beer are fully justified by the need to safeguard public health and do not infringe the principle of proportionality.

40. It is not contested that the prohibition on the marketing of beers containing additives constitutes a barrier to the importation from other member states of beers containing additives authorized in those states, and is to that extent covered by Article 30 of the EEC Treaty. However, it must be ascertained whether it is possible to justify that prohibition under Article 36 of the treaty on grounds of the protection of human health.

41. The court has consistently held (in particular in the judgment of 14 July 1983 in case 174/82 Sandoz bv ((1983)) Ecr 2445) that 'in so far as there are uncertainties at the present state of scientific research it is for the member states, in the absence of harmonization, to decide what degree of protection of the health and life of humans they intend to assure, having regard however to the requirements of the free movement of goods within the Community'.

42. As may also be seen from the decisions of the Court (and especially the judgment of 14 July 1983 in the Sandoz case, cited above, the judgment of 10 December 1985 in case 247/84 Motte ((1985)) ECR 3887, and the judgment of 6 May 1986 in case 304/84 Ministere Public v Muller and others ((1986)) ECR 1511), in such circumstances Community law does not preclude the adoption by the member states of legislation whereby the use of additives is subjected to prior authorization granted by a measure of general application for specific additives, in respect of all products, for certain products only or for certain uses. Such legislation meets a genuine need of health policy, namely that of restricting the uncontrolled consumption of food additives.

43. However, the application to imported products of prohibitions on marketing products containing additives which are authorized in the member state of

production but prohibited in the member state of importation is permissible only in so far as it complies with the requirements of Article 36 of the treaty as it has been interpreted by the Court.

44. It must be borne in mind, in the first place, that in its judgments in the Sandoz, Motte and Muller cases, cited above, the Court inferred from the principle of proportionality underlying the last sentence of Article 36 of the treaty that prohibitions on the marketing of products containing additives authorized in the member state of production but prohibited in the member state of importation must be restricted to what is actually necessary to secure the protection of public health. The court also concluded that the use of a specific additive which is authorized in another member state must be authorized in the case of a product imported from that member state where, in view, on the one hand, of the findings of international scientific research, and in particular of the work of the Community's Scientific Committee for Food, the Codex Alimentarius Committee of the Food and Agriculture Organization of the United Nations (FAO) and the World Health Organization, and, on the other hand, of the eating habits prevailing in the importing member state, the additive in question does not present a risk to public health and meets a real need, especially a technical one.

45. Secondly, it should be remembered that, as the Court held in its judgment of 6 May 1986 in the Muller case, cited above, by virtue of the principle of proportionality, traders must also be able to apply, under a procedure which is easily accessible to them and can be concluded within a reasonable time, for the use of specific additives to be authorized by a measure of general application.

46. It should be pointed out that it must be open to traders to challenge before the courts an unjustified failure to grant authorization. Without prejudice to the right of the competent national authorities of the importing member state to ask traders to produce the information in their possession which may be useful for the purpose of assessing the facts, it is for those authorities to demonstrate, as the Court held in its judgment of 6 May 1986 in the Muller case, cited above, that the prohibition is justified on grounds relating to the protection of the health of its population.

47. It must be observed that the German rules on additives applicable to beer result in the exclusion of all the additives authorized in the other member states and not the exclusion of just some of them for which there is concrete justification by reason of the risks which they involve in view of the eating habits of the German population; moreover those rules do not lay down any procedure whereby traders can obtain authorization for the use of a specific additive in the manufacture of beer by means of a measure of general application.

48. As regards more specifically the harmfulness of additives, the German government, citing experts' reports, has referred to the risks inherent in

the ingestion of additives in general. It maintains that it is important, for reasons of general preventive health protection, to minimize the quantity of additives ingested, and that it is particularly advisable to prohibit altogether their use in the manufacture of beer, a foodstuff consumed in considerable quantities by the German population.

49. However, it appears from the tables of additives authorized for use in the various foodstuffs submitted by the German government itself that some of the additives authorized in other member states for use in the manufacture of beer are also authorized under the German rules, in particular the regulation on additives, for use in the manufacture of all, or virtually all, beverages. Mere reference to the potential risks of the ingestion of additives in general and to the fact that beer is a foodstuff consumed in large quantities does not suffice to justify the imposition of stricter rules in the case of beer.

50. As regards the need, and in particular the technological need, for additives, the German government argues that there is no need for additives if beer is manufactured in accordance with the requirements of Article 9 of the Biersteuergesetz.

51. It must be emphasized that mere reference to the fact that beer can be manufactured without additives if it is made from only the raw materials prescribed in the Federal Republic of Germany does not suffice to preclude the possibility that some additives may meet a technological need. Such an interpretation of the concept of technological need, which results in favouring national production methods, constitutes a disguised means of restricting trade between member states.

52. The concept of technological need must be assessed in the light of the raw materials utilized and bearing in mind the assessment made by the authorities of the member state where the product was lawfully manufactured and marketed. Account must also be taken of the findings of international scientific research and in particular the work of the Community's Scientific Committee for Food, the Codex Alimentarius Committee of the FAO and the World Health Organization.

53. Consequently, in so far as the German rules on additives in beer entail a general ban on additives, their application to beers imported from other member states is contrary to the requirements of Community law as laid down in the case-law of the Court, since that prohibition is contrary to the principle of proportionality and is therefore not covered by the exception provided for in Article 36 of the EEC Treaty.

54. In view of the foregoing considerations it must be held that by prohibiting the marketing of beers lawfully manufactured and marketed in another member state if they do not comply with Articles 9 and 10 of the Biersteuergesetz, the Federal Republic of Germany has failed to fulfil its obligations under Article 30 of the EEC Treaty.

Decision on Costs

Costs

55. Under Article 69 (2) of the rules of procedure the unsuccessful party is to be ordered to pay the costs. Since the Federal Republic of Germany has failed in its submissions, it must be ordered to pay the costs.

Operative Part

On those grounds,
The court
Hereby:

(1) Declares that, by prohibiting the marketing of beers lawfully manufactured and marketed in another member state if they do not comply with Articles 9 and 10 of the Biersteuergesetz, the Federal Republic of Germany has failed to fulfil its obligations under Article 30 of the EEC Treaty;
(2) Orders the Federal Republic of Germany to pay the costs.

THE ASSOCIATION OF SOUTH EAST ASIAN NATIONS

The Association of South East Asian Nations (ASEAN) was originally founded by Thailand, Indonesia, the Philippines, Malaysia and Singapore in 1967. The prior political involvement of the members had been limited and unusually antagonistic. Singapore was expelled from Malaysia in 1965 in the wake of racial riots and concerns over the status of Malays in Singapore. Indonesia had opposed Malaysian independence and had violent territorial disputes with Malaysia over Borneo. Thailand and the Philippines were both members of the American-led South East Asian Treaty Organization (SEATO), an association that proved to be ineffectual. Economic interaction within the region was also limited, with low levels of economic development coexisting with exports primarily of raw materials to the developed world.

Events of the mid-1960s removed some of the political impediments to regional economic cooperation. Indonesian President Sukarno's eclipse by General Suharto led to a reduction in tensions with Malaysia. The *Konfrontasi* between Indonesia and Malaysia was resolved in 1966 and Suharto focused the Indonesian military's attention on suppressing the Communist Party. Indonesia's domestic troubles opened up the possibility of normalizing relations between the largest country in the region and its neighbours. The ongoing Vietnam War threatened to expand the Cold War beyond Indochina and into neighbouring counties in the region. In newly-independent Singapore, Prime Minister Lee Kwan Yew remained a supporter of greater regional cooperation in recognition of his city-state's vulnerability to regional political instability and dependence on external markets.

The Bangkok Declaration signed in 1967 was vague on the specifics of what the organization would accomplish. Indeed, the members did not regard ASEAN as an international organization as such, nor did most foreign governments. At the same time, ASEAN's lack of supranational status has limited its interactions with other organizations. The European Economic Community (EEC) was dubious of ASEAN's ability to accomplish anything independent of its members; and, in fact, the ASEAN–EEC Cooperation Agreement was an agreement between the European Community as a whole and the five individual members of ASEAN.

Both ASEAN and Europe have pursued regional economic and political objectives; however, they have done so with markedly different strategies. While small compared to national governments, the Brussels-based bureaucracies of the European Union employ tens of thousands of employees with a powerful remit to monitor, manage and impose regulations on the domestic economies of the European Union's member-states. In contrast, the ASEAN Secretariat in Jakarta is deliberately limited to a secretarial support role.[1] Where the EEC has focused on the pooling of sovereignty in a variety of policy areas, the members of ASEAN have rejected the supranational approach to regional economic integration. Unlike the European Union's customs union and common external tariff, the ASEAN countries limited their trade integration to the pursuit of preferential trade agreements with one another, reserving trade negotiation powers to their national governments. The ASEAN Free Trade Area (AFTA) signed in 1992 accelerated the process of tariff reduction in the region; however, the internal regulation of markets and economic activity remained with the members. Plans for an ASEAN Economic Community, part of the organization's 'Vision' for 2020, have made ASEAN an attractive locale for foreign direct investment.[2] However, again, actual progress on the practical steps of harmonization, mutual recognition, coordination and institutional reform have not occurred.

AFTA retains the intergovernmental features that have characterized ASEAN since its founding. In this regard, AFTA bears greater resemblance to NAFTA than the European Single Market. Although ASEAN members have often looked at Europe as an example of successful regional integration, South-East Asia is a different region with different interests and realities. At the Bali Summit in 1976, Lee Kuan Yew reflected on how much progress the European Community had made in nineteen years and how many differences of opinion remained.[3] A similar comparison of the extent of ASEAN integration forty years after the Bangkok Declaration (2007) with the European Union forty years after the Treaty of Rome (1998) would find ASEAN still struggling with a free trade area in contrast to a Europe with a consolidated single market, common external tariff and on the verge of launching a single currency.

The actual economic effects of regional integration are more limited in ASEAN than either the European Union or NAFTA. In 2004, while over two-thirds of the trade of European Union member states was with one another and over half of NAFTA member's exports went to each other, under one-quarter of ASEAN trade was intra-regional. This external focus has not been deleterious to economic development, indeed the opposite has been true. Concentrating on external markets has been part of a successful economic strategy for the ASEAN members as it has for most other East Asian economies.[4]

The diversity of domestic political and economic arrangements was also reflected in differing memberships in key international economic institutions, especially the General Agreement on Tariffs and Trade (GATT). Indonesia and Malaysia had long been members of the GATT at the time ASEAN was launched; however, Singapore did not join the international trade regime until 1973, the Philippines followed in 1979 and it was not until 1982 that Thailand joined. Since the 1980s, ASEAN members have experienced rapid economic growth and rising standards of living and all five original ASEAN members were founding members of the World Trade Organization (WTO). As a group, ASEAN members played a collective and positive role in the Uruguay Round negotiations.

ASEAN has experienced modest expansion in membership since its founding in 1967. The original five members were joined by Brunei when it received its independence in 1984. The end of the Cold War ended the security concerns that had overshadowed much of ASEAN's activities from its earliest days.[5] ASEAN's 'Zone of Peace' could now be expanded to include the nations of Indochina, the countries whose previous status as Cold War battlegrounds had contributed to the original creation of ASEAN. Vietnam (1995), Myanmar (1997), Laos (1997) and Cambodia (1999) all joined ASEAN by the end of the twentieth century. The new members, including the Communist government of Vietnam, have expanded the political diversity of an already diverse group of countries.

However, since the creation of the WTO and the expansion of ASEAN to all ten nations of South-East Asia in 1995, ASEAN has not been as unified. Expansion increased the divisions within ASEAN and made collective action more difficult. The heightened politicization of the WTO likewise increased the salience and conflict over negotiations to levels that were not present under the GATT.[6] The 1997 East Asian crisis, which started in Thailand, was particularly intense among ASEAN members. In the decade since the crisis, ASEAN economies have proven to be quite resilient and have begun growing rapidly again, albeit not as rapidly as the 'miracle' years of the 1980s and early 1990s.[7] The slowdown in world trade talks has also led many ASEAN members to pursue bilateral free trade agreements – Singapore has signed one with the United States while Thailand and Malaysia are in negotiations with the Americans and Vietnam is holding talks with the European Union.

Notes

1. P. Tinsulanonda, 'ASEAN: Meeting the Challenges of Asia and the Pacific', in L. G. Martin (ed.), *The ASEAN Success Story: Social, Economic and Political Dimensions* (Honolulu, HI: East–West Center, 1987), p. 5.
2. M. Austria, 'ASEAN's Extra-Regional Linkages', in L. P. Ping, T. S. Yean and G. T. Yu (eds), *The Emerging East Asian Community: Security and Economic Issues* (Kuala Lumpur: Penerbit UKM, 2006), p. 290.

3. See 'Address by Mr Lee Kwan Yew, Prime Minister of Singapore, at the Opening Session of the ASEAN Summit, Bali, on 23 February 1976', below, pp. 149–51.
4. World Bank, *The East Asian Miracle: Economic Growth and Public Policy* (Washington, DC: World Bank, 1993).
5. D. da Cunha (ed.), *Southeast Asian Perspectives on Security* (Singapore: Institute of Southeast Asian Studies, 2000).
6. R. Sally, 'Thai Trade Policy: From Non-Discriminatory Liberalization to FTAs', *World Economy*, 30:10 (2007), pp. 1594–620. See also the documents on the Seattle WTO ministerial included in this volume, below, pp. 282–95.
7. World Bank, *East Asia Update: Solid Growth, New Challenges* (Washington, DC: World Bank, 2006).

ASSOCIATION OF SOUTH EAST ASIAN NATIONS

Statement of S. Rajaratnam (Minister for Foreign Affairs of Singapore) at the ASEAN Conference, Bangkok, 8 August 1967, PRO, FCO 15/23.

> Statement of H.E.S. Rajaratnam
> Minister for Foreign Affairs of Singapore
> Bangkok, August 8, 1967

Mr. Chairman, Your Excellencies, Ladies and Gentlemen,

First of all, on behalf of my Delegation and the Government of Singapore, I would like to thank the Government of Thailand and its people for hosting this Conference of what is today, five countries and in the course of years to come of many more countries of South East Asia. Secondly, on behalf of my Delegation, I would like to extend particular thanks to our Chairman for the tactful, judicious and patient way in which he guided our not always coherent deliberations towards a more than successful conclusion. I would like to take this opportunity to thank the officers who did excellent work in translating our intentions into more concrete form by way of documents and papers.

So, today, after four days of rather pleasant and friendly discussions, we are about to launch the new ASEAN. It is easy to give birth to a new organization but the creation of an organisation of this nature is the most simple of all tasks. It is a more skeleton that we have erected. Now the really difficult task is to give flesh and blood to this concept. We, in Singapore, are not unmindful of the fact that schemes for regional cooperation will run into more rocks than calm waters. Nevertheless, having had four or five days of discussions with my ministerial colleagues, there is one thing that is uppermost in my mind and that is the conviction of my ministerial colleagues in regard to both the inevitability and the desirability of regional cooperation. However, it would be necessary not only for ministers or leaders to take this new regional scheme seriously but also to transmit to its people the need for a new kind of thinking.

For twenty years each of us in this region had been compelled to do things purely on the basis of nationalist fervour. And many of us know that after twenty years of decolonisation, nationalism alone has not provided or fulfilled the expectations by way of happier life, more fruitful life, better living standards to our countries and for our peoples. This realisation has grown and, therefore, it is necessary for us if we are really to be successful in giving life to ASEAN to marry national thinking with regional thinking. We must now think at two levels. We must think not only of our national interests but posit them against regional interests: that is a new way of thinking about our problems. And that is two different things and sometimes they can conflict. Secondly, we must also accept the fact, if we are really serious about it, that regional existence means painful adjustments to those practices, and thinking in our respective countries. We must make these painful and difficult adjustments. If we are not going to do that, then regionalism remains a Utopia.

The last point I would like to stress is that there may be, as has happened to other associations of this kind, misunderstandings as to what ASEAN is all about. So, I would like to stress that those who are outside the grouping should not regard this as a grouping against anything, against anybody. We have approached ASEAN as standing for something, not against anything. If there are people who misunderstand the proposed regional grouping, or manifest hostility towards it, let us explain that it can only be because as in Europe and in many parts of the world, outside powers have vested interests in the balkanisation of this region. We ourselves have learnt the lessons and have decided that small nations are not going to be balkanised so that they can be manipulated, set against one another, kept perpetually weak, divided and ineffective by outside forces.

So, as far as we are concerned, we want to ensure a stable South East Asia not a balkanised South East Asia. And those countries who are interested, genuinely interested, in the stability of South East Asia, the prosperity in South East Asia, and better economic, and social conditions will welcome small countries getting together to pool their collective resources and their collective wisdom to contribute to the peace of the world. The more unstable South East Asia is, the more the peace of the world is also threatened.

So, I would urge people outside the region not to misunderstand this coming together of our five and other South East Asian countries. We want to ensure that ASEAN stands for the interests of ASEANS and therefore by implication for the peace and prosperity of the world. That is all we are interested in. And if other countries think of tomorrow and are willing to help us to achieve this objective, they will be welcomed as friends. And we will also be worthwhile friends to them.

However, in order to win over regard and respect from the outside world, we must first take ASEAN seriously ourselves. There are a lot of people watching what all this is going to amount to. So first we must take our own child seriously. We must convince those that are watching us that we are prepared to make the adjustments and sacrifices necessary to achieve our objective and we are serious about it. The message must get through that this time the South East Asian countries are not going to be like the Balkans during the last two World Wars; that they are not going to be pushed around; once other nations take us seriously, just as we take ourselves seriously; once there is acceptance of our role as a united grouping of Asian countries, then we can bring peace and prosperity to this region as well as to the rest of the world.

Information Department
Ministry of Foreign Affairs
Bangkok, August 8, 1967

Statement of Adam Malik (Minister of Foreign Affairs of Indonesia) at the ASEAN Conference, 8 August 1967, PRO, FCO 15/23.

Statement of H. E. Adam Malik
Presidium Minister for Political Affairs
Minister for Foreign Affairs of Indonesia

Mr. Chairman, Your Excellencies, Dear Friends,

We have arrived today at another milestone in the history of South East Asia.

As you remember, it was about a year ago that I enjoyed the hospitality of the Thai Government when I met here in Bangkok with my colleagues from the Philippines and Malaysia. I had then the opportunity to exchange views not only with them, but also with you, Mr. Chairman.

It was during those exchanges of views that the idea of a new regional cooperation came up for the first time. During the past year all of us patiently worked towards the implementation of that idea, making haste slowly, in order to establish a sound and firm basis on which to build a new association for regional cooperation. It is therefore a great satisfaction to me that today we are able to formalize the birth of this new association.

Mr. Chairman,

Indonesia's thinking regarding the regional cooperation is well known. It is not necessary to elaborate, but I would like to avail myself of this opportunity to recall that Indonesia always wants to see South East Asia develop into a region which can stand on its own feet, strong enough to defend itself against any negative influence from ourside the region. Furthermore, considering our combined natural resources and manpower, such a South East Asia is not just a wishful thinking, if the countries of the region can cooperate effectively with each other.

Of course I realize that differences in outlook do exist among our nations, but I am convinced that we will be able to overcome those differences, provided that we are prepared to approach them with a maximum of goodwill and understanding, of good faith and realism.

Mr. Chairman,

The joint declaration we just signed is only the beginning. Hard work, patience, and perseverance are necessary, if we are to realize the aims and purposes of the association, in order that our peoples will indeed benefit from its achievements.

In conclusion, allow me Mr. Chairman, also on behalf of my delegation, to express my feeling of deep gratitude to the Government and People of Thailand for their warm reception and their generous hospitality. I would also like to thank especially you, Mr. Chairman, for the statesmanship you have shown and for the valuable role you have played while presiding over our deliberations. Thanks to your wisdom and your patience we have arrived at the successful conclusion of our meeting. Profound thanks go also to my other colleagues, and their assistants, for their cooperation and understanding.

Thank you, Mr. Chairman.

Priority Telegram from UK Embassy in Bangkok regarding Declaration Establishing the ASEAN, 8 August 1967, PRO, FCO 15/23, no. 1.

En Clair
PRIORITY   BANGKOK TO FOREIGN OFFICE
Telno. 440   8 August, 1967

UNCLASSIFIED

Addressed to Foreign Office telegram No. 440 of 8 August. Repeated for information to: Kuala Lumpur, Djakarta, Manila, POLAD Singapore, BHC Singapore, Canberra, Wellington, Washington

Declaration establishing the Association of South East Asian Nations (ASEAN) was signed in the Saranrom Palace at 11 a.m. local time today by Malik for Indonesia, Razak for Malaysia, Ramos for Philippines, Rajaratnam for Singapore and Thanat for Thailand.

2. Preamble of Declarations refers to the mutual interests and common problems among the countries of South East Asia and their determination to ensure stability and security from external interference in any form. It also affirms that all foreign bases are temporary and remain only with the expressed concurrence of the countries concerned and are not intended to be used directly or indirectly to subvert the national independence and freedom of States in the area or prejudice the orderly processes of their national development.

3. The Declaration then sets out the aims of the new organization as follows:
   (a) To accelerate the economic growth, social progress and cultural development of the region;
   (b) To promote regional peace and stability through respect for justice and the rule of law and adherence to the principles of the United Nations Charter;
   (c) To promote collaboration in the economic, social, cultural, technical, scientific and administrative fields;
   (d) To collaborate more effectively for the greater utilization of agriculture and industry, the expansion of trade, the improvement of transport and communications and the raising of living standards;
   (e) To promote South East Asian studies;
   (f) To maintain close cooperation with existing organizations with similar aims and purposes.

4. To achieve these aims the following machinery is to be set up:
   (a) An annual meeting of Foreign Ministers;
   (b) A Standing Committee under the chairmanship of the Foreign Minister of

the host country or his representative having as its members the accredited Ambassadors of the other member countries;
(c) Ad hoc and permanent committees of specialists and officials;
(d) A national secretariat in each member country. Bangkok telegram No. 440 to Foreign Office
5. The organization is open to all States in the South East Asian region subscribing to the aforementioned aims, principles and purposes.
6. A Press release accompanying the Declaration states that next year's Ministerial Meeting will be held in Djakarta and that pending and during that meeting the Standing Committee will be located in Djakarta.
7. Please see my immediately following telegram.

Mr. Bullard

Sent 1000Z 8 August
Recd. 1422Z 8 August

Restricted Telegram from UK Embassy in Moscow regarding Soviet Response to South-East Asian Regional Cooperation, 14 August 1967, PRO, FCO 15/23, no. 6.

TO FOREIGN OFFICE

14 August 1967

CLASSIFIED

Addressed to Foreign Office telegram No. 1394 of 14 August, repeated for information to Washington, Singapore, Kuala Lumpur, Djakarta, Bangkok, Manila, Canberra and Wellington.

ASEAN.

Pravda of 13 August carries an authoritative article on ASEAN by one of its political commentators.

2. Following are main points:
- (a) The stated objects of the new association seem unexceptionable. But behind this façade a new military bloc is being built up. The majority of ASEAN's members have links with aggressive blocs: its doors are open to Australia and New Zealand: and there are signs that preparations are being made for South Viet Nam's entry:
- (b) The United States and Britain will seek to exploit the Association for their own ends. It is indicative that a new meeting should be projected under British patronage at Kuala Lumpur, at which Australia, New Zealand, Malaysia, Singapore and Indonesia will discuss joint defence plans:
- (c) This new Association has been brought into being because SEATO, ASPAC, CENTO and ASA are compromised in the eyes of independent Asian countries. The United States is particularly anxious to bring in countries which profess independence in foreign policy:
- (d) Many were surprised at the degree of activity in the organisation of the new bloc shown by Adam Malik. The United States hopes according to Rusk, that Indonesia will make a big contribution to developing the political strength of the 'free world' in Asia: and the Djakarta press has spoken of the role of ASEAN in containing Communism. But those who hope to use the Association to achieve regional leadership or strengthen their military position are making a mistake:
- (e) It is significant that Burma and Cambodia have refused to align themselves with the Association:
- (f) Well tried instruments of cooperation exist already in the form of UNESCO and ECAFE. The Soviet Union has consistently supported

ECAFE as a regional organisation. There is too an increasing awareness in Malaysia, Singapore and the Philippines that normal trade relations with the socialist countries is a way of strengthening their independence.

Sir G. Harrison

Sent 14142 14 August
Recd 15142 14 August

Confidential Summary on the Association of South-East Asian Nations from Giles Bullard (British Embassy in Bangkok) to George Brown (Foreign Secretary), 15 August 1967 PRO, FCO 15/23, no. 7.

CONFIDENTIAL

(1079/67)

SUMMARY

Association of South-East Asian Nations.

1. The establishment of the Association of South-East Asian Nations (ASEAN) is a triumph for Colonel Thanat Khoman, the Thai Foreign Minister (paragraphs 1–3).
2. The Association intends to concentrate on economic and technical problems, but its charter contains the seeds of political disagreement (paragraph 4).
3. Ceylon may join the Association, and possibly Laos also, but no one else, at any rate for the present. Restricting membership to a comparatively small area will help to give the Association a better chance of survival, but a lot will depend on the first year's achievements (paragraphs 5–7)
4. There may be business opportunities for us as a result of ASEAN, but we should not interfere or offer advice. We have already made a contribution; English is the Association's official language (paragraph 8)

BRITISH EMBASSY,
BANGKOK.

(1079/67)
Despatch No. 22
11 August 1967

Sir,

As already reported by telegram a Declaration establishing the Association of South-East Asian Nations (ASEAN) was signed in Bangkok on the 8th of August by the Foreign Ministers of Indonesia the Philippines, Singapore and Thailand and the Deputy Prime Minister of Malaysia. Copies of the Declaration and its accompanying Press Release are enclosed.

2. The setting up of this new regional organisation represents a personal success for Col. Thanat Khoman the Thai Foreign Minister, who composed the first draft of the Declaration last December and has since pursued his objective with his usual energy and rather more than his usual tact. He has had a number of preliminary meetings with Ministers of the other countries concerned, of which the most important was undoubtedly his brief visit to Kuala Lumpur in May at which the Tunku, in order to get Indonesia back into the main

stream agreed to withdraw his previous objections to the setting up of an organisation which would duplicate the aims and membership of his own brain-child, the Association of South-East Asia (ASA). But the Malaysians had also to be persuaded to agree to Singapore's joining the new organisation and to the holding of the five-power meeting in Bangkok instead of in Kuala Lumpur. It was a feat in itself to get the five Ministers to Bangkok so soon after the meeting of the Asian and Pacific Council (ASPAC) and so near the ASA meeting in Kuala Lumpur.

3. To Col. Thanat also must go the credit for the way in which the meeting was staged. The Ministers met first over the weekend for two days of discussions at Bangsaen, a seaside resort some two hours' drive from Bangkok, with a convenient golf-course at which the emphasis was on ease and informality – 'sports-shirt diplomacy' as Thanat put it. A further day of talks in Bangkok produced an agreed declaration ready for signature on the Tuesday morning. Considering the wide field which had to be covered and the differences of opinion, some of them genuine and deeply felt, which had to be resolved, this is a remarkable achievement. Thanat fully deserves the warm tributes to his statesmanship which were paid to him by the other delegates. His status both in South-East Asia and among his own countrymen in Thailand has been increased by the events of the past week.

4. The Declaration is perhaps less precise than its authors would have liked it to be. As expected its aims and purposes are similar to those of the 1961 Bangkok Declaration which established ASA. References to regional peace and security and to the principles of the U.N. Charter have been added, seemingly at the request of the Malaysians but there are no major changes. The emphasis is still on economic and technical cooperation and the raising of living standards. All this is sensible and practical. It is in the preamble that one can detect signs of possible future trouble. Indonesian dislike of being drawn into any kind of regional defensive grouping, which has prevented them from joining ASPAC, is reflected in a clause about the temporary nature of foreign bases itself probably an Indonesian contribution to the original Thai draft. This clause is unpopular with the Malaysians and Filipines and possibly also with the Thais, though as Sir A. Rumbold has already pointed out the United States' bases in Thailand are strictly speaking not foreign bases. Its inclusion together with the choice of Djakarta for the next Ministerial meeting and the acceptance of M. Malik's suggested name for the association are signs of how far the other four countries were prepared to go to secure Indonesian agreement to the draft. The question of a name for the new association must incidentally have occupied the Ministers for some time: the invitations to Tuesday's ceremony gave it the old name of SEAARC (South-East Asian Association for Regional Cooperation).

5. As well as the foreign bases clause a reference to security from external interference has been included in the preamble. This however can be taken to mean whatever the signatories wish. Thanat no doubt intends it to mean Communist China, while Malik is probably also thinking of the Americans. The wording in any case is sufficiently vague not to have deterred the Government of Ceylon from showing interest in the new association and it is possible that Ceylon's application to join under the terms of paragraph 4 of the Declaration will be the first to be received. There are no other likely prospective members except perhaps Laos. Burma and Cambodia under different régimes might be candidates, but not yet. If ASPAC collapses through inanition or through excessive Australian zeal, Japan might wish to join but she is so large and economically powerful that the other countries would think twice about accepting her. Formosa too is a possibility, but not I would guess either Australia or New Zealand. One of the causes of the unreal atmosphere surrounding ASPAC is the presence of these two countries which, though professing Asian sympathies and loyalties, are in fact much closer to the United States or to Western Europe in their way of looking at the area's problems.

6 By contrast the recent ASEAN meeting revealed unsuspected depths of common interest in the participating countries, and a realistic estimate of the difficulties still to be overcome. As M. Rajaratham said in his speech on Tuesday: 'Many of us know that after twenty years of decolonisation, nationalism alone has not provided or fulfilled expectations by way of a happier life a more fruitful life, or better living standards for our countries and for our peoples ... It is necessary for us, if we are really to be successful in giving life to ASEAN, to marry national thinking with regional thinking [and] we must also accept the fact, if we are really serious about it, that regional existence means painful adjustments'. It is this apparently genuine wish for closer cooperation coupled with the limited aims and geographical extent of the new organisation and the realistic approach of the five Ministers concerned which gives the ASEAN Declaration a healthier sound than some of its predecessors and the organisation itself a better chance of survival.

7. What happens now? Presumably the members of ASA will decide at their next meeting to wind up their affairs, perhaps by referring all outstanding projects to the ASEAN Standing Committee, which is already saddled with proposals for regional cooperation in the fields of tourism, shipping, fisheries and trade. Ceylon's application to join, if it materialises will also have to go to the Standing Committee together with any others that may be made. A good deal therefore will depend on events in Djakarta over the next twelve months. ASPAC, after its imposing debut in Seoul in 1966 achieved virtually nothing in the year that followed. We must hope that ASEAN does

not follow the same course. Fortunately M. Malik, who under the terms of the Declaration will be responsible for the Committee's work, seems to have the right approach. In his speech of Tuesday he said. 'I realise what differences in outlook do exist among our nations, but I am convinced that we will be able to overcome those differences, provided we are prepared to approach them with a maximum of good-will and understanding, of good faith and realism ... The joint Declaration we have just signed is only the beginning. Hard work, patience and perseverance are necessary if we are to realise the aims and purposes of the association.'

8. Meanwhile what should our attitude be? As seen from this post it is important that we should not interfere or be suspected of interfering. Colonialism is still a dirty word in South-East Asia, and suspicion of outside interference could fall on non-Communist as well as Communist countries. There may eventually be greater opportunities for doing business in the area, and we should be on the lookout for them. We should also be prepared to help if we are asked, but we should not offer to do so. We should not be well received. If asked whether we approve of ASEAN we need say no more than that we welcome all spontaneous movements of this kind. Our contribution is in fact already a significant one. The Declaration itself, the speeches of the five Ministers, and their discussions at Bangsaen were all in English, their only common language.

9. I am copying this despatch, with enclosures to H.M. Representatives at Kuala Lumpur, Djakarta, Manila, POLAD Singapore, Singapore, Colombo, Canberra, Wellington, Washington, Tokyo, Saigon, Phnom Penn and Vientiane.

I have the honour to be,
with the highest respect,
Sir,
Your obedient Servent,
(Giles Bullard)

Telegram from British Embassy in Manila on the Philippines and ASEAN, 30 October 1967, PRO, FCO 15/23.

CONFIDENTIAL

BRITISH EMBASSY
MANILA
30 October, 1967

Dear Donald,

Before he went off on leave in Japan, the Ambassador took me to call on Ramos, the Foreign Secretary.

The Ambassador had some business to raise with Ramos in his capacity as acting Doyen but apart from this the following points were touched on:

(i) My telegram No: 188-D44/3 196 reports what Ramos told us about the Cambodian frontiers. We have not seen any copy of the Note delivered to the Cambodians and, since sending that telegram, I have heard through other sources that the Note refers to 'actual' frontiers, not 'present' frontiers. We will try to get the authentic wording; perhaps it is the same (French 'actual'). Ramos was rather pleased with himself over this. He maintained that the formula meant nothing at all in practice and was amused that it had not only satisfied the Cambodians but stimulated an immediate invitation to him to visit Cambodia. Unfortunately he could not now go since he ought to do some electioneering (if the Nationalists fail to win in his area, he will get the blame);

(ii) The Ambassador referred to reports that ASEAN might acquire some political and indeed military teeth in the future. He asked whether there was anything in this. Ramos said at once that, in his view, this was an economic association and should remain that way. There would be no pressure by the Philippines to convert it into a political or military association.

(iii) The rest of the discussion was about Sato's visit. Ramos contrived to put the best face possible on this visit and mentioned that the Japanese had promised to lend $ 60 million, whereas, as reported in our Despatch, the Japanese here have told us categorically that only $ 30 million was offered. Having guided the press to speculate before-hand that the Japanese were likely to produce aid amounting to $ 215 million, the Philippines are now somewhat embarrassed and are anxious to conceal the fact that only $ 30 million will be forthcoming. So Ramos' lie was not unexpected.

(G. C. Foster)

D. P. Murray Esq.,
South-East Asia Dept.,

Report of British Embassy in Bangkok on EEC Visit to Thailand, 13 September 1973, PRO, FCO 15/1727, no. 21.

CONFIDENTIAL

BRITISH EMBASSY
BANGKOK

13 September 1973

C W Squire Esq MVO
South East Asian Department
FCO

Dear Bill.
EEC VISIT TO THAILAND

1. Sir Christopher Soames, accompanied by a party of EEC officials, visited Thailand from 4 to 8 September on his way to Tokyo for the meeting of GATT. He came at the invitation of the Thai Government to brief representatives of ASEAN countries and to hear their views on the future relationship between EEC and ASEAN. The following are the main issues they discussed:

    (a) ASEAN allegations of EEC discrimination against them as compared with the Associated African States
    Sir Christopher encountered the view that EEC showed greater concern for the developing states of Africa than for those in South East Asia. He explained the Yaounde Agreement and emphasised that the mono-culture of the African states meant that they were far more dependent on EEC support than were the members of ASEAN, whose economies were more developed and more diversified. He refuted allegations that EEC was not sufficiently interested in South East Asia but pointed out that investment in the region was a matter for the individual members of EEC rather than for EEC itself. His various statements on this subject were reasonably well received but it is doubtful whether ASEAN as a whole is yet convinced of EEC's interest and good intentions.

    (b) Institutional relationship between EEC and ASEAN
    There was some demand from the ASEAN side for the establishment of a formal and institutional relationship. Since it is only very recently, and not with total enthusiasm, that ASEAN has agreed to 'institutionalise' itself in the form of a permanent secretariat (not yet set up) it seems clear that this request sprang less from a practical need than from the Asian predilection for setting up an organisational structure when they do not

know what else to do. Sir Christopher argued that there was no need for a formal relationship at the present stage. This was accepted only reluctantly and certain sections of the Thai press have interpreted it as a rebuff. I cannot speak for ASEAN as a whole but it seems likely that Thailand will wish to reopen the question before too long.

(c) Preferences on individual commodities

Sir Christopher said that though EEC was aware of and was looking into ASEAN views, or more correctly the views of certain members of ASEAN, on certain individual commodities the attitude of ASEAN as a whole towards preferential treatment seemed more general than specific. At his session to brief resident representatives of the Nine he said that he had asked ASEAN members to specify the commodities which were particularly worrying them, though he had been careful to point out that he was not offering to negotiate on these products but only to listen to the cases and arguments put to him.

2. In addition to the briefing which Sir Christopher himself gave to the resident representatives of the Nine David Hannay called on me on 6 September to fill me in on other details. These were:

(a) The role and attitude of Singapore

Rahim Ishak, the Singapore Deputy Minister for Foreign Affairs, had brought a personal letter from Lee Kuan Yew to Sir Christopher saying that Lee was sorry that for protocol reasons he himself could not attend the meeting but that Rahim Ishak knew all his thoughts. Mr Hannay said that if Rahim knew all Lee's thoughts when he left Singapore he had clearly forgotten most of them by the time he arrived here. He rambled incoherently and was very ill-at-ease. He however gave a general tour d'horizon of the area and beyond as seen by Lee Kuan Yew: the Indians were being captured by the Left and were in any case incompetent; the Ceylonese were already captured by the Left and were even more incompetent than the Indians; Tun Razak was 'not bad' but the Malaysians were being captured by the Left too. Rahim had nothing much to say about the Thais but spoke highly of the Indonesians and Sir Christopher got the impression that Lee Kuan Yew is now far more favourably disposed towards Indonesia than he used to be.

Rahim Ishak had spoken both at the official meeting and privately to Sir Christopher about the need to get France more closely re-involved in Indo-China. Lee Kuan Yew's thinking appeared to be that as things are now it is the French who will be the most difficult in getting EEC to look favourably upon South East Asia and that the way to overcome this difficulty is to encourage greater French presence and activity in Indo-China. (Mr. Hannay commented on this that if the French did become more active they would see to it that the advantage accrued to them alone and not to EEC as a whole.)

The Singapore attempt to involve South Vietnam, Cambodia and Laos in the meetings with Sir Christopher was seen as part of a scheme to coax France into greater activity. The Singapore demarche and Rahim Ishak's persistent and rather clumsy pursuit of it somewhat annoyed the Thais. I later heard General Chartichai, the Thai Deputy Minister for Foreign Affairs, remonstrating with my Singapore colleague for having raised the question of the participation of the Indo-China countries at so late a stage. He told the Singapore Ambassador that his country had put Thailand in an administratively impossible position. As it was, because of the lateness of the Singapore demarche and the time it took to get the necessary clearance from other participants, the three Indo-Chinese Ambassadors were not invited to the first meeting, which was the one which would have been of main interest to them since it discussed the broad generalities of policy, but were invited only to the second where, as observers, they had nothing to do but listen to the various ASEAN states putting forward their individual shopping lists. Sir Christopher found it necessary to make it very plain to the ASEAN countries and especially to the Thai hosts that whether the Indo-Chinese Ambassadors were invited or not was a matter for the ASEAN countries and not for him. He told me later that he had been at particular pains to make this clear since he sensed that otherwise an attempt would have been made to place the responsibility upon him and upon EEC.

(b) EEC and ECAFE

Mr Maramis, the new Secretary-General of ECAFE, who was already known to Sir Christopher, asked to see him personally. I had no occasion to speak to Sir Christopher or Mr Hannay after the meeting but I understand that Mr Maramis had sent Sir Christopher a message to the effect that he did not share his predecessor's views on EEC. (U Nyun, the former Secretary-General, affected the view that EEC was an organ of economic imperialism.) I told Mr Hannay that while Mr Maramis could hardly help being a better Secretary-General of ECAFE than U Nyun, it was still too early to decide how in fact he was going to shape. He was certainly acting very much as the new broom but he was up against very strong and entrenched bureaucratic factions and he had already offended some of these factions, including the Indians who were the most entrenched of all. I understand that Mr Maramis hopes to associate ECAFE more closely with EEC and that while leaving the initiative to him Sir Christopher is content to see him make the attempt. Maramis will find however that the U Nyun view of EEC is still strong within ECAFE and this, together with the determination of the various national factions within the ECAFE bureaucracy to maintain the privileged positions they acquired under U Nyun's regime, will make Maramis' road a very uphill one.

(c) ASEAN, EEC and Japan

At a reception during the proceedings I had occasion to speak to several of the younger members of the various ASEAN delegations and I asked them how things were going. With remarkable unanimity they told me that one of their principal concerns was to impress upon the EEC delegation the fact that the EEC countries, jointly and severally, were rapidly losing ground in this area to the Japanese (and, to a lesser degree, to the Americans). They thought that the extent of the inroads by Japan into the economies of the ASEAN countries was not sufficiently understood either in Brussels or in the various EEC countries. They hoped that the delegation would get the message.

I discussed this later both with Mr Hannay and with Sir Christopher. They told me that the question of Japan's activities had indeed come up quite strongly. Sir Christopher had taken note but had again pointed out that investment in South East Asia was a matter for the individual member countries of EEC rather than for EEC itself.

3. When I went to see Sir Christopher off he told me that while he was not dissatisfied with the visit he wondered whether it had been worth while. I said that as I had not been involved in the meetings I could not comment on their practical value but that if I might speak from my Asian experience I thought the visit had probably been a useful public-relations exercise, and I suggested that at this stage that was about all one could reasonably expect.

Arthur de la Mare

Memorandum on EEC/ASEAN Relations, 2 October 1975, PRO, FCO 30/2765.

Mr de Fonblanque

EEC/ASEAN
1. I am sorry about the delay in replying to your minute of 23 September. Even now, and despite the length of this minute, I think I can only offer some general guidance, since there are still too many unknown factors to reach precise conclusions.
2. The first question seems to me to be whether the second paragraph of Article 229 is relevant at all to the Commission's relations with Asean. This turns on whether Asean is an 'international organisation'. That term must mean something, and there must be some kind of dividing line between what is and what is not such an organisation. I doubt whether the Court would take a very strict formal view of what constitutes an international organisation. But equally, I doubt whether it would be right to interpret the term as sufficiently wide and imprecise to cover any kind of informal grouping of states. The term 'international organisation' in its normal usage does suggest some minimum organisational requirements. One thinks, for example, of something with some kind of constitutional document, with its own organs separate from the Member States, and with some kind of legal personality separate from that of the Member States. The clear suggestion from the second paragraph of Article 229 is that the relations are with the organisation and not its Member States, and therefore at least something in the way of an organisational structure separate from the Member States seems required.
3. How far, then, does Asean match up to such requirements? Mr Braithwaite's letter of 11 September suggests that Asean lacks any formal structure. If it is true – and on the face of it, it seems strongly arguable – that Asean is not a real 'international organisation', then certainly there is room to doubt whether Article 229 affords a relevant basis for Commission relations with Asean.
4. It is worth noting also that Article 229 is about the Commission's relations with other bodies, not the Community's (compare Article 229 with Articles 228, 230, 231 and 238). Further, the Commission is, under paragraph 1 of Article 229 only authorised to ensure relations with the organs of the UN, etc – not with the UN itself. While this does give rise to an a contrario argument in relation to paragraph 2, nevertheless, the general flabour of Article 229 as a whole seems to me to be to keep the Commission, when acting under that article, to a fairly low key role: more important matters (Articles 223, 230, 231, 238) are for the Community, not just the Commission.

5. I think we also probably have a considerable interest in not allowing the term 'international organisation' in Article 229 to be given too loose a meaning, not only because of the implications in terms of Article 229 itself, but also because of implications which this would have for the scope of Article 116, which is already beginning to cause one or two difficulties.
6. If Asean is not an international organisation, then there is no scope for Commission action under Article 229.
7. If, however, Asean is to be considered an international organisation, then comes the question of the appropriateness of the relations established with it by the Commission. Article 229 does not say who decides what relations are 'appropriate'. Since it is the Commission which is charged with establishing the relations, the Commission's view on whether they are appropriate would obviously count for a lot; and they presumably do believe that what they are at present engaged on, is 'appropriate'. But appropriateness probably needs to be considered from various points of view: eg appropriate from the point of view of (i) the Commission's policies and interests, (ii) the general Community interest, and (iii) the other organisations' activities and status. There is obviously a lot of scope for argument as to what is the proper interpretation and application of the term 'appropriate relations' in the context of Article 229, in relation to particular circumstances.
8. I doubt whether criticism of the Commission's actions so far would get much support if based solely on the question of 'appropriateness'. But if we can show that there is a risk of trespass on Article 113, then we would be on stronger and more hopeful ground in voicing criticism at the way in which the Commission behave.
9. Of the two particular matters which you mention, discussion of tariff points and nomenclature, seems to me probably all right, given the Commission's role in running the common external tariff, and the summary record of the meeting does suggest in a number of places that the Commission would need to reserve certain matters for consideration by the Member States, so the role of the Member States was not totally ignored. To talk about developments in other international organisations such as the UN could, perhaps, be going a bit beyond what would be proper for the Commission to discuss, but the mere title of the agenda item probably matters less than the actual subjects discussed under that head. I think that the Commission's activities under Article 229 need careful watching. It could easily become a back-door extension of Commission activities, by-passing that control which the Member States can expect to have under Article 113. In terms of Community extended relations generally, an extended Commission use of Article 229 goes well with an extended reliance on Article 116, of which there are already signs.

2 October 1975   A D Watts

'Address by Mr Lee Kwan Yew, Prime Minister of Singapore, at the Opening Session of the ASEAN Summit, Bali, on 23 February 1976', PRO, FCO 15/2173.

ADDRESS BY MR LEE KUAN NEW, PRIME MINISTER OF SINGAPORE, AT THE OPENING SESSION OF THE ASEAN SUMMIT, BALI, ON 23 FEBRUARY 1976

8½ years ago, in August 1967, in Bangkok, the Foreign Ministers of our five countries signed the ASEAN Declaration. The first objective of this Declaration was and is to accelerate economic growth. But all objectives rested on the promise of regional peace and stability.

Over the years, regular meetings of officials and Ministers have made for greater understanding of each other's aspirations and problems. The basic question is how to ensure continuing stability by stimulating economic development to resolve social and political problems. Otherwise increasing disaffection and discontent will fuel incipient insurgencies into full-scale revolutions.

It was as well the pace of co-operation was never forced. Now nations need time to realise that sovereignty does not mean self-sufficiency. The scientific and technological discoveries, which led to the age of jet travel and satellite communications, have welded us into one instant inter-dependent world. In a super-power world of missiles and rockets, and orbiting space stations, independence can be only relative.

8½ years ago in Bangkok, most people assumed that America and the West had a vital interest in, and would help ensure, a non-communist Southeast Asia. Half a million American troops then in South Vietnam were proof that this was so. Today, America and the West are set on detente with the Soviet Union. They have also started a dialogue towards normalisation and cordial relations with the People's Republic of China. America and the West are prepared to live with the new governments of Vietnam, Cambodia and Laos, and for that matter with the new Marxist government of Angola. As never before, the future of non-communist Southeast Asia rests in the hands of the leaders and peoples of non-communist Southeast Asia.

ASEAN is at a crossroad. It has developed into a potentially significant force in the region. Further impetus to realise this potential, to decide the direction and speed ASEAN is to go, can come only from Heads of Government. The simple issue before us is whether we have the will and the vision to reconcile our short-term interests with long-term objectives.

Extensive, at times intense, discussions have preceded this meeting. Agreements have not come about easily. Though we are all agreed on ultimate objectives, it has been difficult to get agreements on the next few steps. Many domestic economic interests, and several different ideas of how to get constructive relations with new governments in the region, have temporarily clouded fundamental issues.

There are two views one can take of these arguments and disagreements. The first is that they reveal a lack of unity of purpose. This is not true. There is unity of purpose in greater regional co-operation. We all seek stability and accelerated economic growth. An ASEAN framework can the better enable us to resolve our economic, social and political problems without outside interference.

The second view is that there were differences in methods and attitudes. This is partly true. We have inherited differs systems. We have developed different administrative machines. We have evolved different styles of political leadership. Healthy argument on ways and means to our agreed goals, is a sign of vigorous life in the ASEAN organisation.

What is crucial is that out of arguments stemming from different perceptions of our common problems, must emerge agreements on the fundamentals of a solution.

There have been arguments on whether ASEAN countries can now take one big step forward towards greater economic and political co-operation. Even the European nations of the EEC, nearly 19 years after they signed the Treaty of Rome in 1957, continue to have strong disagreements from time to time. They could not agree on energy-sharing during the oil crisis of 1973. On monetary union, agreed to in principle, at least two of its major members, Britain and Italy, have to abandon it in practice.

Perhaps the EEC is too advanced to be our model. But, in one respect, we have a situation vaguely analogous to theirs. What gave birth to the EEC was the pressure of a competing and different political and economic system, Comecon, the Soviet Union and the countries of Eastern Europe. Since April last year, the ASEAN countries have to face up to competition from the Marxist-Socialist systems of Vietnam, Laos and Cambodia. We must ensure that differences in political and economic systems between these countries and ASEAN are confined to peaceful competition.

In competition, one party does not seek the destruction of one's competitors. Indeed, competition means the emulation of the strong points of a competitor.

The countries of ASEAN have not been ravaged by war. We have, for the present, the greater capacity to forge ahead. Our economies are in various stages of dynamic growth. If we are able to combine our individual forte's, whether it is national resilence in Indonesia, Rukunegara of Malaysia, the New Society of the Philippines, the traditions of monarchy and Buddhism of Thailand, or Singapore's matter-of-fact habit of facing up to the realition of life, together, we can do what we individually cannot do as well.

We can, as ASEAN, talk with the industrial nations of America, Japan and Western Europe on a more equal basis. With combined strength, we can get better results in long-term co-operation in trade and transfers of technology. We can work more closely and effectively with the countries of Australasia and the Pacific than if we were to go our own separate ways.

In the nature of things, with many Ministers and even more officials, it is difficult to keep all our deliberations secret. It is the business of diplomats, and even more so of newsmen, to ferret out the areas of agreement and of differences. At the end of this meeting, the major capitals of the world will have a shrewd idea of whether ASEAN will crystallise, take definite form, and move ahead in economic, political and diplomatic co-operation.

Let us seize our opportunities for co-operation, for continued security and stability as a more cohesive group, pursuing more coherent policies. Then we can establish more equable and friendly relationships with all the great powers, and their friends and allies in and around the region. Let us give our peoples cause to believe in our policies, that they have been forged to consolidate regional stability, co-operation and progress, and that these policies will eventually spread prosperity over the countries of ASEAN, and also bring benefits to all countries willing to trade and be friends with us.

Mr Chairman, it was at your initiative that we are gathered here at the first Meeting of Heads of Government of ASEAN countries. This Meeting will be memorable for consolidating ASEAN as a regional force in the international community. There has been speculation whether the five governments would accord priority to common issues and interests, those which should bring them closer together, or whether we would pursue our individual pet subjects.

Over the past few months, differences of views have been gradually narrowed. Our energies have been concentrated on those subjects which are of importance to each and every one of us. However, on the eve of the Meeting, before the Heads of Government arrived, full accord had not been reached. I had believed that the salubrious air in Bali would have a soothing effect on harassed officials and ruffled Ministers. But, when I arrived yesterday, I discovered it was you who infused your calm and wise counsel into the Meetings of our Ministers. Thus were the differences resolved before the Heads of Government arrived. This gives me good reason to believe that our deliberations in Bali will be positive and productive.

Dated: February 23, 1976

'Treaty of Amity and Cooperation in Southeast Asia', Denpasar, Bali, 24 February 1976, PRO, FCO 15/2173, no. 30.

KEDUTAAN BESAR REPUBLIK INDONESIA
LONDON

TREATY OF AMITY AND COOPERATION IN SOUTHEAST ASIA

24th FEBRUARY 1976

Preamble

The high contracting parties:

Conscious of the existing ties of history, geography and culture, which have bound their peoples together:

Anxious to promote regional peace and stability through abiding respect for justice and the rule of law and enhancing regional resilience in their relations:

Desiring to enhance peace, friendship and mutual cooperation on matters affecting Southeast Asia consistent with the spirit and principles of the Charter of the United Nations, the ten principles adopted by the Asian-African Conference in Bandung on 25 April 1955, the Declaration of the Association of South East Asian Nations signed in Bangkok on 8 August 1967, and the Declaration signed in Kualalumpur on 27 November 1971:

Convinced that the settlement of differences or disputes between their countries should be regulated by national, effective and sufficiently flexible procedures, avoiding negative attitudes which might endanger or hinder cooperation:

Believing in the need for cooperation with all peace-loving nations, both within and outside Southeast Asia, in the furtherance of world peace, stability and harmony:

Solemnly agree to enter into a Treaty of Amity and Cooperation as follows:

Chapter I: Purpose and Principles

Article 1

The purpose of this Treaty is to promote perpetual peace, everlasting amity and cooperation among their peoples which would contribute to their strength, solidarity and closer relationship.

Article 2

In their relations with one another, the high contracting parties shall be guided by the following fundamental principles:

a) Mutual respect for the independence sovereignty, equality, territorial, integrity and national identity of all nations.
b) The right of every state to lead its national existence free from external interference, subversion or coercion.
c) Non-interference in the internal affairs of one another.
d) Settlement of differences or disputes by peaceful means.
e) Renunciation of the threat or use of force.
f) Effective cooperation among themselves.

Chapter II: Amity

Article 3

In pursuance of the purpose of this Treaty the high contracting parties shall endeavour to develop and strengthen the traditional, cultural and historical ties of friendship, good neighborliness and cooperation which bind them together and shall fulfill in good faith the obligations assumed under this Treaty.

In order to promote closer understanding among them, the high contracting parties shall encourage and facilitate contact and intercourse among their peoples.

Chapter III: Cooperation

Article 4

The high contracting parties shall promote active cooperation in the economic, social, cultural, technical, scientific and administrative fields as well as in matters of common ideas and aspirations of international peace and stability in the region and all other matters of common interest.

Article 5

Pursuant to Article 4 the high contracting parties shall exert their maximum efforts multilaterally as well as bilaterally on the basis of equality, non-discrimination and mutual benefit.

Article 6

The high contracting parties shall collaborate for the acceleration of the economic growth in the region in order to strengthen the foundation for a prosperous and peaceful community of nations in Southeast Asia.

To this end, they shall promote the greater utilization of their agriculture and industries, the expansion of their trade and the improvement of their economic infra-structure for the mutual benefit of their peoples.

In this regard, they shall continue to explore all avenues for close and beneficial cooperation with other states as well as international and regional organizations outside the region.

Article 7

The high contracting parties, in order to achieve social justice and to raise the standards of living of the peoples of the region, shall intensify economic cooperation.

For this purpose, they shall adopt appropriate regional strategies for economic development and mutual assistance.

Article 8

The high contracting parties shall strive to achieve the closest cooperation on the widest scale and shall seek to provide assistance to one another in the form of training and research facilities in the social, cultural, technical, scientific and administrative fields.

Article 9

The high contracting parties shall endeavour to foster cooperation in the furtherance of the cause of peace, harmony and stability in the region.

To this end, the high contracting parties shall maintain regular contacts and consultations with one another on international and regional matters with a view to coordinating their views, actions and policies.

Article 10

Each high contracting parties shall not in any manner or form participate in any activity which shall constitute a threat to the political and economic stability, sovereignty, or territorial integrity of another high contracting party.

Article 11

The high contracting parties shall endeavour to strengthen their respective national resilience in their political, economic, socio-cultural as well as security fields in conformity with their respective ideas and aspirations, free from external interference as well as internal subversive activities in order to preserve their respective national identities.

Article 12

The high contracting parties in their efforts to achieve regional prosperity and security, shall endeavour to cooperate in all fields for the promotion of regional resilience, mutual respect, cooperation and solidarity which will constitute the foundation for a strong and viable community of nations in Southeast Asia.

Chapter IV : Pacific settlement of disputes

Article 13

The high contracting parties shall have the determination and good faith to prevent disputes from arising.

In case disputes on matters directly affecting them should arise, especially disputes likely to disturb regional peace and harmony, they shall refrain from the threat or use of force and shall at all times settle such disputes among themselves through friendly negotiations.

Article 14

To settle disputes through regional processes, the high contracting parties shall constitute, as a continuing body, a high council comprising a representative at ministerial level from each of the high contracting parties to take cognizance of the existence of disputes or situations likely to disturb regional peace and harmony.

Article 15

In the event no solution is reached through direct negotiations, the high council shall take cognizance of the dispute or the situation and shall recommend to the parties in dispute appropriate means of settlement such as good offices, mediation, inquiry or conciliation.

The high council may however offer its good offices, or upon agreement of the parties in disputes, constitute itself into a committee of mediation, inquiry or conciliation.

When deemed necessary, the high council shall recommend appropriate measures for the prevention of a deterioration of the dispute or the situation.

Article 16

The foregoing provisions of this Chapter shall not apply to a dispute unless all the parties to the dispute agree to their application to that dispute.

However, this shall not preclude the other high contracting parties not party to the dispute from offering all possible assistance to settle the said dispute.

Parties to the dispute should be well disposed towards such offers of assistance.

Article 17

Nothing in this Treaty shall preclude recourse to the modes of peaceful settlement contained in Article 33 (1) of the Charter of the United Nations.

The high contracting parties which are parties to a dispute should be encourages to take initiatives to solve it by friendly negotiations before resorting to the other procedures provided for in the Charter of the United Nations.

Chapter V : General provisions

Article 18

This Treaty shall be signed by the Republic of Indonesia, Malaysia, the Republic of the Philippines, the Republic of Singapore and the Kingdom of Thailand.

It shall be ratified in accordance with the constitutional procedures of each signatory states.

It shall be open for accession by other states in Southeast Asia.

Article 19

This Treaty shall enter into force on the date of the deposit of the fifth instrument of ratification with the governments of the signatory states which are designed depositories of this Treaty and of the instruments of ratification or accession.

Article 20

This Treaty is drawn up in the official languages of the high contracting parties, all of which are equally authoritative.

There shall be an agreed common translation of the texts in the English language. Any divergent interpretation of the common text shall be settled by negotiation.

In faith thereof the high contracting parties have signed this Treaty and have hereto affixed their seals.

For the Republic of Indonesia:

_____

SOEHARTO President

For Malaysia:

_____

DATUK HUSEIN ONN
Prime Minister

For the Republic of the Philippines:

_____

FERDINAND E. MARCOS

For the Republic of Singapore:

_____

LEE KUAN YEW
Prime Minister

For the Kingdom of Thailand:

_____

KUKRIT PRAMOJ
Prime Minister

Confidential Memorandum, 'ASEAN Summit: A Thai View', 2 March 1976, PRO, FCO 15/2173, no. 28.

Mr Simons

ASEAN SUMMIT: A THAI VIEW

1. Mr Vitthya Vejjajiva, Counsellor in the Thai Embassy, called on me today to introduce himself. In the course of a long conversation, he made the following points which may be of interest:
ASEAN. He had not yet seen any final documents resulting from the Summit, except for the communique. What he had seen suggested that it had been a generally satisfactory meeting, and he thought that his Government took this view. There had been some disagreement among the ASEAN countries as to what rôle ASEAN should play, and what form co-operation between the member countries should take. Indonesia in particular, before the Summit Meeting, had for some time wanted ASEAN to concern itself more with matters of security, and less with measures of economic co-operation, than the other members had thought desirable. The Indonesians now seemed to have been politely overruled by the majority. There was no question of ASEAN developing security content, though its members would continue to exchange intelligence and tactical information among themselves. Also, although the heads of Government at the Summit had not been able to agree on measures for economic co-operation, they had demonstrated the importance they attached to such measures by directing their economic Ministers to meet swiftly and see what progress they could make on certain specific questions.

2. It was therefore clear that there was now a general political will towards some economic co-operation. It was also significant that the Treaty of Amity and Co-operation for the first time specifically committed ASEAN members to political co-operation on matters of regional importance. (Mr Vejjajiva was here assuming that this passage, which had featured in the draft of the Treaty, had been carried through into the final agreed version, which he had not yet seen.)
Relations with Vietnam. Mr Vejjajiva expressed the hope that ASEAN would eventually be expanded to include the countries of Indo-China. It was essential that ASEAN should not give the impression of confronting Indo-China. Thailand had a special role to play here, since historically she had direct links with both Laos and Cambodia, and was therefore more aware of Indo-Chinese factors and susceptibilities than were the other members of ASEAN. Hanoi's recent denunciation of ASEAN as a tool

of American imperialism was disappointing, but Mr Vejjajiva said that he did not necessarily attach long term importance to this. He thought that the North Vietnamese were in fact attacking Thailand under the guise of a general attack on ASEAN. Also, their denunciation had not been echoed by either Moscow or Peking. Vietnam might try to bully Thailand, but was most unlikely to invade. Thailand had had plenty of experience in preserving her own identity and refusing to be cowed by larger countries. In past history, Thailand and Cambodia had frequently been partners in standing up to Vietnamese bullying, and he thought that this pattern might repeat itself. The Laos had never been able to stand up to the Vietnamese, and would not be able to now. But the Thais and Cambodians had the necessary resolution and national self-confidence to do so, especially if given moral support by the Chinese and Americans.

A K Goldsmith
South East Asian
Department

2 March 1976
cc: Mr L Jones
Research Dept

Cooperation Agreement between the EEC and ASEAN, Kuala Lumpur, 7 March 1980, PRO, FO 970/459.

CO-OPERATION AGREEMENT BETWEEN THE EUROPEAN ECONOMIC COMMUNITY AND INDONESIA, MALAYSIA, PHILIPPINES, SINGAPORE AND THAILAND – MEMBER COUNTRIES OF THE ASSOCIATION OF SOUTH-EAST ASIAN NATIONS

THE COUNCIL OF THE EUROPEAN COMMUNITIES,

of the one part, and

THE GOVERNMENTS OF INDONESIA, MALAYSIA, PHILIPPINES, SINGAPORE AND THAILAND, MEMBER COUNTRIES OF THE ASSOCIATION OF SOUTH-EAST ASIAN NATIONS, hereinafter referred to as ASEAN,

of the other part,

Having regard to the friendly relations and traditional links between the member countries of ASEAN and the Member States of the Community;

Affirming their common commitment to support mutually the efforts of ASEAN and the Community to create and to strengthen regional organisations committed to economic growth, social progress and cultural development and aiming to provide an element of balance in international relations;

Inspired by their common will to consolidate, deepen and diversify their commercial and economic relations to the full extent of their growing capacity to meet each other's requirements on the basis of comparative advantage and mutual benefit;

Affirming their willingness to contribute to the expansion of international trade in order to achieve greater economic growth and social progress;

Conscious that such co-operation will be between equal partners but will take into account the level of development of the member countries of ASEAN and the emergence of ASEAN as a viable and cohesive grouping, which has contributed to the stability and peace in South-East Asia;

Persuaded that such co-operation should be realised in an evolutionary and pragmatic fashion as their policies develop;

Affirming their common will to contribute to a new phase of international economic co-operation and to facilitate the development of their respective human and material resources on the basis of freedom, equality and justice;

Have decided to conclude a Co-operation Agreement and to this end have designated as their plenipotentiaries:

THE COUNCIL OF THE EUROPEAN COMMUNITIES:

Attilio RUFFINI,
President in office of the Council of the European Communities,
Minister of Foreign Affairs of the Italian Republic;

Wilhelm HAFERKAMP,
Vice-President of the Commission of the European Communities;

THE GOVERNMENT OF THE REPUBLIC OF INDONESIA:

Prof. Dr. MOCHTAR KUSUMAATMADJA,
Minister of Foreign Affairs;

THE GOVERNMENT OF MALAYSIA:

TENGKU AHMAD RITHAUDEEN,
Minister of Foreign Affairs;

THE GOVERNMENT OF THE REPUBLIC OF THE PHILIPPINES:

CARLOS P. ROMULO, Minister for Foreign Affairs;

THE GOVERNMENT OF THE REPUBLIC OF SINGAPORE:

S. RAJARATNAM,
Minister for Foreign Affairs;

THE GOVERNMENT OF THE KINGDOM OF THAILAND:

AIR CHIEF MARSHAL Siddhi Savetsila,
Minister for Foreign Affairs;

WHO, Having exchanged their full powers, found in good and due form,

HAVE AGREED AS FOLLOWS:

ARTICLE 1
Most-Favoured-Nation Treatment

The Parties shall, in their commercial relations, accord each other most-favoured-nation treatment in accordance with the provisions of the General Agreement on Tariffs and Trade, without prejudice, however, to the provisions of the Protocol annexed to this Agreement.

ARTICLE 2
Commercial Co-operation

1. The Parties undertake to promote the development and diversification of their reciprocal commercial exchanges to the highest possible level taking into account their respective economic situations.
2. The Parties agree to study ways and means of overcoming trade barriers, and in particular existing non-tariff and quasi-tariff barriers, taking into account the work of international organisations.
3. The Parties shall in accordance with their legislation and in the conduct of their policies:
    (a) co-operate at the international level and between themselves in the solution of commercial problems of common interest including trade related to commodities;
    (b) use their best endeavours to grant each other the widest facilities for commercial transactions;
    (c) take fully into account their respective interests and needs for improved access for manufactured, semi-manufactured and primary products as well as the further processing of resources;
    (d) bring together economic operators in the two regions with the aim of creating new trade patterns;
    (e) study and recommend trade promotion measures likely to encourage the expansion of imports and exports;
    (f) seek insofar as possible the other Parties' views where measures are being considered which could have an adverse effect on trade between the two regions.

ARTICLE 3
Economic Co-operation

1. The Parties, in the light of the complementarity of their interests and of their long-term economic capabilities, shall bring about economic co-operation in all fields deemed suitable by the Parties.
Among the objectives of such co-operation shall be:

- the encouragement of closer economic links through mutually beneficial investment;
- the encouragement of technological and scientific progress;
- the opening up of new sources of supply and new markets;
- the creation of new employment opportunities.

2. As means to such ends, the Parties shall, as appropriate, encourage and facilitate inter alia:
    - a continuous exchange of information relevant to economic co-operation as well as the development of contacts and promotion activities between firms and organisations in both regions;
    - the fostering, between respective firms, of industrial and technological co-operation, including mining;
    - co-operation in the fields of science and technology, energy, environment, transport and communications, agriculture, fisheries and forestry.

    In addition the Parties undertake to improve the existing favourable investment climate inter alia through encouraging the extension, by and to all Member States of the Community and by and to all member countries of ASEAN, of investment promotion and protection arrangements which endeavour to apply the principle of non-discrimination, aim to ensure fair and equitable treatment and reflect the principle of reciprocity.

3. Without prejudice to the relevant provisions of the Treaties establishing the Communities, this Agreement and any action taken thereunder shall in no way affect the powers of any of the Member States of the Communities to undertake bilateral activities with any of the member countries of ASEAN in the field of economic co-operation and conclude, where appropriate, new economic co-operation agreements with these countries.

ARTICLE 4
Development Co-operation

1. The Community recognises that ASEAN is a developing region and will expand its co-operation with ASEAN in order to contribute to ASEAN's efforts in enhancing its self-reliance and economic resilience and social wellbeing of its peoples through projects to accelerate the development of the ASEAN countries and of the region as a whole.
2. The Community will take all possible measures to intensify its support, within the framework of its programmes in favour of non-associated developing countries, for ASEAN development and regional co-operation.
3. The Community will co-operate with ASEAN to realise concrete projects and programmes, inter alia, food production and supplies, development of the

rural sector, education and training facilities and others of a wider character to promote ASEAN regional economic development and co-operation.
4. The Community will seek a co-ordination of the development co-operation activities of the Community and its Member States in the ASEAN region especially in relation to ASEAN regional projects.
5. The Parties shall encourage and facilitate the promotion of co-operation between sources of finance in the two regions.

ARTICLE 5
Joint Co-operation Committee

1. A Joint Co-operation Committee shall be set up to promote and keep under review the various co-operation activities envisaged between the Parties in the framework of the Agreement. Consultations shall be held in the Committee at an appropriate level in order to facilitate the implementation and to further the general aims of this Agreement. The Committee will normally meet at least once a year. Special meetings of the Committee shall be held at the request of either Party.
2. The Joint Co-operation Committee shall adopt its own Rules of Procedure and programme of work.

ARTICLE 6
Other Agreements

Subject to the provisions concerning economic co-operation in Article 3(3), the provisions of this Agreement shall be substituted for provisions of Agreements concluded between Member States of the Communities and Indonesia, Malaysia, Philippines, Singapore and Thailand to the extent to which the latter provisions are either incompatible with or identical to the former.

ARTICLE 7
Territorial Application

This Agreement shall apply, on the one hand, to the territories in which the Treaty establishing the European Economic Community is applied and under the conditions laid down in that Treaty and, on the other hand, to the territories of Indonesia, Malaysia, Philippines, Singapore and Thailand.

ARTICLE 8
Duration

1. This Agreement shall enter into force on the first day of the month following the date on which the Parties have notified each other of the completion of the procedures necessary for this purpose, and shall remain in force for an initial period of five years and thereafter for periods of two years subject to the right of either Party to terminate it by written notice given six months before the date of expiry of any period.
2. This Agreement may be amended by mutual consent of the Parties in order to take into account new situations.

ARTICLE 9
Authentic Languages

This Agreement is drawn up in seven originals in the Danish, Dutch, English, French, German and Italian languages each of these texts being equally authentic.

Background Brief, 'ASEAN's Changing Priorities', June 1992 PRO, FO 973/692.

Background Brief
Foreign & Commonwealth Office, London

June 1992

ASEAN'S CHANGING PRIORITIES

The two main themes emerging from the Fourth Summit Meeting of the Association of South-East Asian Nations (ASEAN), held in Singapore on 27–28 January 1992, were increased economic cooperation and the need to address security issues. The latter will in future be discussed at the Post-Ministerial Conferences (PMCs) which follow Summit meetings. The participants at the Summit also said that ASEAN countries would continue actively to protect the environment, and would strengthen their efforts to overcome drug abuse and trafficking.

When the leaders of Thailand, Malaysia, Singapore, the Philippines and Indonesia formed ASEAN in 1967 (Brunei joined on independence in 1984), their main preoccupation was to improve regional relations following confrontation between Indonesia and Malaysia and Singapore's ejection from Malaysia. There was also unease about the strategic balance of the area following steady British withdrawal from east of Suez and the possibility of American withdrawal from Vietnam, while Communist expansion remained a serious threat. Now, however, the Cold War is over. The Russians will have left their bases at Cam Ranh in Vietnam and the US theirs at Subic Bay in the Philippines by the end of this year, and substantial progress has been made towards ending the conflict in Cambodia: Vietnamese combat troops withdrew in 1989, and the Paris Peace Agreement was signed in October 1991. ASEAN has never been a military alliance, but its members see economic development as depending closely on security and stability.

Many experts believe that the Cambodia issue and fear of a hostile and possibly expansionist Vietnam held ASEAN together. Now, ASEAN needs a new impetus if it is not to decline. Enhanced economic cooperation is the obvious channel to pursue; but observers are aware that ASEAN has been trying to increase economic cooperation for years, and has so far made little progress.

Five members (the Philippines is the exception)[1] have for the past decade been among the world's fastest growing economies. According to UN data, aver-

---

1 The poor state of the Philippine economy is partly due to recent natural disasters and partly to other factors such as dependence on imported energy, heavy indebtedness, economic mismanagement in the past, and a high population growth rate.

age growth of gross domestic product in ASEAN countries, in 1991, was about 6.4 per cent and is projected to rise to 6.9 per cent this year.

This paper has been prepared for general briefing purposes. It is not and should not be construed or quoted as an expression of Government policy.

At the latest Summit, the Heads of Government demonstrated how changing circumstances had bred new challenges. Indeed, they expressed the hope that Vietnam would become a member of the Association within five years – a move which would have been unthinkable a few years ago. To keep their domestic support, ASEAN governments know they must maintain economic growth, which means ensuring access to open markets and an influx of foreign investment. Another problem to be addressed is how to deal with security issues in the light of the declining US presence.

Economic cooperation

The new economic agreement, signed at the January 1992 Summit, covers cooperation in trade, industry, finance and banking, transport and communications. The most significant aspect of the agreement, however, is its commitment to the establishment of an ASEAN Free Trade Area (AFTA) within 15 years from 1 January 1993. This move was originally proposed in 1991 by Anand Panyyarachun, the Thai Prime Minister. Press reports have speculated that it might stall if there is continuing political dislocation in Thailand.

All six Heads of Government agreed on the need for greater economic integration in the face of growing economic regionalism and the prospect of more intense competition for foreign investment from, for instance, the projected Single European Market and North American Free Trade Area (NAFTA). In 1991, ASEAN had a total population of more than 335 million and a gross national product (GNP) of $310,000 million. By contrast, the Single European Market, when it is established at the end of this year, will have more than 350 million consumers and a combined GNP of over $4,370,000 million. The NAFTA, being negotiated between the US, Canada and Mexico, will have a consumer base of 360 million and a combined GNP of about $6,000,000 million.

Indonesia's suggestion of a Common Effective Preferential Tariff (CEPT) was adopted as the mode of transition towards AFTA. This involves the accelerated reduction of tariffs on 15 groups of product (including manufactured goods, processed agricultural items and capital goods) within the 15 years. By then, tariffs on these products are expected to range between nil and a maximum of 5 per cent. The agreement allows members an exclusion list of products they feel unable to expose to increased competition within that timetable. A ministerial-level council will be set up to supervise, co-ordinate and review implementation of the AFTA.

The agreement contrasts with the past unwillingness of the ASEAN countries to engage in close economic cooperation, because they compete for the same overseas markets and foreign investments. However, the free trade area omits the services sector and basic farm products which provide a quarter of the group's exports. More than 80 per cent of ASEAN's exports went to non-ASEAN countries in 1990, compared with the 40 per cent of European Community (EC) exports that went outside that area.

Wider economic links in Asia

At the end of 1990, the Prime Minister of Malaysia, Dr Mahathir Mohammad, proposed the setting up of an East Asia economic grouping, later known as a Caucus (EAEC), to include the ASEAN countries, Burma, China, Hong Kong, the Indochinese countries, Japan, South Korea and Taiwan. Malaysia was seeking endorsement of the Caucus at the ASEAN Summit, but Indonesia wanted it to exist within the larger Asia Pacific Economic Cooperation (APEC)[1] framework. Indonesia feared that the EAEC might lead to a deterioration in relations with the US, ASEAN's main export market – the US had already voiced opposition to the concept of the EAEC, on the grounds that it did not want the world divided into trading blocs.

It was decided that the EAEC would exist alongside the APEC. According to the Singapore Declaration issued at the end of the ASEAN Summit, the EAEC is to be 'a loose consultative forum' for countries in East Asia 'to speak out with one voice against trade restrictions and protectionism'. A Joint Consultative Meeting (JCM) – comprising senior economic and other officials, and the Director-General of ASEAN – was tasked to complete the elaboration of the EAEC and to recommend how it might be brought into operation.

Regional security

Some ASEAN countries have supported the idea of inviting the five Permanent Members of the UN Security Council to accede to ASEAN's 1976 Treaty of Amity and Cooperation (TAC), which binds signatories to resolving disputes peacefully. But Indonesia argued that non-South-East Asian accession could also bring about external interference in the region, and the idea was dropped. However, the Singapore Declaration stated that ASEAN should intensify external dialogues in political and security matters by using the Association's PMCs, which include what ASEAN calls its 'dialogue partners' – the EC, Japan, South Korea, the US, Canada, Australia and New Zealand. The latest Summit approved two new dialogue partners – China and India.

For ASEAN, security has always been a difficult issue. Differences between members over bilateral issues have led the Association away from the idea of a regional security grouping. The Singapore Declaration repeated that ASEAN would work to implement the idea of a Zone of Peace, Freedom and Neutrality

1 APEC comprises: ASEAN members, Australia, Canada, China, Hong Kong, Japan, New Zealand, South Korea, Taiwan and US.

(ZOPFAN) which was proposed as long ago as 1971, and seek to keep nuclear weapons out of the region. However, the imminent withdrawal of US forces from the Philippines appears to be causing ASEAN to reconsider security questions. Singapore, which already allows US warships and aircraft regular access to its ports and airfields, agreed in principle, in January 1992, to a US request to relocate a naval logistics command headquarters from the Philippines to Singapore. It has since been reported that several other ASEAN members are considering allowing the US access to military facilities, to offset the loss of bases in the Philippines.

Indochina

With the withdrawal of Vietnamese combat troops from Cambodia in 1989, and the signing of the Paris Peace Agreement on Cambodia in October 1991, ASEAN now looks set to extend membership to its neighbours in Indochina. At the Singapore Summit, ASEAN members welcomed plans for Vietnam and Laos to become signatories to the TAC – a possible first step towards membership of ASEAN. It is thought that the two States may initial the TAC in Manila in July, when ASEAN Foreign Ministers hold their annual meeting. Late last year, Le Mai, Vietnam's deputy Foreign Minister, said his country now aimed 'to make friends with all nations and to create the peaceful atmosphere for us to concentrate all our efforts on economic development'. Cambodia's accession to the TAC may follow the expected formation of a new Government in Phnom Penh in 1993.

The environment

The Fifth ASEAN Ministerial Meeting on the Environment (AMME) was held on 17–18 February 1992 in Singapore. The meeting adopted the Singapore Resolution on Environment and Development, and an important annex outlining a Common Stand on the UN Conference on the Environment and Development (UNCED), held in Brazil in June. ASEAN's Governments are alarmed by the level of pollution that rapid economic growth has generated in their area, and in the Resolution they agreed to intensify environmental management and protection 'in their common pursuit of sustainable development'. They also affirmed their commitment to participate in international efforts to protect the environment.

ASEAN members' Common Stand on UNCED called for:
- the right to develop and exploit their forests on a sustainable basis, and for developed countries to cease their unilateral bans on the import of tropical timber;
- urgent measures to counter climatic change, aimed at stemming the emission of greenhouse gases by developed countries;
- the control of movements of hazardous waste and of air and water pollution between countries;
- the transfer of funds and technology from the developed countries to encourage environmentally-sound development. (The idea of a US-Asian Environmental Partnership (USAEP) was suggested by President Bush on his visit to Singapore in January. Under this, the US would provide training programmes, equipment and investment to areas where the environment was threatened.)

THE NORTH AMERICAN FREE TRADE AREA

The North American Free Trade Agreement (NAFTA) led to the electoral repudiation of one Canadian Prime Minister, contributed to the electoral defeat of an American President, threatened the governing coalition of a second American President, destroyed the reputation of a Mexican President and left his successor with the seeds of a dire economic crisis. These political consequences were commensurate with the importance of NAFTA in the economic history of the three countries involved. NAFTA represented a profound shift in the international trade strategies of the United States, Canada and Mexico. For all three, it was a watershed agreement.

Both Mexico and Canada had historically been concerned about the domination of their economies by their larger neighbour and had pursued economic policies to lessen their dependence. Since the 1930s, Mexico had pursued economic policies favouring domestic producers and limiting foreign ownership of Mexican industries. The 1938 nationalization of the oil industry – largely owned by American, British and Dutch multinationals – was, until NAFTA, the defining event of Mexican foreign economic policy. The economic slowdown and failure of existing statist policies led Mexican President Carlos Salinas to break with fifty years of tradition and seek a trade pact with the United States. Salinas sought to use NAFTA as part of a wider package of neo-liberal policy reforms to increase the exposure of the Mexican economy to market forces with the objective of creating jobs and attracting foreign direct investment.

In the years before NAFTA, rather than pursuing import-substitution strategies, Canada followed a strategy of both domestic subsidy and international engagement through involvement in multilateral international institutions, thus diluting the direct influence of the United States over its economy. Faced with stubbornly high unemployment, the Progressive Conservative Party of Prime Minister Brian Mulroney, like its conservative counterparts in the United States and United Kingdom, became converted to neo-liberalism and the efficacy of the market. Concerns that the consequences of rising American protectionism and anxieties about the stalled General Agreement on Tariffs and Trade (GATT) negotiations pushed Canadian policymakers to cut a separate, bilateral deal with the United States. A trade agreement with the United States promised greater access to capital to develop Canada's natural resources and the potential of greater export sales for outwardly-oriented Canadian companies to Canada's largest customer.

For its part, the United States' historical attachment to multilateral trading agreements was strained by the lack of progress on negotiations over the Uruguay Round. Desiring a boost to foreign trade, the Americans sought to put bilateral free trade agreements in place while they continued to push for a multilateral agreement. This dovetailed nicely with the Reagan administration's (and later the Bush administration's) view of opening foreign markets to American products and investment as a means of creating exports, jobs and overseas earnings. Many also saw a trade agreement with Mexico as providing part of a solution to the problem of illegal Mexican migration to the United States. To the extent that a trade agreement would raise incomes in Mexico and provide jobs for Mexicans, the more attractive staying in Mexico would become, thus reducing the flow of illegal workers into the United States.[1]

With the American economy struggling through a recession, economics and trade policy were a prominent issue during the autumn 1992 presidential election campaign. President George H. W. Bush, whose administration had negotiated NAFTA, was strongly in support of NAFTA and ideologically committed to a free trade agenda. For independent presidential candidate Ross Perot, who received nearly 20 per cent of the vote in the election, NAFTA epitomized the sort of 'one-way' international trade agreement that he criticized for the outsourcing of American jobs and the decline of the United States' manufacturing base. In the presidential debates, Perot made a standard critique of free trade for a developed economy, arguing that relatively high-wage American workers would be unable to compete with low-cost Mexican producers. If NAFTA was approved, Perot claimed, American workers would hear 'a giant sucking sound' as their jobs drained out of the United States across the Rio Grande into Mexico. Governor Bill Clinton, the winner of the 1992 election, took a middle position. He had supported granting President Bush negotiating authority for the agreement, but due to concerns about potential labour and environmental aspects of the agreements reserved judgement on the outcome of the negotiations. In this position, Clinton's reluctance to be forced into taking a position – especially one on someone else's terms – was apparent, and the debate transcripts included here demonstrate the nuances to his position on NAFTA.[2]

After his election, Clinton renegotiated several environmental and labour side agreements to make NAFTA more palatable to the unions and environmental groups who were important constituencies within the Democratic Party. Even so, many unions vehemently opposed the agreement. As the trade agreement was negotiated under so-called 'fast-track' authority, both houses of Congress needed to approve the unamended agreement. Problematically for Clinton, most Democratic Congressional Representatives baulked at ratifying the agreement. Although the Republican Party was largely united in support of NAFTA, aggressive lobbying by labour unions and Ross Perot's political organization meant that a substantial majority of Democrats opposed the agreement. As the crucial Congressional vote approached in November 1993, NAFTA's approval remained in doubt even with the side agreements and Clinton's promise of worker retraining funds for displaced workers and other pro-labour programmes.[3]

With the Congressional vote hanging in the balance, the climax of the American ratification process came in a television debate between Vice President Al Gore and Perot. Perot, whose folksy debating style in the 1992 campaign had earned him plaudits, came to the debate as the leader of the opposition to foreign trade agreements and was widely expected to prevail over the wooden Vice President. However, Gore's earnestness and unexpected showmanship – particularly his presenting Perot with a picture of Reed Smoot and Willis Hawley, authors of the 1930 Tariff Act – matched Perot's, while his grasp of the details of NAFTA was far superior. In the ninety-minute debate, Gore was widely credited with successfully explaining a complicated agreement to a mass audience, ably rebutting Perot's criticisms and – most crucially – bolstering flagging support for the agreement among Democrats on Capitol Hill.[4] Perot, in contrast, was seen as a poorly-informed, ill-tempered, argumentative bully.

The support of the Republican Party, Clinton's side agreements, Gore's debate performance and a sprinkling of presidentially-sanctioned Congressional pork-barrel politics led the United States House of Representatives to approve NAFTA by a narrow margin in November 1993, and the United States Senate followed suit by a large margin shortly thereafter. The Mexican Senate, dominated by President Salinas's Party of Institutional Revolution, ratified the agreement nearly unanimously. However, the trials and tribulations of the approval process were not complete. In large measure due to having forced the unpopular NAFTA agreement though the House of Commons, the Progressive Conservatives were overwhelmingly defeated in the 1993 Canadian general election. The new Liberal government of Jean Chretien baulked at implementing the agreement.[5] Only once the United States had guaranteed that several concessions granted to Mexico would also be granted to Canada did Chretien allow the agreement to come into force.

Subsequent economic studies have argued that, over the next decade, NAFTA had an insignificant impact on the net number of new jobs in the United States and a substantial number over the long term in Mexico – where large job losses resulting from the 1995 peso crisis had initially occurred.[6] The political consequences were more rapid. President Bush lost the 1992 election largely on economic issues – including NAFTA – to Bill Clinton, who campaigned under the informal slogan of 'it's the economy stupid'. In losing the televised NAFTA debate with Gore, Perot lost his political influence and effectively ended his political career. He made a second run for the presidency in 1996, but generated far less enthusiasm than he had four years previously. More importantly, his share of the vote plummeted by more than half, from the 19 per cent he had received in 1992 to 9 per cent in 1996, a figure that approximated other unsuccessful third-party candidates in recent American history. Canadian Prime Minister Kim Campbell lost her riding in the 1993 election defeat that saw a mere three members of her Progressive Conservative Party returned to Canada's House of Commons. Upon her forced retirement from politics, she became a visiting fellow at Harvard University's Kennedy School of Government, where she was joined by a fellow NAFTA refugee, Carlos Salinas, who had left Mexico in the wake of the 1995 collapse of the peso.

Notes
1. J. Sen, 'The North American Free Trade Agreement', in G. Sampson and S. Woolcock (eds), *Regionalism, Multilateralism, and Economic Integration: The Recent Experience* (New York: United Nations University Press, 2003), pp. 135–66.
2. See The Third Clinton-Bush-Perot Presidential Debate, 19 October 1992, below, pp. 177–86, especially pp. 181–2.
3. H. Milner, *Interests, Institutions and Information: Domestic Politics and International Relations* (Princeton, NJ: Princeton University Press, 1997), pp. 213–14. For a list of some of these proposals, see 'U.A.W. Wants Trade Payoff in Jobs', *New York Times*, 1 January 1994, below, pp. 256–8.
4. B. Clinton, *My Life* (New York: Random House, 2004), p. 891.
5. See Jonathan Ferguson, 'NAFTA: Canada's Concerns', *Toronto Star*, 30 November 1993, below, pp. 252–5.
6. United States International Trade Commission, *The Impact of Trade Agreements: Effect of the Tokyo Round, US–Israel FTA, US–Canada FTA, NAFTA, and the Uruguay Round on the US Economy*, Investigation TA-2111-1 (Washington, DC: USITC, 2003), pp. 122–3.

THE NORTH AMERICAN FREE TRADE AGREEMENT

The Second Clinton-Bush-Perot Presidential Debate, 15 October 1992, Edited Transcript, Commission on Presidential Debates, http://www.debates.org/pages/trans92b1.html.

The Second Clinton-Bush-Perot Presidential Debate

October 15, 1992
Richmond, Virginia

Moderator: Carole Simpson
Candidates: George Bush, Bill Clinton, Ross Perot

CAROLE SIMPSON: Good evening and welcome to this second of three presidential debates between the major candidates for president of the US. The candidates are the Republican nominee, President George Bush, the independent Ross Perot and Governor Bill Clinton, the Democratic nominee.

My name is Carole Simpson, and I will be the moderator for tonight's 90-minute debate, which is coming to you from the campus of the University of Richmond in Richmond, Virginia.

Now, tonight's program is unlike any other presidential debate in history. We're making history now and it's pretty exciting. An independent polling firm has selected an audience of 209 uncommitted voters from this area. The candidates will be asked questions by these voters on a topic of their choosing – anything they want to ask about. My job as moderator is to, you know, take care of the questioning, ask questions myself if I think there needs to be continuity and balance, and sometimes I might ask the candidates to respond to what another candidate may have said.

Now, the format has been agreed to by representatives of both the Republican and Democratic campaigns, and there is no subject matter that is restricted. Anything goes. We can ask anything.

After the debate, the candidates will have an opportunity to make a closing statement.

So, President Bush, I think you said it earlier – let's get it on.

PRESIDENT GEORGE BUSH: Let's go.

SIMPSON: And I think the first question is over here.

AUDIENCE QUESTION: Yes. I'd like to direct my question to Mr. Perot. What will you do as president to open foreign markets to fair competition from American business and to stop unfair competition here at home from foreign countries so that we can bring jobs back to the US?

ROSS PEROT: That's right at the top of my agenda. We've shipped millions of jobs overseas and we have a strange situation because we have a process in Washington where after you've served for a while you cash in, become a foreign lobbyist, make $30,000 a month, then take a leave, work on presidential campaigns, make sure you've got good contacts and then go back out.

Now, if you just want to get down to brass tacks, first thing you ought to do is get all these folks who've got these 1-way trade agreements that we've negotiated over the years and say fellas, we'll take the same deal we gave you. And they'll gridlock right at that point because for example, we've got international competitors who simply could not unload their cars off the ships if they had to comply – you see, if it was a 2-way street, just couldn't do it. We have got to stop sending jobs overseas.

To those of you in the audience who are business people: pretty simple. If you're paying $12, $13, $14 an hour for a factory worker, and you can move your factory south of the border, pay $1 an hour for labor, hire a young – let's assume you've been in business for a long time. You've got a mature workforce. Pay $1 an hour for your labor, have no health care – that's the most expensive single element in making the car. Have no environmental controls, no pollution controls and no retirement. And you don't care about anything but making money. There will be a job-sucking sound going south.

If the people send me to Washington the first thing I'll do is study that 2000-page agreement and make sure it's a 2-way street.

One last point here. I decided I was dumb and didn't understand it so I called a 'Who's Who' of the folks that have been around it, and I said why won't everybody go south; they said it will be disruptive; I said for how long. I finally got 'em for 12 to 15 years. And I said, well, how does it stop being disruptive? And that is when their jobs come up from a dollar an hour to $6 an hour, and ours go down to $6 an hour; then it's leveled again, but in the meantime you've wrecked the country with these kind of deals. We got to cut it out.

SIMPSON: Thank you, Mr. Perot. I see that the president has stood up, so he must have something to say about this.

BUSH: Carole, the thing that saved us in this global economic slowdown has been our exports, and what I'm trying to do is increase our exports. And if indeed all the jobs were going to move south because there are lower wages, there are lower wages now and they haven't done that. And so I have just negotiated with the president of Mexico the North American Free Trade Agreement – and the prime minister of Canada, I might add – and I want to have more of these free trade agreements, because export jobs are increasing far faster than any jobs that may have moved overseas. That's a scare tactic, because it's not that many. But any one that's here, we want to have more jobs here. And the way to do that is to increase our exports.

Some believe in protection. I don't; I believe in free and fair trade, and that's the thing that saved us. So I will keep on as president trying to get a successful conclusion to the GATT Round, the big Uruguay Round of trade which will really open up markets for our agriculture particularly. I want to continue to work after we get this NAFTA agreement ratified this coming year. I want to get one with Eastern Europe; I want to get one with Chile. And free and fair trade is the answer, not protection.

And, as I say, we've had tough economic times, and it's exports that have saved us, exports that have built.

SIMPSON: Governor Clinton.

GOVERNOR CLINTON: I'd like to answer the question, because I've actually been a governor for 12 years, so I've known a lot of people who have lost their jobs because of jobs moving overseas, and I know a lot of people whose plants have been strengthened by increasing exports.

The trick is to expand our export base and to expand trade on terms that are fair to us. It is true that our exports to Mexico, for example, have gone up and our trade deficit has gone down; it's also true that just today a record high trade deficit was announced with Japan.

So what is the answer? Let me just mention three things very quickly. Number one, make sure that other countries are as open to our markets as our markets are to them, and, if they're not, have measures on the books that don't take forever and a day to implement.

Number two, change the tax code. There are more deductions in the tax code for shutting plants down and moving overseas than there are for modernizing plant and equipment here. Our competitors don't do that. Emphasize and subsidize modernizing plant and equipment here, not moving plants overseas.

Number three, stop the federal government's program that now gives low-interest loans and job training funds to companies that will actually shut down and move to other countries, but we won't do the same thing for plants that stay here.

So more trade but on fair terms – and favor investment in America.

The Third Clinton-Bush-Perot Presidential Debate, 19 October 1992, Edited Transcript, Commission on Presidential Debates, http://www.debates.org/pages/trans92c.html.

The Third Clinton-Bush-Perot Presidential Debate

19 October 1992
East Lansing, Michigan
From Commission on Presidential Debates

Moderator, Jim Lehrer
Candidates: George Bush, Bill Clinton, Ross Perot

JIM LEHRER: Good evening. Welcome to this third and final debate among the three major candidates for president of the US. Governor Bill Clinton, the Democratic nominee, President George Bush, the Republican nominee, –

(APPLAUSE)

– and independent candidate Ross Perot.

(APPLAUSE)

I am Jim Lehrer of the MacNeil-Lehrer Newshour on PBS. I will be the moderator for this debate, which is being sponsored by the Commission on Presidential Debates. It will be 90 minutes long. It is happening before an audience on the campus of Michigan State University in East Lansing.

The format was conceived by and agreed to by representatives of the Bush and Clinton campaigns, and it is somewhat different than those used in the earlier debates. I will ask questions for the first half under rules that permit follow-ups. A panel of 3 other journalists will ask questions in the 2nd half under rules that do not.

As always, each candidate will have 2 minutes, up to 2 minutes, to make a closing statement. The order of those, as well as that for the formal questioning, were all determined by a drawing.

Gentlemen, again welcome and again good evening.

[...]

CLINTON: I don't have any criticism of Mr. Perot. I think what I'd like to talk about a minute, since you're asking the question, is the General Motors issue.

I don't think there's any question that the automobile executives made some errors in the 1980s, but I also think we should look at how much productivity has increased lately, how much labor has done to increase productivity and how much management has done. And we're still losing a lot of auto jobs, in my judgment, because we don't have a national economic strategy that will build the industrial base of this country.

Just today I met with the presidents and the vice presidents of the Willow Run union here, near here. They both said they were Vietnam veterans supporting me because I had an economic program to put them back to work. We need an investment incentive to modernize plant and equipment; we've got to control the health care costs for those people – otherwise we can't keep the manufacturing jobs here; and we need a tough trade policy that is fair, that insists on open markets in return for open markets. We ought to have a strategy that will build the economic and industrial base.

So I think Mr. Perot was right in questioning the management practices. But they didn't have much of a partner in government here as compared with the policies the Germans and the Japanese followed, and I believe we can do better. That's one of the things I want to change. I know that we can grow manufacturing jobs. We did it in my state, and we can do it nationally.

LEHRER: Mr. President, do you have a response?

BUSH: To this?

LEHRER: Yes.

BUSH: Well, I wondered, when Governor Clinton was talking to the auto workers, whether he talked about his and Senator Gore's favoring CAFE standards, fuel efficiency standards, of 40 miles per gallon. That would break the auto industry and throw a lot of people out of work.

As regarding Mr. Perot, I take back something I said about him. I once said, in a frivolous moment, when he got out of the race: If you can't stand the heat, buy an air conditioning company. And I take it back, because I think – he said he made a mistake. And the thing I find is if I make a mistake, I admit it. I've never heard Governor Clinton make a mistake.

But one mistake he's made is fuel efficiency standards at 40 to 45 miles a gallon will throw many auto workers out of work, and you can't have it both ways. There's a pattern here of appealing to the auto workers and then trying to appeal to the spotted owl crowds or the extremes in the environmental movement. You can't do it as president: you can't have a pattern of one side of the issue one day and another the next.

So my argument is not with Ross Perot; it is more with Governor Clinton.

LEHRER: Governor, what about that charge? Do you want it both ways on this issue?

CLINTON: Let's just talk about the CAFE standards – that's the fuel efficiency standards. They are now 27.5 miles per gallon per automobile fleet. I never said – and I defy you to find where I said – I gave an extensive environmental speech in April, and I said that we ought to have a goal of raising the fuel efficiency standards to 40 miles a gallon. I think that should be a goal. I have never said we should write it into law if there is evidence that that goal cannot be achieved. The National Science Foundation did a study which said it would be difficult for us to reach fuel efficiency standards in excess of 37 miles per gallon by the year 2000.

I think we should try to raise the fuel efficiency. And let me say this. I think we ought to have incentives to do it, I think we ought to push to do it. That doesn't mean we have to write it into the law.

Look, I am a job creator, not a job destroyer. It is the Bush administration that has had no new jobs in the private sector in the last 4 years. In my state, we're leading the country in private sector job growth.

But it is good for America to improve fuel efficiency. We also ought to convert more vehicles to compressed natural gas. That's another way to improve the environment.

LEHRER: Mr. Perot, based on your experience at General Motors, where do you come down on this? This has been thrown about, back and forth, during this campaign from the very beginning about jobs and CAFE standards.

PEROT: Well, everybody's nibbling around the edges. Let's go to the center of the bull's-eye, the core problem. And believe me, everybody on the factory floor all over this country knows it. You implement that NAFTA, the Mexican trade agreement, where they pay people a dollar an hour, have no health care, no retirement, no pollution controls, et cetera, et cetera, et cetera, and you're going to hear a giant sucking sound of jobs being pulled out of this country right at a time when we need the tax base to pay the debt and pay down the interest on the debt and get our house back in order.

We've got to proceed very carefully on that. See, there's a lot I don't understand. I do understand business. I do understand creating jobs. I do understand how to make things work. And I got a long history of doing that.

Now, if you want to go to the core problem that faces everybody in manufacturing in this country, it's that agreement that's about to be put into practice. It's very simple. Everybody says it'll create jobs. Yes, it'll create bubble jobs.

Now, you know, watch this – listen very carefully to this. One-time surge while we build factories and ship machine tools and equipment down there. Then year after year for decades, they will have jobs. And I finally – I thought I didn't understand it – called all the experts, and they said, oh, it'll be disruptive for 12 to 15 years.

We haven't got 12 days, folks. We cannot lose those jobs. They were eventually saying, Mexican jobs will eventually come to $7.50 an hour, ours will eventually go down to $7.50 an hour. Makes you feel real good to hear that, right?

Let's think it through here. Let's be careful. I'm for free trade philosophically, but I have studied these trade agreements till the world has gone flat, and we don't have good trade agreements across the world.

I hope we'll have a chance to get into that tonight, because I can get right to the center of the bull's-eye and tell you why we're losing whole industries in this country.

LEHRER: Just for the record, though, Mr. Perot, I take it, then, from your answer, you do not have a position on whether or not enforcing the CAFE standards will cost jobs in the auto industry?

PEROT: Oh, no, it will cost jobs, but that's not – let me say this. I'd rather, if you gave me 2 bad choices –

LEHRER: Okay.

PEROT: I'd rather have some jobs left here than just see everything head south, see?

LEHRER: So that means – in other words, you agree with President Bush; is that right?

PEROT: No, I'm saying our principal need now is to stabilize the tax base, which is the job base, and create a growing, dynamic base. Now please, folks, if you don't hear anything else I say, remember where the – millions of people at work are our tax base.

One quick point. If you confiscate the Forbes 400 wealth, take it all, you cannot balance the budget this year. Kind of gets your head straight about where the taxes, year in and year out, have gotta come from. Millions and millions of people at work.

LEHRER: Yes, sir.

BUSH: I'm caught in the middle on NAFTA. Ross says, with great conviction, he opposes the North American Free Trade Agreement. I am for the North American Free Trade Agreement. My problem with Governor Clinton, once again, is that one time he's gonna make up his mind, he sees some merit in it, but then he sees a lot of things wrong with it. Then the other day he says he's for it, however then we've got to pass other legislation.

When you're president of the US, you cannot have this pattern of saying well, I'm for it but I'm on the other side of it. And it's true on this and it's true on CAFE.

Look, if Ross were right when we get a free trade agreement with Mexico, why wouldn't they have gone down there now? You have a differential in wages right now. I just have an honest philosophical difference. I think free trade is going to expand our job opportunity. I think it is exports that have saved us when we're in a global slowdown, a connected global slowdown, a recession in some countries. And it's free trade, fair trade that needs to be our hallmark, and we need more free trade agreements, not fewer.

LEHRER: Governor, quick answer on trade and I want to go on to something else.

(APPLAUSE)

CLINTON: I'd like to respond to that. You know, Mr. Bush was very grateful when I was among the Democrats who said he ought to have the authority to negotiate an agreement with Mexico. Neither I nor anybody else, as far a I know, agreed to give him our proxy to say that whatever he did was fine for the workers of this country and for the interests of this country.

I am the one who's in the middle on this. Mr. Perot says it's a bad deal. Mr. Bush says it's a hunky-dory deal. I say on balance it does more good than harm if, if we can get some protection for the environment so that the Mexicans have to follow their own environmental standards, their own labor law standards, and if we have a genuine commitment to reeducate and retrain the American workers who lose their jobs and reinvest in this economy.

I have a realistic approach to trade. I want more trade, and I know there are some good things in that agreement. But it can sure be made better.

Let me just point out, just today in the Los Angeles Times Clyde Prestowitz, who was one of President Reagan's leading trade advisers and a life-long conservative Republican, endorsed my candidacy because he knows that I'll have a free and fair trade policy, a hard-headed, realistic policy, and not get caught up in rubber-stamping everything the Bush administration did. If I wanted to do that, why would I run for president, Jim? Anybody else can run the middle class down and run the economy in a ditch. I want to change it.

(APPLAUSE)

LEHRER: We've got about 4 –

BUSH: I think he made my case. On the one hand, it's a good deal but on the other hand I'd make it better. You can't do that as president. You can't do it on the war, where he says well, I was with the minority but I guess I would have voted with the majority.

This is my point tonight. We're talking about 2 weeks from now you've gotta decide who's gonna be president. And there is this pattern that has plagued in him the primaries and now about trying to have it both ways on all these issues. You can't do that. And if you make a mistake, say you made a mistake and go on about your business, trying to serve the American people.

Right now we heard it. Ross is against it. I am for it. He says on the one hand I am for it and on the other hand I may be against it.

LEHRER: The governor –

(APPLAUSE)

CLINTON: That's what's wrong with Mr. Bush. His whole deal is you've gotta be for it or against it, you can't make it better. I believe we can be better. I think the American people are sick and tired of either/or solutions, people being pushed in the corner, polarized to extremes.

GOVERNOR CLINTON (continuing): I want think they want somebody with common sense who can do what's best for the American people. And I'd be happy to discuss these other issues, but I can't believe he is accusing me of getting on both sides. He said trickle-down economics was voodoo economics; now he's it's biggest practitioner.

(Laughter and applause)

He promised – he – you know – let me just say –

BUSH: But I've always said trickle-down government is bad.

CLINTON: I could run this string out a long time, but remember this, Jim. Those 209 Americans last Thursday night in Richmond told us they wanted us to stop talking about each other and start talking about Americans and their problems and their promise, and I think we ought to get back to that.

I'll be glad to answer any question you have, but this election ought to be about the American people.

(APPLAUSE)

LEHRER: Mr. Perot.

PEROT: Is there an equal time rule tonight?

BUSH: Yes.

PEROT: Or do you just keep lunging in at will? I thought we were going to have equal time, but maybe I just have to interrupt the other 2. Is that the way it works?

LEHRER: No, it's – Mr. Perot, you're doing fine. Go ahead. Whatever you want to say, say it.

PEROT: Now that we've talked all around the problem about free trade, let's go again to the center of the bull's- eye.

LEHRER: Wait a minute. I was going to ask – I thought you wanted to respond to what we're talking about.

PEROT: I do, I do.

LEHRER: All right.

PEROT: I just want to make – foreign lobbyists, this whole thing. Our country has sold out to foreign lobbyists. We don't have free trade. Both parties have foreign lobbyists on leaves in key roles in their campaigns. And if there's anything more unwise than that, I don't know what it is. Every debate I bring this up, and nobody ever addresses it.

I would like for them to look you in the eye and tell you why they have people representing foreign countries working on their campaigns. And you know, you've seen the list, I've seen the list, we won't go into the names, but no wonder they – if I had those people around me all day every day, telling me it was fair and free, I might believe it. But if I look at the facts as a businessman, it's so tilted, the first thing you ought to do is just say, guys, if you like these deals so well, we'll give you the deal you gave us.

Now, Japanese couldn't unload the cars in this country if they had the same restrictions we had, and on and on and on and on and on. I suggest to you that the core problem – 1 country spent $400 million lobbying in 1988, our country. And it goes on and on. And you look at a who's who in these campaigns around the 2 candidates. They're foreign lobbyists taking leaves. What do you think they're going to do when the campaign's over? Go back to work at 30,000 bucks a month representing some other country. I don't believe that's in the American people's interest.

I don't have a one of them, and I haven't taken a penny of foreign money, and I never will.

(APPLAUSE)

LEHRER: Mr. President, how do you respond to that? Mr. Perot's made that charge several times. The fact that you have people working in your campaign who are paid foreign lobbyists.

BUSH: Most people that are lobbying are lobbying the Congress. And I don't think there's anything wrong with an honest person who happens to represent an interest of another country for making his case. That's the American way. And what you're assuming is that that makes the recipient of the lobbying corrupt or the lobbyist himself corrupt. I don't agree with that.

But if I found somebody that had a conflict of interest that would try to illegally do something as a foreign – registered lobby, the laws cover this. I don't know why – I've never understood quite why Mr. Perot was so upset it, because one of the guys he used to have working for him, I believe, had foreign accounts. Could be wrong, but I think so.

PEROT: And as soon as I found it out, he went out the door.

(Laughter)

BUSH: Well –

(APPLAUSE)

But I don't – I think you got to look at the integrity and the honor of the people that are being lobbied and those that are lobbyists. The laws protect the American taxpayer in this regard. If the laws are violated so much, but to suggest if somebody represents a foreign country on anything, that makes him corrupt or against the taxpayer, I don't agree with that.

PEROT: One quick relevant specific. We're getting ready to dismantle the airlines industry in our country, and none of you know it. And I doubt in all candor if the president knows it. But this deal that we're doing with BAC and US Air and KLM and Northwest, guess who's on the president's campaign big time: a guy from Northwest. This deal is terribly destructive to the US airline industry. One of the largest industries in the world is the travel, tourist business. We won't be making airplanes in this country 10 years from now if we let deals like this go through.

If the president has any interest tonight, I'll detail it to you; I won't take 10 minutes tonight. All these things take a few minutes. But that's happening as we sit here today.

We hammerlock the American companies – American Airlines, Delta – the last few great we have, because we're trying to do this deal with these 2 European companies. And never forget, they've got Airbus over there, and it's a government-owned, privately owned, consortium across Europe. They're dying to get the commercial airline business. Japan is trying to get the commercial airline business.

I don't think there are any villains inside government on this issue, but there's sure a lot of people who don't understand business. And maybe you need somebody up there who understands when you're getting your pocket picked.

(APPLAUSE)

CLINTON: Jim.

LEHRER: Governor, I'm sorry, but that concludes my time with – well, you...

CLINTON: Why, I had a great response to that.

LEHRER: All right, go ahead, quick, quickly.

CLINTON: Just very briefly. I think Ross is right and that we do need some more restrictions on lobbyists. We ought to make them disclose the people they've given money to when they're testifying before congressional committees; we ought to close the lawyers' loopholes; they ought to have to disclose when they're really lobbying. And we ought to have to limit – we ought to have a much longer period of time, about 5 years, between the time when people can leave executive branch offices and then go out and start lobbying for foreign interests. I agree with that.

We've wrecked the airline industry already because of all these leverage buyouts and all these terrible things that have happened to the airline industry. We're going to have a hard time rebuilding it.

But the real thing we got to have is a competitive economic strategy. Look what's happening to McDonnell Douglas; even Boeing is losing market share – because we let the Europeans spend $25-$40 billion on Airbus without an appropriate competitive response.

What I want America to do is to trade more but to compete and win by investing in competitive ways. And we're in real trouble on that.

(APPLAUSE)

House of Commons Debates, Official Record, 3rd Session, 34th Parliament (Canada), 15 (25 May 1993), pp. 19610–19.

Mr. Wappel: [...]

[W]hy are we here? The hon. member from the New Democrats pointed out that the government is ramming the NAFTA legislation through the House of Commons this week. That is a tragedy. That is why its members are not here. That is why they do not put up any speakers. They want to ram NAFTA through the House of Commons as quickly as possible. So what have they done? They have put a notice of motion for closure. What does that mean? It means no debate.

How did I find this out, besides reading about it in the newspapers? I wanted to speak on third reading of the NAFTA legislation and I called our critic and I asked him to please put me on the list. He said he was sorry but there was no room. I asked what he meant. He explained that because of the closure motion we are only going to be able to debate NAFTA at third reading for one day. As we all know there are certain periods of time allocated for debate and only so many people can fit into those slots. There are 80 of us in the Liberal Party, all of whom wished to say a few words about this nefarious legislation. We are not going to be able to because there is a certain rank and precedence, and quite properly so, of the critics and associate critics of the various departments that are particularly concerned with NAFTA.

I get an opportunity to say a few words now at report stage on different amendments. That is why I am standing today, first of all, to deal with this first group of amendments. Seven amendments are proposed in the first group and there is one in particular that I would like to talk about and support, and it is Motion No. 1, not surprisingly, moved by the hon. member for Kenora – Rainy River, my colleague. It would be very interesting to see if anybody on the government benches gets up to explain what is wrong with this amendment. What is wrong with the government members on the other side agreeing with this particular amendment?

We all know that they are not going to agree with anything. Not only that, they are not going to tell the Canadian people why they do not agree with anything. They think that a document which contains 4,300 pages is perfect. There is not a word, not a comma, not a crossed *t*, not a dotted *i* that is missing. Everything is absolutely perfect and cannot possibly be improved.

Who could believe that? Who would have the audacity to make a statement like that? It is the government members on the other side of the House. It is hard to believe they all insist that this document is perfect, that there cannot possibly be any improvements. It is inconceivable to them that anybody on this side of the House might possibly have some good ideas which could make the NAFTA legislation a little bit better. Better for whom? For Canada.

I look at this motion and what does it talk about? It talks about the freedom of association and the ability for us in Canada to organize our workers and to permit our workers to organize in a free and democratic county.

I am not going to read the entire motion because it is four paragraphs but I want to précis it. It is there for a reason and what does it suggest? First of all it says we should be able to have the freedom of association. We should be able to have independent public and private sector unions that play a part in conducting the democratic process in this country.

It is interesting that my colleague moved a motion dealing with unions. What happened to the New Democratic Party members? Where are their motions dealing with unions? It was the hon. member for Kenora – Rainy River who was concerned about workers. I commend him for that and I know that the working people of Canada will remember that in the months to come.

In any event he goes on to suggest that there should be retraining programs and adjustment programs for workers displaced as a result of this agreement. We know, despite all the rhetoric on the other side that there are going to be workers displaced because of this agreement.

We know that in the riding of Scarborough West, the riding I am privileged to represent, the Scarborough GM van plant just closed. We know for a fact that was due to the free trade agreement. All the workers who were displaced know that. Everybody in Scarborough knows that. The families of those workers know that. The spin-off industries that are going to be affected by that plant closure know that. And my hon. friend, the member for Kenora – Rainy River knows that. The reason he moved this motion was to provide that there be retraining and adjustment programs for workers displaced as a result of the agreement.

I ask myself: What is wrong with that? What is wrong with putting in a few words to protect those people who might just be adversely affected by the North American free trade agreement?

My friends over there would have us believe that this 4,300 pages of an agreement is absolutely perfect and incapable of amendment. They would have us believe that nobody is going to be adversely affected by the North American free trade agreement.

Of course that is not true. Everybody knows it is not true. Therefore my hon. friend has moved an amendment to provide for the protection of those workers who will suffer as a result of the North American free trade agreement which the Conservatives are going to ram through this House this week without adequate debate. There is absolutely no reason to do so, none whatsoever.

They are not going to stand up today and tell us why they are doing this and they are not going to stand up today and tell us what is wrong with Motion No. 1 moved by my colleague. I will tell you why, Mr. Speaker. It is because there is nothing wrong with it. There is absolutely nothing wrong with that amendment. But because it is an amendment, because it is a change from what has been drafted and what has been agreed upon, it is absolutely inconceivable that the other side would even think about supporting it.

That is a tragedy. How can we proceed with this agreement with that kind of mind-set? How can we on this side make any sort of constructive recommendations, do anything in the way of bettering a bill? One of our jobs in opposition is to constructively criticize, to offer suggestions. How can we do that when the minds on the government side are closed? They will not listen. They will not do anything except ram through the agreement.

This is not some fanciful idea I have, but I predict that by midnight on Thursday, if this government has its way, this deal will be passed unamended by this House of Commons and that government will be judged for that sort of action.

Mr. Simon de Jong (Regina – Qu'Appelle): Mr. Speaker, it gives me great pleasure to join the debate this evening on the first part of the amendments dealing with the North American free trade agreement. My remarks will be general because the amendments specifically deal with the environment and social policy.

We heard much from the Conservative benches during the Canada-U.S. Free Trade Agreement debate and now in dealing with NAFTA about the changing nature of our world, globalization, the need for international trade, et cetera. I have no dispute with much of what they say as indeed we have seen a tremendous globalization, particularly starting in the 1960s, picking up speed in the 1970s and then well into the 1980s.

We see both positive and negative results. We see the positive side where there has been tremendous economic development in parts of the world particularly in parts of Asia where tremendous growth is occurring. There is no doubt about that. The People's Republic of China, Korea, Taiwan, Thailand, India and I believe very soon Vietnam, will experience a tremendous increase in their rate of growth.

Yet one also has to stand back and wonder what benefit this growth has been to the ordinary people in many of those countries. I had the occasion to visit some of those countries. I saw the huge skyscrapers going up, apartment buildings that in terms of the rents are comparable to those in downtown Vancouver, Toronto or New York. There are the very expensive clothes and the Mercedes. But in the shadows of it all is the beggar. There are people who are still working for the equivalent of $1 to $1.50 a day. Much of their so-called prosperity is on the backs of the poor.

When it occurs and when the workers are able to demand a little bit more as they now are in Korea and Taiwan, those industries are being moved to mainland China, to Thailand, to Vietnam or to North Korea. There is this continuous shift searching for very cheap labour, as though that is the important component.

Of course with globalization, we have now opened our borders to these countries and now our Canadian workers have to compete against them. We see Canadian companies, the large retail organizations, setting up their own manufacturing units. The hammers, other tools, clothing or whatever are all manufactured especially for them under contract to what essentially are sweatshops so that they can provide Canadian consumers with supposedly cheap goods. I imagine the mark-up between the factory gates in the Third World and the time the item reaches the consumer here is quite substantial.

We are asked to continue this with this agreement, to have our own North American version of an Asian backwater so to speak, our own source of cheap labour. That is what this is all about: the ability of our ownership class to have access to cheap labour.

The government has the gall to suggest that this is good for Canada, that this is good for the men and women who work, make and produce the things we need in this country, who pay their taxes and keep this country going. This government claims that this frontal assault to the average Canadian is a good thing.

We have seen the results of the Canada-U.S. Free Trade Agreement. We have seen hundreds of thousands of jobs leave Canada. Of course it was the combination of the free trade agreement and the high Canadian dollar that priced our goods out of the market and allowed this huge exodus of capital and manufacturing jobs out of Canada.

What I do not understand about the Tories is that there is a simple thing they have never figured out. It is that people need to earn incomes in order to buy the goods and services the businesses are offering. If Canadian men and women cannot earn the dollars in good jobs, then they cannot buy. It is no wonder we have this recession. It is no wonder we have lost the confidence of the consumers. It is no wonder we have the deficit. It is because more Canadians are out of work and are not able to pay taxes. Instead they are drawing UI and welfare.

That is a recipe for disaster. Why is this government acting against the self-interests of Canada, of this nation? It has a job to protect and govern this country. Why in Heaven's name is it so adamantly on this course that is going to do further harm and cripple our country?

The government is of course driven by ideology. I would suggest in some ways the neo-conservatives over there are the purest ideologues left in this country. They are driven by ideology. They are not driven because something is good for the country or because it makes common sense. They are driven because they feel this is the right thing to do.

Therefore, we are down this neo-conservative path that the Americans have finally rejected. I suspect that the Americans will not pass this agreement because they have come off the neo-conservative binge and have assessed the damage it has done to their country. They have seen the type of economic malaise that exists in the United States in the numbers of unemployed and the deficit they have. They have come off that. It is a question of time a matter of months before finally we in Canada can get off this same ride the neo-conservatives have put us on.

What a ride it has been. We have the highest per capita debt in the world. We have the highest level of unemployment of the industrialized countries. They have crippled this country. Of course in one sense we can understand it. These people believe in little or no government. They will leave behind a government and a country so in ruin and laden with such a weight of debt that the government will not be able to do anything.

These people have succeeded in down-scaling government and one would almost think they did it deliberately. In fact, there are some who suggest that David Stockman who was the budget bureau director under Ronald Reagan is now openly admitting that they ran up the deficit in order to justify cutbacks to social services down the road. It was part of the neo-conservative agenda to destroy government. That is what these people have done. What a record.

Of course when we deal with NAFTA that is part of the scenario. It is part of the grand design. They burden us with huge amounts of debt. They deregulated so that now we do not have any viable transportation system left in this country. They have done it with communications. They have done it across the board. They have weakened our cultural institutions. They have tied our hands with the Canada-U.S. Free Trade Agreement. Now I suppose the height of their accomplishment is NAFTA where Canadian workers are going to have to compete with the Mexican workers who earn $1, $1.50 or $2 an hour.

What an accomplishment in eight or nine years of various governments, including past Progressive Conservative governments as well as Liberal governments often crowded by the CCF and the New Democratic Party. We have built institutions in this country to help protect and enrich the lives of Canadians and to make this one of the most decent, civilized countries in the world. In nine short years these folks driven by neo-conservative ideology have brought us to our knees. They have crippled Canada. I am afraid it will take a long time to heal from the abuses inflicted on us.

I am not against international trade. There are some good models we could follow. The Conservatives during the 1988 election said that we should look at Europe. I agreed. The Europeans got together and formed a social agreement. It was not just an agreement on trade but an agreement on social policies, labour standards and the environment to ensure that the whole matter was not dragged down to the lowest common denominator of Greece, Spain and Portugal. There are plans afoot to raise those countries to higher levels, but in this agreement there is no such guarantee. We will be forced down to the lowest common denominator.

For that reason my party and I are opposed. We will do everything possible to protect Canada, our way of life and our standard of living.

Mr. Bill Blaikie (Winnipeg Transcona): Madam Speaker, I too would like to participate in the debate tonight.

As I listened to the hon. member for Regina – Qu'Appelle I was struck by the passion with which he spoke. I actually contrasted it with my own mood tonight. It is one of despair to some degree. As once again we are debating something that has been compared to a constitutional debate changing the economic constitution of North America under the threat and indeed the reality of closure.

When the government moved closure on second reading of this legislation I asked the Chair at that time to intervene on behalf of Parliament, to protect Parliament from becoming a rubber stamp and to protect Parliament from the tyranny of a majority that simply regards any prolonged debate on something of this importance as a nuisance. There was a time when closure came after the opposition had dragged the debate on for a while. Now the government House leader if we are not prepared to agree to limit the debate before the debate starts feels justified in moving time allocation. If we do not agree before the debate starts we get a motion of time allocation.

That is not the purpose of closure or time allocation. If at a certain point the government feels the debate has gone on long enough it does not take it long to move time allocation. It can take the political risk of cutting the debate off. The opposition can take the political risk of dragging the debate on. We do not even get to do that. We do not get to let the Canadian people make some kind of judgment about whether or not the debate has gone on for too long. Right off the bat we have time allocation, and all of this at the same time as we are allegedly down in the United States negotiating parallel or side agreements to the very agreement we are seeing rammed through the House at this particular time.

It is embarrassing to think the Canadian negotiating stance is that we are negotiating but in the meantime we are going to pass the bill and the implementing legislation as is. It is only embarrassing if one looks at it with any kind of national self-respect. I guess it is not embarrassing if one looks at it through the eyes of the Conservatives because the fact is that they like this agreement just the way it is. They really do not want to improve it. It is so transparent. They like it the way it is because the idea of putting in tougher environmental standards or tougher labour standards goes against their particular view of the world.

That is where the hon. member for Regina – Qu' Appelle was right on when he said this was an ideological fixation on the part of the government. It is fond of thinking that somehow the New Democrats are the ideological ones, but this is the most ideological government we have had in Canadian history. It has rewritten the ideological fabric of Canadian society.

What the government is doing in these agreements is trying to enshrine its ideology beyond its own political existence as a government so that regardless of what happens to it its particular view of the world will be enshrined in these agreements for a long time to come, particularly if we get a Liberal government after the next election because the Conservatives will have done all the dirty work for the right wing of the Liberal Party.

These agreements will not be changed and, as I have said before, they will outlast the Conservatives. They will go far beyond the reach of their political life as a government.

The Minister of Finance said it well this morning when he was answering questions in the House respecting the North American free trade agreement. He said: 'Why are not people out there exploiting these opportunities that the North American free trade agreement creates?' Creates for whom?

I want to say two things. I think the word exploit tells us a lot. These agreements are really all about exploiting the people of Mexico, the people of Canada and, for that matter, the people of the United States. It is about exploiting the working people of those three countries by pitting them against each other in a new form of so-called competition. The opportunities are not for Canadian workers. The only opportunities they have are to be faced with ultimatums from their employers to take a $3 an hour cut in wages or lose their jobs as is the case with a number of firms in my riding and in Winnipeg generally. Those are the only opportunities that exist for Canadian workers.

The opportunities are there for Canadian exporters of a certain kind: people who are willing either to export or to relocate in Mexico and take advantage of those low wages. Those are the opportunities, but what are the opportunities for? They are opportunities for exploitation. We should just reverse exploiting opportunities and talk about opportunities for exploitation because that is what it is.

All the statistics about how Canada is benefiting from the free trade agreement only have to do with exports. They do not say anything about jobs. They do not say anything about social well-being. They do not say anything about the environment. All they talk about is certain kinds of export statistics.

Theoretically we could have a handful of companies in Canada employing only a handful of people who are very successful at exporting all kinds of things to other countries. This would make our economic statistics look great except for the fact that a whole lot of people who used to have jobs do not have them any more. I suggest to the minister that to the extent he believes these statistics, and I am not sure he does, he is suffering from what the famous philosopher Alfred North Whitehead once called the fallacy of misplaced concreteness. That is investing certain abstractions with a reality that hides what is really going on. To have the Minister of Finance, the minister of trade, or whoever does it from day to day here get up to talk about these wonderful export statistics is a good example of the fallacy of misplaced concreteness.

The concrete reality is that Canadians everywhere have either lost their jobs, are losing their jobs, are being asked to accept a lower wage, a wage rollback, or in a variety of other ways are being asked to forfeit the standard of living and degree of social justice we have achieved in the last 40 years to 45 years in the name of competition.

I had my nomination meeting a week or so ago within about 48 hours of the tragedy in Thailand where a factory was burned and somewhere in the neighbourhood of 250 women died. It struck me that there was a competitive factor, a factory that was a good investment according to all the rhetoric we hear on the other side. It probably was very productive. It probably had very high productivity, low overhead, cheap wages and no union. The list goes on of the ways the factory in which those 250 women died met all the standards of competition, efficiency and productivity. This was a place for people to invest, invest in death.

That is what we are being asked to applaud time and again in this House, the fact that we are turning the world into a place where decisions to invest in places like that factory in Thailand are called good when they should be called bad.

[...]

Mr. Lyle Dean MacWilliam (Okanagan – Shuswap): Madam Speaker, about 10 years ago the Prime Minister was first elected to the House of Commons. As a matter of fact I think it was in his very first speech in the House that he said: 'Give us 20 years and you will not recognize this country'.

The Prime Minister has had less than 10 years and already if we look at the economic situation in Canada we are fast becoming a Third World economic basket case. It is quite a legacy to have left us; it is quite a legacy to have left the Canadian people. Although the Prime Minister may soon be gone that legacy will indeed live on through the enshrinement of the policies and the ideological commitment of this government in both the free trade agreement and the proposed North American free trade agreement.

These agreements are a way of enshrining the government's corporate agenda. None of us on this side of the House has any difficulty with the idea of reducing trade barriers, reducing tariff barriers, increasing opportunities for Canadian workers or increasing opportunity for Canadian business.

These free trade agreements really do not have a lot to do with that. What they do have to do with is opening up the Canadian market for exploitation from multinational corporations, be they U.S. multinationals or other multinationals operating through the United States. They have basically opened up the opportunity to exploit not only Canadian workers but Canadian resources.

With the proposed signing of the North American trade agreement between Canada, the United States and our now our newest partner, Mexico, this exploitation will be furthered to include the Mexican workers, the Mexican economy and the Mexican environment where basically all the pieces of the puzzle if you like have been put into place through the FTA and now through the North American trade agreement.

The United States and the multinational corporations operating in the United States will have been an opportunity to exploit cheap Canadian resources and cheap Mexican labour.

As my colleague for Regina – Qu' Appelle mentioned earlier in his presentation, these agreements do not have the kind of social charters that are necessary to guarantee equality in terms of opportunity for workers and in terms of basic standards for health, environmental safety, and educational opportunities.

The social charter should be very much a part of this agreement to ensure that countries such as Mexico, a developing Third World nation, brings its working conditions, environmental conditions, its health and labour standards up to the level that Canadian workers and Canadian people have enjoyed.

Without those guarantees, this is exactly what President Clinton has been talking about when he has said he will not sign this agreement unless there are parallel agreements that guarantee certain provisions for workers and certain provisions for environmental standards. He will not sign the agreement because he is aware that without these parallel accords, without these extenuating provisions, what happens as we have already seen through the free trade agreement is a downward spiral to the lowest common denominator.

Rather than raising the wages and working conditions of our brothers and sisters in Mexico up to the standards that Canadian workers have traditionally enjoyed, what will happen is that the working standards for Canadian workers and U.S. workers will spiral downward to the lowest common denominator. That in the long run is not going to be healthy for the Canadian economy, nor will it be healthy for the United States economy which is why we have seen Ross Perot.

We all know Ross Perot was one of the U.S. presidential leadership candidates. This man was a multibillionaire. He knew a good deal when he saw one. He knows how to make a good buck. He took one look at that trade agreement, shook his head and said if this agreement is signed all we are going to hear is one great sucking sound as U.S. jobs go south of the border. He was speaking on behalf of U.S. workers and U.S. industry.

I want to say that if this agreement is signed in Canada and Canada signs into the agreement as it is now written, all we are going to hear is an even greater sucking sound as Canadian jobs and Canadian resources are also drawn south of the border.

This agreement coupled with the free trade agreement that we are now experiencing, the radical restructuring of our economy as a result of its signing four years ago, provide that opportunity for the multinationals, the transnationals to access Canadian resources and Mexican labour.

They have got all the pieces of the puzzle put together and it is a level playing field for the multinationals where they can move capital and labour to wherever they see the best fit. If you reread it to the lowest common denominator where labour is cheapest and environmental standards are the most lax, it means it will allow them to move these factors around like pieces of a giant jigsaw puzzle. Canadian workers, and I submit Canada's economy, will suffer significantly as a result of this.

It is interesting that while Mr. Clinton has said this agreement cannot be signed unless these other provisions for environmental standards, health and safety standards of workers are also met, here we are in this House of Commons today with this government ramming through this agreement, calling closure on the rewriting of our economic constitution, probably one of the most important questions that this House has faced in many, many years. The rewriting of Canada's economic constitution through the signing of this agreement will set us on an irreversible path of economic and political union with the United States in a few short years.

It will be a path that is well delineated. Without a blink of an eye this government on the most important question facing this House, the most important question facing the Canadian people, denies the opportunity for debate even in this House of Commons, even in this Parliament, through the calling of closure, through the calling of time allocation.

Time and time again we have seen this government use and abuse this parliamentary procedure to ram through its political and ideological agenda and abrogate its responsibility to the Canadian people by castrating the process of Parliament. Those are pretty strong words, but that is exactly what is happening through the calling of time allocation on this motion.

A few months ago when we had the opportunity to debate the rewriting of our social constitution through the holding of the referendum in the fall, this government spent limitless amounts of money and went to no ends to ensure that information was provided to every part of this country. People were inundated with information on the referendum and why they should support the government's position on the referendum.

Here we have a question that the Canadian people need to address and should have the opportunity to address, a question that is ever as important as the referendum question was. I submit it is even more important because it is the rewriting of our economic constitution, and this government has not taken the opportunity to provide information to the Canadian people. It has not taken the opportunity to involve the Canadian people through a possible referendum process in itself. It does not even involve the members of Parliament who are here representing their own constituents and allow them the opportunity to debate this issue.

This is a very sad day when the government calls closure on a motion as important and as critical as the signing of this economic constitution for Canada, the signing of this North American trade agreement. It is a shameful day when that abusive privilege is given the opportunity as it has been through the calling of closure on this motion.

Mr. Chris Axworthy (Saskatoon – Clark's Crossing): Madam Speaker, it is almost five years since this House debated the U.S. – Canada Free Trade Agreement after the last election and after the majority of Canadians voted against the free trade agreement, but of course free trade agreements did not start there.

There were other efforts to sell out Canada before, but the modern free trade trend did start at least just before the 1988 free trade agreement. It began, of course, with the appointment of the Macdonald Commission, the Royal Commission by the then Liberal government, and the report by the Macdonald royal commission which mapped out the free trade agenda for Canada which the Conservative government has so carefully followed.

It is important to note the amount of support for free trade agreements like the U.S. – Canada Free Trade Agreement and like the Mexico deal in the Liberal Party at that time and indeed today. If we look across the country at Liberal premiers we will see, for example, the Liberal premier of Quebec and the Liberal Government of Quebec strongly in support of the North American free trade agreement. We should not forget that the Liberals talk out of both sides of the mouth when dealing with these important matters facing Canadians. We should also remember that rather than take the position of scrapping the free trade agreement with the United States and having nothing to do with the North American free trade agreement with Mexico, the Liberals talk only about making changes to that agreement even though both President Bush and President Clinton have indicated that this sort of renegotiation is simply not possible.

We now have this government again, against the wishes of Canadians, ramming through the North American free trade agreement with Mexico. It is not providing ample opportunity for this House to debate it or even for Canadians to debate the consequences of what surely will be essentially a new economic constitution for this country, making worse what has already been made intolerable for Canadians by the Canada, U.S. Free Trade Agreement and entrenching the loss of sovereignty even further than was done by the Canada, U.S. Free Trade Agreement.

Basically what is being tried now is essentially the same as before, an economic agenda being driven by the marketplace with no concern for the costs to individuals, the costs to families, the costs to communities, but letting the big business community controlled almost all offshore to decide to use Canadian resources, American capital and Mexican labour to produce the products that might be sold both in this part of the world and in others.

Since the signing of the free trade agreement some estimates have indicated over a million jobs lost in Canada and in Saskatchewan one in nine manufacturing jobs has been lost since the free trade agreement.

The experience that Canada has had with the free trade agreement signed with the United States has not been one which would suggest we would want to go even further, that we would want to pursue this approach yet again.

Some of the government supporters will say things might have been worse but for the free trade agreement. First of all it is hard to see how they could have been worse. I think if you try to tell those 4.2 million Canadians who are either unemployed or on social assistance that the free trade agreement in fact helped them they would laugh because they simply could not see how that could be the case. When we have a country in which 16 per cent or 17 per cent of Canadians are not participating in the productive work force it is quite clear that the economy is not working for Canadians.

No matter what the numbers or the figures are with regard to the value of manufacturing products sold to the United States over the last year, if Canadians are not working we cannot say that the economy is working. If it is working in one sense who is it working for? Certainly not for Canadians, but it may be working for large multinational corporations which so freely contribute to the coffers of the Conservative Party for its election efforts and which worked so hard and spent so much money in the last election to get the Conservative Party elected.

The world is changing. There is no doubt about that and New Democrats recognize that as much as anybody else. The question is how we are going to respond to that change. Are we going to give up control over Canada and Canadian resources and Canadian jobs and the Canadian economy? Or are we going to try to map out a strategy which enables Canada to respond to the changing times, to the changing world, so as to maintain jobs in Canada as best we can and to create new jobs in Canada. Basically we have a choice. We can throw up our hands as this government wants to do and leave all these decisions to the international marketplace, dominated as it is by huge corporations which have enormous problems competing with each other but have a great deal of ease finding ways to work with each other so as to benefit themselves.

We can throw up our hands or we can try to develop a strategy, a plan which enables us to compete in the world and still keep jobs here in Canada.

It is odd but the Conservative government continues to ignore the fact that all successful economies around the world have strategies, have plans and have a vision for the way in which their economy will develop. Most of those successful economies have plans which have been developed, not alone by government, but with business and very often with workers; also there is a consensus, an agreement, a commitment to work together to solve the country's economic problems and to maintain a decent standard of living and a decent employment rate for their citizens.

The basket case economies, the economies that do not work, like Canada's, are those that follow this neo-conservative agenda of just throwing economic decisions out into the international marketplace. The United States, Canada, Britain, Australia and New Zealand are really the only countries that have attempted to respond in this way.

We should take some lessons from countries that have successful economies, from the economies of Asia, Japan, northern Europe and in particular from those northern European countries that have a long and distinguished social democratic tradition in which jobs came first and jobs continue to come first. Those countries are also experiencing difficulties with the world economy, but surely we in Canada would look with glee at an unemployment rate of 6 per cent, which Sweden has, rather than the one of some 12 per cent which we have.

Even through the good times, through Liberal governments and Conservative governments alike, we had unemployment rates stubbornly high, twice as high as those in those social democratic countries because those countries put jobs first. Canada, in its economic policy development, has never put jobs first. We have constantly, both Liberal and Conservative governments at the federal level, attacked inflation by creating unemployment, attacked interest rates by creating unemployment and attacked problems with the dollar by creating unemployment. That is not an acceptable policy to pursue.

We all know that the Canadian Catholic bishops have said that not only is that not an acceptable policy, but it is an immoral policy, that this government's policies are immoral, not just wrong but immoral. Nobody should be able to do that sort of thing to Canadians and their families.

Who wants this deal? Do the 4.2 million Canadians who are out of work or on social assistance? Do the Canadians struggling to maintain their families on inadequate incomes as they see their real income decline over the last decade? Do Canadians who are struggling to maintain their homes and pay their mortgages want this free trade deal with Mexico? Of course they do not. The only people who want this free trade are the Conservative Party, some Liberal provincial governments and also the supporters of that party, the big business community. They want it so that they can take advantage of the opportunities for themselves without having to care about what is good for Canadians or for Canada. It is in the self-interest of the large corporations, but it is not in Canada's interest and it should not be pursued for that very reason.

In closing I would just like to draw a contrast with the common market in Europe which is much more about planned development and strategies than this government is pursuing with the United States and Mexico. It is also much more about raising standards of regions and countries that are less well off than others. That would be a much better approach to take than this one of throwing the whole economic decisions making open to the big business community.

We cannot, in all consciousness, support a deal which does not protect the environment and protect health care standards for workers in Mexico.

Mr. Jerry Pickard (Essex – Kent): Madam Speaker, as I look around the House I do not see many people who are very happy with the legislation that we are dealing with tonight.

Many amendments to NAFTA have been brought forward. Our party feels that there are many things about this agreement which are totally unacceptable. Certainly there are things about the agreement that must be changed before any consideration is given to expanding our trade.

As Liberals, we are a party that has always looked upon trade as something that is very beneficial to this country. We realize that our country's greatness has grown because we are a great trading nation. It was a Liberal government that brought in the North American auto pact, which brought prosperity in manufacturing year after year after year, that brought hundreds of thousands of jobs and a great job surplus to this nation. Trading dollars throughout the world made Canada prosperous and always has.

However, since the day that the free trade agreement was brought in with the United States and the auto pact was changed, we found a real loss in jobs. We found a dragging down of our economy. We found that Canadians were suddenly going from a very prosperous nation to a position where we were seeking jobs, where we were concerned about the recession, we were concerned that our brothers, our neighbours, our cousins were all out of work. We are in very difficult straits. I have to think that the government opposite must have concerns about this because what did it do before the debate started? It forced time allocation on this debate.

In other words, it said: 'We are going to push this through as hard and as rapidly as possible so that the Canadian public does not hear all of the concerns we have with the 4,000 pages of this NAFTA proposal'.

We feel that those proposals should be debated very thoroughly, very fully, so that all possible avenues of improvement are put forward. The government, on the other hand, has set its own agenda. That agenda, unfortunately, is very politically partisan. We have an upcoming election and there is reason to believe that the Conservatives are trying to get the NAFTA off the floor of the House of Commons and passed as quickly as possible so that it is not the election issue that it should be, so that it is not debated fully and Canadian people do not see the negatives that are coming forward. They are almost trying to throw a blanket or table cloth over the whole issue, push it through as rapidly as possible and leave the Canadian people in the dark.

I believe that is a very poor practice. It is not an acceptable practice in modern societies. However, that is what is being done today.

Why are we dealing with closure on the NAFTA agreement when the other two nations involved are not even finished negotiating the complete deal at this point? Why are we being pushed so hard at this point to talk on the issue? Why are my colleagues here tonight only being given 10 minutes to stand up and deal with the issue?

It comes down to jobs. It comes down to labour problems.

[...]

It is very unfortunate when we look at the policies that are coming in we are going to have to deal with job losses by the thousands. We are talking about people in Canada that are going to be replaced in the job market.

Madam Speaker, I am glad they are having their side debate. Not only are they showing a lack of respect in this House but they are showing a lack of respect for anyone trying to speak as well. I find that rather appalling by three people who just walked into the House. I find it appalling that they are trying to stop people from saying what in fact is happening.

Pay scales in the United States can be as low as $2, $3, $4 an hour and pay scales in Mexico $1 an hour. I know that many Canadian jobs are going to be put up in comparison. All I have to do is look at below what a corporate entity will do.

If you or I are managing a large corporation our job is to look at profits. If I can hire people for $3, $5, $7 an hour less in Mexico than they would work in Canada, I am certainly going to do what is going to make my corporation the most profits.

We see that occurring time after time. Corporations are paying Mexican workers very low wages. They are pumping their waste products into the Gulf of Mexico and the Pacific Ocean. As a result the environmental concerns are not being looked after. The Maquiladora corridor is something that has been a bone of contention with environmentalists for years. However nothing has been done on the big business side to clean that up.

We are putting workers at very low wages against Canadian workers. We are putting the environmental standards of Mexico against Canadian standards. Corporations are going to start putting Canadian jobs in Mexico and in other areas. NAFTA certainly is leading in that direction.

We are going to end up with a major problem. I am very pleased that my colleague put forward this motion. What will happen to these workers who are being displaced? My colleague has suggested that when this many workers lose their jobs they must be given an opportunity for retraining. They must be given an opportunity to seek other types of skills so that they can become part of our labour force again.

In my own area of Windsor and Essex county we have lost over 5,000 manufacturing jobs since NAFTA was signed. I perceive that we are going to lose many more manufacturing jobs because of this government's policies and direction.

The government is not putting forward funds or providing retraining opportunities for those people who are out of work. I am talking about 5,000 jobs in Essex county but I could well be talking about 300,000 jobs in Ontario. I could well be talking about the potential for as many as a million people to be replaced, their potential to be shifted from one area to another. We are talking about very large numbers of people who will certainly be in a position to seek other kinds of training or employment without those positions being placed.

I also could refer to the agrifood industry which has been very hard hit. The benefactors of the free trade agreement were supposed to be many people in agriculture. Certainly those people have lost hundreds of jobs. The largest employer in my riding, Heinz Corporation, has lost hundreds of jobs since the implementation of this agreement. Other small producers have just been totally wiped out.

We saw plants in our area close one a day for many days. That went on for months. Now we are sitting in one of the highest unemployment areas in the country where before it was very prosperous. I am afraid that this North American free trade agreement is going to bring further devastation to my area.

'NAFTA Debate: Gore vs. Perot', on Larry King Show, CNN, 9 November 1993.

NAFTA Debate: Gore vs. Perot

ANNOUNCER: Welcome to a special edition of Larry King Live. The North American Free Trade Agreement. A deal to knock down trade barriers between Mexico, Canada, and the United States. Good or bad for Americans? Tonight, Vice President Al Gore meets Ross Perot, as Larry King and CNN present The NAFTA Debate. Now, from Washington, Larry King.

LARRY KING, Host: Good evening. We need to tell you off the top about some ground rules that have been agreed to by the vice president, Mr. Perot, and CNN. We have no studio audience here. Neither the vice president nor Mr. Perot have any staffers in the studio, nor may they talk with any assistants during the telecast. No representative of either side are in the control room while we are on the air. Our guests may use notes, visual aids if they wish. We have no debate clock. This is no formal statement-and-rebuttal format. There's no time limit on questions or answers. The program will go 90 minutes.

To be fair about deciding who got to sit where, we tossed a coin earlier today. The vice president won, and chose the inside seat. Viewer calls will be screened and chosen by the producer of this program, who will make every effort to assure balance. The call-in number in the United States is (202) 408–1666. Overseas, (202) 408–4821. We'll give you those numbers again later. We'll start with the vice president. We're going to swing back and forth, and then include your phone calls.

When President Bush signed this in San Antonio, he was on our show, and then a few nights later I was with you and then-president-then-governor, now President-Elect, Clinton, asked about this, NAFTA, and the president said, to the best of my memory, 'Well, I'm basically for it. I want to see the side agreements and I want to hear what the unions object to, and then I'll come back and sort of let you know.' But it was not a definitive yes. What changed?

Vice President AL GORE: Well, we negotiated two side agreements that protect labor and protect the environment. And, not until the two side agreements were completed did we agree to support NAFTA. Now, this is a good deal for our country, Larry, and let me explain why.

KING: But, you were hedging earlier?

Vice Pres. GORE: Well, we said from the very beginning that we wanted to improve the basic arrangement, which we did with the side agreements. And the reason why this is so important can be illustrated by the story of a good friend of mine that I grew up with, named Gordon Thompson, who lives in Elmwood, Tennessee, with his wife Sue and his son Randy. He makes tires for a living. He's a member of the United Rubber Workers, and he's for this because he's taken the time to look at how it affects his job and his family. We make the best tires in the world, but we have a hard time selling them in Mexico because they have a 20 percent tax, collected at the border, on all of the tires that we try to sell. Now, when they make tires and sell them into the United States, the tax at the border is zero. So it's a one-way street. NAFTA changes that. It makes it even-Steven.

KING: So he'll make more tires.

Vice Pres. GORE: Well, his job will be more secure, they'll make more tires, they'll be able to sell more tires. His son will have a better chance of going into that line of work, if that's what he should decide he wants to do, and, remember this – I mean, people think, 'Well, they don't buy tires.' Mexico bought 750,000 new cars last year. The Big Three sold them only 1,000, because they have the same barriers against our cars. Those barriers will be eliminated by NAFTA. We'll sell 60,000, not 1,000, in the first year after NAFTA. Every one of those cars has four new tires and one spare. We'll create more jobs with NAFTA.

KING: Weren't you a free-trader always, Ross?

ROSS PEROT: I am a free-trader now.

KING: Do you favor some sort of NAFTA?

Mr. PEROT: Absolutely.

KING: Then what's your rub?

Mr. PEROT: The problem is this is not good for the people of either country.

KING: Either country.

Mr. PEROT: You have my – yes. I think the important thing for everybody watching this show tonight to remember, this is not an athletic contest. This is not a question of who wins, whether I win or the vice president wins. This is a question of do the people of the United States and the people of Mexico win? Now, that's the important issue, and I'm sure we're in agreement on that.

My concern is very simple. I look at many years experience in maquiladora programs, and –

KING: These are the –

Mr. PEROT:– here is what I see. This – we have a lot of experience in Mexico. I've been accused of looking in the rear-view mirror. That's right. I'm looking back at reality, and here is what I see after many years. Mexican workers' life, standard of living and pay, has gone down, not up. After many years of having U.S. companies in Mexico, this is the way Mexican workers live all around big new U.S. plants. Now, just think if you owned a big U.S. company and you went down to see your new plant, and you found slums all around it, your first reaction would be, 'Why did you build a plant in the middle of slums?' And your plant manager would say, 'Oh, there were no slums here when we built the plant.' And you say, 'Well, why are they here now?' They said, 'This is where the workers work.'

KING: Your agreement would have been a different NAFTA, right?

Vice Pres. GORE: And I would suggest –

Mr. PEROT: This would be a NAFTA that gives the people – now, what are the rules here? Do I answer his questions or yours?

KING: Well, mine, or both. This is freewheeling now.

Mr. PEROT: OK, but, the point being, this is – there it is. Here it is on a more personal basis. Livestock in this country, and animals, have a better life than good, decent, hardworking Mexicans working for major U.S. companies. And here's one just to look at.

KING: Now, all this –

Mr. PEROT: Now, here's a good, decent man working his heart out, making his cardboard shack. And the cardboard came from boxes that were used to ship the goods down there.

Vice Pres. GORE: Can I say something about this picture?

Mr. PEROT: This – I didn't interrupt you.

KING: OK, now, guys.

Mr. PEROT: Now, maybe it just –

KING: Is this – now, your concept would have been what, Ross? If this was a bad deal, what would you –

Mr. PEROT: All I'm saying is if after 10 active years – this has been in effect since the '60s, but let's say 10 active years, you would think the standard of living of the Mexican worker would begin to come up. Instead, it continues to go down, by design. Thirty-six families own over half the country –

KING: So, you're –

Mr. PEROT: Eighty-five million people work for them in poverty, U.S. companies, because it is so difficult to do business in this country, they can't wait to get out of this country and go somewhere else, and, if possible, get labor that costs one-seventh of what it costs the United States.

Vice Pres. GORE: How would you change it? How would you change it?

Mr. PEROT: Very simply. I would go back and study – first, we look at this. It doesn't work.

Vice Pres. GORE: Well, what specific changes would you make in it?

Mr. PEROT: I can't – unless you let me finish, I can't answer your question. Now, you asked me and I'm trying to tell you.

Vice Pres. GORE: Right. Well, you brought your charts tonight, so I want to know what specific changes you would like to make in the treaty.

KING: That's a fair question. If you're against it – let him respond, OK?

Mr. PEROT: How can I answer if you keep interrupting me?

KING: All right.

Vice Pres. GORE: Go ahead. Go ahead.

Mr. PEROT: OK. Now, first, study the things that work. The European Community has had a similar experience. They got to Spain, Portugal, countries like that, where the wages were different, people didn't have rights, so on and so forth, and they made them come up the economic scale. In 1904, Theodore Roosevelt wrote a beautiful simple statement. And, basically, he said something very similar to what Congressman Gephardt recently said. He said, 'Under no circumstances can we lower the standard of living of the working American.' Therefore, any trade agreement we enter into must require a social tariff, I would say, that makes it an even playing field, then gives Mexico an incentive to raise the standard of living with those people, which it does not have now.

Vice Pres. GORE: OK, can I respond now?

Mr. PEROT: They have lowered the standard of living for those people.

KING: OK.

Vice Pres. GORE: OK. Now, so, your basic response is you would change it by raising tariffs –

Mr. PEROT: Now, I just started, but you interrupted.

Vice Pres. GORE: – on Mexico –

Mr. PEROT: That's the first thing I would do.

KING: Well, let's do it one by one.

Vice Pres. GORE: All right.

Mr. PEROT: It's the first thing I would do.

Vice Pres. GORE: OK, now, I've heard Mr. Perot say in the past, as the carpenter says, 'Measure twice and cut once.' We've measured twice on this. We have had a test of our theory, and we've had a test of his theory. Over the last five years, Mexico's tariffs have begun to come down because they've made a unilateral decision to bring them down some, and, as a result, there has been a surge of exports from the United States into Mexico, creating an additional 400,000 jobs, and we can create hundreds of thousands more if we continue this trend. We know this works. If it doesn't work, you know, we give six months' notice and we're out of it. But, we've also had a test of his theory.

KING: When?

Vice Pres. GORE: In 1930, when the proposal by Mr. Smoot and Mr. Hawley was to raise tariffs across the board to protect our workers. And, I brought some pictures too. You brought some pictures?

KING: [crosstalk] – of protectionist?

Vice Pres. GORE: This is a picture of Mr. Smoot and Mr. Hawley. They look like pretty good fellas. They sounded reasonable at the time. A lot of people believed them. The Congress passed the Smoot-Hawley Protection Bill. He wants to raise tariffs on Mexico. They raised tariffs, and it was one of the principal causes – many economists say the principal cause – of the Great Depression in this country and around the world. Now, I framed this so you can put it on your wall if you want to.

Mr. PEROT: Thank you. Thank you. Thank you.

KING: Would raising tariffs produce another –

Mr. PEROT: You're talking two totally different unrelated situations. Now, you do need to measure twice and cut once, but, then, if you have a program that is failing, you should not institutionalize it. See, the Mexican program has failed. It's failed the people of Mexico, it's failed the people of the United States. These numbers they give of exports from the United States are not realistic numbers. For example, they count in the government figures automobile parts going into Mexico to be put into cars made by U.S. car companies in Mexico and shipped back to the United States to be sold as if Mexican consumers bought those parts. But it didn't happen.

Then, if you take a – let's just say you have a piece of glass crystal, that you spend $100 making it in this country. You're going to send it to Mexico to have $10 of additional work done to it. They count it as a $100 export, and then they count it as a hundred – you come into Mexico from the U.S., then they count it as $110 import back in the United States. Now, then, when you look at how they count, the real export figures to Mexican consumers are tiny. The used factory equipment coming from U.S. factories going into Mexico, new factories going to Mexico –

KING: Are not bought?

Mr. PEROT: No. No, no. It's a – Zenith moves equipment from the U.S. into Mexico. That's used equipment. Then we count that as if Mexican consumers bought it. Nobody bought anything. Old equipment just came to Mexico.

Vice Pres. GORE: Let me respond to that if I can because, unfortunately, there's a grain of truth to that, but it's so tiny that it's – I mean, it's not a half-truth, it doesn't quite rise to that level. There are a few things in that category, but the vast majority, 80 to 90 percent, are exports that stay in Mexico and are bought there. Here's what's happened to our trade surplus, and these figures are net figures. It takes into account everything that he's talking about in that small category.

In 1987, before Mexico started lowering its taxes at the border, its tariffs, we had a $5.7 billion trade deficit with Mexico. After five years, the goods we make and sell into Mexico, the volume has been growing twice as fast as the goods they make and sell in the United States. So, last year we had a $5.4

billion trade surplus. Now, if that trend continued for another two years, and NAFTA will, by removing those barriers, greatly accelerate it, we will have a larger trade surplus with Mexico than with any country in the entire world.

KING: Why are trade unions so opposed to it then?

Vice Pres. GORE: Well, some of them –

KING: I mean, it's your friend who makes the tire, and he's a union member, he's going to benefit from this. Why are the unions aligned with Ross Perot? Why do we have this alignment of Ross Perot, unions, Jesse Jackson, Pat Buchanan, and Ralph Nader?

Vice Pres. GORE: Because some of them make the same mistake that, with all due respect, Mr. Perot makes. They confuse the bad trade deals in the past with this one, which is the first time we've been able to get one that's even-Steven with zero on – zero taxes on both sides. You know, I told you about my friend Gordon Thompson. The international president of his union opposes NAFTA. Gordon Thompson has taken the time to look at the facts, and he supports NAFTA. Let me tell you who else has taken the time. Every living former president of the United States, in both parties. The two-termers and the one-termers. Every former secretary of state, every former secretary of defense, secretary of treasury. Every living Nobel Prize winner in economics, conservatives, liberals, every one in between. They'd never agreed on anything –

KING: Well, that fact –

Vice Pres. GORE: Wait, let me just finish this one point. And distinguished Americans from Colin Powell to Tip O'Neil to Rush Limbaugh, Ross Perot, Jr., the head of his business, Mort Meyerson, Orville Swindle, the head of United We Stand, the last time, and Ross Perot, Sr., supported it until he started running for president and attempting to bring out the politics of fear.

KING: Ross?

Mr. PEROT: Will I be able to speak –

KING: You sure may.

Mr. PEROT: – for a second or two? From time to time?

KING: You may, you – you're on.

Mr. PEROT: Because there's a lot of inaccuracies here. Let's go to the Big Picture and skip the personal stuff. People who don't make anything can't buy anything. Let's start with that. We are 85 percent of the market. Canada is 11 percent of the buying power.

KING: Of the total of the three markets.

Mr. PEROT: And Mexico is only 4 percent. People who don't make anything cannot buy anything. Never forget that. Now, then, let's look at these exports. See, here's Mexico, 4 percent; Canada, 11 percent; the United States, 85 percent. We're the biggest buyer of goods and services in the world. Please remember that tonight, that's one of our aces. Now, then, here's the real export story. You get down here, these are the phony exports down here. Here are the real exports here, about $7.7 billion. You take this thing into pieces. You take this big number here and take it right down to here, and that's what you're really talking about. And, just remember this. If you want to trade, you trade with people who make money. You don't trade with people who oppress their workers and they don't have any money.

Now, it's true – let's – Now, a good deal will sell itself, folks, just plain talk. Four former presidents came out for it and couldn't sell it. All the secretaries of state came out for it and couldn't sell it. We had satellite going across 200 auditoriums across the country. That didn't sell it. Got Lee Iacocca for it. That didn't sell it. Thirty million dollars coming out of Mexico, and that is rotten and that is wrong, and that didn't sell it. Thirty, thirty-five million dollars coming out of corporate America to try to get out of this country, go south of the border and hire that cheap labor, and that didn't sell it.

KING: Let me know when you –

Mr. PEROT: This dog just didn't hunt. Now, today they don't have the votes in the House of Representatives. We're in the third quarter. They can get them because they're buying them big-time with your tax money. We're working the halls night and day to make sure it doesn't happen. You can play a key role in it. But, sure, they all tried to sell it to you, and the fact that they couldn't demonstrates that this deal is not good for our country.

KING: All right, let me get a break and then – but, it doesn't impress you that every former president supports this?

Mr. PEROT: It impresses me that they couldn't do it.

Vic. Pres. GORE:– But it's not over with, yet.

LARRY KING, Anchor:– [unintelligible] that they support it?

Mr. PEROT: That they showed – those are the guys that cut the worst trade deal in history. He's already talked about it.

Vice. Pres. GORE: It's not – it's not over.

Mr. PEROT:– Wait just a minute, now! They did the Japanese deals, they did the Chinese deals –

KING:– We'll have the vice –

Mr. PEROT:– that cost you two million jobs.

Vice. Pres. GORE:– Do you think they fooled Colin Powell? Do you think they fooled Colin Powell?

Mr. PEROT: He's a great soldier, doesn't know anything about business.

KING: We'll have the vice president respond –

Vice. Pres. GORE:– Do you think they fooled Lee Iacocca?

Mr. PEROT: They must have.

KING:– with Vice President Gore Ross Perot after this.

[Commercial break]

LARRY KING, Host: We're back on Larry King Live. We'll be going to your phone calls in about 15 minutes. And we're going to cover as much of this as possible. We're going to be getting to jobs and other aspects of it. But I want the vice president to respond to Mr. Perot, who's made some charges here that this is being bought.

Vice. Pres. GORE: Well, all of the – there's been more money spent against the NAFTA than for it, for sure. You can just look at the commercials. Every dollar that has been spent lobbying for it has been publicly disclosed. That is not true of the other side, and I would like to suggest to Mr. Perot –

KING:– You say they're hiding the –

Vice. Pres. GORE: Well, I think it would be a good idea, seriously, if you would publicly disclose the finances of your organization lobbying against it. They have not released the money spent, the contributors, where it's coming from, how much of it Mr. Perot's, where the rest of it is coming from.

But there was another statement I wanted to respond to, also. And that is that Mexico doesn't buy a lot of products, that they're too poor to buy a lot of products. There's a big misunderstanding in the minds of some people about that. They are buying a lot of products. In fact, they're our second largest customer for manufacturing goods. They will be one of the largest customers overall if the trends continue. They already are. Seventy percent of everything that they buy from a foreign country comes from the United States because we're so close to them and because they prefer our products.

KING: And this treaty would increase jobs here? –

Vice Pres. GORE:– Oh, no question about it –

KING:– Because there was an announcement today that it would be minimal either way.

Vice. Pres. GORE: There have been 23 studies of the impact of NAFTA on jobs in the United States.

Twenty-two of them have shown that it will cause an increase in jobs in the United States. The one that didn't showed that there would be a decline in illegal immigration, and they counted all of the illegal immigrants as holding jobs. And when they were taken out of the picture, they said that was a decline. Everybody else says it increases jobs in the United States.

KING: On those points, Ross –

Mr. PEROT: OK. Government studies are kind of like weather forecasters before balloons, even, and certainly before radar.

KING: You don't trust them.

Mr. PEROT: Let me give you three. Let me give you three. Now we're back down to common sense. Number one – you remember in the tax and budget summit when they said, 'Watch my lips, no new taxes'? Then they gave you a big tax increase and they told you if you would pay it they would balance the budget, pay off the debt, and we'd live happily ever after. See? Now then, the new president had to raise taxes again because that one didn't work. And you picked up the difference.

Now, let's go to Medicare. When Medicare was first conceived in 1965 –

Vice. Pres. GORE:– Are we talking about NAFTA, or –

Mr. PEROT: I'm talking about government forecasts.

Vice. Pres. GORE: Well, can we talk about NAFTA?

Mr. PEROT: Excuse me, Larry, I don't interrupt. May I finish?

KING: No, but he brought up a specific point –

Mr. PEROT:– Could I finish?

KING:– Yeah, but of course.

Mr PEROT: I'm saying all government forecasts – how come the facts are –

Vice. Pres. GORE:– Well, I don't want to sit here and listen to you just take shots at President Clinton on other subjects.

Mr. PEROT: Well, excuse me, I haven't taken a shot at it. He wasn't here in 1965. I'm saying –

Vice. Pres. GORE: Well, no, but you talked about –

Mr. PEROT: No, the, the –

Vice. Pres. GORE:– We tried to reverse trickle-down economics, and we're proud that we did.

Mr. PEROT: The, the tax and budget summit occurred before he became president.

Vice. Pres. GORE: Yeah, you went on from that, though. Why don't we talk about NAFTA?

Mr. PEROT: Excuse me. All I said was he had to raise taxes again. That's hardly a cheap shot.

Vice. Pres. GORE: Well, on the wealthy, on the wealthy.

Mr. PEROT: Oh, my goodness!

KING: Back to the point.

Mr. PEROT: That's the campaign promise.

KING: Let's try to stay on point. He says –

Mr. PEROT: I agree, I agree –

KING: He says – are you spending more money than the other side?

Mr. PEROT: Larry, I would really like to finish. I don't interrupt him, and if I could finish –

KING: OK.

Mr. PEROT: Let me give these two examples. We've talked about the inability to forecast the debt – right? – and the fact that we have to keep paying more taxes. Then when Medicare came along in 1965, they said it would cost us $9 billion in 1990. It cost us $109 billion. Then, when Medicaid came along, they said it would cost $1 billion in 1990. It cost $76 billion in 1990.

KING: Meaning that you don't trust any government forecast?

Mr. PEROT: I'm saying they basically come out with phony numbers. He's talking about exports –

KING:– You're saying –

Vice. Pres. GORE:– Can I respond?

KING: Hold it. You're saying the forecasts on NAFTA are phony?

Mr. PEROT: Yes. Then, let's take the next one. We say that we're spending more money against NAFTA than they're spending for it? That is not even close to truth. It is a matter of record how much record how much Mexico has spent. It is a matter of record how much USA/NAFTA has spent. You take –

Vice. Pres. GORE:– Why isn't it a matter of record –

Mr. PEROT:– I, I–

Vice. Pres. GORE:– how much you all spent. Can that be a matter of public record? Can you release those numbers?

Mr. PEROT: I really would appreciate being able to speak.

KING: All right, go ahead, it was a question he raised before –

Mr. PEROT:– I really would –

Vice. Pres. GORE: It's a fair question, isn't it?

Mr. PEROT: Excuse me –

Vice. Pres. GORE: I raised it earlier.

Mr. PEROT: It was my understanding tonight we'd have a format where you would ask the questions.

KING: OK.

Mr. PEROT: I would be able – I am not able to finish.

KING: But if he makes a statement – I'm just trying to balance so that he answers yours –

Mr. PEROT: Well, excuse me, I would like – I would like to finish a sentence, just once before the program's over.

Now, we are not able to buy time. If you are anti-NAFTA, you cannot buy time on the networks. We have had to go buy local station time. We cannot buy network time because the networks won't sell it. That's the covers on how much you're spending. We didn't run 10-page supplements in the New York Times, et cetera, et cetera.

Vice. Pres. GORE: OK, now, I'd like to respond to that, OK?

KING: Let him finish, he's got one more thing.

Vice. Pres. GORE: All right, go ahead. I do want to respond.

KING: For the benefit of both of you, our time is equal, you both have spoken equally tonight in time. We're keeping time in the control room so that we're fair.

Mr. PEROT: All right. And on the manufacturing goods, second largest manufacturing goods- second largest manufacturing goods, they send all this phony turn-around stuff and count it as though we sold it to Mexican citizens. Now, people who don't make any money can't buy anything. When you look at the Mexican worker, and you go to the Miami Herald, and you look at the man who works for Zenith in Mexico, and you compare him to his counterpart who works for Zenith in the United States, this poor man makes $8.50 a day. You know what his dream is? To someday have an outhouse. You know what his big dream is? To some day have running water. You know why these people are desperate for running water. Because Mexico ignores their pollution and environmental laws –

KING:– But this all is without NAFTA.

Vice. Pres. GORE: Yeah, that's all happening now –

Mr. PEROT:– Excuse me, excuse me, but this is the prelude to NAFTA. They have strong environmental laws that they don't enforce – now, just one second –

Vice. Pres. GORE:– Let me respond to that –

KING:– Let him respond to that, and then we'll have –

Vice. Pres. GORE:– OK. First of all, you will notice, and the audience will notice, that he does not want to publicly release how much money he's spending, how much money he's received from other sources to campaign against NAFTA. I would like to see those public releases that other side has made.

Now, let me come to the point – he talked about accuracy of forecasts and numbers. I watched on this program, right here at this desk, when the war against Iraq was about to take place, and you told Larry King, 'This is a terrible mistake because it will lead to the death of 40,000 American troops.' You said you had talked to the person who had 'ordered the caskets.' You were wrong about that. You said on 'Larry King' just before the election that after Election Day, there would be 100 banks that would fail, costing the taxpayers $100 billion. You were wrong about that.

Now, the politics of negativism and fear only go so far.

KING:– All right –

Vice. Pres. GORE:– You started out as –

KING:– take a break, and I'll have Ross respond. We'll come back on 'Larry King Live' –

Mr. PEROT:– That has nothing to do with – but we'll have to fool with it, and I'll be happy to.

KING: OK, we'll come right back on 'Larry King Live.' We've got a lot to go, your calls, too. Don't go away.

[commercial break]

KING [in progress] – President finish his statement and Mr. Perot respond, and then we'll get to some specifics and your phone calls.

Vice Pres. GORE: Well, you're getting to the key issue there because Bill Clinton and I were elected to do something about what's happening to working men and women to this country.

KING: Correct.

Vice Pres. GORE: They've been losing their jobs. There has been unfair competition from foreign countries that don't let our products in even though we buy their products. This will help to stop that. Some people want to stay with the status quo, just keep things the way they are. We want to open up these barriers. And let me give you a specific example. Valmont Electric Company in Danville, Illinois, less than a year ago was trying to sell products into Mexico. They've got a 13 percent tax at the border. We have zero tax coming the other way. They closed down in Danville, 400 jobs lost. They opened up in Mexico with 100 jobs down there, and now they ship their products duty free back into the United States through the Alliance Airport, which is the free trade zone that Mr. Perot's company has set up for – it's kind of a private free trade zone outside of Dallas –

KING: You're saying Mr. Perot –

Vice Pres. GORE: And they take Valmont Electric's products and distribute them through the United States duty free. Now, if we passed NAFTA, that 13 percent tax that they have at their border would be gone, and companies like Valmont could stay here in the United States, sell their products in Mexico, and not have to go down there to get over the barrier.

KING: Are you saying that Mr. Perot is personally benefiting by attacking NAFTA?

Vice Pres. GORE: I think he has set it up so that he will benefit financially either way. But if NAFTA passes – I mean, if NAFTA is defeated, this family business that has a free trade zone outside of Dallas will continue to distribute products coming from Mexico into the rest of the United States. What is the deal with Alliance?

Mr. PEROT: I think what the – I'll explain it, but we see here tonight is why our country is four trillion dollars in debt, going a billion dollars in debt every working day. Nobody everybody focuses on the real problems. Now, I'm going to try to say this as simply as I can. Alliance Airport is in Fort Worth, Texas, not in Mexico. Alliance Airport is owned by the city of Fort Worth, not my son. Do you shake head on that?

Vice Pres. GORE: No, the –

Mr. PEROT: Alliance Airport, check the FAA, is owned by the city of Fort Worth.

Vice Pres. GORE: You don't have ownership of Alliance Carter Incorporated.

Mr. PEROT: The airport. Now, I'm going to – please.

KING: Let him finish.

Mr. PEROT: Let's have an unnatural event and try not to interrupt me. Now, my son owns land adjoining the airport. Now, the purpose of that land is to build factories and warehouses to be – so that industrial goods can be moved by rail and by air. Just – now, watch my lips. The jobs will be created in Texas. Texas is in the United States. The workers will be United States citizens. They will be paid U.S. wages. It is a job creator in the United States of America. And all of this other silly putty throw up – for example, the free trade zone concept goes back to the 1930s. It is nothing new about the free trade zone concept. You have to apply to the U.S. government to get it, and if it didn't make sense I guess they wouldn't have given it to him. But it is not aimed at doing business with Mexico.

Vice Pres. GORE: You're not involved in it?

Mr. PEROT: Mexico will be a tiny little pipe of this whole operation. Okay, if – I am putting my country's interest far ahead of my business interest.

KING: You would do wetter with NAFTA?

Mr. PEROT: I would – no. When I'm in a room with corporate America, the first thing they say is, 'Perot, why don't you keep your mouth shut. You could with your resources make more money than anybody else.' Here is the NAFTA game. Buy U.S. manufacturing companies cheap right after NAFTA passes that are labor intensive that make good products that have marginal profits, close the factories in the U.S., move the factories to Mexico, take advantage of the cheap labor, run your profits through the roof, sell the company stock at a profit, go get another one.

Vice Pres. GORE: That's what they do now. That's what they're doing right now.

KING: Are they doing that now?

Vice Pres. GORE: And they're using Alliance Carter Incorporated in part to do it.

Mr. PEROT: Oh, come on, come on. You're talking about something like a trickle of water coming over Niagara Falls as opposed to the gusher. You know it.

Vice Pres. GORE: Now, you say it's your son's business but isn't –

Mr. PEROT: Now, do you guys never do anything but propaganda?

Vice Pres. GORE: Isn't your business also –

Mr. PEROT: Would you even know the truth if you saw it?

Vice Pres. GORE: Oh, yes –

Mr. PEROT: I don't believe you would. We've been up here too long.

Vice Pres. GORE: Let me ask you a question.

Mr. PEROT: Please let me finish. This is not Crossfire, is it, Larry?

KING: No.

Mr. PEROT: May I finish?

Vice Pres. GORE: And then I'd like to ask a question.

Mr. PEROT: All right, I have tried to explain with countless interruptions that this creates jobs in the United States. I am extremely proud of what my son is doing. I want to answer the question that he jumped in to ask. I own a minority interest in the airport. This – everything I'm doing makes it next to impossible for my family to ever do anything south of the border, and I could care less, okay?

KING: You do no business in Mexico or going to?

Mr. PEROT: I have no – look, I will put my country's interest in front of making money.

Vice Pres. GORE: Let me know when I can respond.

Mr. PEROT: And I don't ever want to make money at the expense of other people. Now, I got interrupted a minute ago when you shifted it back –

KING: One other thing could finish with.

Vice Pres. GORE: No, I'd like to respond on this.

KING: The financing of the anti-NAFTA campaign, it had not been answered and he asked it.

Mr. PEROT: Okay, fine, I'll answer it. See, again, he throws up propaganda. He throws up gorilla dust that makes no sense.

KING: What is it then?

Mr. PEROT: May I finish?

KING: Yeah.

Mr. PEROT: Okay. Most of the television time I bought during the campaign. That is a matter of public record. I have had two television shows since the campaign in the spring. They cost about $400,000 a piece. Those were network shows. Then we just did a NAFTA show, but we have to buy the time locally. I don't have the figures yet on what that cost me or I'd be glad to tell you.

KING: You're spending –

Mr. PEROT: I had to buy – no, I buy the television time because I don't want to take the members money for that. They understand that, they approve of that.

Vice Pres. GORE: Can I – it's not all his money, and we don't know because they do not –

Mr. PEROT: No, but television time – I just told you.

Vice Pres. GORE: Well, but – see, they do not release the records, but I accept your response because you have said that now –

Mr. PEROT: If it makes you feel better to see the checks and the bills from the network –

Vice Pres. GORE: It's okay for you interrupt but not me?

KING: Okay, all right –

Vice Pres. GORE: Now, hold on. You just said that you would –

KING: Let's go back to jobs.

Vice Pres. GORE: You just said that you would release the records, and I appreciate that. Now, this –

Mr. PEROT: It has nothing to do with what's going to happen to our country.

Vice Pres. GORE: Well, we need to know who's trying to influence it.

Mr. PEROT: I am paying for it, it's that simple.

KING: We got the answer.

Vice Pres. GORE: Now, on this – this Alliance business is connected to the jobs issue.

KING: Why is it important?

Vice Pres. GORE: Well, because right now we've got these barriers that we cannot surmount to sell into Mexico. We have been trying for years to get an even relationship so that their tariffs, their barriers, their taxes at the border will be eliminated. A lot of companies now have an incentive to leave the United States and locate down there. We heard about auto parts. Right now there is 13 percent tax at the border collected by Mexico on U.S. auto parts.

KING: All right, all right –

Vice Pres. GORE: Wait a minute, let me finish. This is important, Larry. And there is less than one half of one percent tariff the other way. That big growing market down there, in a few years they're going to buying a million cars a year. In order to sell into that market, these companies now have an incentive to pull up stakes and move down there. This business, which is not just his son's business, and there's nothing dishonorable about it at all. But here is the brochure for it, and here is the prospectus. And here are the two principle – what look like the principle investors there, Mr. Perot and the American eagle. And in the prospectus it says – okay, see it there. And in the prospectus it says that this is an ideal national distribution center for products coming out of Mexico. Plus, they have – he has lobbied the taxpayers to spend more than 200 million dollars in taxpayer funds in this project –

Mr. PEROT: Who is he?

Vice Pres. GORE: That takes you and your business.

Mr. PEROT: No, I'm not lobbying anybody.

Vice Pres. GORE: There's nothing illegal about it.

Mr. PEROT: I haven't done it. I don't – I haven't lobbied anybody.

Vice Pres. GORE: You've never hired a lobbyist?

Mr. PEROT: I – in my life? You mean on the airport?

Vice Pres. GORE: Both.

KING: No, on the airport.

Vice Pres. GORE: On the airport.

Mr. PEROT: I don't hire lobbyists. This is my son's project. I went to the airshow and haven't been out there – oh, probably been 18 months since I've been out there.

KING: What's the relevance?

Vice Pres. GORE: Well, the relevance is that if the free trade – if NAFTA is defeated then –

KING: What?

Vice Pres. GORE: Then this free trade zone that he has is still in business. If it's good enough for him, why isn't it good enough for the rest of the country?

KING: Do you say he's doing this for personal profit?

Vice Pres. GORE: I said before that I think he is in a position to benefit either way. And he was in favor of NAFTA, again, made speeches in favor of it, wrote in favor of it in your book before you started running for president. You started getting a response from people –

KING: Let's ask this then, what turned you against it if you were in favor of it?

Mr. PEROT: Well, conceptually I am for free trade. I am, if we ever get back to the subject, for a good agreement with Mexico. I am deeply concerned about the 85 million people who live in poverty and don't have any rights. I am deeply concerned about workers who when they go on strike U.S. companies call in goons, bring in the state police, shoot several workers, kill one, injure dozens, put the workers back to work and cut wages 45 percent. Those are things that are wrong. We can do this right. I am not in favor of a one political party country. The PRI runs the country. President Salinas will pick his successor. President Salinas went to the 36 families who own over 54 percent of the gross domestic product and asked them for 25 million dollars a piece. Fortunately for their families one of them leaked it to the New York Times and they didn't have to pay. That's Mexico. He will pick his successor not the Mexican people. Read the State Department's annual report on human rights; a journalist being killed, people in the opposing political parties being put in prison and killed and tortured.

This is not a free society, and yet for some reason the same people who are willing to put our troops at risk around the world to make sure people are protected, once we get to Mexico, ignore all of that.

KING: Are you not anyone that supports a fascist kind of state?

Mr. PEROT: I'm saying this is not – I'm concerned any agreement we do should give the Mexican people a decent life and over a period of time should give them some purchasing power. If I'm going to do business with somebody – let's just say if the U.S. is going to do business with another country, let's do business with a country whose people can buy things. Let's go –

KING: You don't think President Salinas is a progressive.

Mr. PEROT: President Salinas is almost out of office. I'm worried to death about who follows him.

Vice Pres. GORE: Can I respond on that?

Mr. PEROT: When you treat people the way they treat people, it's a matter of time until they loose power. And they've had it for a lot of years, and they keep it by force. But whether it's labor and management or countries and people, you oppress people long enough and you got to change, and that will happen.

Vice Pres. GORE: Let me respond to this because some of what he is saying here is true. Mexico is not yet a full democracy. They do not yet have full protection for human rights. They do not yet have the kind of living standard and labor standards and environmental protection standards that we would like them to see, but they've been making tremendous progress. And the progress has been associated with this new relationship to the United States. The decisions in Mexico will ultimately be made by the people in Mexico. The question is whether or not we will have the ability to influence what they and their government decide. The best way to eliminate our influence down there is to defeat NAFTA. The best way to preserve it is to enter into this bargain, continue the lowering of the barriers. We've got a commitment that they're going to raise their minimum wage with productivity. We've got an agreement for the first time in history to use trade sanctions to compel the enforcement of their environmental standards. As they begin to develop and locate better jobs farther south, we cut down on illegal immigration. Now, one of the reasons why all of the living former presidents and the other folks that I mentioned are supporting this is because this is the kind of choice that comes along only once every 40 or 50 years. This is a major choice for our country of historic proportions. Sometimes we do something right; the creation of NATO, the Louisiana Purchase, Thomas Jefferson did the right thing there, the purchase of Alaska. These were all extremely controversial choices, but they made a difference for our country. This is such a choice – if we make – if we should happen to give into the politics of fear and make the wrong choice, the consequences would be catastrophic. If we make the right choice, we have a chance to encourage Mexico to continue on the path they have been travelling.

KING: Ross is not saying he wants the status quo. He wants a different treaty, am I correct?

Vice Pres. GORE: He wants to raise tariffs on Mexico.

Mr. PEROT: Just a second. Let's look at reality –

KING:– And then we'll take our first call. Go ahead.

Mr. PEROT: Let's look at reality instead of theory. There's a major U.S. chemical plant in Mexico that digs holes in the ground, dumps the chemical waste in those holes, bulldozes over those holes, and contaminates the water supply for the people in that area. A disproportionate number of the babies born in the shantytown around that plant are born without a brain. Now, I don't care if you're poor or rich. If your baby is born without a brain because a U.S. company is willing to take advantage of workers to that extent, that's wrong. Now, if there's any question about it, the xylene, the chemical xylene, in the water content in a ditch coming out of that plant is 53,000 times the amount permitted in the United States. This outfit, big Democratic group-backing the Democratic Party – here's the videotape that shows them digging the holes, putting the chemicals in the ground. It shows one child whose foot is horribly burned from chemicals, and it shows the classic worker abuse –

Vice Pres. GORE:– Can I respond? Can I respond?

Mr. PEROT: I pass it on to Vice President Gore –

Vice. Pres. GORE:– Yeah, thank you –

Mr. PEROT: Because I know he cares, and I'm not – I'm not trying to play doctor with you.

Vice Pres. GORE: I agree with you on this, I agree with you on this.

Mr. PEROT: I know you care deeply about these things.

Vice Pres. GORE: Yeah, can I answer?

Mr. PEROT: I know you're a good man, but the laws are on the books, they're not enforced.

Vice Pres. GORE: Yeah –

KING: NAFTA would what? Change them? Not change them?

Mr. PEROT: Well, they have this little side agreement, but the facts are Mexico is so sensitive about its sovereignty they're not about to let us go down there and get into the middle of their – the Rio Grande River, all right folks, the Rio Grande River is the most polluted river in the Western Hemisphere –

Vice Pres. GORE: Wait a minute. Can I respond to this first?

KING: Yeah, let him respond –

Mr. PEROT: The Tijuana River is the most – they've had to close it –

KING: But all of this is without NAFTA, right?

Vice Pres. GORE: Yeah, and let me respond to this, if I could, would you –

Mr. PEROT:– Larry, Larry, this is after years of U.S. companies going to Mexico, living free –

KING:– But they could do that without NAFTA.

Mr. PEROT: But we can stop that without NAFTA and we can stop that with a good NAFTA.

Vice Pres. GORE: How do you stop that without NAFTA?

Mr. PEROT: Just make – just cut that out. Pass a few simple laws on this, make it very, very clear

Vice Pres. GORE: Pass a few simple laws on Mexico?

Mr. PEROT: No.

Vice Pres. GORE: How do you stop it without NAFTA?

Mr. PEROT: Give me your whole mind.

Vice Pres. GORE: Yeah, I'm listening. I haven't heard the answer, but go ahead.

Mr. PEROT: That's because you haven't quit talking.

Vice Pres. GORE: Well, I'm listening. How do you stop it without NAFTA?

Mr. PEROT: OK, are you going to listen? Work on it. Now, very simple – just tell every company south of the border if they operate that way they cannot ship their goods into the U.S. at any price period, and they will become choir boys overnight. See, Mexico is a country that can't buy anything. Japan, everybody else in the world is going to flood into Mexico if NAFTA is passed so that they can get cheap labor –

KING: OK, I gotta get a break in and –

Vice Pres. GORE:– When we come back I want to respond to this.

KING: The vice president will respond and then we'll go to your phone calls on Larry King Live. We'll be right back.

[Commercial break]

Vice Pres. GORE: [off-mike] Are you going to give me a chance to respond to this?

KING: OK – [on-mike] OK, if we keep responding and responding, we're never going to get some calls, but I'll have the vice president respond on the Stefan Chemical, and then quickly to calls. Quick.

Vice Pres. GORE: Oh, thank you. Well, if we defeat NAFTA, we'll lose all leverage over the enforcement of Mexico's environmental laws.

KING: Ross says we just pass a law to –

Vice Pres. GORE: That wouldn't effect Mexican companies or the investments from other countries. But the problem has been not so much their laws, but the enforcement of their laws. We can probably agree on that. This side agreement that we negotiated gives us the ability to use trade sanctions to compel the enforcement of their environmental laws.

KING: Let me get some calls in –

Vice Pres. GORE:– A major step forward –

KING:– and by the way, I must tell our audience that we're keeping kind of score, so we're fair. We always try to be fair, and each party has had equal time right to this minute in talking. We go to Washington, D.C., as we being phone calls. Hello?

WASHINGTON, D.C., CALLER: Hello. My question is for Mr. Perot.

KING: Yes.

WASHINGTON, D.C., CALLER: How can the United States expect to compete on a long-term basis in an increasingly interdependent economic world, while Europe and the Pac Rim nations unite through their own respective trade alignments?

Mr. PEROT: Very simple – we've got the most productive workforce in the world. We're the biggest buyer of goods and services in the world. We're the market everybody wants to sell to. Our problem is we do the world's dumbest trade agreements. You go back to the agreements we've done all over the world, you'd be amazed that adults did them. We're about to do another one, but the American people have stopped it and it's dead in the House of Representatives. It's time we draw a line in the sand, and we've done it.

Now, here's the key – you want to buy and sell with people who have money. You want to trade with partners who have money, but then if you make a one-sided deal with Japan, they get all the benefits, we get all the problems. Then, you come to Mexico. It's an emerging nation. You want to help it. You put in this tariff that as they raise the standard of living of their people, the tariff goes away. If anybody wants to do things like destroy people's life by dumping chemicals and all that and polluting the Rio Grande River and destroying the Tijuana River and the beaches in San Diego – and the life in San Diego pretty soon – you just say you can't ship your good to the U.S.

KING:– Ross, his question was –

Mr. PEROT:– You can help Mexico and do it –

KING:– Ross –

Mr. PEROT:– No – You can't compete – go put your primary effort with people who have money to spend. Then, because we want to help emerging nations, help nations like Mexico. But you're primary effort has to be – and believe me, you say, does everybody want to do business with us? More than anything else in the world, because we buy a lot.

KING: Please try to limit answers, so we can get our calls in.

Vice. Pres. GORE: I'd like to respond to that quickly. Could I?

KING: Yeah.

Vice. Pres. GORE: Let me give you a quick example. Mattel just announced that if NAFTA is passed, it will move a plastics factory from Asia to Mexico. Instead of getting the plastic from China, it will get the plastic from the United States. With NAFTA, we will enlarge what is already the largest consumer market in the world with the addition of a country that buys 70 percent of all of its foreign products from the United States of America. It will position us to compete effectively with the rest of the world. That's why a lot of these other countries are a little nervous about it.

One of the trade officials in Japan described this as 'sneaky protectionism' and raised a lot of questions about it. It will benefit us in our trading relationship with Asia and Europe, and we're right now in the middle of the negotiations with the GATT – that's the larger world trade agreement. If we pass NAFTA, we will be able to use the leverage to drop the barriers against our products in other countries.

KING: Fairview Heights, Ill., hello?

ILLINOIS CALLER: Hello, Larry. Vice President Gore, I understand the United States will spend $7 billion to clean up the pollution left by multinational companies in Mexico, much of it polluting our rivers. I would like to know why we're going to spend that money, and couldn't be better spent here at home?

Vice. Pres. GORE: Well, Mexico will join in, so will the Inter-American Bank, and so will the polluters who have caused the problem. And we should clean up that pollution that Mr. Perot was talking about so eloquently earlier whether we have NAFTA or not. With NAFTA, we will have the cooperation of Mexico and other countries in this hemisphere in doing that.

KING: Aren't you –

Mr. PEROT:– May I cut in briefly?

KING: Yeah, sorry.

Mr. PEROT: It will cost us several billion dollars in tariff losses. It will cost us at least $15 billion and probably more to build infrastructure. And we will have a $20–40 billion bill on pollution alone. Now, guess who's going to pay that? All you hard-working taxpayers that still have jobs, go look in the mirror and ask yourselves why the government's policies have caused four out of five of you to have to lower your standard of living. Ask yourselves why your government sent two million jobs to Asia alone, manufacturing jobs, in the 1980s. [To Vice Pres. Gore] Now, you agree with that number?

Vice. Pres. GORE: All of that happened before NAFTA –

Mr. PEROT:– You agree with two million, or not?

Vice. Pres. GORE:– and before we took office.

Mr. PEROT:– That's not the point. Is it a good number?

Vice. Pres. GORE: Oh, we've lost a lot of jobs to lousy trade deals in the past because they weren't fair, they weren't fair.

Mr. PEROT: Well, we agree that we've made –

Vice. Pres. GORE:– Let me finish, now –

Mr. PEROT:– Excuse me, excuse me.

Vice. Pres. GORE: Thank you very much, I'll let you finish. I like that line. I appreciate that. The fact is that we have the opportunity with NAFTA to stop this kind of stuff. All of the problems that Mr. Perot talks about will be made worse if NAFTA is defeated. We have an opportunity to make all of them better if we pass NAFTA.

Listen, Larry – the whole world is poised, waiting for America's response to Mexico's decision to say 'yes.' We have knocked on their door for 20 years trying to get them to stop being protectionist –

KING:– Are you saying this embarrasses us if we –

Vice. Pres. GORE:– Well, of course it does, but it's far more important than just embarrassment. It diminishes our ability, it would diminish our ability to open other markets overseas. The GATT round would probably not be completed if NAFTA were defeated.

KING: All right, I've got an exact break here. We'll come right back, half hour to go. We'll take your phone calls. Don't go away.

[Commercial break]

LARRY KING, Anchor: We're back with the NAFTA debate on Larry King Live and back to your phone calls for Vice President Al Gore and Ross Perot. Nanimo, British Columbia. Hello.

CALLER: Hi. It's Nanimo. I'd like to know what Mr. Perot and Mr. Gore have both learned from the previous free trade agreement between Canada and the U.S.

KING: Both learned? Ross?

ROSS PEROT: Well, just by watchin' it. First thing, thousands of people joined United We Stand America out of Canada. I couldn't figure out why so I checked – they were mad at NAFTA. Then I watched the election – the Conservative Party had 155 seats and the prime minister. There's a message here for both political parties in the United States. After the dust cleared, they had two seats in parliament, no prime minister. The reason –

KING: NAFTA?

Mr. PEROT: Reason – NAFTA. Why? Huge numbers of manufacturing jobs left Canada, came into the United States because of a 15 percent wage differential. We pay our workers less than Canada. Now, when you've got a seven-to-one wage differential between the United States and Mexico, you will hear the giant sucking sound –

Al GORE, Vice President of the United States: Now, wait –

Mr. PEROT:– there's a political lesson, there's a business lesson –

KING:– a quick – I'm going to ask you to limit the answers so we can move on.

Vice Pres. GORE: But this is an important question and it's important to realize that only one of the parties in that election campaigned against the basic NAFTA treaty – that was the socialists. They lost seats. They only got nine seats out of 258 and now the person who won has been talking with the – President Clinton. This has been a good deal for both Canada and the United States. Both have gained jobs; both have gained trade flows; both have become more competitive in the world marketplace as a result.

Mr. PEROT: And there is a tooth fairy and there is an Easter Bunny.

KING: Bethesda, Maryland. Hello.

CALLER: Good evening, Larry. I'd like to ask the vice president specifically to answer, in terms of a time limit, how long – how many years? Five, eight, 10 years will it be before we see these new jobs in America that are supposed to be out there?

KING: Job swing, how long?

Vice Pres. GORE: Well, we're already seeing a great many new jobs. We have seen 400,000 new jobs just in the last five years because of Mexico's unilateral decision to lower the barriers to U.S. products. We'll see 200,000 jobs, it is estimated, over the next several years –

KING: But there'll be a dip first, right?

Vice Pres. GORE:– in the wake of NAFTA. No, no, no. We think – absolutely not.

KING: Unions are wrong?

Vice Pres. GORE: Oh yes, I think they're wrong.

KING: The trade unions are wrong about fearing a dip?

Vice Pres. GORE: Absolutely. Now, there is always, in our economy, a churning of the economy –

KING: Five hundred thousand jobs –

Vice Pres. GORE:– with or without NAFTA, that is the case, but the net change is positive with NAFTA. Now, there are all kinds of estimates – virtually all of them show job gains, as I've said before. Some of them show very large job gains, but the importance of NAFTA goes beyond that because again, it gives us the ability to open up markets in the rest of the world because other countries – let me give you a specific example to illustrate this. Computers in the United States will –

KING: A business he knows –

Vice Pres. GORE:– we sell into Mexico – they have a 20 percent tariff on our computers. After NAFTA, they will have a zero percent tariff on our computers, but the 20 percent will still apply to Asia and to Europe, so with the transportation advantage and a 20 percent price advantage, who are they going to buy their computers from? They're going to buy lots of them from us. Now, that gives us an advantage and when you sell more products, you make more products. When you make more products, you hire more people.

Mr. PEROT: Quickly. If you believe that, I've got a lot of stuff in the attic I can sell you. Second, if this is all true, why is corporate America downsizing? If this is all true, why do we have the largest number of college graduates this year unable to find jobs since at any time in the '40s? If this is all true, why is that everywhere I go in a hotel, I've got a college graduate comin' up to the room, bringin' food, carrying bags, so on and so forth, waiting till they get their job? If this is all true, why isn't our economy booming? You see, it just doesn't fit, folks. Just go –

Vice Pres. GORE:– I'd like to answer –

KING: OK.

Mr. PEROT:– look at reality.

Vice Pres. GORE: I'd like to answer the question if I could.

KING: OK.

Mr. PEROT: We –

Vice Pres. GORE:– no, because, see while we have a $5.6 billion trade surplus with Mexico, we have a $49 billion deficit with Japan, a $19 billion deficit with China, a $9 billion deficit with Taiwan – those are trade problems. Mexico is a trade opportunity. If we use the opportunity to pry open the markets in the rest of the world, we'll change this. All of the problems that he talks about? That's what we want to change. We don't accept the status quo. We want to fight for working men and women and NAFTA is part of it.

KING: Zagreb, Croatia, hello.

CALLER: Good evening. My question is this. Mr. Perot, since you obviously have many, many criticisms about the NAFTA agreement, can you give us specific answers as to an alternative to it? If you don't like it, tell us what, really, we should be doing?

KING: Can you over – view a treaty you would sign?

Mr. PEROT: Yes, I will do it again. First, we've got to have a clear understanding with Mexico that we can only do business with a country that gives its people a decent standard of living and respects human rights. Because we are all humans – every human life is precious.

KING:– and that would be the first part of it?

Mr. PEROT:– every human life is precious. If you don't treat your workers fairly and if you don't treat your people fairly, history teaches us that that produces stress that will take may be a century to cure. It's in Mexico's interest to do that.

Then, their workers will come up the economic scale; we'll put in a social tariff that drops as they bring their workers' pay and benefits up. If we pass NAFTA and we pass health care and your competitor goes to Mexico, you will either have to go to Mexico or go out of business. I can give you a whole list of things like that.

KING: You would have a tariff that swings?

Mr. PEROT: The way we're set now. No, it's a social tariff – as they bring their people up, we drop the tariff. When it's head-to-head competition and their people have equal pay and benefits as ours –

KING: What's wrong with that?

Mr. PEROT:– there is no tariff and we've brains and wits and off we go. That's good for Mexico and it protects our people.

KING: Why is that bad?

Vice Pres. GORE: Well, it – it kind of goes back to the Smoot – Hawley idea –

Mr. PEROT:– oh, come on –

Vice Pres. GORE:– seriously, for this reason – for this reason. The idea that we can isolate ourselves from the rest of the world and only do business with 'perfect' countries that do everything the way we want them to do is pretty unrealistic. His proposal, as I understand it, is to raise tariffs and call it a social tariff and use that to keep products out from any country that doesn't meet our standards in all things.

Mr. PEROT:– I said Mexico –

Vice Pres. GORE:– now, let me finish, please. Now, you take –

Mr. PEROT:– tiny little market –

Vice Pres. GORE:– that kind of approach to Mexico and you defeat NAFTA, you've lost the partnership we've been building with Mexico for a generation and more. But beyond that, here's the central point. We have to realize that we, unilaterally, cannot change the entire world. We can't force every country in the world that we want to trade with to meet our standards in everything that we would like to see them meet.

Now, the fundamental – the guts of this whole thing is the reason why some people listen to what he's saying is that they think if a country has wages lower than we have, then it's fundamentally unfair to trade with them even when it's totally even in all other respects. If that were the case – if low wages were the determinant of where you locate businesses, then Haiti would be an economic powerhouse; Bangladesh would be a powerhouse. We have problems – trade problems – with countries that have wages higher than we have, like Germany and they have fewer barriers than we do and higher wages because, Larry, the secret is, productivity – our working men and women are the most productive of any nation on the face of the Earth. You give us the opportunity to sell our products unimpeded, without these trade barriers and – that we've been having to deal with, into these other countries – we'll knock the socks off the workers of any other country in this world.

KING: Why doesn't that make sense to you?

Mr. PEROT: Well, it wouldn't make sense to most people over six years old.

KING: Why?

Mr. PEROT: If I have to explain it to the audience, they'd probably – I don't think I will. Bangladesh and Haiti? They all got that. Well, I won't waste your time on that one. You understand that that –

Vice Pres. GORE: No, but they have the lowest wages.

Mr. PEROT: That's not the point. Everybody out there understands why Bangladesh and Haiti are not like Mexico, so I won't waste my time. Secondly –

Vice Pres. GORE: – but tell me, I mean, humor me if you would and –

Mr. PEROT: – no, I won't. I don't think I can. Now, next thing. It's pretty simple stuff. We've been out-traded by everybody. All we've got to do is explain very nicely to Mexico that they out-traded us on this deal. We've got to make a fair deal with them. They'll huff and puff for a few days. They'll be back. We'll make a good deal. For a very simple reason. They need us. We don't need them. Now then, we go to Japan – send a horse trader over to Japan. Send somebody that knows how to negotiate and just explain to them that they was the most one-sided trade deals in the world. We've got to reopen 'em; we've got to make 'em fair and they'd say 'What do you mean?' I say 'We'll just take the same deal we gave you.' They would look at you like 'Good gracious sakes alive! You mean, you want the same deal we've had for years?' That's fair. Then you start to negotiate and say, well, a fall-back position – 'We'll just take the deals that ya'll made with Europe because they're a whole lot better than the ones you made with the U.S.'

You know what the problem is folks? It's foreign lobbyists – are wreckin' this whole thing. Right here, Time magazine just says it all – it says 'In spite of Clinton's protests, the influence-peddling machine in Washington is back in high gear.' The headline, Time magazine – 'A Lobbyist's Paradise.'

Vice Pres. GORE: I'd like to respond to that.

KING: OK.

Mr. PEROT: We are being sold out by foreign lobbyists. We've got 33 of them working on this in the biggest lobbying effort in the history of our country to ram NAFTA down your throat.

KING: Allright, let him respond.

Vice Pres. GORE: I'd like to respond.

Mr. PEROT: The good news is it ain't working.

KING: OK, Ross.

Mr. PEROT: I'll turn it over to the others.

Vice Pres. GORE: OK, thank you.

KING: And we've got another call.

Vice Pres. GORE: One of President Clinton's first acts in office was to put limits on the lobbyists and new ethics laws, and we're working for lobby law reform right now. But, you know, we had a little conversation about this earlier, but every dollar that's been spent for NAFTA has been publicly disclosed. We don't know yet –

KING: He says –

Vice Pres. GORE: Tomorrow – perhaps tomorrow we'll see, but the reason why, and I say this respectfully, because I served in the Congress and I don't know of any single individual who lobbied the Congress more than you did, or people in your behalf did, to get tax breaks for your companies. And it's legal.

Mr. PEROT: You're lying. You're lying now.

Vice Pres. GORE: You didn't lobby the Ways and Means Committee for tax breaks for yourself and your companies?

Mr. PEROT: What do you have in mind? What are you talking about?

Vice Pres. GORE: Well, it's been written about extensively and again, there's nothing illegal about it.

Mr. PEROT: Well that's not the point. I mean, what are you talking about?

Vice Pres. GORE: Lobbying the Congress. You know a lot about it.

Mr. PEROT: I mean, spell it out, spell it out.

Vice Pres. GORE: You didn't lobby the Ways and Means Committee. You didn't have people lobbying the Ways and Means Committee for tax breaks?

Mr. PEROT: What are you talking about?

Vice Pres. GORE: In the 1970's.

Mr. PEROT: Well, keep going.

Vice Pres. GORE: Well, did you or did you did you not? I mean, it's not –

Mr. PEROT: Well, you're so general I can't pin it down. I mean, 1970 – [crosstalk]

Vice Pres. GORE: I'm not charging anything illegal. It's this blunderbuss attack on all lobbyists.

[crosstalk]

Mr. PEROT: Wait just a minute. Wait just a minute. Let's talk about the lobbying reforms – that's the biggest sham in history. All you had to do was take a pledge. The pledge is like a pledge to quit drinking. We don't have lobbying reform under Clinton. We will get it, but we don't have it yet. And this stuff they've come up with is nothing, and if you look at who's running all these economic negotiations, it's a who's who of former foreign lobbyists now in the Clinton administration.

KING: McLean, Virginia, hello.

CALLER: Sir, this is for Mr. Perot.

KING: Yeah, go ahead.

CALLER: Sir, over the past five years, and I think you probably know this, the U.S. has nearly tripled its electronics exports to Mexico, worth about $6 billion. Now that's produced a lot of high-tech, good-paying jobs in America. Now if Congress does the right thing and passes NAFTA and removes the tariffs on these products, how can you believe that this wouldn't increase our exports, create more jobs, create more exports for America?

Mr. PEROT: Well I think you're seeing, counted in that figure, every piece of electronics that goes to Mexico, does a turn-around in an assembly plant, and comes back to the United States. I am certain you're seeing all the radios that go down and get put in cars that come back to United States. If we strip it down to the real electric products that the Mexican people buy that stay in Mexico, it would be a fraction of that sum.

Vice Pres. GORE: Did you see the Wal-Mart that opened in Mexico City on the news?

KING: Largest one in the –

Vice Pres. GORE: Largest one in the world, if I understand it. They have 72 cash registers ringing constantly with people in that – in Mexico taking American products out of that store. We have this image of them being so poor that they can't possibly buy any electronic equipment or anything else that we make. They are poorer than we are. But you know what? They spend more per person on American products than any other country except. [crosstalk] Let me finish, let me finish, because this is very important. Japan, if you take everything that Japan buys, only 2 percent of it comes from the United States. If you take everything that Mexico buys, it's 800 percent larger, and if you take what they buy from foreign countries, 70 percent of everything they buy from other countries come from us. They prefer American products. If we lower those trade barriers and get rid of them altogether, we will have an export surge into Mexico and we'll have a partnership with Mexico that will help us remove the trade barriers in the rest of the world.

KING: Fairfax, Virginia, hello. I should bring it down. Fairfax, Virginia, with Vice President Al Gore and Ross Perot, hello.

CALLER: Companies can come into Mexico by, you know, thousands and set up manufacturing of products using the cheap Mexican labor, and I think that that is the biggest threat to the loss of U.S. jobs. Is this correct?

Vice Pres. GORE: No, it's not correct, because American workers are more than five times more productive than their counterparts in Mexico because they have better tools, they have better training, they have a better infrastructure. There are lots and lots of companies that moved down to Mexico and decided that they would rather move back to the United States. I've got a whole long list of them. General Motors is one of them, that moved down while Mr.

Perot was on the board. He may have voted against that, but they have – I don't know, but they now moved, started moving jobs back from Mexico, back to the United States. Let me give you another example. Norm Cohen in Charlotte, North Carolina, is in the textile business. 15 years ago, he tried to sell his products in Mexico – he had the price, he had the quality, he couldn't sell. Why not? He went in and investigated. His Mexican counterparts got a little mail-out from the Mexican government every month with a listing of all the foreign companies, including American companies, that wanted to sell in competition into Mexico. They were given an opportunity to put an 'X' beside the name of any company they didn't want to compete with. He got some investors and opened up a company in Mexico. Now NAFTA not only eliminates the taxes at the border, it eliminates practices like that 'x marks the spot,' and if NAFTA passes, Norm Cohen has plans right now to shut that factory in Mexico down and move 150 jobs back to Charlotte, North Carolina.

KING: Want to respond?

Mr. PEROT: If I have to.

KING: Don't have to.

Mr. PEROT: First off, the whole textile thing is a joke. Talk to anybody in the textile business and they will tell you if their competitors go to Mexico, they will have to go to Mexico. They will also tell that the Mexicans have spent a fortune building textile plants and are building them now in Cuba, where labor is next to nothing. Next, the GM bringing back jobs into this country is a sham used in the union negotiation. Next, the Mexican – the U.S. worker is five times more productive than the Mexican worker – big joke of the century. The Mexican worker is a good worker, he is an industrious worker. He quickly gets up to 70 percent as productive, and after three to five years, is 90 percent as productive, and only makes $1/7$ as much. You cannot compete with that in the good ol' USA, particularly with our benefits, retirement, and so on and so forth. It's just that simple. It's a tilted deck.

KING: Mexico City, hello.

Vice Pres. GORE: It's not just that simple.

CALLER: Hi. The subject has come up about the possibility of Japanese taking over if NAFTA doesn't go through. I'm American; I've been living in Mexico City for many years. There are thousands of Japanese here. They are waiting. They are lurking. What are you people doing? Why [call cuts off]

Vice Pres. GORE: Let me answer that.

KING: What's the finish of it, ma'am? All right, I didn't hear the end of it.

Vice Pres. GORE: Yeah, she said what are you doing, why don't you wake up.

Mr. PEROT: Does he get to answer first every time?

KING: I think the question was for him

Vice Pres. GORE: You go ahead and answer.

Mr. PEROT: No, you go ahead.

Vice Pres. GORE: I'd like to answer it, but you go first.

Mr. PEROT: Let him go ahead, he can have it. I know – as I long as I get a brief follow up.

KING: Well, I think the question was for you.

Mr. PEROT: It will only take a minute to kill this snake, go ahead.

KING: Go ahead, kill it.

Vice Pres. GORE: You're talking about the question, not me, right?

Mr. PEROT: No, the question. Absolutely. Excuse me.

KING: Go ahead, it's for you.

Mr. PEROT: It's just this basic. There's a constant in the Clinton administration. Any time they get cornered, they go into what I call 'the sky is falling routine' – the presidency is at stake, the Japanese are coming.

KING: No, the question was – she says there are Japanese –

Mr. PEROT: – next thing we'll have is 'The British are coming.' You know, the ghosts are coming. Look, the Japanese cannot just wander into Mexico, do anything they want to do, dump across our border unless we're stupid enough to let them. Now, if our foreign lobbyists stay wired in the way they are now, we'll probably say 'Ooh, this is wonderful.' I can tell you about Japanese deals that have been cut through our foreign lobbyists. I can tell you a deal that's buried in this agreement that gives a $17 million benefit to Honda – it's buried. I can show it to you in print. It's there big time. I can show you a deal –

KING: Benefits a single company?

Mr. PEROT: – you bet. I can show you a deal on Tennessee whiskey that'll make you just wonder what the heck is going on. The sky is not falling, the Japanese are our friends –

Vice Pres. GORE: Well, let me respond –

Mr. PEROT: – they're not a threat.

KING: OK. All right.

Vice Pres. GORE: Let me respond. Both automobile manufacturers, including Honda in Marysville, Ohio, Nissan in Tennessee, Saturn in Tennessee, all of the companies in Detroit – they benefit because that Mexican tariff is brought down to zero. Every other American from Tennessee – whiskey benefits – every American business potentially benefits if they want to sell in Mexico –

Mr. PEROT: And they –

Vice Pres. GORE: Hold on, hold on, because I want to respond to her question. This is extremely important. President Salinas has a trade mission to Japan the month after the vote on NAFTA. If we don't take this deal, you can bet that Japan will try to take this deal. They'll be in there in a New York minute. Europe will try to get this deal. They are concerned about us taking this deal. Listen, we – Larry, we ought to thank our lucky stars that the Mexican people have had the vision and courage to strike out on the American path toward the ideas of Thomas Jefferson, toward democracy, toward free markets, and now they just want to know 'Can we take 'yes' for an answer?'

KING: In the interest of time, Ross, is there – are there things about this treaty you like?

Mr. PEROT: Oh, sure, but here's the Honda deal –

KING: – are there any – is there anything about it –

Mr. PEROT: Here it is, folks, as they say – it's in the book. There's the Honda deal. Here is the Tennessee whiskey deal.

KING: Al, is there anything about the deal you don't like?

Mr. PEROT:— now, stay with me one second. Here is the deal on Tennessee whiskey. Only in the state of Tennessee, authorized to produce only in the state of Tennessee —

Vice Pres. GORE: No —

Mr. PEROT:— this is foreign lobbying big-time. This is what's wrong with our country. This is what you and I will clear up through government reform.

KING: That's protection of a brand name. I mean, that's protection of a brand name. One of the things about this treaty is it protects intellectual property.

Mr. PEROT: Why just that brand name?

Vice Pres. GORE: Well, it's not just that brand name. If you'll look at the line above it, it says 'Bourbon Whiskey.' That doesn't have — that's not a brand name.

Mr. PEROT: Stay with me. Tennessee whiskey —

Vice Pres. GORE:— and Tennessee whiskey —

Mr. PEROT:— authorized to produce only in the state of Tennessee —

Vice Pres. GORE: No, but that refers to the other one. It recognizes — it deals with all bourbon —

KING: Bourbon is only from Kentucky, right?

Mr. PEROT:— caught in the middle of the act, folks. No place to run, no place to hide.

KING: I think Bourbon is only —

Vice Pres. GORE: It's two different brand names.

KING: Is there anything about —

Vice Pres. GORE: Excuse me. Just so you're clear about that. Those are brand names and one of the things we've been trying to get in our trade dealings with other countries is protection for what's called intellectual property. And it's a good thing, too, because Mexicans now prefer U.S. brand name products. That's why they're going in and out of that Walmart so fast.

KING: All right, there's a six-month out if it's turned down, right?

Vice Pres. GORE: Yeah, that –

KING:– let me, let me –

Vice Pres. GORE:– now, let's talk about that for a minute. If we don't – if I'm wrong and he's right, then you give six months notice and you're out of it.

KING: Ross, what's wrong with that?

Mr. PEROT: Now, here's the way we get out of it. If the House of Representatives lets this go through, the whole House of Representatives is running in 1994 and a third of the Senate, we've got a little song we sign. 'We'll remember in November' when we step into that little booth. If we have to, we the people, the owners of this country, we'll clean this mess up in Washington in '94.

KING: Are you saying you will –

Mr. PEROT:– and. And. We'll make sure that we put the six-month tail on this thing in 1995 and if you think these guys will, you believe in the tooth fairy.

Vice Pres. GORE:– well –

KING: Ross, are you saying that you're going to work against congressmen who vote for it?

Mr. PEROT: I'm not – our people are really angry about this. Working people all across the United States are extremely angry. There is no way to stop 'em. They are not going to tolerate having their jobs continued to be shipped all over the world –

Vice Pres. GORE: I'd like to say something about that.

Mr. PEROT:– we've got to have a climate in this country where we can create jobs in the good old U.S.A. –

KING: OK – [blocked]

[crosstalk]

Mr. PEROT:– that is one thing that the president and vice president should do for us and they're not.

Vice Pres. GORE: Excuse me. I'd like to say something about that. Because that's a direct political threat against anybody who votes for this. This is a choice between the politics of fear and the politics of hope. It's a choice between the past and the future. It's a choice between pessimism and optimism. It's a choice between the status quo – leave things as they are – enact new tariffs on Mexico and I don't know who else, or move forward into the future with confidence. We're not scared. We're not a nation of quitters. We're not a nation that is afraid to compete in the world marketplace and when we face a choice as important as this one, it is extremely important that we make the right decision. This is a fork in the road. The whole world is watching.

KING: What's going to happen in eight days?

Mr. PEROT: I love the way these guys turn around on a dime. They've been out making speeches that everybody ought to get a depression check every time they get their eyes checked or their glasses checked and the president's made a stream of speeches telling us how insecure we are. Now, suddenly, they figure out that we are a strong, proud people and –

Vice Pres. GORE: We are –

Mr. PEROT:– and we are not going to let this trade agreement go through and create further damage to this great country. We – let me make sure I say this before we go off the air tonight. I'll give you one reason that will just stick – why we can't continue to do these agreements.

KING: Thirty seconds for each.

Mr. PEROT: If we keep shifting our manufacturing jobs across the border and around the world and deindustrializing our country, we will not be able to defend this great country and that is a risk we will never take.

Vice Pres. GORE: He started off as head of United We Stand. I'm afraid he's going to end up as head of Divided We Fall. Everything that he is worried about will get worse if NAFTA is defeated. We want jobs for America's working men and women. We want to get rid of the barriers that have prevented us from selling what we make in other countries. This is an historic opportunity to do that.

KING: Thank you both for this historic evening. The vote in Congress is eight days away. You'll be hearing lots more about it. Thanks to Ross Perot and Vice President Al Gore. For everyone here at Larry King Live and for the superb staff that put this all together, the best in the business. Thanks for joining us and good night.

'Canada Prepared if NAFTA Fails; Movement Afoot to Arrange Bilateral Deal with Mexico', *Globe and Mail* (Toronto), 13 November 1993.

The Mexican government and senior Canadian business leaders have held discussions in recent weeks over proceeding with a bilateral free-trade deal if the U.S. House of Representatives votes against NAFTA this Wednesday.

Senior members of the Chretien government, including International Trade Minister Roy MacLaren and Finance Minister Paul Martin, have been briefed about the idea and are said to be enthusiastic.

One well-placed source in Ottawa said: 'Right now, it would be irresponsible for anyone in the Canadian government to go running around saying what-if.' But little doubt is left that if NAFTA does go down in Washington, Ottawa will be quick off the mark to hammer out some arrangement with Mexico, and maybe even extend the deal to Chile.

Thomas d'Aquino, president of the Business Council on National Issues, and Ted Newall, president of Calgary-based Novacorp Chemicals Ltd., say that bilateralizing would be a bold foreign economic policy coup for the new Liberal government and potentially reap a bonanza for Canadian companies.

'This would let Canadian entrepreneurs win a head start in the Mexican market ahead of their U.S. competitors,' said Mr. Newall, who spent 40 minutes discussing the idea with Mexican President Carlos Salinas de Gortari last week in Mexico City.

'The President said it is a very interesting idea, but the first job is to make sure we get this through the U.S. Congress.'

The two businessmen argue that for Canada to jump into the breach where the United States fears to tread would send a powerful signal to Latin America and Asia that Canada is stepping out from under the American shadow with an aggressive, forward-looking trade posture.

They said the Liberal Party's policy platform articulates this type of trade diversification as a counterweight to dependence on the United States.

In a letter to Prime Minister Jean Chretien, dated Nov. 10, Mr. d'Aquino, on behalf of the business council, urged the new government to implement a bilateral free-trade deal with Mexico should Congress veto NAFTA.

'Such a move, we are convinced, would make a great deal of sense in the context of building Canadian-Mexico trade links.'

In an interview, Mr. d'Aquino said that by implementing NAFTA with Mexico, Canada would indirectly be doing the United States a favour by keeping the agreement alive until a future date when Washington might change its mind and sign on. 'All together, it's a made-in-heaven idea.'

Although the Mexicans are loath to say so publicly for fear of rocking the NAFTA boat in Washington, Mr. Salinas's government has signalled it would welcome a quick Canadian offer to go ahead if the United States were to pull out.

Congressional rejection of the deal would undoubtedly spark a fierce anti-U.S. backlash in Mexico and could cause significant political trouble for Mr. Salinas as he gets ready to hand over the reins of power to a successor next year.

'Canada could do very well if, on the day after Congress turned NAFTA down, a delegation of Roy MacLaren, Paul Martin and Andre Ouellet got off a plane and said: 'We're still interested in keeping this thing alive; let's talk,' 'one senior Mexican official said.

The thinking is, that by extending a hand of friendship to Mexico at a highly vulnerable time, and when the Mexican government has invested so much of its political capital in NAFTA, Canada would win enormous gratitude.

NAFTA would be tailored to eliminate provisions relevant to the United States.

One idea being floated is a possible decision by Mexico's state-owned oil company, Pemex, to move its big Houston procurement office to Calgary. The company expects to buy $1-billion worth of oil field equipment over the next several years – business Alberta's oil service suppliers would salivate over.

More prosaically, after getting used to thinking of itself as the fifth wheel in the U.S.-Mexico free-trade negotiations, Canada would suddenly find itself the only nation with free-trade access to both the U.S. market and Mexico. That means companies wishing to produce for the North American market could do so without paying tariffs only if they located in Canada.

Canadian trade officials said that, in a bilateral NAFTA, Canada's auto plants would benefit from a gradual lifting of Mexican car import restrictions, while the tight Mexican auto decree would continue to apply to cars made in the United States. For Detroit's Big Three or Japanese auto companies, this would make Canada something of an investment magnet.

But wary of being seen to be intruding in the U.S. Congressional debate over NAFTA, the Canadian government has not broached the idea directly with Mexico City.

As well, the two-week-old Liberal administration is still adjusting to the responsibilities of power and hasn't yet had an opportunity to devise a NAFTA fall-back position.

'It's a matter to be taken up on the 18th,' said another Mexican official, alluding to the Nov. 17 congressional ratification vote. 'No one wants to create any distraction from the current effort in Washington to persuade undecided congressmen.'

In any event, trade officials in Ottawa, Mexico City and Washington are, for now, still assuming that NAFTA will squeak through Congress.

'NAFTA Backers Must Speak Now', Crain's Detroit Business, 15 November 1993, p. 6.

Some blue-collar workers think their jobs will be saved by giving the North American Free Trade Agreement the ax. We hope they have long memories. Regardless of how the U.S. House votes on NAFTA on Wednesday, the exodus of low-skill, low-wage jobs abroad will continue. But the golden opportunity for the United States to position itself more securely in a world economy dominated by trading blocs will be lost. That's why we need to remember which members of Congress are caving in to the populist appeals of Ross Perot and organized labor.

A NAFTA defeat will hurt Michigan – especially its auto, office-furniture and agriculture industries. According to the U.S. Department of Commerce, Michigan has 254,000 jobs dependent on exports to Mexico and Canada -/the most of any state in the union. We're still a nuts- and-bolts state, and we can sell a heck of a lot of both to Mexico as its own industrialization grows. But not if our companies have to pay high tariffs.

The anti-NAFTA camp would have us believe that U.S. companies have no stake in their communities, that they're poised greedily at the southern border, waiting to leap across the moment the trade accord is signed. That simply isn't true. Mexican workers are not as productive as U.S. workers. And the transportation problems in that country do not make it an attractive investment site.

The vehemence of the anti-NAFTA faction is interesting. President Clinton and NAFTA supporters in Congress may hold some trump cards in what labor holds dear in the 1994 Congress: health care and a proposed minimum-wage increase, to name two.

Late last week, about 50 members of the House were undecided, more Democrats than Republicans. The Wall Street Journal ran a list of them on its editorial page last Thursday. The Michigan delegation, dominated by Democrats, is mostly on the record against NAFTA. By week's end, two Republicans from Michigan – Fred Upton of St. Joseph and Dave Camp of Midland, were undecided but leaning in favor of NAFTA.

So who ya gonna call? That's the question today. It's important for the business voice to be heard, from small and midsize businesses. Some Detroiters who have business ties in other states – vendors, plants or satellite offices – may want to review The Journal's list of undecided congresspeople from those states. You can reach congressional offices by calling (202) 224-3121.

'The National Interest: House Members Have Clear Obligation to Free Trade', *Houston Chronicle*, 16 November 1993, p.10.

There are times when members of the U.S. House are obligated to put the national interest ahead of all other interests which have a claim on their consideration. The vote Wednesday on the North American Free Trade Agreement is one of those times.

The overall national interest in approving the trade pact is clear and compelling. The objections to it are on the margins and in narrow interests. It is no accident that no serious-minded case has ever been made against NAFTA as wrong for the country on a fundamental basis.

There is no such case. In the almost 50 years since World War II, the United States, at times almost single-handedly, has pushed the world into an unparalleled period of prosperity through freer trade among nations. Despite ups and downs and alarms and excursions, Americans have persevered and the world – not least this country – has prospered from the engine of trade.

NAFTA is one of the great achievements of America's long march to free trade. So are the currently stalled – waiting on NAFTA – negotiations for the latest liberalization of the General Agreement on Tariffs and Trade, which governs how the world trades.

If NAFTA does not win congressional approval, the GATT round may well fail also – because America turned protectionist.

This newspaper would not like to have on its conscience what the House members who vote against NAFTA will have on theirs should it not win approval. The last such congressional vote against free trade – the Smoot-Hawley Act in 1930 – produced the Great Depression.

Intellectually, the members of the House know all this. But the politics of special- and narrow interests have become so pervasive that many members struggle with the feeling they cannot vote the greater national interest. It is not true. They can vote the national interest. The people expect them to.

Dennis Wharton, 'H'wood: Muy Bueno, eh? Valenti Sees Doors Opening as House Passes NAFTA Treaty', *Daily Variety*, 18 November 1993, p. 1

(Washington) – President Clinton's solid win on NAFTA in the House of Representatives Wednesday represents good news for a U.S. entertainment industry heavily dependent on open markets worldwide.

That's the claim of Jack Valenti, head of the Motion Picture Assn. of America, who said the North American Free Trade Agreement 'helps frame the future. In that future, trade barriers must come down (and) access to markets must be granted to all. Either we export or we shrink. There is no middle ground.'

Pundits had expected a close vote, but the 234–200 victory gave Clinton plenty of breathing room. Among Democrats, the vote was 102 for and 156 against; Republicans favored the measure by 132 to 43. The lone independent voted against the pact.

Specifically, the NAFTA agreement requires Mexico – with a long tradition of copyright piracy – to begin strictly protecting intellectual property. The result could be a boom in the sale of U.S. videos in Mexico.

NAFTA also carries lingo requiring greater protection from signal theft of U.S. satellite programming beamed into Mexico, a provision that should result in greater development of cable programmers such as HBO Ole and TNT Latin America.

Another clause in NAFTA allows Mexican cinema owners to reduce from 50% to 30% the percentage of films that are of Mexican origin.

In Canada, NAFTA's passage means little for the entertainment industry. Canada has had a 'cultural exemption' since 1987 under a prior agreement with the U.S. but has never used it.

Though the Senate must also put its stamp of approval on NAFTA before the accord becomes law, passage there is considered a certainty. A Senate vote could come as early as this weekend.

The MPAA also believes passage of NAFTA will set a precedent for greater copyright protection in all Latin American countries.

Hollywood support for NAFTA is linked hand-in-hand with MPAA's hope for successful completion of the General Agreement on Tariffs and Trade (GATT) in Europe. The feeling among MPAA member companies has been that GATT talks will collapse if NAFTA fails and that Hollywood would thus lose a golden chance to roll back TV program quotas and other restrictions on 'cultural' products from the U.S. embraced by European Community countries.

Eric Smith, general counsel of the International Intellectual Property Assn., a trade group that represents the film, recording and book publishing industries, said passage of NAFTA 'will significantly improve (President Clinton's) chance for securing a strong GATT agreement.'

Meanwhile European officials, particularly the French, continue in their pronouncements that they will not sign any world trade agreements that do not provide for some exemptions for cultural products and activities.

Many Europeans fear that free trade in cultural goods and an end to government subsidies would give the Americans a greater edge and accelerate the dominance of American culture on their continent. The more protectionist-minded among the Europeans are likely to view the passage of NAFTA as one more reason why their trade block – the European Community – should play hard ball against the Americans – and their newly formed trade block.

The administration also had stressed the impact of NAFTA's passage on the Asia Pacific Economic Cooperation forum, which began Wednesday in Seattle and includes delegations from 13 nations, plus Hong Kong and Taiwan. That summit also is expected to include discussion of American copyright issues.

'NAFTA All Clear in Mexico', *Record* (Kitchener-Waterloo, Canada), 23 November 1993, p. A5.

(Mexico City) – The North American free trade agreement cleared its last legislative hurdle when the Mexican Senate overwhelmingly voted its approval.

The trade pact, which will link the United States, Canada and Mexico in a $6.3 trillion free trade zone scheduled to go into effect on Jan. 1, 1994, won late Monday by a margin of 56–2 after nearly 12 hours of speeches.

The big victory was not unexpected since the governing Institutional Revolutionary party of President Carlos Salinas de Gortari holds 61 of 64 seats in the Senate.

Under Mexican law, a vote of the lower House of Deputies was not required to approve the treaty legislation.

NAFTA passed its toughest test last week when it was ratified by the U.S. House of Representatives following protracted lobbying by President Bill Clinton. It later easily passed the U.S. Senate.

The Canadian Parliament approved the pact in May, but Prime Minister Jean Chretien has said he wants some parts reworked before he will proclaim it.

Chretien wants better rules on what constitutes a subsidy and what sort of sanctions should be imposed for trade violations. He also wants the same protection for energy resources that Mexico won for its oil industry.

Trade officials from both sides are discussing clearer definitions of subsidies and dumping.

In Mexico City, Senate commerce committee chairman Carlos Sales Gutierrez, arguing for NAFTA, described the pact as an 'exceptional instrument' for Mexico's economy.

But, following the line of Salinas in recent statements, he advised his colleagues that 'the treaty will not do everything, not automatically or immediately.'

Senator Roberto Robles Garnica of the leftist Democratic Revolution party said his party opposed NAFTA because 'it has nothing to do with the needs and longings of the Mexican people.'

Senator Porfirio Munoz Ledo, also of the Democratic Revolution party, said the agreement favored Mexico's powerful neighbors to the north.

He said NAFTA was a 'colonial-type pact' that will 'turn our country over to the foreigners.'

Sales Gutierrez accused Munoz Ledo of making 'false statements.'

'The country you see and the country I see are very different, sir,' Sales Gutierrez said.

Many NAFTA opponents in Mexico worry that opening the borders will give the United States greater control of their economy, politics and culture.

They also say Mexico will be unable to control the flood of American and Canadian investors setting up shop south of the border because they will receive the same treatment as Mexican companies under NAFTA.

Free trade proponents say NAFTA will create jobs in Mexico and help raise the standard of living.

NAFTA will phase out most trade barriers in the next 15 years and could eventually include other countries in Latin America.

Jonathan Ferguson, 'NAFTA: Canada's Concerns; Liberals Demand Trade Rules that Put Everyone on Same Footing; Canada Wants Protection from U.S. Political Winds', *Toronto Star*, 30 November 1993, p. A13.

(Ottawa) – The rules are loaded in favor of the United States, says Prime Minister Jean Chretien, and he wants them back in balance.

Chretien has said he won't proclaim the North American Free Trade Agreement into law by Jan. 1 unless the deal has a method of resolving disputes and defining subsidies and dumping that are more equitable to Canada.

Parliament approved the trade deal during Brian Mulroney's final days in power but it is still up to the new government to proclaim it.

The NAFTA would create a North American free trade bloc of about 360 million people and about $7 trillion in combined economic output, bigger than the European Community.

The vast majority of that – $5.9 trillion in economic output – comes from the United States.

DISPUTES

Settling disputes was on Canada's list of demands when Trade Minister Roy MacLaren sat down yesterday with U.S. counterpart, Mickey Kantor, in Washington.

In both NAFTA and its predecessor, the Free Trade Agreement, the rules are loaded in favor of the big importing country (the United States) and against the small exporting country (Canada), high-ranking Liberals said.

The Americans not only have the might, but a system for launching trade actions that is more politicized and susceptible to domestic industry pressure than is Canada's.

Since the Canada-U.S. deal took effect Jan. 1, 1989, there has been an upswing of increasingly aggressive American unfair trade actions against Canada.

These punitive and U.S. actions have affected trade in key Canadian exports including softwood lumber, steel, magnesium and pork.

The problem is not with U.S. laws, intended to curb unfair imports into the American market, but with their 'arbitrary rules of application' and the effectiveness of the dispute settlement mechanism in overturning instances of unfair application, the Liberals said.

'These laws have become an increasingly aggressive instrument for unilateral unfair American trade actions that are invariably highly protectionist in nature,' one Liberal insider said.

'The Prime Minister believes only a more effective dispute process, one that arrives at decisions faster and leaves no room for foot-dragging if the American don't like the decisions, can curb this trend.'

He referred to the party's campaign Red Book, now the government's political bible, to underline Chretien's position. It states:

'The mechanism for resolving disputes under the FTA is often lengthy and costly, draining away resources from businesses that should be focusing on research and development, marketing and retooling.'

The Red Book slammed Brian Mulroney's Progressive Conservative government for giving up a chance to correct the flaw during the NAFTA negotiations.

What the Tories agreed to in the Canada-U.S.-Mexico pact, the Liberals said, may make it harder for Canada to resolving unfair trade disputes that arise from in the original deal.

The free trade deal established a unique system of panels, made up of appointed experts from both countries, to make binding decisions when cross-border disputes arise and negotiations fail.

The system established under the free trade deal remains largely intact in the new pact. But some trade analysts believe technical changes under the NAFTA make it more likely that the U.S. will challenge panel decisions.

For example, a new step allows a country to appeal a panel decision that goes against it.

That change alone, said Gordon Ritchie, deputy trade negotiator in the Canada-U.S. deal, provides the Americans with a new tool with which to harass Canadian exporters.

'It merely adds to the time, expense and uncertainty for Canadian companies hit by an unfair U.S. trade action,' said Ritchie, now an Ottawa-based trade consultant.

Liberal insiders acknowledge that negotiating a better method of settling trade disputes takes a back seat to improving the definitions of what constitutes subsidies and dumping.

Ambiguities about subsidies and dumping are blamed by the Liberals as the major reasons U.S. industries are able to launch harassing trade actions against Canadian exporters.

'Subsidies and dumping are the front-and-centre issues in these new talks.'

SUBSIDIES

Without agreement on what subsidies are, Chretien says, free trade partners are free to use their own definitions to trigger disputes – and the U.S. has, over softwood lumber, pork and other products since the original deal took effect on Jan. 1, 1989.

As things stand, if the U.S. government finds that Canada has subsidized exporters and that those subsidies have caused injury to U.S. producers, it can slap duties on the Canadian goods as a punishment.

Canada and the United States agreed to establish committees to improve definitions of subsidies within seven years. But those groups barely got off the ground. The North American pact says it's up to panels made up of experts from both countries who base their decisions on the laws of each country.

Pierre Pettigrew, an international trade expert with Samson Belair Deloitte & Touche, says a negotiated subsidies code would help 'level the playing field' between Canada and the U.S.

'Curbing Washington's arbitrary use of punitive trade laws in response to political pressure from U.S. industries unhappy with Canadian competitors would be a significant step forward,' Pettigrew says.

'A subsidies code gets at the root of the problem because it helps remove the leeway the Americans now enjoy to define trade-distorting subsidies the way they see fit, or interpreting the law in a manner that politically satisfies domestic industries.'

Nobody expects Ottawa and Washington to agree on a subsidies code before Jan. 1. Chretien is expected to settle for a firm undertaking from the U.S., with an iron-clad deadline, to remove the ambiguities.

The heart of Chretien's argument is that the U.S. system is so politicized that its definition of what constitutes a trade-distorting subsidy is subject to arbitrary changes.

The Liberals refer to the long-running dispute over Canadian softwood lumber exports as the classic illustration of how the U.S. system is stacked against Canada.

The U.S. initally said the provinces' low stumpage fees weren't a subsidy. But Canadian exports increased and Washington decided three years later they were. To avoid U.S. duties, Ottawa added its own 15 per cent export duty.

Now, Washington is claiming that British Columbia's ban on raw log exports constitutes a subsidy, even though three Northwest states have an identical ban.

DUMPING

Under its anti-dumping laws, the Americans are free to hammer a Canadian company for charging prices that merely compete with U.S. producers.

Canadian steel-producing giants like Stelco and Dofasco, for example, are struggling with continued U.S. charges of unfair pricing despite strong evidence to the contrary.

The tariffs Washington slapped on the Canadian steel producers under its anti-dumping laws have been dismissed by the industry, and Ottawa, as 'pure harassment.'

Dumping occurs when companies sell goods in foreign markets at prices lower than the domestic price or below their full cost. The domestic industry must prove it was injured by the foreign dumping before tariffs are levelled.

Like subsidies, Canada and the United States agreed under the 1989 free trade deal to improve definitions of what constitutes dumping within seven years but made no headway.

Under the North American pact, the two countries agreed to refer all disputes about dumping to a panel with members from both countries.

High-ranking Liberals say Chretien interprets that move as the two parties agreeing to drop their commitment to develop a set of rules and definitions.

Leaving it up to a panel, the Liberals say, means the process can be drawn out by the U.S., adding to the time, expense, and uncertainty for Canadian companies.

The way things now stand, the U.S. could simply rewrite its anti-dumping laws when it wants a panel to decide in its favor.

'The Prime Minister wants a firm commitment from Washington that a detailed and transparent anti-dumping code will be negotiated, and that its application when disputes arise will be dealt with quickly and without political interference,' a Liberal insider said.

Canada also has anti-dumping laws but even U.S. trade officials acknowledge Canada's system is less susceptible to domestic pressure and political interpretation of the laws.

'U.A.W. Wants Trade Payoff in Jobs', *New York Times*, 1 January 1994, p. 43.

(Detroit, 31 December 1993) – Looming over the Edsel Ford Freeway near the General Motors Corporation headquarters here, a billboard recently proclaimed one of the many benefits vaunted by supporters of the North American Free Trade Agreement: 15,000 new auto-related jobs in the United States in the first year.

The billboard is gone now, but the promise is far from forgotten by one group defeated in the free-trade battle: the United Automobile Workers union.

'We're going to be waiting and looking with bated breath for those 15,000 good-paying jobs,' said Owen F. Bieber, president of the U.A.W.

Union leaders were not impressed recently when the Ford Motor Company announced that it would shift production of some vehicles among its American, Canadian and Mexican plants as a result of the trade agreement, recalling 300 workers in Mexico and creating 550 new jobs north of the border.

All told, Ford said, the move could lead to 6,000 new auto-related jobs. But those jobs, Ford said, would be created in the United States and Canada. And some of them, Ford said, would not be new jobs, but 'job equivalents' – that is, overtime worked by already employed workers.

Such fuzziness, the U.A.W. claims, has overtaken other once-clear benchmarks set by the North American Free Trade Agreement's proponents before the agreement passed.

Before the passage, boosters including President Clinton asserted that in the first year of the agreement, the Big Three would export 60,000 cars to Mexico, compared with 7,700 currently. But recently, top executives of the Big Three – like their critics before the trade accord passed – have cast doubt on that number.

'The 60,000 number – I have to tell you, I have not ever discussed that number, nor do I know the origin of it,' Robert J. Eaton, the chairman of the Chrysler Corporation, told reporters.

'Well, they do know where it came from,' Mr. Bieber retorted, pointing out that the American Automobile Manufacturers Association, the Big Three's trade association, pushed the number. 'If it was false, then they had an obligation to say, wait a minute. We're for Nafta, but don't get us into a box where we're going to be expected to sell 60,000 cars.'

Now that the auto makers are in that box, Mr. Bieber clearly relishes keeping them there, insisting that they sell all 60,000 and create all 15,000 new jobs. 'By God, I'll tell you this, we're going to keep tabs of how many are sold there, and we're going to remind people of this,' he said.

Parts Supplier Movements

While he does not expect the auto makers to move assembly plants to Mexico overnight, Mr. Bieber said he thought they would begin pushing their parts suppliers to relocate there in pursuit of lower-cost labor.

In a recent interview at Solidarity House, the U.A.W.'s headquarters here, Mr. Bieber reflected both on his recent defeat on the trade agreement and on what most auto analysts regard as his recent victory over the Big Three in national labor contract negotiations. As he spoke about the future of labor and of his union – whose diverse but declining membership includes not only auto workers but state employees and jai alai players – he adopted a wait-and-see attitude toward Mr. Clinton, whose support he acknowledged he needs to fulfill a broad legislative agenda.

'I have great respect,' Mr. Bieber allowed with the faintest of grins, 'for his ability to get people to vote his way.'

Indeed, Mr. Bieber has not taken the big picture of him with Mr. Clinton off his office wall, despite the irony that the President's scribble has acquired since the trade agreement vote: 'with thanks for all your help.'

'We worked hard in 1992 to help elect Bill Clinton President of the United States,' Mr. Bieber said. 'I have no regrets.'

Fourth and Final Term at U.A.W.

At 65, Mr. Bieber, a hulking man and a tenacious bargainer, is serving his fourth and final term as U.A.W. president. He will retire in 1995, ending a career with the U.A.W. that began in 1949.

In contrast to the time Mr. Bieber started negotiating for auto workers, the legal deck is now stacked heavily against labor, he said, which he contends is one reason union membership is declining. The U.A.W.'s membership has dropped from 1.5 million in 1979 to about 850,000 today.

To restore labor's bargaining power, Mr. Bieber said, Mr. Clinton needs to finish making his appointments to the National Labor Relations Board. Mr. Bieber contends that the board tilted drastically toward management during the Reagan-Bush years.

Mr. Bieber also said the President should lobby for the so-called striker-replacement bill. That proposal, which Mr. Clinton has said he strongly supports, would make it illegal for companies to replace striking workers permanently, a practice that became much more common in the last decade. The bill was held up by a Republican filibuster in the Senate.

'The President can help himself tremendously among the trade-union movement by going out and actively campaigning for the right of the Senate to vote' on the bill, Mr. Bieber said. 'To say, 'permanently replace' – you might as well say you don't have the right under law to strike, when you have a situation with a shortage of jobs and a large unemployment pool.'

With the playing field leveled again, Mr. Bieber said, unions would begin to grow, which he argued is the best way to preserve the country's middle class.

'You can't just keep talking about good high-paying jobs,' he said.

But Mr. Bieber acknowledged that his union had suffered because of inroads overseas competitors had made in the auto industry, seizing about a quarter of the domestic market for new cars and trucks.

To help stem the flow of industrial jobs overseas, Mr. Bieber said, the U.A.W. will continue fighting for Mr. Clinton's health-care plan. While the union favors a single-payer approach, Mr. Bieber said, Mr. Clinton's plan, as presented, offers the best hope for restraining health-care costs for large employers, which will help keep their labor costs competitive.

THE WORLD TRADE ORGANIZATION, 1994

The failure of the United States to ratify the International Trade Organization (ITO) after the Second World War meant that for nearly fifty years the world's international trading system was operating under a temporary, allegedly impermanent, framework. It was not until 1995 that the creation of the World Trade Organization (WTO) marked a significant change from the 'provisional' General Agreement on Tariffs and Trade (GATT) arrangements that had been in existence since 1947. Not only did the WTO create an international institution to manage trade negotiations, it also provided the means for the development of international trade law. While still relying upon the support and cooperation of its members to function, the WTO codified many rules and procedures and created a Dispute Settlement Mechanism (DSM) that allowed for rapid decisions and gave the WTO the power to sanction retaliation against members found to be in breach of WTO rules.[1] This was a fundamental change from the GATT where countries which lost disputes could not only delay decisions, but could veto any sanctions against themselves, effectively stripping the GATT of any effective enforcement power.[2]

In the 1980s, a major breakthrough in international trade appeared unlikely. The international trade agenda appeared to have stalled. Europe had embarked upon the Single Market, but it was seen as a step towards the creation of a protectionist 'Fortress Europe', rather than as a supporter of freer international trade.[3] Protectionist sentiments were also on the rise in the United States Congress as competition from East Asia, especially Japan, threatened the profitability of venerable American textile, steel and automobile companies. The corresponding job losses undermined the American labour movement's support for free trade and weakened the Democratic Party's traditional position of support for an open international trading regime. A series of legislative acts in the United States strengthened the unilateral component of American trade policy and enabled the United States to sanction countries it deemed to be using 'unfair' trading practices. In a related vein, the Reagan and Bush administrations' negotiations with Canada and later Mexico signalled a break from the long-standing American commitment to multilateral institutions in favour of bilateral and regional negotiations.[4]

While these new actions proved popular with American business and labour, they heightened anxiety in Europe, Japan and the developing world that they would suffer from increased American unilateralism. In the Uruguay Round (1986–94), the European Union and Japan each for their own reasons came to endorse the creation of the WTO as an international institution to support worldwide trade negotiations and arbitrate disputes. The European Union had previously been a supporter of discretion and negotiation over binding rules and commitments, so accepting the WTO and its DSM represented a change in policy. In the WTO, Europe saw a codification of international trading rules as both the international counterpart to the domestic liberalization of the Single European Act and as a means of reining in American unilateralism. Japan, for its part, sought a multilateral legal framework to protect it from a series of restrictive trade practices, such as the so-called Voluntary Export Restrictions extracted by the Americans from an increasingly reluctant Japanese government.[5]

Europe and Japan could also join the Americans in supporting the Uruguay Round's commercial, investment and intellectual property provisions – which protected the interests of developed countries in dealings with the developing world.[6] The agreement on trade-related aspects of international property rights (TRIPS) sought to bring legislation on patents, copyrights and licenses in the developed and developing world into closer alignment. This served to allow extensive interference in the domestic regulatory activities of countries which had previously had more liberal attitudes towards intellectual property rights – typically developing countries.[7]

The WTO's broader powers also brought it broader scrutiny at the domestic level than had existed for its predecessor. While trade under the GATT had been widely seen as a technical issue with limited domestic salience, increasing globalization placed the WTO in the forefront of domestic political debates. This was true not only in smaller, trade-dependent economies, but also in the larger economies of the developed world. As trade liberalization increased, the domestic groups affected by greater economic exchange in the world economy also increased. While many groups, exporting corporations and consumers especially, experienced the benefits of larger markets, reduced prices and greater consumer choice, others were not so fortunate. Labour in the developed world began to experience the consequences of heightened competition from low-wage economies, initially in labour-intensive industries such as textiles, but rapidly advancing into all forms of manufacturing and extending into the service sector. Job losses and economic disruption were not confined to the developed world. In January 2005, the expiration of the Multi-Fiber Arrangement and its system of national quotas led to a surge in exports of textiles from China and the sudden impoverishment of textile producers in Africa and South Asia, all of whom lost their guaranteed quotas. Rapid economic change also had severe environmental consequences for the developing world, especially in countries where environmental regulations were relatively lax compared to those in Europe and the United States.

Both the members of groups adversely affected by globalization and those concerned that the WTO reflected the interests of corporations and developed countries over those of civil society and the developing world organized a protest against the WTO at its ministerial conferences. Large street protests by approximately 40,000 demonstrators had disrupted the 1998 ministerial meeting in Geneva, but worldwide attention was drawn to anti-globalization protestors during the failed 1999 WTO ministerial conference in Seattle.[8] Surrounded by pitched street battles between the protesters and police supported by National Guard troops, many delegates were unable to reach the conference site and negotiations were limited. The planned launching of the next major round of trade negotiations with a focus on development issues was delayed until the next ministerial meeting in Doha – where the government of Qatar ensured that street protests did not occur.

The Doha Development Round held out the promise of prioritizing the interests of developing nations in international trade talks. Prior trade talks tended to focus on the issues of importance to the major economies, primarily those of the United States, Europe and Japan. The Doha Round sought to put the emphasis on opening wealthier markets to agricultural and manufactured goods from developing countries. In subsequent meetings in Hong Kong, Geneva and Potsdam, agriculture proved to be a major sticking point as the European Union was reluctant to dismantle the system of subsidies contained within its Common Agricultural Policy and the United States proved unwilling to compromise on its own agricultural support system. While the trade talks were nominally intended to promote the development prospects of poorer countries, it was evident that there would be serious obstacles to reaching an agreement that did not address the interests of the wealthier economies.

Meanwhile, the prospects of a major multilateral agreement received a political setback in the United States. Under the 'fast-track' negotiating authority which a Republican Congress approved for President George W. Bush, the United States had made rapid progress in bilateral free trade talks. Between 2002 and 2007, the Americans ratified free trade agreements with countries ranging from Australia to Singapore and Bahrain.[9] However, it was less successful at the multilateral level, experiencing difficulties reaching agreement on issues of development with poorer countries and on agricultural issues with Europe. In July 2007, the new Democratic-controlled Congress refused to extend President Bush's 'fast-track' negotiating authority. This has put a damper on current international negotiations and put the future of international trade talks in doubt despite some efforts by American and European politicians to reinvigorate them.[10]

Notes:
1. J. Stiglitz and A, Charlton, *Fair Trade for All* (London: Oxford Unviersity Press, 2007), pp. 82–3.
2. I. M. Destler, *American Trade Politics*, 4th edn (Washington, DC: Institute for International Economics, 2005), p. 221.
3. B. Hanson, 'What Happened to Fortress Europe?: Trade Policy Liberalization in the European Union', *International Organization*, 52:1 (1998), pp. 55–86.
4. See the section on The North American Free Trade Area, above, pp. 169–258.
5. A. Brown, *Reluctant Partner: A History of Multilateral Trade Cooperation 1850–2000* (Ann Arbor, MI: University of Michigan Press, 2003), pp. 153–5.
6. G. Sen, 'The United States and the GATT/WTO System', in R. Foot, S. N. MacFarlane and M. Mastanduno (eds), *US Hegemony and International Organizations* (London: Oxford University Press, 2003), pp. 115–38.
7. D. Drezner, *US Trade Strategy: Free Versus Fair Trade* (New York: Council on Foreign Relations, 2006), p. 61.
8. Kerry Murakami, 'Geneva Sounded WTO Warning That Went Unheeded in Seattle', *Seattle Post-Intelligencer*, 10 March 2000, below, pp. 293–5.
9. Drezner, *US Trade Strategy*, p. 16.
10. Gordon Brown, UK Statement to the International Monetary and Financial Committee. International Monetary and Financial Committee, 17 September 2006, below, pp. 312–17.

WORLD TRADE ORGANIZATION

Cordell Hull, Statement on Tariffs and an International Tariff Congress, *Congressional Record,* **64th Congress, 1st Session, 8 July 1916, pp. 10653 – 4.**

Mr. HULL of Tennessee.

Now, Mr. Chairman, the truth is that in Germany the tariff law is not enacted primarily for revenue at all. It is enacted in a manner that the gentleman from Massachusetts [Mr. GILLETT], and those who think as he does, would enact a tariff law, primarily to allow the manufacturers and other special classes and interests to get together and fix up such schedules as satisfy their selfish business purposes at the expense of the masses of the people. The Government has practically nothing to do with it. They appoint a board of business men there, who meet, and after full conference and a decision as to just how much the people will stand without an open revolt, recommended it to the Parliament, and it becomes a law. One result of that class system would have been that Germany would have been in charge of the socialists before now if this war had not broken out.

Mr. SIMS. Will my colleague yield?

Mr. HULL of Tennessee. I will.

Mr. SIMS. What amount of revenue does Germany collect from all other sources compared with the amount of tariff?

Mr. HULL of Tennessee. She gets about $760,000,000 of receipts from many sources. I am sorry that I have not time to go into that again now.

Mr. SIMS. But which would show that the tariff taxes of Germany are much less in proportion to the amount raised than they are in this country?

Mr. HILL. Does not the gentleman know that it is not the manufacturing interests of Germany that control legislation, but it has been, and absolutely, for years the agrarian classes?

Mr. HULL of Tennessee. I am only stating the authorities I have with respect to the German tariff commission. I am only surprised, though, that they have not fallen into the hands of the agrarians a long time earlier.

Mr. Chairman, notwithstanding that since the Civil War our revenue system has been lopsided in its effects, the chief taxes having been imposed on consumption, the people have borne this heavy and unequal burden with small complaint.

Another new factor arising out of the European war necessarily enters into our present revenue considerations. A lesson every nation has long since learned is that during a period of general war tariff taxation becomes utterly unreliable as a means of meeting either ordinary or extraordinary expenditures. Nations, therefore, no longer hesitate, when such wars come, to turn at once to internal duties as the only certain dependence for suitable and adequate revenues. Whatever may be the tariff policy of the political party in charge of this Government in normal or peace times it is likewise compelled under the conditions to seek the chief amount of revenue from internal taxation. It would be worse than economic folly at present to our shattered customs resources as a means of securing any substantial and certain amount of additional revenue. This plain truth, demonstrated by every war, needs no elaboration.

I desire at this time most strongly to point to the fact that whatever views or purposes any political party may profess in regard to an early general revision of the tariff, any such proposed revision made within the next two years would be far worse than no revision. It would be the merest guess and haphazard revision. The most intelligent revision of the tariff that could possibly be made under existing conditions would within two years after the war require a still more general revision in order to meet the new changes in commercial, economic, and financial conditions resulting from the war. No economic truth is more universally recognized than the fact that any tariff revision attempted when the cost of production, prices, and trade conditions in other commercial countries are wholly unnatural, abnormal, and out of joint, would be unintelligible, irrational, and entirely futile. Its chief effect would be to create dreaded suspense, confusion, and practical demoralization in all domestic business affairs until a later revision could be had.

Viewed from any standpoint, the citizen must be selfish, greedy, and shortsighted who would demand or seriously suggest tariff revision before normal conditions develop and reveal themselves.

At the close of the war Europe, commercially and industrially speaking, will be flat on her back. She will be most seriously handicapped by high prices, high wages, inflated currency, destroyed capital, scarcity of skilled labor, loss of export trade, high taxes, burdensome interest, extreme scarcity of all raw materials, and great depletion of her stock of manufactures, both for export and domestic purposes. The principal countries at war will be paying greater annual interest charges than the total amount of taxes annually levied by the United States Government. With these tremendous handicaps, no intelligent person expects Europe to be able to rehabilitate herself commercially and industrially within any short period of time. Many of her best markets have forever been lost to the United States.

Since this Government now has in operation an honest, fair, sound, and well-balanced system of tariff taxation, to which all business has become adjusted, it would be both unwise and suicidal commercially to start an agitation or propaganda to materially change or modify the existing system within the next two or three years and before the manifest results of the European war upon trade, finance, and industry the world over shall become known.

In the meantime the Underwood law, which, notwithstanding its lack of opportunity to be fully tried out, has so far proven so wise, equitable, and beneficial, that it should from every viewpoint continue in permanent operation. It will surely accomplish its share in safeguarding the Treasury and will work no injustice to any legitimate business interests in this country. Whenever new facts shall be developed through the proposed tariff commission or other source which suggest a change in the rate upon a given item here and there and now and then, such change can be promptly made to a competitive basis, with the result that in the end each phase of the present tariff law will become practically and intelligently adjusted to the new conditions to follow the war. This course would avoid the evil and injurious effects on business of constant and useless tariff agitation extending over the next few years.

In my judgment the life of the modernized ultra-high protective tariff system as heretofore developed in this and one or two other leading countries has reached its end. Apart from its essential injustice to the people, this system has become a positive menace to the peace of all trade countries. It is naturally utilized for purposes of rank discrimination, practical boycotting, undue preferences, and other irritating practices. It also involves, in its logical development, as in Germany, subsidies, bounties, rebates, and drawbacks. The trade practices growing out of the very spirit and operation of these so-called scientific high protective tariff systems have been a source of constant controversy and irritation among the leading commercial nations. It is a matter of common knowledge that the operation of the many unfair, injurious, and trouble-making trade practices and the strenuous trade conquests pursued under these systems chiefly contributed to the outbreak of the present European war.

If I were President of the United States I should, at a later and suitable date, propose to the governments of all commercial nations that at the close of the present European war an international trade conference be held in the city of Washington for the purpose of establishing a permanent international trade congress, the function and duty of such congress to comprise the consideration of all international trade methods, practices, and policies which in their effects are calculated to create destructive commercial controversies or bitter economic wars, and to formulate agreements with respect thereto, designed to eliminate and avoid the injurious results and dangerous possibilities of economic warfare, and to promote fair and friendly trade relations among all the nations of the world.

In the face of Europe's awful condition, it is the shallowest pretense that our giant industries, instead of encouraging their representatives here to perform a patriotic duty by imposing upon them what is comparatively a nominal tax for increased armaments, would threaten to block preparedness legislation and to hold it up unless they are protected by the most exorbitant tariff rates against the millions of former skilled laborers who now lie sleeping in their graves in Europe; against run-down foreign factories that are standing idle; against the women who in a feeble way are trying to turn out enough goods for domestic necessities; against those desolated countries, which, like the South following the Civil War, can not hope to rehabilitate themselves either physically or commercially or financially for years to come.

Senate Debate on the World Trade Organization (Uruguay Round Agreements Act), *Congressional Record*, 103rd Congress, 2nd Session, 30 November 1994, pp. S15079 – 87.

Mr. MOYNIHAN. Mr. President, on July 8, 1916, in a speech on the House floor, Cordell Hull, then a young Congressman from Carthage, TN – the same town from which our distinguished Vice President, presiding officer in exceptional circumstances comes – called for a permanent international trade congress.

It was a hugely prescient idea. He understood that the inability of the European powers – the established ones – to accommodate the enormously increased economic importance of Germany had, in considerable measure, led to the First World War.

He saw that trade was a source of conflict as far back as conflict is recorded and that it should be subject to the same kinds of rules and procedures internationally that we had established in our internal arrangements.

Our Constitution is very careful to see that trade disputes, which are really the bulk of the litigation that takes place in our courts, are given validity across State boundaries and that the trading partners, knowing that whenever disputes arise, if litigated, the decisions will be held valid everywhere in the Union, are all the more disposed to entering such contracts. This is a point which Alexander Hamilton made in his Report on Manufacturers given to the Congress in 1791.

Hull saw the extension of this great understanding to a world market. That was the beginning of the century. Two vast wars and much turmoil in between bring us to the end of the century and to the completion of that vision. It reached its nadir in 1930 when, in the Smoot-Hawley Tariff Act of that year, we raised tariffs to an average of 60 percent in our country. Imports dropped by two-thirds; exports dropped by two-thirds; the British went off free trade, establishing a colonial empire's imperial preference; the prosperity feared in Japan began. In 1933, in a parliamentarily correct election, Adolf Hitler became chancellor. War was 6 years away – 5. Not even that, Mr. President.

[...]

[I]n 1934, Cordell Hull began the reciprocal trade agreements program, an arrangement whereby the Executive could enter trade agreements and Congress would approve. It was a brilliantly innovative device, and every President [...] since has held to this proposal, this basic construct.

It cannot be too much stated or stressed that the agreement before us today was proposed under President Ronald Reagan, to whom we send the great good wishes of the Senate on this first occasion that we have met since his announcement of his illness. It was largely negotiated by President Bush's representatives, notably Carla Hill, who has been indomitable in support of this measure, and it was concluded, as the majority leader observed, a year ago in Geneva. The formal signing took place in Marrakesh in Morocco this spring, but the work was done a year ago. It took a long time to do it, 3 years longer than expected, because more was done than in past trade agreements.

Most important, we have brought agricultural interests into the GATT. I hope the Senator from Nebraska will take note of that, that agricultural products are now under the GATT. They have never been previously; it has been a manufactured goods affair. And the export subsidies which have so bedeviled our exports of agricultural goods are to be severely cut back, a concession finally made from the European Union, which is one of the reasons this bill comes to us 3 years later than originally expected.

The bill provides protection for intellectual properties, our largest growth industries in this country, which have been bedeviled by widespread piracy, and it creates a WTO. This World Trade Organization is no more than a rather pale image of the International Trade Organization which was contemplated at the end of World War II. The Bretton Woods agreements of 1944 proposed the International Bank for Reconstruction and Development, which we know as the World Bank and the International Monetary Fund; they did not get to the details of an international trade organization, but they clearly anticipated that one would be proposed and adopted.

President Truman did, indeed, propose that there be such an organization with many more powers than the WTO will have. It failed of adoption in the Congress. The House Foreign Affairs Committee never acted, principally due to opposition in the Senate Finance Committee, as the distinguished former chairman, future chairman knows.

[...] [T]here has been a great deal of talk about this new organization as if it is something very new and very large and threatening. May I make the simple point that the GATT, which began, in the absence of an ITO, as simply an informal arrangement – a British Treasury official, Eric Wyndham-White, whom I had the privilege to know, with just a small secretarial staff, ran it on a very informal basis – over 40 years, the staff of the General Agreement on Tariffs and Trade has reached 450 persons. The staff estimates that, with the new responsibilities that the World Trade Organization will devolve onto the GATT in consequence, the 450 would acquire 15 additional employees.

Four hundred sixty-five persons in the WTO. [...] [T]hat is one-third the size of the Capitol Police force, scarcely a daunting prospect of world government. The dispute settlement decisions that were made in the GATT were arbitration decisions really, given agreements, given the rules. Over the last 40 years, there have been about four such cases a year that have come to be completed.

Under the GATT arrangement, there was a veto, and, for example, Europeans on agricultural products were repeatedly saying, 'Well, yes, the panel decided the American exports were being unfairly discriminated against, but we even so will not accept it.'

[...]

I simply make the point that we are not creating anything new in this World Trade Organization. We are simply codifying the practice of consensus, which has been the practice of the GATT.

May I make the point that I wonder if my friend from Oregon knows: That there has not been a vote in the GATT for 35 years. Yes, this is not a litigious organization in that sense. When there is a dispute – and contract disputes are the bread and butter of the American judicial system, and properly so – the parties concerned pick nonpartisan arbiters from other countries. They make their case and may live with the results. That is what a system of law is about.

[...]

I urge the adoption of this legislation.

Mr. President, on July 8, 1916, in a speech on the House floor, Cordell Hull, then a Democratic Congressman from Tennessee, called for a 'permanent international trade congress' to formulate agreements to dismantle destructive trade practices. Today, over 78 years later, it is with great honor that I, as chairman of the Committee on Finance, bring to the floor of the Senate legislation that will finally realize that vision.

Mr. President, over the past several weeks, a number of persons have observed, quite accurately, I believe, that we are about to cast a vote of monumental importance – on a par with the historic and defining votes on the League of Nations and the Marshall Plan. The legislation that we take up this morning will approve and implement the largest, most comprehensive trade agreement the international community has yet witnessed. If this Senate approves the Uruguay Round Agreements Act, as I fully expect it shall, that action will represent nothing less than the culmination of 60 years of American trade policymaking – policymaking that began with Cordell Hull's Reciprocal Trade Agreements Program in 1934 and that has, ever since, been carried out in the best bipartisan traditions of this body.

Mr. President, it was only 8 years ago, September 1986, in Punta del Este, Uruguay, that trade ministers from around the world gathered to launch the eighth round of multilateral trade negotiations under the auspices of the General Agreement on Tariffs and Trade – the GATT, a provisional arrangement that has served as a forum for trade agreements since 1948.

The ministers' goals were ambitious – indeed, too ambitious for the timetable they contemplated. They sought to strengthen the rules governing international trade, to bring trade in agriculture, services, and textiles under the rules, to protect intellectual property and trade-related investment. Such far-reaching objectives could not be reached in 4 years, as they had planned. Not until December 1993, rather than 1990, was final agreement struck. But that agreement was one that largely achieved their objectives.

Objectives, I must point out, that were both shared and guided by the Congress of the United States. The Congress laid down the United States objectives for the Uruguay round in the Omnibus Trade and Competitiveness Act of 1988, goals shared by the executive branch and sought by negotiators under three American Presidents, Republican and Democrat alike. I am pleased to report that, as a result of the endeavors of the administrations of Presidents Reagan, Bush, and Clinton, in close consultation with the Congress, the agreement before us today largely meets the standards set forth by the Congress 6 years ago. Not in total, we must acknowledge, as I suppose the objectives of other countries were likewise qualified in the give-and-take of negotiation. But met in large part.

Optimistic reports on the economic impact of the Uruguay round abound. The GATT organization itself estimates that, in 10 years' time, U.S. gross domestic product [GDP] will increase by $122 billion annually as a result of this agreement. Our own Council of Economic Advisors estimates an annual increase in U.S. GDP of $100 to $200 billion. Other studies suggest smaller increases, but it is notable that all economic analyses are positive – a singular event in the world of economists.

The economic benefit of many aspects of the Uruguay round, such as improved intellectual property protection and rules for services trade, are difficult to quantify here and now. But its simplest aspect alone presents a compelling case – that is, the nearly $750 billion in tariff, meaning tax, cuts to be made worldwide. The largest tax cut in world history. A tax cut of $32 billion over 10 years on products imported into this country alone. And an average tax cut of 40 percent on the products we export to the rest of the world. I would ask my colleagues: What other economic measure could we consider with such far-reaching effect?

Most importantly, the Uruguay round means jobs – 300,000 to 700,000 more American jobs once fully implemented. And these will be good jobs, for jobs engaged in producing exported goods typically pay 13 percent more than the average.

Much will be made during this debate, I expect, of the decline in manufacturing jobs over the last decade, attributing such in large part to the failings of American trade policies. Indeed, employment in manufacturing has declined between 1979 and 1993 – falling from 21 to 18 million – even though employment in the nonagricultural sector of the economy has increased by almost 25 percent. But why, we must ask?

In significant part because American companies have succeeded in becoming the most productive in the world. From 1979 to 1993, while manufacturing employment declined by 14 percent, productivity increased substantially so that industrial production in the manufacturing sector increased by 38 percent. The result – more output, fewer workers. Repeating our experience in agriculture, where the mechanization of production released thousands of workers from the field: in 1930, over 21 percent of America's workers were engaged in agricultural production, but by 1993, less than 3 percent of the work force was employed in the farm, forest, or fishery sectors – and less than 1 percent of the work force was employed as farmhands.

In these circumstances, difficult as they may be for the workers affected, we should look upon trade not as the villain, but as an opportunity. Trade among countries should not be avoided; indeed, it cannot be avoided in an open society, any more than can be the effect of advancing communications or innovative technologies. If we approach trade as friend, rather than foe, we will find ways to sell more of our goods abroad, employing more rather than fewer Americans.

In fact, the United States is in the best position among trading nations to take great advantage of the more open markets that come with the Uruguay round. For the United States today is at the height of its global competitiveness. Americans should note with some degree of satisfaction the recent report of the World Economic Forum which rates the United States as the world's most competitive nation. We have returned to the top ranking for the first time since 1985, Japan is now a distant second.

Of this fact I would remind those who have voiced concerns about the impact of this agreement on U.S. sovereignty. There are legitimate concerns here, which have been legitimately addressed. Again in a bipartisan fashion. But others who speak of a loss of sovereignty prey on the fears of American workers, uncertain about their future in a global economy. Let us remind American workers of their ability to think, create and innovate, not to fail or fall prey to outside forces beyond their control. That is not the kind of thinking by which American workers built the most competitive economy in the world. Nor is there reason to succumb to such thinking now.

Rather, we must remember that our economy is the largest single market in the world, a market which others seek, recognizing its value. To those who fear that we will constantly be out-voted in the new World Trade Organization, established in the Uruguay round, I would say that there is little reason for concern. The WTO simply codifies the practice of consensus in the GATT and there has not been a vote in the GATT on a trade policy matter for 35 years. To those who suggest that the WTO will have the power to override our own governing of our market, I would say but one thing – look to the Constitution. We yet govern ourselves, with the authority to regulate commerce with foreign nations given to the Congress. And with the Congress also rests the authority to take the necessary and proper steps to carry out international agreements, as recognized by the Supreme Court in the seminal Missouri versus Holland decision – on a migratory bird convention, of all matters – in 1920.

It is the Congress which, since the disaster of the Smoot-Hawley Act of 1930, has chosen with care the arrangements whereby U.S. trade policy is made. Having learned the lessons of Smoot-Hawley – the two-thirds drop in trade that followed, worldwide depression, the rise of totalitarian regimes, and in the wake of such events, the Second World War.

In the aftermath of such, the Congress sought a better arrangement for trade policymaking in this country. Beginning with the Reciprocal Trade Agreements Program of 1934, the Congress has determined that the President should negotiate liberalizing trade agreements and the Congress should embody those agreements in legislation which it considers, debates, and votes on. In 1974, the Congress chose to create special procedural rules – we know them today as the fast track – to ensure that these trade liberalizing policies would continue.

But these arrangements do not preclude the Congress from performing its constitutional duties of regulating foreign commerce. Indeed, the Congress has chosen these arrangements in the belief that they best serve our commercial interests. Likewise, mechanisms have been created with this implementing bill to ensure that the congressional voice is heard should the World Trade Organization not serve American interests. Congress will have the opportunity to demand withdrawal from this organization on 6 months' notice as permitted under the agreement itself.

Indeed we should withdraw if the worst fears of the opponents are realized. If foreign governments pursue repeated, and unfounded, challenges to U.S. law. But that is not the likely scenario. The United States is not a protectionist country. And it is those countries which are so that must be concerned about the WTO, not the United States.

We seem to forget that it was the United States, and the Congress in the 1988 Trade Act, that sought the strengthened rules that come with the World Trade Organization. Why? Because although we consistently have been more successful than the average in GATT litigation, we have too often been frustrated in our successes. During the period leading to the passage of the 1988 Trade Act, we won three GATT cases against the Europeans – on pasta, citrus, and canned fruit – only to be frustrated by their stalling tactics. The European Community blocked the adoption of those three panel reports, preventing formal GATT approval of the panel's decisions. And throughout 1988, the Europeans first blocked and then further delayed the establishment of a dispute settlement panel to hear a U.S. challenge to EC production subsidies on oilseeds. Four cases, all of great consequence to our agricultural community. Is it any wonder that the

Congress, in 1988, urged our negotiators to achieve a more effective and expeditious dispute settlement system?

Under the new WTO rules, these stalling tactics will not be allowed. And the United States, I might note, has nothing to fear from a tougher dispute settlement system. We have been victorious more often than most under the GATT, and there is every reason to expect that trend to continue. Under the GATT, we have prevailed in 70 of the 87 cases that we have brought. That is a remarkable success rate of roughly 80 percent. When challenged, we have also prevailed more than most – in 55 of the 75 cases brought against us, or nearly 75 percent of the time.

Most important, we should keep in mind that, in the first 43 years of the GATT, there have only been 88 panel decisions. If we include the cases that did not culminate in panel decisions, that number grows to 207. That averages to less than five cases a year. There is thus no grounds for fearing that hundreds of our laws will be challenged in the WTO.

Thus, the crucial fact to be remembered: It is the United States that stands to benefit most from the World Trade Organization's improved, and more effective, rules for settling disputes among trading partners.

We are on the brink of realizing these benefits. This is not the International Trade Organization [ITO], established in the Havana Charter of March 1948, that the Congress turned its back on. The ITO was a more ambitious arrangement. It included, as the WTO does not, provisions on full employment and economic reconstruction, on technology transfer and access to capital, on private cartels and international commodity agreements.

The ITO died at the hands of the Congress, due in no small part to the intense opposition of the Committee on Finance of that day. The business community joined in that opposition, ironically because of concerns that the ITO Charter fell too far short of their ideals of free trade. In the end, only one committee of Congress, the House Committee on Foreign Affairs, even held hearings on the Habana Charter. There were no votes. The ITO Charter simply withered in the face of intractable opposition.

In contrast, the World Trade Organization of 1994 is a more modest arrangement than that envisioned by the Habana Charter. But its principal purpose is the same – to provide a sound institutional framework for the conduct of trade among nations. To provide a forum for resolving disputes that inevitably arise among people who trade together. In recognition that the prosperity of all depends upon the peaceful resolution of such conflicts and the continuing conduct of international trade. And in 1994, unlike in 1948, the Finance Committee and the business community join together in support of the World Trade Organization.

Let us not replicate our unfortunate experience with the International Trade Organization, over 40 years ago. Instead, let us emulate the bipartisan spirit that has developed over the past decade as we have ratified, with little or no dissent, four important conventions negotiated under the auspices of the International Labor Organization [ILO].

Mr. President, I look forward to the coming debate, and I urge the Senate, once the debate is over, to act in that bipartisan spirit and approve the Uruguay Round Agreements Act.

[...]

Mr. HOLLINGS. [...] What happens, and let me put it to bed immediately, agriculture is the most protected, subsidized of all of America's produce. We all know it. We vote for the price support programs. We put in the Export-Import Bank to finance it. We put in export promotion programs, and everything else. I believe in those things, and they have been successful.

Right to the point, on Intel and steel, steel, as the Senator reads from the New York Times, we use, coming out of the distinguished Finance chairman's committee, Super 301 and being able to threaten retaliation. We did not retaliate, but we threatened retaliation to open up the market. Then we got in so-called agreements, voluntary restraint agreements, on steel, on automobiles, yes, on semiconductors. Intel benefits from the managed trade that they say they are all against.

But under GATT, Madam President, I can tell you the European Commission and the booklet on Japan in their particular findings already have found our voluntary restraint agreements are GATT illegal, our Super 301 is GATT illegal. And that, in and of itself, is enough to kill this particular agreement – should kill it.

What disturbs this particular Senator is the attitude that somehow when they bring in trucks and those kinds of things, and technology, they assume the lack of intellect or experience on the other side. We know about exports. I can list down from Bosch and all the fuel injectors for the Toyotas and Mercedes. I can list our General Electric friends. I brought them in 35 years ago to make bulbs, light bulbs. Then they made cellular radios. And now they make what? Magnetic resonance images, health care, the most sophisticated instrumentality there is. And do you know what? We took the market. Florence, SC, took the market from Tokyo. We ship over half of what we produce in Florence, SC, to Tokyo. We know about exports and we know about automobiles.

The Japanese have been dumping, dumping automobiles at less than cost.

I had, as chairman of the Commerce Committee, lined up a couple years ago on the 1989 figure of a loss of $3.2 billion that the Japanese lost in selling cars in the United States of America, I had Ford and Chrysler ready to testify to start into dumping. General Motors chickened out. That is why we do not do it. The business leadership said, rather than spending for lawyers on dumping cases, we are just going to move on out. That is our problem.

[...]

And that brings me right to the point. There are two different trading systems in this global competition. Do not say, 'We are competent. We can compete. We can compete.'

We know that the American industrial worker is the most productive, our research is the best, our technology is the best. What is inadequate, downright dumb, is us, the Government, right here. That is what is not competing. Do not sell me off about we are against the American workers and all that and give me the patriotism.

What happens is, there are two different systems entirely. We follow Adam Smith, David Ricardo, competitive advantage, free markets, open markets, open competition. The Japanese and all the countries in the Pacific rim follow the federalist Alexander Hamilton of closed markets. They measure the wealth of a country not by what it can buy, but by what it can produce. And their decisions are made as to whether or not it weakens the economy or strengthens the economy.

And all of these Senators run around moaning and groaning about fair play and quit cheating and we want a fair trade and all those kinds of things.

There is no moral question of fairness or unfairness. It is a calculated, definitely successful method of trade.

And not only are all the Pacific Rim countries following it, read the most recent issue of Business Week and you will find, Madam President, that Business Week says Eastern Europeans coming in from communism into capitalism are following not the American system but the Pacific rim system of design for market share. That is what it is – the strength of a country.

And we are running around talking about the price of consumers. When the poor Senator says we have got 200 jobs for trucks in Oregon, we have got 300 jobs for trucks in North Carolina, he does not understand what he says, because he says we are the largest manufacture of that particular equipment. Well, it is the largest, 500 jobs. We are talking about jobs. Transportation equipment in the United States in the last 5 years has lost 278,000 jobs. And that is why the Senator can stand on the floor and say the largest we have got has only got 300 jobs in North Carolina and 200 jobs in Oregon.

Going to those particular two systems, what happens over the years. We failed to compete as a government intentionally. We sacrificed, if you please, our economy to keep the alliance together under the cold war.

And let us go immediately now to the Tokyo round and where we are at this particular time, because we heard all of these arguments under Ambassador Strauss in the previous administration in 1979, under President Carter.

What is particularly annoying is that the leadership in this town, Republican and Democrat, fail to recognize reality and the real competition that they are in. That is the frustration of the American voter that you faced here just a couple of weeks ago and it continues. It is not over now.

Oh, they can run around and take away from committees and they can run around and cut this and say we all are going to be subject to the same rules, but if we do not get this Government competitive on jobs, on creating an industrial backbone that we are fast draining off, we all should go down the tube. We do not have to pass term limits. They will limit you. You go in to bat in 2 years, 4 years from now, we all will see the result. They promised me the jobs.

The actual figure, undisputed – and we had eight separate hearings in the Committee of Commerce, very few people were around, but they were covered by C-SPAN – we have lost 3.2 million jobs under what we got. Now here, instead of creating jobs, they talk about what is going to happen in the future.

We heard that in 1979, that we were going to all burst out with all of these jobs. We have lost jobs. The average worker who has really got a job – a lot of people are back into part-time jobs and everything else of that kind, those are the only ones created – are making 20 percent less.

And what happens? This is a trade debate, the General Agreement on Tariffs and Trade. And what happens on trade? An average of a $100 billion deficit. Not exports. Yes, exports might go up X percent, Y percent, G percent, 50 percent, 300 percent, but never, never more than imports. Imports are coming in faster.

Yes, exports create jobs, but imports lose the jobs, and we are losing them at $100 billion a year. And, according to their own measure, every billion dollars represents 20,000 jobs. So we are losing 2 million jobs a year.

This year, 1994, that is a $150 to $160 billion trade deficit. That is 3 million jobs lost. And they continue to think they are leading. 'This is a wonderful moment in history. The allies will wonder whether we continue to lead.' Continue to lead. That is nonsense.

We are losing. The poor President goes out to the Far East a couple of weeks ago with a $150 billion hole in his pocket and a tin cup, begging the Japanese to finance the debt. Where do you think you get the debt? Right here. This is not competing, this particular Government here, that we are all part of. We are losing.

The Japanese leaders – I have been in conferences with them. They are aghast, over the years, at our lack of competing here and enforcing our own dumping and trading laws. So after all those deficits in the balance of trade, by 1985 we had, yes – former Secretary of State Baker, he was Secretary of Treasury, and ran the White House – he devalued the dollar in 1985 with the Plaza Agreement and put the United States of America up for a half-price sale and the Japanese came running and bought up the Metro Goldwyn Mayer, all the studios out there in your back yard – the Plaza, Algonquin Hotel – bought up everything. They bought up the farms. We did not have to worry about shipping beef to the Japanese. They just bought up the farms and shipped back their own beef at half price. Come on.

What has been going on is that we are in a disastrous decline – a disastrous decline. The headline just before the election said 'Rising Tide Fails to Lift.' There is no rising tide. We are losing jobs. We have 40 million hungry in America. I wrote a book on hunger. It used to be 12 million. Now there are 40 million out there. How many homeless? Millions are homeless. How many on, heavens above, half the take-home pay?

So they are all for the family. What breaks up the family? When you are only getting half, 20 percent, of what you were making, the wife has to go out and you get the latchkey children. So they think it is a moral thing, that we have to get the wives and the mothers to look after children more. It is economic decline. They look after the children trying to earn bread to put it on the table. Who is causing latchkey children? We are.

In crime? They are all against crime – three strikes and you are out. Build more prisons. There are 64,000 textile jobs in the Bowery in New York, sewing jobs; there are 60,000 out there in Los Angeles, in Watts. They get $6.30 an hour and get all the requirements. We burden our system, business: Clean air, clean water, minimum wage, plant closing notice, parental leave, Social Security, Medicare/Medicaid, safe working place, safe machinery – on and on, up and up. Those jobs move to Mexico and now to the Pacific rim, all gone. And you have a little candidate running all around here with his blow-dry, hollering, 'Enterprise zone, enterprise zone.' We are taking, today, the enterprise out of the zone. That is what causes the crime, when we lose the jobs that we have there in the inner city: Newark, New York, Los Angeles, Chicago, Cleveland. Go around the country and find out what is happening. That is what the American people say: Get off your duffs and start competing here. Because this Tokyo round has been a disaster.

Madam President, what has been the change? One, they talk about tariffs. Back in 1947, tariffs were nothing – absolutely nothing, relatively speaking. The average tariff in Japan is 2 percent. The average tariff here is 4 percent. Cut it 50 percent? That is not the case. It is nontariff barriers. That is why Ambassador Kantor went working all year long. He had this GATT agreement back in December. He has been working all year long to get an agreement with the Japanese, but he comes around and says, 'We will all work under the same rules.' We are not going to all work under the same rules. We are not going to open up any markets.

If they thought so, they put him on notice out there in Malaysia and Indonesia. The trade executive in Indonesia said we are not going along with it.

Kuala Lumpur, Malaysia, today expressed its objection to any efforts for enforcing trade liberalization. Minister of International Trade and Industry, Ricardo Seed, said it is mooting market liberalization. No APEC member should push another member to open its markets.

So what did they do? They came away and said open them by the year 2020, 25 years from now, and they hail that as, 'We have progress. We are opening up markets. We are creating jobs,' when we are going down the tubes. We are killing every economic or job opportunity that you could possibly think of. That is one particular change.

The other particular change is America's security is like on a three-legged stool. We have the one leg, the values of the country – strong. Feeding the hungry in Somalia, building democracy in Haiti.

The second leg, the military leg or power – unquestioned.

The third leg is our economic strength. And if one is fractured or tips, the security tips, and that is the condition we are in. We are on the way, as England. Years back, they told England, 'Don't worry; instead of a nation of brawn, you will be a nation of brains. Instead of producing products, you will produce services and be a service economy. Instead of creating wealth, you will handle it and be a financial center.' And England has gone to hell in a hand basket, economically. We can prove that. It came out in the hearings. We are on the same road, and I am trying to get us off that road, and not listen to these shibboleths about creating jobs and technology. We are losing all of the technology jobs.

What we have now, with the fall of the wall, Madam President, the big change is that we have an opportunity to quit sacrificing the economy and refurbish that third leg of the stool, our economic strength. I hope we can go after this in a deliberate way and understand that it is not the rule of the jungle or anything else.

We have a virtual veto under the present GATT. We lose our veto under this GATT. I have 50 witnesses and they cannot point to me where I have a veto and they have to go to it.

I see now I am pretty well limited in my time. Let me yield to the distinguished Senator from Ohio and reserve the remainder of my time.

The PRESIDING OFFICER. The Senator from Ohio is recognized.

Mr. METZENBAUM. [...] I rise in opposition to the passage of GATT, The General Agreement on Tariffs and Trade. Before I discuss my concerns with the agreement, let me frankly say I wish I could support the President on this matter, especially in light of recent events. I strongly believe the President has been misunderstood and unfairly maligned. He has done much to improve the direction of this country and deserves far more praise than he has received. But I am frank to say that I have many deep concerns about this agreement and I just cannot support it.

Today, I want to focus on the impact of this agreement on children. Up to now, there has been virtually no discussion about this critical issue. I recently held a hearing of the Labor Subcommittee on International Child Labor Abuses and, frankly, I was deeply shocked by what I heard. Around the world today, as many as 200 million children are subjected – 200 million children are subjected – to abusive labor practices in sweat shops, in mines, in factories, and in the fields. The more advanced and mobile our productive technology gets, the more easily it can be run by children in impoverished countries.

Walk into a clothing store like the Gap, or The Limited. You will have a very hard time finding any garments made in the United States. I did that the other day, just to explore for myself. It is very difficult to find anything made in the United States. But you do find clothing made in low-wage countries such as Thailand, China, the Philippines, Brazil, Honduras, Korea, and so many other countries. In many of these countries, a substantial percentage of the apparel industry is comprised of children, and working conditions are horrendous. Child labor is also widely used in many other countries in the production of toys, in carpets, in jewelry, and in numerous other exports.

I ask unanimous consent [...] that a list of these countries be printed in the Record in full.

There being no objection, the material was ordered to be printed in the Record, as follows:

Countries With Documented Child Labor Violations

Bangladesh – Children make up an estimated 40 percent of garment industry workers there, despite national laws that prohibit employment of children under the age of 14.

Brazil – 1,300 children under the age of 14 work illegally in the footwear industry, which exports $1.4 billion worth of merchandise to the U.S.

China – Children between the ages of 10 and 16 spend 14 hours a day working for foreign-owned companies

Colombia – Children as young as 11 work in the fresh cut flower industry where they are exposed to toxic substances present during and after the spraying of pesticides.

Cote D'Ivoire – Children as young as three years old work in the gold mining industry

Egypt – Children in the export-oriented leather industry average 11.7 years of age and work an average of 12.8 hours a day.

India – India has the largest number of child workers in the world: an estimated 100 million, including some as young as five in the silk and fireworks industries.

Indonesia – Children make up a portion of the export industry workforce, for which they work an average of 7–13 hours a day, 7 days a week. They earn an average of $4 a week for their work.

Lesotho – Children under the age of 14 work in at least ten different foreign owned factories that assemble garments exported to the United States.

Mexico – Many children under the age of 14 are found working in the maquiladoras, which are affiliates of American-owned companies that assemble goods for export.

Morocco – Children as young as eleven work in leather workshops, where they are exposed to toxic chemicals and work with hazardous machinery.

Nepal – Five year olds working 15 hours a day in Nepal's carpet export industry earn approximately $25 for a carpet that will retail in the U.S. for $4,000.

Pakistan – Millions of children suffer under a system of 'bonded labor', a situation in which children pay off their parents' debts through forced labor. It is estimated that 50,000 children in the bonded labor sector will die before the age of 12 because of disease and malnutrition.

The Philippines – Children work long hours in unhealthy and crowded conditions and are paid less than one-third of the minimum wage.

Portugal – Children are paid 10 percent of an adult's wages working in the garment industry that exports $60 million in merchandise annually to the U.S.

Tanzania – Children make up 30 percent of the workforce in the sisal (rope and yarn) industry, which exports $2 million in merchandise to the U.S.

Thailand – Children working in the leather industry, which exports products to the U.S., are given amphetamines to keep up their strength during their 15 hour days.

Source: *By the Sweat and Toil of Children: The Use of Child Labor in American Imports.* U.S. Department of Labor, 1994.

Mr. METZENBAUM. Global trade may bring great riches to multinational corporations and even to some developed nations, but for millions of children around the world it is an unmitigated disaster, bringing oppressive working conditions, rampant illiteracy, unbroken cycles of poverty, and an ever-widening gap between rich and poor.

Incredibly, the GATT Treaty not only ignores this problem, it will encourage even more employers to exploit the children of the Third World in the manufacture of goods for the U.S. and other developed markets.

I am a cosponsor of Senator Harkin's bill to ban the importation of goods made with child labor. But in a recent letter, U.S. Trade Representative Mickey Kantor informed me that GATT would actually make that bill illegal under the new World Trade Organization's rules. Now, Mickey Kantor is a longtime friend, one who has done superb work as the U.S. Trade Representative. But according to Mickey Kantor, under the GATT Treaty, 'the United States could not block the importation of a product made by child labor consistent with our obligations under the GATT.'

How can we approve a treaty that not only ignores the problem of international child labor, but actually prevents us from doing anything about it in the future?

I suspect that the American people, as well as most of my colleagues, have no idea of the scope or depth of this problem. So let me set forth some basic facts.

We are talking about children – kids forced into slavery, subjected to torture and physical abuse, all in the name of free trade, to produce goods for U.S. markets. Instead of meeting this problem head on, GATT will only make it worse.

Today, in many developing nations, millions of children are paid pennies an hour for their labor.

Many of these children will die of disease, exhaustion, physical abuse, or starvation.

Those who are lucky enough to survive the horrors of forced child labor will never lead a normal adult life.

By working instead of going to school, child laborers are doomed to perpetuate the cycle of poverty.

It is outrageous that these conditions exist, and we are talking about passing the GATT Treaty and not doing a damned thing about it. Even worse, they are doing nothing to address the problem. GATT will not help – it will simply hurt, by limiting our ability to address this problem in the future.

Scott Sunde, 'Chaos Closes Downtown; Police Use Rubber Pellets, Tear Gas Against Thousands; Demonstrators Delay Start of Trade Meeting for Hours; Schell Orders Curfew; National Guard Called', *Seattle Post-Intelligencer*, 1 December 1999, p. A1.

(Seattle) – Withstanding tear gas, rubber pellets and nightsticks, thousands of protesters faced down the World Trade Organization and police in Seattle yesterday, forcing authorities to order a curfew and call out the National Guard.

After night fell, police swept through downtown, pushing protesters out of the curfew area with a blanket of tear and pepper gas. The battle continued late into the night on Capitol Hill.

Protesters forced cancellation of the WTO's opening ceremonies yesterday morning at the Paramount Theater and for much of the day faced down outnumbered police on streets littered with the refuse of chaos: protest signs, spent tear-gas canisters and broken glass.

Protesters all along planned to occupy downtown and to halt the opening ceremonies. One protester summed up the day in white paint on a bank's picture window, writing 'We win.'

'Those who were protesting the opening of the WTO in fact were successful today,' police Chief Norm Stamper said.

The unrelenting, daylong street battles prompted Gov. Gary Locke to call out the National Guard.

But when asked whether police were in control of the demonstrations, Mayor Paul Schell – who declared a state of civil emergency and the 7 p.m.–7:30 a.m. curfew – said yes.

'This administration had people who marched in the '60s – the last thing I wanted was to be mayor of a city that called in the National Guard,' Schell said.

Then he nudged Stamper, who hemmed before saying, 'From a public-safety standpoint, yes.'

Still, protesters raged through the streets, while gangs used the cover of chaos to commit strong-arm robberies and loot some businesses, including a Starbucks at Sixth and Stewart.

In addition to 200 or more riot-trained guardsmen who are to deploy today, Locke also ordered 300 more state troopers to Seattle.

This is the first time in modern history that the National Guard has been called into Seattle, and the curfew is apparently the first since World War II, when a U.S. Army general ordered Japanese Americans off the streets at night.

Stamper defended his 1,200 officers.

'Our police officers, in my judgment, did an extraordinary job against all odds.'

But Ed Joiner, assistant chief, said officers may have waited too long before taking action.

While the police had been in negotiations with dozens of protest groups for months, the chief said the city underestimated the number who hadn't asked permission to demonstrate and were bent on anarchy.

He said the National Guard was a 'last-ditch' contingency.

Police made 60 arrests by midnight, but Schell rejected suggestions that mass arrests would have defused the melee.

'You can't just arrest people for no reason,' Schell said. He also suggested the city lacked room to house an army of detainees, and police officials said mass arrests would have taken too many officers off the street.

Top Clinton administration officials, meanwhile, declined to criticize Seattle officials.

'The city today faced very difficult situation,' said Gene Sperling, a national economic adviser. 'None of us ... have the facts to try to second-guess and critique the situation.'

Though protesters seemed to be everywhere, few took part in violence, broke windows, painted slogans on walls or fought police. On some street corners, spontaneous carnivals broke out. People danced. Jugglers juggled, and a woman practiced her Hula-Hoop. A young man strode through the crowd on stilts.

'I'm really bummed out that a few hundred out-of-control protesters are undermining the important, peaceful message brought downtown today by tens of thousands of demonstrators,' said an exhausted Ron Judd, executive secretary of the King County Labor Council-AFL-CIO after 25,000 union members marched through downtown. 'A hundred and fifty out-of-control anarchists that we suspected all along might be a problem are getting all the attention.'

Judd said some of the anarchists had taken labor signs and were pretending to be union members.

Most protesters had also cleared out of downtown by the time police began enforcing the curfew between Interstate 5 and the waterfront and Yesler Way north to Denny Way.

After dark, police moved west down Pike Street to the Seattle Sheraton, shooting flash-bang concussion grenades and tear gas at a crowd of more than 1,000. Two platoons of police in riot gear followed protesters down Pike Street, firing tear gas.

'We are cleaning the streets,' one police officer said.

Protesters, stopped at Third and Pike, screamed in response: 'Animals, you animals, go back to your jungle, you animals!'

Late last night, police bomb squads rushed to a parking garage at Pine Street and Boylston Avenue on Capitol Hill to investigate a possible explosive device and to explode it.

Just before 10 p.m., an officer ran from the garage and yelled, 'Fire in the hole!' A small explosion followed, destroying what officers said was an unattended briefcase but not a bomb.

About 300 to 400 protesters were nearby. Some had been chased out of downtown by police and tear gas to Capitol Hill. Others were locals angry that police were there.

'Off our hill! Off our hill!' protesters near Seattle Central Community College chanted at police. Many set off fireworks, including some from the roof of a church.

At 10 p.m., police set off three concussion grenades, then fired a dozen rounds of tear gas, forcing many protesters to flee.

Exactly who set off the first riot of the day was in dispute.

'I have been a medic for the protesters all day long,' a Colorado man named Bob said. 'And even though I saw some things people might say were violent, I think the police overreacted.'

In one incident, police shot tear gas into a peaceful crowd and at a lone protester at Pine and Fifth who was simply waving a Mexican flag.

Amber Lewis, an 18-year-old journalism student from Emory College in Atlanta, was standing on trash can when tear gas hit her full in the face.

'This isn't supposed to happen to us,' she said through tears, sitting on the sidewalk while two women rinsed her eyes with a saline solution.

At Fourth and Pike, five overturned trash containers littered the intersection, and was was set ablaze as the echo of tear-gas guns sounded in the distance.

'Not a good night to go shopping,' deadpanned a police officer.

Those who tried to go about their business risked being drawn into the mess.

Late in the day, protesters at Sixth and Stewart hijacked an Emerald City Garbage Disposal truck on its way to the dump, blocking it with newspapers and trash cans to use it for protection against police.

The driver of the truck, whose name was not known yesterday, said over his cellular telephone that he felt annoyed, not threatened.

'Some of us have got to go to work,' he told a reporter. 'I wish they (the police) would use tear gas so I can just go.'

The driver later moved the debris and drove away.

The manager of Ben Bridge Jewelers at Fourth and Union looked at the crowd of protesters and police just outside the bars of his closed shop, shaking his head and rubbing eyes stinging with tear gas.

Most downtown businesses closed early, though Emmanuel Marianakis, owner of Olympic Broiler, said he planned to stay open until the authorities told him to close.

'No matter whether they're demonstrators or with WTO, they have to eat,' Marianakis said, 'and I sell food.'

Several Metro buses were boarded by protesters who assaulted drivers, pulled battery plugs and slashed tires, said King County Executive Ron Sims, who promised more security today.

Reacting to rumors that the WTO would leave Seattle, Terry Laggner-Brown, spokeswoman for the Washington Council of International Trade, denied the rumors. The council brought the WTO to Seattle.

'I'm standing here in the WTO press office, and I can assure you that this meeting will continue,' she said. 'It's taking place as we speak.'

Delegates from 135 countries were prevented from attending meetings at the Paramount in the morning, but business proceedings were held in the afternoon as police squeezed delegates through lines of protesters to the Washington State Convention and Trade Center. Some delegates were roughed up in the process, but none were reported injured.

The National Lawyers Guild faxed an angry letter to Schell yesterday afternoon, complaining of excessive police force. The guild, with 150 legal observers at the protests, claimed rubber bullets were fired by police at least twice and said officers beat a television cameraman and chased down a woman to dose her with pepper spray.

Stamper refused to confirm that rubber bullets were used, but other officials said much smaller and less-dangerous rubber pellets and bean bags were used.

There were apparently no serious injuries, though Harborview Medical Center treated three people who had been gassed. Virginia Mason Medical Center treated five for gas and one for a minor rubber pellet injury. Swedish Medical Center treated three for gas and one for injuries from a fistfight.

The huge and orderly labor march seemed to calm things midday, but violence flared later on Fourth Avenue near Pike and Union Streets. It began when a small group of self-styled anarchists started throwing bottles at police, and used hammers and crowbars to shatter store windows.

'I don't think it's right to hurt someone,' said Rain, a 17-year-old who joined in the rampage. 'But property destruction is not violent ... And we're not just going to lay down and say, 'Peace, love, let me give you a flower, piggie.'

Protesters from several groups, labor marchers and University of Washington students then set trash containers and protest signs afire. King County deputies responded by lobbing in a dozen tear-gas grenades.

Young people were running, rubbing their eyes, but other protesters rushed to take their place and the deputies threw more canisters. Some protesters tossed the canisters back.

Windows were broken at the Bank of America on Pike between Fourth and Fifth, as well as at Starbucks, Washington Mutual Bank, Warner Bros., Banana Republic, Nordstrom, FAO Schwarz and McDonald's. A red 'A' – the symbol for anarchy – was spray-painted on some buildings.

'Remarks by the President to Farmers, Students from the Seattle-Tacoma Area Who Study Trade, and Area Officials', Seattle, 1 December 1999.

THE WHITE HOUSE
Office of the Press Secretary
(Seattle, Washington)

For Immediate Release December 1, 1999
REMARKS BY THE PRESIDENT
TO FARMERS, STUDENTS FROM THE SEATTLE-TACOMA
AREA WHO STUDY TRADE, AND AREA OFFICIALS
Weyerhauser Facility
Transit Shed – Terminal 5
The Port of Seattle, Washington

THE PRESIDENT: Thank you very much. Good afternoon. John, thank you for your introduction and thank you for your example. I want to say a little more in a minute about the points that you made, but I thank you for being here.

[...]

Last year, Seattle sold $34 billion in exports to foreign markets, making it the largest exporter among all American cities – everything from airplanes to apples. The control tower I just climbed, therefore, offers an interesting vantage point, not only of what was once a condemned toxic waste site and is now a wonderful, flourish economic asset; but in a larger sense, a vantage point of the 21st century world that I think we ought to be building for our children.

It's a perfect place to talk about what we came here to the WTO meeting in Seattle to do – to open markets and expand opportunities, not only for our people, but for people all around the world; from the world's newest business, e-commerce, to the world's oldest business, farming. We came to talk about trade, and to talk about trade in the context of an increasingly globalized society.

Now, I want to say just a few words about all the rather interesting hoopla that's been going on here. We need to start and ask ourselves some basic questions: Do you believe that on balance, over the last 50 years, the United States has benefited from world trade? I do.

There wouldn't be nearly as many family farmers left in America as there are today – with all the mechanization and the modernization – if we hadn't been able to sell our products around the world, because we can produce more at higher quality and lower cost than any other country in the world, in so many products. Today, we have about 4 percent of the world's people. We enjoy about 22 percent of the world's income. It is pretty much elemental math that we can't continue to do that unless we sell something to the other 96 percent of the people that inhabit this increasingly interconnected planet of ours.

Now, if you look at where the farmers in our country are today – whether they're row crop farmers like most of them in my home state of Arkansas, growing soybeans and rice and cotton and wheat; or people who grow fruit in Washington State, or vegetables here and on the East Coast – one of the biggest problems we've got is low prices because of the Asian financial crisis. And it's been a terrible burden. In addition to low prices, many of our farmers have been victimized by terrible, terrible weather problems. And, finally, they deal with market after market after market where they could sell even more than they do if the markets were more open.

I personally believe for the farmers who are in our national farm programs, we're going to have to adjust our national laws if we are going to stop having an annual appropriation of the surplus that's as big as what we've been doing over the last couple of years. But, over and above that, for the farmers – like the people that run our apple orchards that aren't in the farm programs, we've got to keep fighting to open these markets.

Now, we do that against a background of people who are raising more and more questions about the global trading system and about the process of globalization in general.

When I see all these people in the streets here, I'd like to point out that among a lot of people who are peacefully protesting here in the best American tradition, are protesting in part because the interests they represent have never been allowed inside the deliberations of the world trading system. And I went all the way to Geneva last year to talk to the WTO to tell them we had to change that, we needed to open this system up.

For most of the last 50 years, trading issues, when they were finally decided, were the private province of CEOs, trade ministers and the politicians who supported them. Now we know we have to continue to open markets, we're reaching out to places like China. We're trying to do more with developing nations. We're trying to build more partnerships with governments and industry and labor and management. But we can't do any of it unless there is a broader consensus on trade that reaches deep into our country and to other countries.

So I say that for those who came here to peacefully make their point, I welcome them here because I want them to be integrated into the longer-term debate. To those who came here to break windows and hurt small businesses or stop people from going to meetings or having their say, I condemn them; and I'm sorry that the mayor and the governor and the police officers and others have had to go through this. But we need to make a clear distinction between that which we condemn and that which we welcome. (Applause.)

I'm convinced we do have to open the WTO and the world trading system to greater public scrutiny and to greater public participation. Because unless real people, like this apple farmer from Washington, can say, this is how I fit in the global economy, this is why my family and I are better off than we otherwise would be, over the long run we're not going to be able to continue to bring the world together, which I think is important to America economically and I think it is very important politically that we continue to work closely with countries and encourage them to follow good rules of law and adopt good economic policies and to be good neighbors and not hostile neighbors.

There are a lot of opinions being expressed here among a lot of the folks that are out in the streets, and representatives of groups that I will meet with later today, that I do not agree with. But I am glad that there is such intense interest in this meeting, because it shows that people really do care about this now; and, therefore, trade decisions, like other decisions we make in the Congress and in Washington and in the state houses around the country, have to become part of the democratic process.

You know, every elected official here will tell you that there are some decisions that you really have to consult heavily with the people you represent before you make, and other decisions you know they've just sort of given you a contract on. They say, oh, well – the people in North Dakota, I know, Congressman Pomeroy or Senator Conrad, and I don't understand that issue very much, but whatever decision they make is okay with me because I trust them.

And it's not that way any more here, with trade. We have to bring people into this tent. And we have to do it in an effective way. But I think, at least for people like me – and I haven't even succeeded in bringing harmony, I know, within my own party about this – but I do not see how we can have the country and the future we want unless America continues to be a leading force for expanding trade – expanding markets for goods and services; expanding the reach of international commerce; doing it on fair and decent terms; being sensitive to the burdens that the poorest countries have; and understanding that, while a concern for labor or the environment could be twisted to be an excuse for protectionism, it is not wrong for the United States to say we don't believe in child labor, or forced labor, or the oppression of our brothers and sisters who work for a living around the world. And we don't believe that growing the economy requires us to undermine the environment.

You know, you just look at this port here. What they're doing with multimodal transportation here is saving huge amounts of energy, dramatically reducing greenhouse gas emissions as it promotes economic growth. You're going to see the growth, in my opinion, in the next several years of alternative fuels, much of it coming out of America's farming areas, which will dramatically reduce greenhouse gas emissions, reduce global warming and accelerate economic growth. So I strongly believe that if we want to get everybody together and move forward, we are going to have to listen to people who have legitimate economic concerns, legitimate environmental concerns, legitimate labor concerns.

But one of the things that I think we've got to be clear on, everybody has to decide, do you think we are better off or worse off with an increasingly integrated global economy where productive Americans have a chance to sell their goods and services and skills around the world. I think we're better off. That's the number one core decision we ought to make up our mind as a country we agree about. (Applause.)

Now, I want this new trade round at the WTO to be about jobs, development, and broadly shared prosperity and about improving the quality of life and work for ordinary people all around the world. It isn't right for me to ask for the good things I want for America's working families without wanting to provide those opportunities for others who are willing to work for them.

The impact of this round could be quite profound. Since the first trade round 50 years ago, we've cut major nations' tariffs on manufactured goods by 90 percent. During the same period, global trade has grown fifteen-fold, and we've seen the most rapid, sustained economic growth – not just in the United States, but throughout the world – in any period of human history, because we're working together.

Are there difficulties? Are there problems? Are there disagreements? Of course, and there always will be. That's why you have to have some system to resolve them. Whatever system you adopt, will there always be a mistake made by somebody, somewhere, sometime? Of course. We're all human.

But we need to keep our eyes on the objective, and increasing economic cooperation is in the interest of the ordinary citizens of the United States and the rest of the world. If we expand access, and we do it on fair terms, and we're sensitive to the legitimate difficulties these poor countries face, we can also advance the cause of the environment and labor conditions without it becoming a shield for protectionism and trying to take unfair advantage of countries that are poorer than we are. I believe that.

But, again, let's keep our eyes on the big issue: we cannot grow the American economy in the 21st century unless we continue to sell more to a world that is prospering and that is more connected, increasingly, in information technology and travel – not only with us, but with everyone else in the world.

The typical American – let's just take apples, for example – the typical American eats 20 pounds of fresh apples each year. And this is a pander to Washington state, I am not the typical American; I eat more. (Laughter and applause.) This is a pander, I admit.

But the typical European consumes about 46 pounds of apples a year. So America exported $353 million worth of apples last year. More than a quarter of the total, 46,000 metric tons, were shipped here, from Seattle – Red Delicious from the Lake Chelan region; Granny Smiths from the Columbia Basin; Winesaps, Fujis, Galas grown in Washington state, boxed and bound for Mexico, Malaysia, and more than 40 other countries around the world.

I have worked very hard to open these markets. We opened the Japanese market for the first time to Washington State's apples in our administration. Then we fought to get the barriers down in Washington, in Mexico and elsewhere. And we're making some progress.

But it is very important to recognize – go back to John, or go back to – those of us who come from farming states. Farmers are the lifeblood of our country. They are better at what they do, thank goodness, than any group of people on Earth. But we cannot preserve family farms unless we sell more of what we grow to more people around the world, because the structure of agriculture we have, to make a living, has to produce a lot more food than all of us can consume.

And that is a good thing. That can be a gift to the rest of the world. It can free other countries to work on what they need to do – to develop the capacities of their people, to focus on diversifying their own economies. And we have to find a way to reach agreements to do that.

Five years ago, we joined with our trading partners to put agriculture on the WTO agenda. We made some progress then; we pledged to come back and do more. Today, our agenda here is to fight and win for the family farmers of the United States. (Applause.) We want to level the playing field. We don't want any special preferences. We just want agriculture to be treated as fairly as any other sector in the global economy.

I know that's long overdue and I believe it is the due of every farm family in America, whether an apple farmer in the Cascades, a banana farmer in the Cameroon, any farmer deserves a chance to compete. It is not just American farmers that would be benefitted from this. Some of the poorest countries in the world would get the biggest benefits out of this trade round if we continue to tear down barriers to agricultural exports. They shouldn't have to compete against state-owned enterprises, restrictive regulations, the size of other countries' government grants.

In the European Union, for example, which accounts for 85 percent of the world's agricultural export subsidies, half of the overall budget is spent on agriculture. Now, I appreciate their support for their rural communities. We've always wanted to support our rural communities. But we have to work out a system going forward where everybody can do what they do best. And then people have to be given time and support and investment to make the transitions into the new economy. That's all I'm asking for and that's all I would ever ask for, for people here in the United States.

We have to lower tariff barriers; they're too high. On average, official rates abroad are five times as high as they are here in America. Taking apples as an example, it was just mentioned tariff rates are 45 percent in Korea and 30 percent in China. One of the reasons that our people in our economic team, Charlene Barshefsky and her group and Gene Sperling when they went to China, they negotiated a steep cut in the tariff in China to 10 percent by the year 2004. That's more apple sales from Washington. It will help more family farmers.

We will also work to reduce domestic supports that don't support trade, so much as distort it by paying farmers to overproduce and drive prices down – and we see that in a lot of places in the world. That should not be the case. We know that our farms can produce a vast and varied supply of food at affordable prices in a way that helps to reduce hunger and malnutrition around the world. We also should see that the promise of biotechnology is realized by consumers as well as producers in the environment, ensuring that the safety of our food is guaranteed by science-based and absolutely open domestic regulations. And we should maintain market access based on sound science.

I want to say to the people of Europe and all around the world, I would never knowingly permit a single pound of any American food product to leave this country if I had a shred of evidence that it was unsafe and neither would any farmer in the United States of America. (Applause.) I say to people around the world, we eat this food, too, and we eat more of it than you do. Now, if there's something wrong with anything we do, we want to know about it first. But we need to handle this in an open, honest way.

It shouldn't be just about politics and emotionalism and short-term advantage. We need an open system. There is a reason we have confidence in the federal bodies that analyze the safety of our food. They may not be perfect, but nobody believes they are in anybody's hip pocket. They are the world's best experts. We have an orderly, disciplined system here for evaluating the safety of not only our food, but our medicine. And we ask all of our trading partners to do the same and to deal with us in a straightforward manner about this.

But everybody must understand we have nothing to hide and we are eating this food, too. Nobody is trying to do anything under the table, in secret, in an inappropriate way. But neither should our farmers be subject to unrealistic delays and unfair discrimination based on suspicion unsupported by the latest scientific examination. Let's handle this in an open, fair, scientific way. That's the right way to do this. (Applause.)

Now, after I leave you, I am going to go meet with the trade ministers that are here from more than 100 countries. It's a great honor for Seattle, for the State of Washington and for the United States to have these people come here and to try to come to terms with a lot of these very difficult issues. I want to talk about how we can make sure that ordinary working people all across the world feel that they have a stake in an improving global economic system. I want to assure them that we have to do what is necessary to make sure that economic competition lifts people up everywhere.

Now, there are people, again, I say, who honestly believe that open trade stacks the deck against ordinary people. Thirty percent of the growth we've gotten in this country, 30 percent, between 1993 and the time of the Asian financial crisis, came because of expanding trade. We had some pretty good farm years in there too, folks. It's hard to remember it's been so bad the last year or so, but we had some pretty good years.

And we have got to figure out a way not only to sell the idea but to make it real, that we can continue to pursue these objectives in a way that lifts people's quality of life up and lifts the ordinary living standards for people throughout the world. We can do that.

Now, let me finally say that I know these questions won't be easy. One of the things I've learned in all trade cases is that it once again reaffirms the wisdom of the Italian Renaissance political philosopher Machiavelli, who said – I'm paraphrasing here, but this is almost exactly right – he said, there is nothing so difficult in all of human affairs as to change the established order of things. Because the people that are going to win will always be somewhat uncertain of their gain; whereas, the people who will lose are absolutely sure of what they are going to lose.

So this will require some amount of imagination and trust and humility and flexibility. But if we're going to have a world, rule-based trading system, then we have got to make it work for ordinary folks. But we in America, we have to take the lead in continuing to make the main point. The world is a better place today after 50 years of more open trade than it would have been if we hadn't had it. Americans are better off today after 50 years of open trade than they would have been if we hadn't had it.

And what has helped us will help the poorest countries in the world, the wealthy countries and the countries in between if we find a way to continue to draw together, and to deal with the legitimate concerns of the legitimate protestors in the streets of Seattle.

And, you know, to me it is a very exciting time. This is a high-class problem, and we ought to treat it as a 21st century challenge worth our best efforts. If we do, I think we'll get a good result.

Thank you very much. (Applause.)

Kerry Murakami, 'Geneva Sounded WTO Warning That Went Unheeded in Seattle', *Seattle Post-Intelligencer*, 10 March 2000, p. A1.

In May 1998, 40,000 protesters took to the streets of Geneva. They threw paint bombs and bottles at banks and corporate offices, reportedly causing $3 million in damage, and overturned the Jamaican delegate's car – all in protest of the World Trade Organization.

Four months later, Seattle's corporate and political leaders were trying to persuade the WTO to come here.

Why didn't those leaders heed the warning in the shattered glass and overturned cars of Geneva?

In part because business leaders who extended the invitation and city officials who helped clinch the deal knew little about what the city would face.

The riots had not been big news in the United States. Neither Seattle paper carried articles about them.

Deputy Mayor Maud Daudon, then-City Council President Sue Donaldson and then-council Budget Committee Chairwoman Martha Choe said they were unaware of the street violence in Switzerland when they pitched Seattle to a selection team from the White House in September 1998.

They and other city officials said they didn't learn about Geneva's problems until after Seattle's selection the following January.

But interviews with the principals involved in inviting the WTO here, and a review of internal correspondence obtained by the Seattle Post-Intelligencer, suggest city and business leaders – out of complacency or perhaps a sense of euphoria about stepping onto the international stage – asked few questions.

In an e-mail to an aide to Sen. Slade Gorton, R-Wash., last September, the city's federal lobbyist, Steve Johnson, wrote: 'In the euphoria of pursuing the event, the Seattle Host Committee (Ray Waldman, Pat Davis of the Port, along with our business leaders and electeds) had little understanding of the mind-boggling security considerations associated with having the world focus its discontent with trade policy in Seattle.'

By comparison, officials in Honolulu – one of three finalists to host the conference – said they were aware of the problems in Geneva and took the possibility of mass protests seriously.

'It was all over the international news and CNN. I think that's where I first heard about it was on CNN,' said Brenda Foster, an aide to Hawaii Gov. Benjamin Cayetano. 'Anybody watching the news and in particular paying attention to international news would have known about it.'

In fact, part of Honolulu's pitch, Foster said, was that the island offers insulation from protesters.

'Anarchists can't just drive five hours up the freeway to get here,' Foster said, referring to protesters from Eugene, Ore., who helped disrupt the WTO conference in Seattle.

A few, like Seattle Port Commissioner Pat Davis, co-author of Seattle's bid proposal, said they might have been aware of Geneva's riot, but didn't think much about it at the time. 'It just didn't register,' she said.

Even when Geneva's riot became widely known, most viewed it as a European phenomenon that wouldn't happen here.

Ray Waldman, executive director of the Seattle Host Organization, has told council WTO investigators that he and Davis flew to Geneva last May, where they were given a tape of news broadcasts of the riots there. Waldman said he gave it to Seattle police.

Waldman said he had a vague notion there was some sort of protest in Geneva, but figured it was the normal sort of non-violent protests that happen at trade conferences.

The investigators say Waldman told them that he had lived and traveled in Europe for decades and was aware of a core of radical students and activists who can be mobilized for a variety of causes.

'We don't have anything like that in the U.S.,' he told the investigators. 'I tended to discount the possibility of extreme violence.'

James Kelly, president of the Urban League and a member of the citizens panel, said he is 'kind of flabbergasted by (Waldman's) response.'

Hawaii's Foster, who attended the University of Washington, said she took the potential of mass riots seriously.

Whether Geneva's riot was ample warning of riots in Seattle is a matter for debate. But the debate came only after the Battle of Seattle.

In a self-assessment written after the conference, the Seattle Host Organization acknowledged that civic leaders should have found out more before inviting the WTO to town.

The report, 'Lessons Learned,' was written by Bill Stafford, Washington Trade Alliance president, and Mariana Parks, Microsoft public relations director. They wrote that, 'When recruiting (future) meetings, we should find out more about the conference and its logistics. How controversial is the meeting? Is it likely to draw protesters? Was tear gas required at the last meeting?'

So why didn't they see trouble coming?

In hindsight, maybe they should have, acknowledged Cliff Traisman, the city's intergovernmental affairs director, and Keith Orton, the office's international affairs expert.

In the year leading up to the Seattle WTO meeting, President Clinton began talking about inviting China into the organization. The collapse of trade discussions last fall dumped a list of unresolved issues on the Seattle conference. Events seemed to conspire against a calm meeting here.

Swept up in the excitement

The city became involved after Port of Seattle Economic Development Director Don Lorentz heard during a tourism conference that President Clinton wanted to host the next WTO conference, and Rita Hayes, the U.S. ambassador to the WTO, encouraged Seattle to apply.

Lorentz said he left Geneva either immediately after the conference there, on May 14 or early on the 15th. Had he been in downtown Geneva on May 15, he would have seen first-hand what was in store for Seattle – the WTO under siege.

He said he heard about it later, and didn't think much of it.

Back home, business leaders – including Davis and Waldman – hurriedly wrote the bid. City officials technically never agreed to host the WTO, but gave their blessing when Mayor Paul Schell's aides and council members helped woo the selection team on Sept. 30 and Nov. 13.

'You have to remember 40 cities were going after the WTO,' Traisman said. 'Why would any of them pursue the WTO if they expected what was going to happen?'

In October of that year, in the time between the selection committee's two visits, the City Council voted not to pursue the 2012 Olympic Games. In that case, the United States Olympic Committee required the mayor and the City Council to submit a formal bid. There was no such requirement for the WTO – the city seemed swept up in the excitement.

Doha Ministerial Declaration, 14 November 2001, World Trade Organization, WT/MIN(01)/DEC/1.

WORLD TRADE
ORGANIZATION

WT/MIN(01)/DEC/1
20 November 2001
(01-5859)

MINISTERIAL CONFERENCE
Fourth Session
Doha, 9–14 November 2001

MINISTERIAL DECLARATION
Adopted on 14 November 2001

1. The multilateral trading system embodied in the World Trade Organization has contributed significantly to economic growth, development and employment throughout the past fifty years. We are determined, particularly in the light of the global economic slowdown, to maintain the process of reform and liberalization of trade policies, thus ensuring that the system plays its full part in promoting recovery, growth and development. We therefore strongly reaffirm the principles and objectives set out in the Marrakesh Agreement Establishing the World Trade Organization, and pledge to reject the use of protectionism.

2. International trade can play a major role in the promotion of economic development and the alleviation of poverty. We recognize the need for all our peoples to benefit from the increased opportunities and welfare gains that the multilateral trading system generates. The majority of WTO Members are developing countries. We seek to place their needs and interests at the heart of the Work Programme adopted in this Declaration. Recalling the Preamble to the Marrakesh Agreement, we shall continue to make positive efforts designed to ensure that developing countries, and especially the least-developed among them, secure a share in the growth of world trade commensurate with the needs of their economic development. In this context, enhanced market access, balanced rules, and well targeted, sustainably financed technical assistance and capacity-building programmes have important roles to play.

3. We recognize the particular vulnerability of the least-developed countries and the special structural difficulties they face in the global economy. We are committed to addressing the marginalization of least-developed countries in international trade and to improving their effective participation in the multilateral trading system. We recall the commitments made by Ministers at

our meetings in Marrakesh, Singapore and Geneva, and by the international community at the Third UN Conference on Least-Developed Countries in Brussels, to help least-developed countries secure beneficial and meaningful integration into the multilateral trading system and the global economy. We are determined that the WTO will play its part in building effectively on these commitments under the Work Programme we are establishing.

4. We stress our commitment to the WTO as the unique forum for global trade rule-making and liberalization, while also recognizing that regional trade agreements can play an important role in promoting the liberalization and expansion of trade and in fostering development.

5. We are aware that the challenges Members face in a rapidly changing international environment cannot be addressed through measures taken in the trade field alone. We shall continue to work with the Bretton Woods institutions for greater coherence in global economic policy-making.

6. We strongly reaffirm our commitment to the objective of sustainable development, as stated in the Preamble to the Marrakesh Agreement. We are convinced that the aims of upholding and safeguarding an open and non-discriminatory multilateral trading system, and acting for the protection of the environment and the promotion of sustainable development can and must be mutually supportive. We take note of the efforts by Members to conduct national environmental assessments of trade policies on a voluntary basis. We recognize that under WTO rules no country should be prevented from taking measures for the protection of human, animal or plant life or health, or of the environment at the levels it considers appropriate, subject to the requirement that they are not applied in a manner which would constitute a means of arbitrary or unjustifiable discrimination between countries where the same conditions prevail, or a disguised restriction on international trade, and are otherwise in accordance with the provisions of the WTO Agreements. We welcome the WTO's continued cooperation with UNEP and other inter-governmental environmental organizations. We encourage efforts to promote cooperation between the WTO and relevant international environmental and developmental organizations, especially in the lead-up to the World Summit on Sustainable Development to be held in Johannesburg, South Africa, in September 2002.

7. We reaffirm the right of Members under the General Agreement on Trade in Services to regulate, and to introduce new regulations on, the supply of services.

8. We reaffirm our declaration made at the Singapore Ministerial Conference regarding internationally recognized core labour standards. We take note of work under way in the International Labour Organization (ILO) on the social dimension of globalization.

9. We note with particular satisfaction that this Conference has completed the WTO accession procedures for China and Chinese Taipei. We also welcome the accession as new Members, since our last Session, of Albania, Croatia, Georgia, Jordan, Lithuania, Moldova and Oman, and note the extensive market-access commitments already made by these countries on accession. These accessions will greatly strengthen the multilateral trading system, as will those of the 28 countries now negotiating their accession. We therefore attach great importance to concluding accession proceedings as quickly as possible. In particular, we are committed to accelerating the accession of least-developed countries.

10. Recognizing the challenges posed by an expanding WTO membership, we confirm our collective responsibility to ensure internal transparency and the effective participation of all Members. While emphasizing the intergovernmental character of the organization, we are committed to making the WTO's operations more transparent, including through more effective and prompt dissemination of information, and to improve dialogue with the public. We shall therefore at the national and multilateral levels continue to promote a better public understanding of the WTO and to communicate the benefits of a liberal, rules-based multilateral trading system.

11. In view of these considerations, we hereby agree to undertake the broad and balanced Work Programme set out below. This incorporates both an expanded negotiating agenda and other important decisions and activities necessary to address the challenges facing the multilateral trading system.

WORK PROGRAMME
Implementation-Related Issues and Concerns

12. We attach the utmost importance to the implementation-related issues and concerns raised by Members and are determined to find appropriate solutions to them. [...] We agree that negotiations on outstanding implementation issues shall be an integral part of the Work Programme we are establishing, [....] In this regard, we shall proceed as follows: (a) where we provide a specific negotiating mandate in this Declaration, the relevant implementation issues shall be addressed under that mandate; (b) the other outstanding implementation issues shall be addressed as a matter of priority by the relevant WTO bodies, which shall report to the Trade Negotiations Committee, established under paragraph 46 below, by the end of 2002 for appropriate action.

Agriculture

13. We recognize the work already undertaken in the negotiations initiated in early 2000 under Article 20 of the Agreement on Agriculture, including the

large number of negotiating proposals submitted on behalf of a total of 121 Members. We recall the long-term objective referred to in the Agreement to establish a fair and market-oriented trading system through a programme of fundamental reform encompassing strengthened rules and specific commitments on support and protection in order to correct and prevent restrictions and distortions in world agricultural markets. We reconfirm our commitment to this programme. Building on the work carried out to date and without prejudging the outcome of the negotiations we commit ourselves to comprehensive negotiations aimed at: substantial improvements in market access; reductions of, with a view to phasing out, all forms of export subsidies; and substantial reductions in trade-distorting domestic support. We agree that special and differential treatment for developing countries shall be an integral part of all elements of the negotiations and shall be embodied in the Schedules of concessions and commitments and as appropriate in the rules and disciplines to be negotiated, so as to be operationally effective and to enable developing countries to effectively take account of their development needs, including food security and rural development. We take note of the non-trade concerns reflected in the negotiating proposals submitted by Members and confirm that non-trade concerns will be taken into account in the negotiations as provided for in the Agreement on Agriculture.

14. Modalities for the further commitments, including provisions for special and differential treatment, shall be established no later than 31 March 2003. Participants shall submit their comprehensive draft Schedules based on these modalities no later than the date of the Fifth Session of the Ministerial Conference. The negotiations, including with respect to rules and disciplines and related legal texts, shall be concluded as part and at the date of conclusion of the negotiating agenda as a whole.

Services

15. The negotiations on trade in services shall be conducted with a view to promoting the economic growth of all trading partners and the development of developing and least-developed countries. We recognize the work already undertaken in the negotiations, initiated in January 2000 under Article XIX of the General Agreement on Trade in Services, and the large number of proposals submitted by Members on a wide range of sectors and several horizontal issues, as well as on movement of natural persons. We reaffirm the Guidelines and Procedures for the Negotiations adopted by the Council for Trade in Services on 28 March 2001 as the basis for continuing the negotiations, with a view to achieving the objectives of the General Agreement on Trade in Services, as stipulated in the Preamble,

Article IV and Article XIX of that Agreement. Participants shall submit initial requests for specific commitments by 30 June 2002 and initial offers by 31 March 2003.

MARKET ACCESS FOR NON-AGRICULTURAL PRODUCTS

16. We agree to negotiations which shall aim, by modalities to be agreed, to reduce or as appropriate eliminate tariffs, including the reduction or elimination of tariff peaks, high tariffs, and tariff escalation, as well as non-tariff barriers, in particular on products of export interest to developing countries. Product coverage shall be comprehensive and without *a priori* exclusions. The negotiations shall take fully into account the special needs and interests of developing and least-developed country participants, including through less than full reciprocity in reduction commitments, in accordance with the relevant provisions of Article XXVIII *bis* of GATT 1994 [...]. To this end, the modalities to be agreed will include appropriate studies and capacity-building measures to assist least-developed countries to participate effectively in the negotiations.

TRADE-RELATED ASPECTS OF INTELLECTUAL PROPERTY RIGHTS

17. We stress the importance we attach to implementation and interpretation of the Agreement on Trade-Related Aspects of Intellectual Property Rights (TRIPS Agreement) in a manner supportive of public health, by promoting both access to existing medicines and research and development into new medicines and, in this connection, are adopting a separate Declaration.
18. With a view to completing the work started in the Council for Trade-Related Aspects of Intellectual Property Rights (Council for TRIPS) on the implementation of Article 23.4, we agree to negotiate the establishment of a multilateral system of notification and registration of geographical indications for wines and spirits by the Fifth Session of the Ministerial Conference. We note that issues related to the extension of the protection of geographical indications provided for in Article 23 to products other than wines and spirits will be addressed in the Council for TRIPS pursuant to paragraph 12 of this Declaration.
19. We instruct the Council for TRIPS [...] to examine, *inter alia*, the relationship between the TRIPS Agreement and the Convention on Biological Diversity, the protection of traditional knowledge and folklore, and other relevant new developments raised by Members pursuant to Article 71.1. [...]

RELATIONSHIP BETWEEN TRADE AND INVESTMENT

20. Recognizing the case for a multilateral framework to secure transparent,

stable and predictable conditions for long-term cross-border investment, particularly foreign direct investment, that will contribute to the expansion of trade, and the need for enhanced technical assistance and capacity-building in this area as referred to in paragraph 21, we agree that negotiations will take place after the Fifth Session of the Ministerial Conference on the basis of a decision to be taken, by explicit consensus, at that Session on modalities of negotiations.

21. We recognize the needs of developing and least-developed countries for enhanced support for technical assistance and capacity building in this area, including policy analysis and development so that they may better evaluate the implications of closer multilateral cooperation for their development policies and objectives, and human and institutional development. To this end, we shall work in cooperation with other relevant intergovernmental organisations, including UNCTAD, and through appropriate regional and bilateral channels, to provide strengthened and adequately resourced assistance to respond to these needs.

22. In the period until the Fifth Session, further work in the Working Group on the Relationship Between Trade and Investment will focus on the clarification of: scope and definition; transparency; non-discrimination; modalities for pre-establishment commitments based on a GATS-type, positive list approach; development provisions; exceptions and balance-of-payments safeguards; consultation and the settlement of disputes between Members. Any framework should reflect in a balanced manner the interests of home and host countries, and take due account of the development policies and objectives of host governments as well as their right to regulate in the public interest. The special development, trade and financial needs of developing and least-developed countries should be taken into account as an integral part of any framework, which should enable Members to undertake obligations and commitments commensurate with their individual needs and circumstances. Due regard should be paid to other relevant WTO provisions. Account should be taken, as appropriate, of existing bilateral and regional arrangements on investment.

INTERACTION BETWEEN TRADE AND COMPETITION POLICY

23. Recognizing the case for a multilateral framework to enhance the contribution of competition policy to international trade and development, and the need for enhanced technical assistance and capacity-building in this area as referred to in paragraph 24, we agree that negotiations will take place after the Fifth Session of the Ministerial Conference on the basis of a decision to be taken, by explicit consensus, at that Session on modalities of negotiations.

24. We recognize the needs of developing and least-developed countries for enhanced support for technical assistance and capacity building in this area, including policy analysis and development so that they may better evaluate the implications of closer multilateral cooperation for their development policies and objectives, and human and institutional development. To this end, we shall work in cooperation with other relevant intergovernmental organisations, including UNCTAD, and through appropriate regional and bilateral channels, to provide strengthened and adequately resourced assistance to respond to these needs.
25. In the period until the Fifth Session, further work in the Working Group on the Interaction between Trade and Competition Policy will focus on the clarification of: core principles, including transparency, non-discrimination and procedural fairness, and provisions on hardcore cartels; modalities for voluntary cooperation; and support for progressive reinforcement of competition institutions in developing countries through capacity building. Full account shall be taken of the needs of developing and least-developed country participants and appropriate flexibility provided to address them.

Transparency in Government Procurement

26. Recognizing the case for a multilateral agreement on transparency in government procurement and the need for enhanced technical assistance and capacity building in this area, we agree that negotiations will take place after the Fifth Session of the Ministerial Conference on the basis of a decision to be taken, by explicit consensus, at that Session on modalities of negotiations. These negotiations will build on the progress made in the Working Group on Transparency in Government Procurement by that time and take into account participants' development priorities, especially those of least-developed country participants. Negotiations shall be limited to the transparency aspects and therefore will not restrict the scope for countries to give preferences to domestic supplies and suppliers. We commit ourselves to ensuring adequate technical assistance and support for capacity building both during the negotiations and after their conclusion.

[...]

WTO Rules

28. In the light of experience and of the increasing application of these instruments by Members, we agree to negotiations aimed at clarifying and improving disciplines under the Agreements on Implementation of Article VI of the GATT 1994 and on Subsidies and Countervailing Measures,

while preserving the basic concepts, principles and effectiveness of these Agreements and their instruments and objectives, and taking into account the needs of developing and least-developed participants. In the initial phase of the negotiations, participants will indicate the provisions, including disciplines on trade distorting practices, that they seek to clarify and improve in the subsequent phase. In the context of these negotiations, participants shall also aim to clarify and improve WTO disciplines on fisheries subsidies, taking into account the importance of this sector to developing countries. We note that fisheries subsidies are also referred to in paragraph 31.

29. We also agree to negotiations aimed at clarifying and improving disciplines and procedures under the existing WTO provisions applying to regional trade agreements. The negotiations shall take into account the developmental aspects of regional trade agreements.

Dispute Settlement Understanding

30. We agree to negotiations on improvements and clarifications of the Dispute Settlement Understanding. The negotiations should be based on the work done thus far as well as any additional proposals by Members, and aim to agree on improvements and clarifications not later than May 2003, at which time we will take steps to ensure that the results enter into force as soon as possible thereafter.

Trade and Environment

31. With a view to enhancing the mutual supportiveness of trade and environment, we agree to negotiations, without prejudging their outcome, on:
    (i) the relationship between existing WTO rules and specific trade obligations set out in multilateral environmental agreements (MEAs). The negotiations shall be limited in scope to the applicability of such existing WTO rules as among parties to the MEA in question. The negotiations shall not prejudice the WTO rights of any Member that is not a party to the MEA in question;
    (ii) procedures for regular information exchange between MEA Secretariats and the relevant WTO committees, and the criteria for the granting of observer status;
    (iii) the reduction or, as appropriate, elimination of tariff and non-tariff barriers to environmental goods and services.

We note that fisheries subsidies form part of the negotiations provided for in paragraph 28.

32. We instruct the Committee on Trade and Environment, in pursuing work on all items on its agenda within its current terms of reference, to give

particular attention to:
- (i) the effect of environmental measures on market access, especially in relation to developing countries, in particular the least-developed among them, and those situations in which the elimination or reduction of trade restrictions and distortions would benefit trade, the environment and development;
- (ii) the relevant provisions of the Agreement on Trade-Related Aspects of Intellectual Property Rights; and
- (iii) labelling requirements for environmental purposes.

Work on these issues should include the identification of any need to clarify relevant WTO rules. The Committee shall report to the Fifth Session of the Ministerial Conference, and make recommendations, where appropriate, with respect to future action, including the desirability of negotiations. The outcome of this work as well as the negotiations carried out under paragraph 31(i) and (ii) shall be compatible with the open and non-discriminatory nature of the multilateral trading system, shall not add to or diminish the rights and obligations of Members under existing WTO agreements, in particular the Agreement on the Application of Sanitary and Phytosanitary Measures, nor alter the balance of these rights and obligations, and will take into account the needs of developing and least-developed countries.

33. We recognize the importance of technical assistance and capacity building in the field of trade and environment to developing countries, in particular the least-developed among them. We also encourage that expertise and experience be shared with Members wishing to perform environmental reviews at the national level. A report shall be prepared on these activities for the Fifth Session.

Electronic Commerce

34. [...] electronic commerce creates new challenges and opportunities for trade for Members at all stages of development, and we recognize the importance of creating and maintaining an environment which is favourable to the future development of electronic commerce. We instruct the General Council to consider the most appropriate institutional arrangements for handling the Work Programme, and to report on further progress to the Fifth Session of the Ministerial Conference. We declare that Members will maintain their current practice of not imposing customs duties on electronic transmissions until the Fifth Session.

Small Economies

35. We agree to a work programme, under the auspices of the General Council,

to examine issues relating to the trade of small economies. The objective of this work is to frame responses to the trade-related issues identified for the fuller integration of small, vulnerable economies into the multilateral trading system, and not to create a sub-category of WTO Members. The General Council shall review the work programme and make recommendations for action to the Fifth Session of the Ministerial Conference.

Trade, Debt and Finance

36. We agree to an examination, in a Working Group under the auspices of the General Council, of the relationship between trade, debt and finance, and of any possible recommendations on steps that might be taken within the mandate and competence of the WTO to enhance the capacity of the multilateral trading system to contribute to a durable solution to the problem of external indebtedness of developing and least-developed countries, and to strengthen the coherence of international trade and financial policies, with a view to safeguarding the multilateral trading system from the effects of financial and monetary instability. The General Council shall report to the Fifth Session of the Ministerial Conference on progress in the examination.

Trade and Transfer of Technology

37. We agree to an examination, in a Working Group under the auspices of the General Council, of the relationship between trade and transfer of technology, and of any possible recommendations on steps that might be taken within the mandate of the WTO to increase flows of technology to developing countries. [...]

Technical Cooperation and Capacity Building

38. We confirm that technical cooperation and capacity building are core elements of the development dimension of the multilateral trading system, and we welcome and endorse the New Strategy for WTO Technical Cooperation for Capacity Building, Growth and Integration. We instruct the Secretariat, in coordination with other relevant agencies, to support domestic efforts for mainstreaming trade into national plans for economic development and strategies for poverty reduction. The delivery of WTO technical assistance shall be designed to assist developing and least-developed countries and low-income countries in transition to adjust to WTO rules and disciplines, implement obligations and exercise the rights of membership, including drawing on the benefits of an open, rules-based multilateral trading system. Priority shall also be accorded to small,

vulnerable, and transition economies, as well as to Members and Observers without representation in Geneva. We reaffirm our support for the valuable work of the International Trade Centre, which should be enhanced.

39. We underscore the urgent necessity for the effective coordinated delivery of technical assistance with bilateral donors, in the OECD Development Assistance Committee and relevant international and regional intergovernmental institutions, within a coherent policy framework and timetable. In the coordinated delivery of technical assistance, we instruct the Director-General to consult with the relevant agencies, bilateral donors and beneficiaries, to identify ways of enhancing and rationalizing the Integrated Framework for Trade-Related Technical Assistance to Least-Developed Countries and the Joint Integrated Technical Assistance Programme (JITAP).

40. We agree that there is a need for technical assistance to benefit from secure and predictable funding. We therefore instruct the Committee on Budget, Finance and Administration to develop a plan for adoption by the General Council in December 2001 that will ensure long-term funding for WTO technical assistance at an overall level no lower than that of the current year and commensurate with the activities outlined above.

41. We have established firm commitments on technical cooperation and capacity building in various paragraphs in this Ministerial Declaration. We [...] also reaffirm the understanding in paragraph 2 on the important role of sustainably financed technical assistance and capacity-building programmes. We instruct the Director-General to report to the Fifth Session of the Ministerial Conference, with an interim report to the General Council in December 2002 on the implementation and adequacy of these commitments in the identified paragraphs.

Least-Developed Countries

42. We acknowledge the seriousness of the concerns expressed by the least-developed countries (LDCs) in the Zanzibar Declaration adopted by their Ministers in July 2001. We recognize that the integration of the LDCs into the multilateral trading system requires meaningful market access, support for the diversification of their production and export base, and trade-related technical assistance and capacity building. We agree that the meaningful integration of LDCs into the trading system and the global economy will involve efforts by all WTO Members. We commit ourselves to the objective of duty-free, quota-free market access for products originating from LDCs. In this regard, we welcome the significant market access improvements by WTO Members in advance of the Third UN Conference on LDCs

(LDC-III), in Brussels, May 2001. We further commit ourselves to consider additional measures for progressive improvements in market access for LDCs. Accession of LDCs remains a priority for the Membership. We agree to work to facilitate and accelerate negotiations with acceding LDCs. We instruct the Secretariat to reflect the priority we attach to LDCs' accessions in the annual plans for technical assistance. We reaffirm the commitments we undertook at LDC-III, and agree that the WTO should take into account, in designing its work programme for LDCs, the trade-related elements of the Brussels Declaration and Programme of Action, consistent with the WTO's mandate, adopted at LDC-III. We instruct the Sub-Committee for Least-Developed Countries to design such a work programme and to report on the agreed work programme to the General Council at its first meeting in 2002.

43. We endorse the Integrated Framework for Trade-Related Technical Assistance to Least-Developed Countries (IF) as a viable model for LDCs' trade development. We urge development partners to significantly increase contributions to the IF Trust Fund and WTO extra-budgetary trust funds in favour of LDCs. We urge the core agencies, in coordination with development partners, to explore the enhancement of the IF with a view to addressing the supply-side constraints of LDCs and the extension of the model to all LDCs, following the review of the IF and the appraisal of the ongoing Pilot Scheme in selected LDCs. We request the Director-General, following coordination with heads of the other agencies, to provide an interim report to the General Council in December 2002 and a full report to the Fifth Session of the Ministerial Conference on all issues affecting LDCs.

Special and Differential Treatment

44. We reaffirm that provisions for special and differential treatment are an integral part of the WTO Agreements. We note the concerns expressed regarding their operation in addressing specific constraints faced by developing countries, particularly least-developed countries. In that connection, we also note that some Members have proposed a Framework Agreement on Special and Differential Treatment (WT/GC/W/442). We therefore agree that all special and differential treatment provisions shall be reviewed with a view to strengthening them and making them more precise, effective and operational. In this connection, we endorse the work programme on special and differential treatment set out in the Decision on Implementation-Related Issues and Concerns.

ORGANIZATION AND MANAGEMENT OF THE WORK PROGRAMME

45. The negotiations to be pursued under the terms of this Declaration shall be concluded not later than 1 January 2005. The Fifth Session of the Ministerial Conference will take stock of progress in the negotiations, provide any necessary political guidance, and take decisions as necessary. When the results of the negotiations in all areas have been established, a Special Session of the Ministerial Conference will be held to take decisions regarding the adoption and implementation of those results.
46. The overall conduct of the negotiations shall be supervised by a Trade Negotiations Committee under the authority of the General Council. The Trade Negotiations Committee shall hold its first meeting not later than 31 January 2002. It shall establish appropriate negotiating mechanisms as required and supervise the progress of the negotiations.
47. With the exception of the improvements and clarifications of the Dispute Settlement Understanding, the conduct, conclusion and entry into force of the outcome of the negotiations shall be treated as parts of a single undertaking. However, agreements reached at an early stage may be implemented on a provisional or a definitive basis. Early agreements shall be taken into account in assessing the overall balance of the negotiations.
48. Negotiations shall be open to:
    (i) all Members of the WTO; and
    (ii) States and separate customs territories currently in the process of accession and those that inform Members, at a regular meeting of the General Council, of their intention to negotiate the terms of their membership and for whom an accession working party is established.
    Decisions on the outcomes of the negotiations shall be taken only by WTO Members.
49. The negotiations shall be conducted in a transparent manner among participants, in order to facilitate the effective participation of all. They shall be conducted with a view to ensuring benefits to all participants and to achieving an overall balance in the outcome of the negotiations.
50. The negotiations and the other aspects of the Work Programme shall take fully into account the principle of special and differential treatment for developing and least-developed countries embodied in: Part IV of the GATT 1994; the Decision of 28 November 1979 on Differential and More Favourable Treatment, Reciprocity and Fuller Participation of Developing Countries; the Uruguay Round Decision on Measures in Favour of Least-Developed Countries; and all other relevant WTO provisions.
51. The Committee on Trade and Development and the Committee on Trade

and Environment shall, within their respective mandates, each act as a forum to identify and debate developmental and environmental aspects of the negotiations, in order to help achieve the objective of having sustainable development appropriately reflected.

52. Those elements of the Work Programme which do not involve negotiations are also accorded a high priority. They shall be pursued under the overall supervision of the General Council, which shall report on progress to the Fifth Session of the Ministerial Conference.

Statement by President George W. Bush Announcing Temporary Safeguards for the US Steel Industry, Washington, DC, 5 March 2002.

President Announces Temporary Safeguards for Steel Industry

Statement by the President

Free trade is an important engine of economic growth and a cornerstone of my economic agenda. My Administration has successfully launched new global trade talks, reignited the movement for free trade within our own hemisphere, and helped bring China and Taiwan into the World Trade Organization. To open even more markets to American products, I have urged the Senate to grant me the trade promotion authority I need to create jobs and greater opportunities for U.S. workers and farmers.

An integral part of our commitment to free trade is our commitment to enforcing trade laws to make sure that America's industries and workers compete on a level playing field. Free trade should not mean lax enforcement. Consistent with this commitment, last June I launched a three-part initiative designed to restore market forces to world steel markets. This initiative includes international discussion to encourage the reduction of excess global steel capacity and negotiations to eliminate market-distorting subsidies that led to the current glut of capacity. I also called upon the United States International Trade Commission (ITC) to investigate the impact of imports on the U.S. steel industry under section 201 of the 1974 Trade Act. The ITC subsequently found that increased steel imports are a substantial cause of serious injury to our domestic industry.

Today I am announcing my decision to impose temporary safeguards to help give America's steel industry and its workers the chance to adapt to the large influx of foreign steel. This relief will help steel workers, communities that depend on steel, and the steel industry adjust without harming our economy.

These safeguards are expressly sanctioned by the rules of the World Trade Organization, which recognizes that sometimes imports can cause such serious harm to domestic industries that temporary restraints are warranted. This is one of those times.

I take this action to give our domestic steel industry an opportunity to adjust to surges in foreign imports, recognizing the harm from 50 years of foreign government intervention in the global steel market, which has resulted in bankruptcies, serious dislocation, and job loss. We also must continue to urge our trading partners to eliminate global inefficient excess capacity and market-distorting practices, such as subsidies.

The U.S. steel industry must use the temporary help today's action provides to restructure and ensure its long-term competitiveness. Restructuring will impact workers and the communities in which they live, and we must help hard-working Americans adapt to changing economic circumstances. I have proposed a major expansion of the National Emergency Grants program to assist workers affected by restructuring with effective job training and assistance. I have also proposed direct assistance with health insurance costs that will be available to workers and retirees who lose their employer-provided coverage. And I support coordinated assistance for communities and a strengthened and expanded trade adjustment assistance program. America's workers are the most highly skilled in the world, and with effective training and adjustment assistance we will help them find better, higher paying jobs to support their families and boost our economy.

Gordon Brown (Chancellor of the Exchequer), UK Statement to the International Monetary and Financial Committee. (International Monetary Fund), 14th Meeting, Singapore, 17 September 2006.

We are meeting in Singapore at a time of global economic opportunity. World growth is strong, not least because of continued rapid expansion here in Asia.

But there are also heightened global risks:
- Global economic imbalances persist and the threat of their unwinding in an uncontrolled way remains;
- Global inflation is rising with upward revisions to over half of all country forecasts in the IMF WEO;
- Further sustained rises in oil and energy prices since the Spring Meetings creates risks to world growth;
- The stalling of the Doha round of world trade talks.

It is vital that all of us – global institutions, politicians and business – rise to these challenges. We must make the case confidently for the benefits of globalisation, and commit to policies that maximise globalisation's benefits and minimise its risks – to ensure sustained growth and prosperity for all countries.

The UK has set out a progressive approach to reform. To make globalisation work we must show that the route to prosperity lies not in isolationism and protectionism but in greater global economic openness. Prosperity is greatest in outward-looking trading nations, not closed economies. And we look to the world delivering a shared consensus on how best we cope with globalisation.

First, we need to urgently push forward a trade agreement. With the stalling of the Doha round of world trade talks we are seeing a much wider rise of protectionist feeling.

Without trade growth, the world will be poorer. World Bank estimates suggest further trade reform could lift up to 95 million people out of extreme poverty, making trade growth far from a zero sum game with positive benefits for both rich and poor. Countries stand to benefit from an extra $300 billion in world growth every year.

Our proposal is for least developed countries to decide, plan and sequence reforms to their trade policies in line with their country-led development programmes and international obligations.

The UK calls for bold leadership and a new willingness from pro-free trade leaders in both government and business to revive the negotiations.

Without some compensating mechanism the benefits of trade liberalisation are spread unevenly between countries. Support for the capacity to trade through funding for infrastructure and communications is essential to help developing countries participate effectively and fairly in the global trading system. As US Treasury Secretary, Hank Paulson, has said we must think creatively about how to help those who fall behind.

Before the WTO ministerial in Hong Kong in December 2005, rich countries made 'aid for trade' pledges. The UK alone committed to spend £100m a year by 2010 on the institutions and people needed to support trade. Our total support for aid for trade, including support for infrastructure – like roads, ports, power and telecommunications – is expected to increase by 50% by 2010/11. This would equate to $750m a year in 2010. Together European countries and the European Commission will increase assistance to a total of €2 billion a year by 2010. Japan has promised US$10 billion over three years and the US a total of US$2.7 billion a year by 2010.

The UK calls for all countries to turn their commitments into concrete and credible financing, within a new 'aid for trade' framework which cuts red tape and builds the infrastructure that businesses in poor countries need to compete. This allows the developing world to see the trade regime as fair, turn the rhetoric of Doha into positive progress, and address the critics of globalisation by showing all countries can share its benefits.

The Fund and the Bank continue to have an important role in taking this agenda forward.

Second, we need to make our global institutions fit for the challenges ahead. The international financial community learned valuable lessons following the Asian crisis. That was why we saw an effort unprecedented in recent times to reform and galvanise the international system.

- Global institutions can only be effective if they have legitimacy and credibility with its membership. As the shape of the global economy changes, one of the central challenges for all international organisations is to respond to these changes. The UK welcomes progress on the next stage of reform: the two year quota reform package for the IMF that is currently with the governors. It is vital that the IMF takes the lead in showing it can adjust its governance to reflect rapid global economic change. This package contains an immediate quota allocation to quickly correct the most extreme imbalances and agreement to embark on fundamental reforms of the quota system over the next two years. And to ensure the continuing effectiveness and legitimacy of the fund the UK will continue to push for an increase in developing country share and at least tripling the basic vote for Africa as well as a more transparent system for calculating an IMF members' quota share.
- At the Spring meetings, ministers agreed that IMF surveillance needed to be reformed to keep pace with the global, multilateral nature of today's economies.

- In the modern, increasingly integrated global economy, the primary role of surveillance should be on supporting IMF members' shared objective of maintaining the stability of the global economy. So surveillance – the Fund's analysis of the national economic policies – needs to focus more clearly on managing the global implications of national policy. This requires a strengthened framework to provide the incentives to the Fund to produce accurate, persuasive and influential surveillance, based on high-quality analysis and candid assessment.
- A long standing objective for the UK has been to see surveillance strengthened by making it more independent and objective. The IMF have made good progress on this issue in recent years but we continue to believe that institutional reform at the IMF may be needed to more clearly delineate surveillance and lending activities.
- The UK thinks it is right that the IMF should consider a new surveillance decision to focus on policies that support external stability. We also support an annual remit which bases surveillance on each country's policy frameworks. Together, these reforms will make IMF surveillance more transparent, independent and credible while still being accountable to fund members, thereby helping countries to recognise that international cooperation can yield more than talk but also policy improvement.
- The IMF and World Bank also play a critical role in the anti-money laundering and counter-terrorist financing framework and they should ensure that they maintain their commitment to this area of work. The UK therefore will propose that they strengthen their joint-work with the financial action task force to focus its delivery of technical assistance to where its impact is greatest, particularly in those jurisdictions that have failed to recognise international standards.

Third, we need to show we can mitigate the impacts of globalisation that do create hardship and insecurity. Developed countries must continue to support developing countries in their structural reforms, creation of security nets and help finance their infrastructure and investment in their people.

Education in particular is vital to a country's future. Empowering people through education is at the heart of poverty reduction and fighting pandemic diseases such as AIDS and creating the skills and ability to participate in a global economy. Yet every day more than 100 million primary children do not go to school. More than half of the world's out-of-school children are girls, and eight out of ten live in South Asia or sub-Saharan Africa. Achieving the education Millennium Development Goals (MDGs) needs to be addressed as a matter of urgency. Rich and poor countries must work together to ensure that by all children, irrespective of birth or gender, can have the opportunity to fulfil their potential through education.

To achieve a step change in health, education and growth, last year the world community pledged to deliver an additional $50 billion of aid. As a key donor and key contributor to the additional $50 billion promised in 2015, the UK set an example by committing to spend at least $15 billion on aid for education over the next ten years. But too often the key constraint for developing countries is not just the volume of resources – but whether they are predictable and long-term to enable them to take on recurrent financial obligations, such as teachers salaries.

So in April in Mozambique, President Guebuza, President Mandela and Graca Michel launched a global campaign for children's education – setting out the need for long term and predictable financing. Building on this in May in Abuja, African Finance and Education Ministers, committed to developing 10-year education plans and to present their progress at the Annual Meetings. 15 African countries have now completed fully costed, ambitious plans. On Sunday they will be publishing detailed summaries of these plans. Implementation will reduce by 50 per cent the number of African children not receiving schooling. 25 million children going to school who would not have done. We need to make sure that these plans are matched to the financing commitments made by donors. So, the UK calls for an international donor conference to achieve that.

This year we have made significant progress in launching the International Finance Facility for Immunisation, which will provide $4 billion to prevent 5 million childhood deaths. The UK also calls for the launch of the first pilot advance market commitment (AMC) before the end of the year. AMCs are a powerful market-based mechanism to accelerate the development and availability of priority new vaccines against diseases, like malaria, TB, aids and pneumococcus, which kill millions of people in developing countries each year. For example, pneumococcal disease kills 1.6 million people a year, most of them children. A successful AMC for a pneumococcal vaccine could save 5.4 million lives by 2030.

September 2006 marks the tenth anniversary of the HIPC Initiative. The HIPC Initiative has made a significant contribution in alleviating the burden of unpayable debt in 29 countries, writing off $70 billion and reducing debt payments from an average of nearly 24% of Government revenues to 11%, and freeing up significant resources for health, education and poverty reduction. And so we will continue to work together to ensure completion of the HIPC Initiative; so that all creditors participate; and to ensure that the initiative is securely and fully financed. We welcome the decision to ensure that all potentially eligible countries are able to benefit from debt relief.

We also strongly welcome the progress that has been made in implementing the Multilateral Debt Relief Initiative in the IMF, IDA and the AfDF, which is freeing up billions of dollars in additional resources for investment in services and infrastructure and to make progress towards the MDGs. We share the objective of ensuring that countries that have benefited from debt relief do not reaccumulate unsustainable debt. the primary responsibility for borrowing lies with borrowing countries themselves and we urge the Fund and the Bank to increase their support in helping governments to manage debt effectively. At the same time it is essential that creditors lend responsibly. The joint Debt Sustainability Framework is central to this. We will continue to work with the Fund and the Bank to strengthen the DSF, and urge all official creditors, including export credit agencies, to use the framework to guide their lending decisions. We urge the Fund and the Bank to be active in facilitating and supporting stronger creditor coordination.

The Fund and the Bank must continue to strengthen their collaboration, and we look forward to the report of the External Committee which provide an opportunity to cement a stronger partnership both institutionally and on the ground. For the Fund and the Bank to give countries the support countries they must ensure comprehensive coverage of all issues critical to the MDGs.

Finally, developed countries must focus on how we can adapt and compete in a globalised world and find our comparative advantage. Because this means moving up the value added chain each country needs to emphasize the rising importance of education and skills.

- In the UK, we are taking action to tackle our historic skills deficit and will publish Lord Leitch's final report alongside the Pre-Budget Report that will recommend a shared national commitment to a world class skills base, doubling current rates of improvement and meeting the challenge of global change.

Governments alone cannot pursue a progressive globalisation agenda. We must also involve businesses-the engines of wealth creation-to create an alliance of global companies and globally minded governments.

Despite this global economic uncertainty, economic growth in the UK is stronger and more balanced:

- business investment is growing more quickly than private consumption as the economy rebalances. It has risen by around 1¾ per cent in each of the first two quarters and by 4¼ per cent over the previous year. And, on the basis of the latest revisions, business investment grew by 3 per cent in 2005, twice as fast as previously thought. Whole economy investment has risen in every year of this government, making this the first government in 40 years to

avoid any years of negative investment growth.
- exports growth is also strengthening, up by 8.5 over the past year compared with 4.8 per cent in 2005.
- employment is at a record high, up 220,000 over the past 12 months. And the latest data show this expansion to be wholly in the private sector with public sector employment falling slightly
- and we continue to close the productivity gap with our major competitors. GDP per capita has increased by 47 per cent per cent in the UK since 1997, compared with 34 per cent in Germany, 39 per cent in France, 44 per cent in the USA, 29 per cent in Japan and 34 per cent in Italy. We know that if we are to sustain growth in the future we must never be complacent and always be vigilant to risks. So that is why I have said I supported the proactive forward-looking action taken by the Bank of England in August and why we will continue to base public sector pay settlements on our 2 per cent inflation target.

COPYRIGHTS AND PERMISSIONS

'Editorial: Trade Agreements', *Journal of the National Union of Manufacturers* (June 1946), pp. 686–7. Copyright © CBI, reproduced with permission.

Letter from National Union of Manufacturers, Sir Leonard Browett (Director) and Sir Patrick Hannon (President), to Sir Stafford Cripps (President of the Board of Trade), 21 October 1946; 'Confidential Note of a Meeting Held at the Board of Trade on the 25th February 1947, Between the National Union of Manufacturers and Mr. Marquand, Mr. Helmore, Mr. Holmes, Mr. Summerscale, Miss Fisher and Mr. Sydenham-Clarke of the Board of Trade', PRO, BT 11/3242. Reproduced with permission from the National Archives (Kew, Surrey).

'Chapter V. Retaliation and Other Indirect Consequences', Board of Trade Economic Group Report on Long-Term Problems and Consequences of Failure to Approve ITO, 8 July 1947, PRO, BT 11/3544, pp. 69–74. Reproduced with permission from the National Archives (Kew, Surrey).

Confidential Note on a Meeting with the FBI on 20 February (1947) attended by Mr Helmore (Secretary for Overseas Trade), Mr Holmes, Mr Summerscale, Mr Cohen, Miss Fisher and Mr Marquand; E. J. Elliot (Federation of British Industries) to E. A. Cohen (Board of Trade), 1 April 1948; R. J. Shackle (Board of Trade) to E. J. Elliot (Federation of British Industries), 8 April 1948,, PRO, BT 11/3254. Reproduced with permission from the National Archives (Kew, Surrey).

Jacob Viner, 'Conflicts of Principle in Drafting a Trade Charter', *Foreign Affairs*, 25:4 (June 1947), pp. 612–28. Copyright © Council on Foreign Relations, www.foreignaffairs.org. Reprinted by permission of Foreign Affairs.

Clair Wilcox, 'The London Draft of a Charter for an International Trade Organization', *American Economic Review*, 37:2 (May 1947), pp. 529–41. Copyright © American Economic Association, reproduced with permission.

Memorandum on Imperial Preference, Loans from the United States and Tariff Negotiations between the United States and United Kingdom, 14 October 1947, PRO, PREM 8/490. Reproduced with permission from the National Archives (Kew, Surrey).

'Resolution on the Havana Charter', First Draft Prepared by the International Headquarters of the International Chamber of Commerce, 10 May 1948, PRO, BT 11/3721. Reproduced with permission from the National Archives (Kew, Surrey).

Notes for Prime Minister Winston Churchill in Preparation for Meeting with Jean Monnet regarding United Kingdom Association with the European Coal and Steel Community, 25 May 1954; Memorandum for Prime Minster Anthony Eden on Meeting of the Ministerial Committee Meeting on Relations with the ECSC, 4 July 1956, PRO, PREM 11/1340. Reproduced with permission from the National Archives (Kew, Surrey).

'Record of Conversation between the Secretary of State [Foreign Secretary Selwyn Lloyd] and the Netherlands Ambassador on July 15, 1960', PRO, PREM 11/3774, no. 140. Reproduced with permission from the National Archives (Kew, Surrey).

'Press Conference by President de Gaulle, Paris, 14th January 1963', Assembly of the Western European Union, 'The Political Year in Europe', 1963. Copyright © Western European Union.

Remarks, made by President Charles de Gaulle at his Fifteenth Press Conference, 16 May, 1967. Copyright © French Press and Information Service, French Embassy, Washington, DC.

Sir Con O'Neill (Head of UK Delegation to the European Communities), 'Valedictory Despatch', 3 May 1965, PRO, PREM 13/306. Reproduced with permission from the National Archives (Kew, Surrey).

'Record of a Meeting Between the Prime Minister [Harold Wilson], and the Foreign Secretary [George Brown] and the Acting Vice-President [Albert Coppé] and Other Members of the High Authority of the European Coal and Steel Community at the British Embassy, Luxembourg, on 8th March 1967', PRO, PREM 13/1495. Reproduced with permission from the National Archives (Kew, Surrey).

Memorandum for Non-Cabinet Ministers, 'Ten Reasons Why Britain Should Join the Common Market', December 1970, PRO, PREM 15/62. Reproduced with permission from the National Archives (Kew, Surrey).

'Record of Conversation between the Chancellor of the Duchy of Lancaster [Sir Geoffrey Rippon] and the Portuguese Foreign Minister [Dr Rui Patricio]', 8 March 1972, PRO, PREM 15/887. Reproduced with permission from the National Archives (Kew, Surrey).

'Cassis' Decision, Judgement of the European Court of Justice, Rewe-Zentral AG v. Bundesmonopolverwaltung für Branntwein, 20 February 1979, European Court of Justice, Case 120/78. Copyright © European Communities, 1998–2008, reproduced with permission.

German Beer Purity Law Decision, Judgement of the European Court of Justice, Commission of the European Communities v. Federal Republic of Germany, 12 March 1987, European Court of Justice, Case 178/84. Copyright © European Communities, 1998–2008, reproduced with permission.

Statement of S. Rajaratnam (Minister for Foreign Affairs of Singapore) at the ASEAN Conference, Bangkok, 8 August 1967; Statement of Adam Malik (Minister of Foreign Affairs of Indonesia) at the ASEAN Conference, 8 August 1967; Priority Telegram from UK Embassy in Bangkok regarding Declaration Establishing the ASEAN, 8 August 1967; Restricted Telegram from UK Embassy in Moscow regarding Soviet Response to South-East Asian Regional Cooperation, 14 August 1967; Confidential Summary on the Association of South-East Asian Nations from Giles Bullard (British Embassy in Bangkok) to George Brown (Foreign Secretary), 15 August 1967; Telegram from British Embassy in Manila on the Philippines and ASEAN, 30 October 1967, PRO, FCO 15/23. Reproduced with permission from the National Archives (Kew, Surrey).

Report of British Embassy in Bangkok on EEC Visit to Thailand, 13 September 1973, PRO, FCO 15/1727, no. 21. Reproduced with permission from the National Archives (Kew, Surrey).

Memorandum on EEC/ASEAN Relations, 2 October 1975, PRO, FCO 30/2765. Reproduced with permission from the National Archives (Kew, Surrey).

'Address by Mr Lee Kwan Yew, Prime Minister of Singapore, at the Opening Session of the ASEAN Summit, Bali, on 23 February 1976'; 'Treaty of Amity and Cooperation in Southeast Asia', Denpasar, Bali, 24 February 1976; Confidential Memorandum, 'ASEAN Summit: A Thai View', 2 March 1976, PRO, FCO 15/2173. Reproduced with permission from the National Archives (Kew, Surrey).

Cooperation Agreement between the EEC and ASEAN, Kuala Lumpur, 7 March 1980, PRO, FO 970/459. Reproduced with permission from the National Archives (Kew, Surrey).

Background Brief, 'ASEAN's Changing Priorities', June 1992 PRO, FO 973/692. Reproduced with permission from the National Archives (Kew, Surrey).

House of Commons Debates, Official Record, 3rd Session, 34th Parliament (Canada), 15 (25 May 1993), pp. 19610–19. Copyright © Canadian House of Commons. Reproduced with permission.

'NAFTA Debate: Gore vs. Perot', on Larry King Show, CNN, 9 November 1993. Copyright © CNN licensing, reproduced with permission.

'Canada Prepared if NAFTA Fails; Movement Afoot to Arrange Bilateral Deal with Mexico', *Globe and Mail* (Toronto), 13 November 1993. Copyright © The Globe and Mail, reproduced with permission.

'NAFTA Backers Must Speak Now', Crain's Detroit Business, 15 November 1993, p. 6. Copyright © Crain's Detroit Business, reproduced with permission.

'The National Interest: House Members Have Clear Obligation to Free Trade', *Houston Chronicle*, 16 November 1993, p. 10. Copyright © Houston Chronicle.

Dennis Wharton, 'H'wood: Muy Bueno, eh? Valenti Sees Doors Opening as House Passes NAFTA Treaty', *Daily Variety*, 18 November 1993, p. 1. Copyright © Daily Variety, reproduced with permission.

'NAFTA All Clear in Mexico', *Record* (Kitchener-Waterloo, Canada), 23 November 1993, p. A5. Copyright © Canadian Press, reproduced with permission.

Jonathan Ferguson, 'NAFTA: Canada's Concerns; Liberals Demand Trade Rules that Put Everyone on Same Footing; Canada Wants Protection from U.S. Political Winds', *Toronto Star*, 30 November 1993, p. A13. Copyright © Torstar Syndication Services, reproduced with permission.

'U.A.W Wants Trade Payoff in Jobs', *New York Times*, 1 January 1994, p. 43. Copyright © *New York Times*.

Scott Sunde, 'Chaos Closes Downtown; Police Use Rubber Pellets, Tear Gas Against Thousands; Demonstrators Delay Start of Trade Meeting for Hours; Schell Orders Curfew; National Guard Called', *Seattle Post-Intelligencer*, 1 December 1999, p. A1. Copyright © Seattle Post-Intelligencer, reproduced with permission.

Kerry Murakami, 'Geneva Sounded WTO Warning That Went Unheeded in Seattle', *Seattle Post-Intelligencer*, 10 March 2000, p. A1. Copyright © Seattle Post-Intelligencer, reproduced with permission.

INDEX

Abbeville, wool trade **1**.40–1
Addington, H. U.
    on American tariffs **1**.137–9
    letter to George Canning (1824) **1**.137–9
Agricultural Protection Society for Great Britain and Ireland, on Corn Laws (1844) **1**.376
agricultural trade
    'Causes of Trade Depression' (1886) **3**.36–9
    fair trade **3**.23–4, 36–9
        cf. mining **1**.307
    protectionism **3**.111–12
    taxation **1**.307–13
    see also grain trade
Alison, Alexander, *Universal Free Trade* (1852) **2**.48–52
'The Allies' Economic Combine' (1916) **3**.215–17
Alsace-Lorraine, recommendations, Paris Economic Conference (1916) **3**.244–5
America
    'America and the British Corn Law' (1842) **1**.370–2
    American Press's Response to Paris Conference (1916) **3**.210–11
    'The American Tariff' (1828) **1**.144
    Anglo-American relations 1812–30 **1**.129–35
    Anglo-American Treaty abstract (1795) **1**.75–8

Arguments against the Dingley Bill (1897) **3**.157–9
autotrade tariff, French, 1930 **3**.282–9
commercial policy **1**.131–2
Continental System **1**.111–20
cotton trade **1**.152–3
Dependence of the British Empire on the United States, Cabinet Report (1916) **3**.219–28
depression, 'Our Tariff and the Depression' (1931) **3**.300–10
Dingley Tariff Act (1897)
    Arguments against the Dingley Bill (1897) **3**.157–9
    The Fruits of American Protection (1907) **3**.160–4
'Economic Policies of the Government' (1931) **3**.296–9
Free Trade and the European Treaties of Commerce (1875) **2**.299–303
'Free Trade' (1890) **3**.149–51
The French and American Tariffs Compared (1861) **2**.179–86
French autotrade tariff (1930) **3**.282–9
The Fruits of American Protection (1907) **3**.160–4
General Convention of Agriculturists and Manufacturers (1827) **1**.141–2
Hamilton, Alexander **1**.131–2
Hull, Cordell **3**.296–9
ITO
    Report on Failure to Approve (1947) **4**.10–17

FBI meeting (1947) 4.18–22
McKinley tariff law 3.154–6
The McKinley Tariff Robbery and Fraud (1892) 3.154–6
The New American Tariff (Simmons-Underwood) and the Wool Industry of Bradford (1914) 3.175–82
Non-Intercourse Law (1809–10) 1.113–17
Panama Canal 3.223, 225, 226–7
Paris Economic Conference (1916) 3.210–11
post-war commercial relations, British Empire (1916) 3.218–28
post-war protection (1824) 1.137–61
protectionism 3.157–9, 160–4
Radio Address, 'Forgotten Man' (1932) 3.311–13
Reciprocity Pact 3.170–2
Reciprocity Treaty (1854) 2.126–8
Reciprocity with the United States (1911) 3.168–9
Report of the Committee on Commerce (1824) 1.140
Roosevelt, Franklin D. 3.311–13
Sheffield and the American tariff (1890) 3.152–3
Simmons-Underwood tariff 3.175–82
Smoot-Hawley Tariff Act (1930) 3.265–323
Smoot, Reed, 'Our Tariff and the Depression' (1931) 3.300–10
tariff battles (1880–1914) 3.145–82
Tariff Bill 1.132, 143
tariff duties collected (1930) 3.290–1
'Tariff of Abominations' (1828) 1.133
tariff policy 1.133
tariffs 1.132, 133, 137–9, 140, 3.173–4
Treaty of Commerce (1806) 1.112–20
'The Underwood Act, 1913' 3.173–4
Walker tariff 1.133
Wells, David A. 2.299–301
wool trade 1.150–2
see also North American Free Trade Agreement; Smoot-Hawley Tariff Act (1930)
Anglo-American relations (1812–30) 1.129–35

Anglo-American Treaty abstract (1795) 1.75–8
Anglo-French commercial relations 1.242–80
 Baron Freville 1.257–9
 Baron Louis 1.256–7
 John Bowring 1.243–5, 254–9
 Chamber of Commerce, Boulogne-sur-Mer 1.246–51
 Count Tanneguy Duchâtel 1.257–9
 prohibitions, removal demands 1.246–51, 252–3
 George Villiers 1.254–9
Anglo-French Commercial Treaty (1786) 1.1–6, 44–67
 Board of Trade minutes (1785) 1.44–9
 William Eden 1.52, 53–4, 56
 iron trade 1.50–1
 letters
  William Eden to Lord Carmarthen (1786) 1.52
  William Eden to Robert Liston (1786) 1.56
  Daniel Hailes to the Marquis of Carmarthen (1786) 1.58–63
  Manchester Manufacturer Charles James Fox (1787) 1.65–7
  William Pitt to the Marquis of Stafford (1786) 1.55
  William Pitt to William Eden (1786) 1.53–4
  Ralph Woodford to Robert Liston (1786) 1.57, 64
 linen trade 1.46–7
 metals trade 1.50–1
 Minutes of the Committee of Trade (1786) 1.50–1
 opposition 1.3–4
 William Pitt 1.3, 53–4, 55
 tobacco trade 1.48–9
 Ralph Woodford 1.57, 64
Anglo-French Commercial Treaty (abortive; 1852) 2.117–25
 James Booth 2.120–5
 Lord John Russell 2.117–20
Anglo-French Treaty (1860) 2.137–73
 Michel Chevalier, *The History of Political Economy* (1869) 2.143–7

Richard Cobden to John Bright (1860)
2.148–52
Richard Cobden to Arlés Dufour (1860)
2.153
The French Treaty, a Mockery, a Delusion, and a Snare (1860) 2.164–8
H. Reader Lack, *The French Treaty and Tariff of 1860* (1861) 2.154–60
Robert Andrew Macfie 2.164–8
Sir Louis Mallet 2.207–11
Memorandum on Modifications of the Anglo French Treaty (1871) 2.207–11
'The Past and the Future' (1885) 3.7–9
silk trade 2.139
George Frederick Young 2.164–8
Anglo-Irish commercial relationship 1.1–6
Anglo-Irish relations (1779–85) 1.7–43
Anglo-Prussian commercial relations 1.260–5, 268–80
Lord Palmerston 1.266–7
Anglo-Zollverein commercial relationship 1.239–41, 260–5
Arbitration Instead of War (1848) 2.41–3
Arguments against the Dingley Bill (1897) 3.157–9
aristocracy and Corn Laws (1846) 1.383–5
ASEAN *see* Association of South East Asian Nations
Ashworth, Henry
 'Our Colonies: Their Commerce and their Cost' (1862) 2.334–7
 Corn Laws 2.35–40
 free trade 2.35–40
 Recollections of Richard Cobden and the Anti-Corn-Law League (1877) 2.35–40
Association of South East Asian Nations (ASEAN) 4.125–68
 Address, Opening Session (1976) 4.149–51
 'ASEAN Summit: A Thai View' (1976) 4.157–8
 'ASEAN's Changing Priorities' (1992) 4.165–8
 background 4.125–8
 Giles Bullard, Summary of ASEAN (1967) 4.138–41

Cooperation Agreement between the EEC and ASEAN (1980) 4.159–64
EEC
 Cooperation Agreement between EEC and ASEAN (1980) 4.159–64
 Memorandum on EEC/ASEAN Relations (1975) 4.147–8
 Report on EEC Visit to Thailand (1973) 4.143–6
Foreign and Commonwealth Office, 'ASEAN's Changing Priorities' (1992) 4.165–8
G. C. Foster, Telegram on the Philippines and ASEAN (1967) 4.142
Lee Kwan Yew, Address, Opening Session (1976) 4.149–51
Adam Malik, statement, ASEAN Conference (1967) 4.132–3
Arthur de la Mare, Report on EEC Visit to Thailand (1973) 4.143–6
priorities, changing (1992) 4.165–8
H. E. S. Rajaratnam, statement, ASEAN Conference (1967) 4.129–31
Report on EEC Visit to Thailand (1973) 4.143–6
Summary of ASEAN (1967) 4.138–41
Telegram on the Philippines and ASEAN (1967) 4.142
Telegram regarding Declaration Establishing the ASEAN (1967) 4.134–5
Telegram regarding Soviet Response to South-East Asian Regional Cooperation (1967) 4.136–7
'Treaty of Amity and Cooperation in Southeast Asia' (1976) 4.152–6
Atkinson, Edward, 'Arguments in Favour of Discrimination' (1897) 3.157–9
Atkinson, Solomon
 The Effects of the New System of Free Trade upon our Shipping, Colonies and Commerce (1827) 1.190–201
 letter to William Huskisson 1.190–201
 manufacturing industries 1.195–6
 shipping/navigation 1.193–5
 timber trade 1.193
Australia
 Gower Evans 2.348–51
 fair trade 3.26–8, 40–3

free trade **2**.323–6, 348–51
Free Trade and the European Treaties of Commerce (1875) **2**.348–51
Freedom and Independence for the Golden Lands of Australia (1852) **2**.323–6
growth/prosperity **3**.51–5
John Dunmore Lang **2**.323–6
meat duty **3**.364–9
Ottawa Imperial Economic Conference (1931–2) **3**.364–9, 382–3, 384–5
Henry Parkes **2**.348–51
Proposed Conditions of the Treaty of Independence Continued (1852) **2**.323–6
'Protection in Young Communities' (1882) **3**.51–5
'The Riddle of Ottawa' (1932) **3**.384–5
Royal Commission on Depression in Trade and Industry, 'Minority "Fair Trade" Report' (1886) **3**.40–3
treaties of commerce **2**.348–51
see also New South Wales (colony); Victoria (colony)
Austria
George von Bunsen **2**.289–91
'Commercial Treaty with Austria' (1866) **2**.196–206
Free Trade and the European Treaties of Commerce (1875) **2**.283–91
Sir Louis Mallet **2**.196–206
treaties of commerce **2**.196–206, 216–17
Max Wirth **2**.283–9
autotrade
meeting prior to Ottawa Imperial Economic Conference (1932) **3**.346–8
French tariff, Smoot-Hawley Tariff Act (1930) **3**.282–9
'U.A.W. Wants Trade Payoff in Jobs' (1994) **4**.256–8

Baden Powell, George, 'Protection in Young Communities' (1882) **3**.51–5
Barkworth, J. B.
fair trade **3**.30–3
'The Fair-Trade Party' (1886) **3**.30–3
'Protection for Home Agriculture' (1886) **3**.30–3
Bateman, Lord, *Lord Bateman's Plea for Limited Protection* (1877) **2**.257–61

Beauchamp, Lord **1**.11
Beer Purity Law Decision, ECJ (1987) **4**.110–24
Belgian and German Commercial Treaties, terminating (1897) **3**.90–5
Belgium
Belgian Association, 'Congress of Political Economists at Brussels' (1847) **2**.73–8
Memorandum on Terminating the Belgian and German Commercial Treaties (1897) **3**.90–5
Paris Economic Conference (1916) **3**.189–91, 209
treaties of commerce **2**.217
Bennet, P., speech to Central Suffolk Agricultural Society (1846) **1**.381–2
Bennett, Richard, Ottawa Imperial Economic Conference (1931–2) **3**.327
Berlin Decree
article on Continental System (1806) **1**.82–4
A Key to the Orders in Council (1812) **1**.106–13, 117
Besant, Annie
fair trade **3**.17–22
imports/exports **3**.19–20
wealth, meaning of **3**.17–22
'What is Really Free Trade' (1881) **3**.17–22
Bismarck, Prince, 'Protection in Germany' (1881) **3**.83
blockade, Continental System **1**.98–100
Board of Trade
Anglo-French Commercial Treaty (1786) **1**.44–9
Economic Group Report on Failure to Approve ITO (1947) **4**.10–17
ITO **4**.23–6, 58
National Union of Manufacturers **4**.23–6
Booth, C., 'Fiscal Reform' (1904) **3**.129–32
Booth, James, Anglo-French Commercial Treaty (abortive; 1852) **2**.120–5
Bourne, S.
fair trade **3**.56–8
'Imperial Federation in its Commercial Aspect' (1886) **3**.56–8

Bowring, John
  Anglo-French commercial relations **1.**243–5, 254–9
  Election Address (1841) **1.**367–8
  First Report on the Commercial Relations between France and Great Britain (1834) **1.**254–9
Bradford
  Dingley Tariff Act (1897) **3.**178–9
  Gorman-Wilson tariff **3.**178
  McKinley tariff law **3.**177–8
  The New American Tariff (Simmons-Underwood) and the Wool Industry of Bradford (1914) **3.**175–82
  wool trade **3.**175–82
bread tax
  'The Bread-Taxing Bishops and the Bible-Reading People' (1840) **1.**356–8
  'Manifestations of Public Feeling on the Bread Tax' (1840) **1.**353–4
  petitions **1.**359–60
  see also grain trade
Bright, Jacob
  fair trade **3.**34–5
  Manchester Chamber of Commerce **3.**34–5
British Empire
  dependence on United States (1916) **3.**218–28
  Panama Canal **3.**223, 225, 226–7
  post-war commercial relations with United States (1916) **3.**218–28
British Empire League
  Joseph Chamberlain **3.**74–5
  Commercial Union of the Empire (1891) **3.**67–71
  Report of Inaugural Meeting of the League (1896) **3.**72–3
  Report of Speech of the Right Hon. Joseph Chamberlain (1896) **3.**74–5
Bromley, John, Ottawa Imperial Economic Conference (1931–2) **3.**360–1
Browett, Sir Leonard
  letter to Sir Stafford Cripps (1946) **4.**8–9
  National Union of Manufacturers (1946) **4.**8–9
Brown, Gordon, UK Statement to the IMF (2006) **4.**312–17

Bullard, Giles, Summary on ASEAN (1967) **4.**138–41
Bunsen, George von **2.**289–91
Burdett, Sir Francis, Corn Laws **1.**327
Burke, Mr **1.**10, **2.**320–1
Burroughes, H. N., Election Address (1841) **1.**366
Bush, George H. W.
  Second NAFTA Presidential Debate (1992) **4.**173–6
  Third NAFTA Presidential Debate (1992) **4.**177–86
Bush, George W., US steel industry temporary safeguards (2002) **4.**310–11

Caldwell, Sir James, Report on the Manuscripts of Mrs Stopford-Sackville (1779) **1.**12
Canada
  'Canada Prepared if NAFTA Fails' (1993) **4.**244–5
  'Canada's Answer' (1911) **3.**170–2
  Canadian National League **3.**168–9
  'The Canadian Tariff' (1881) **3.**49–50, 56–8
  'Colonial Preference and Imperial Reciprocity' (1908) **3.**138–41
  Sir W. Laurier **3.**165–7
  and Mexico **4.**244–5
  and NAFTA
    'Canada Prepared if NAFTA Fails' (1993) **4.**244–5
    disputes (1993) **4.**252–3
    dumping (1993) **4.**254–5
    House of Commons Debates (1993) **4.**187–202
    'NAFTA: Canada's Concerns' (1993) **4.**252–5
    subsidies (1993) **4.**253–4
  Ottawa Imperial Economic Conference (1931–2) **3.**329–92
  Reciprocity Pact **3.**170–2
  Reciprocity Treaty (1854) **2.**126–8
  Reciprocity with the United States (1911) **3.**168–9
  'Tariff Reform in Canada' (1910) **3.**165–7

see also Ottawa Imperial Economic Conference (1931–2)
Canadian National League, *Reciprocity with the United States* (1911) 3.168–9
Canning, George, Corn Laws **1**.322–5
Cardwell Memorandum on Commercial Policy towards Russia (1854) **2**.131–6
Carey, Henry Charles, *The French and American Tariffs Compared* (1861) **2**.179–86
Central Society for the Protection of British Agriculture and Industry
  Corn Laws **1**.391–4
  'The Ghost of a Dead Monopoly' (1846) **1**.391–4
Central Suffolk Agricultural Society
  P. Bennet, speech **1**.381–2
  Corn Laws **1**.381–2
Chamber of Commerce, Boulogne-sur-Mer, Anglo-French commercial relations **1**.246–51
Chamber of Commerce, Havre, tariffs **1**.252–3
Chamberlain, Joseph
  British Empire League **3**.74–5
  free trade vs tariff reform **3**.115–18
  Report of Speech of the Right Hon. Joseph Chamberlain (1896) **3**.74–5
'Chamberlain bubble' **3**.116
The Chamberlain Bubble **3**.121–3
The Charter of the Nations (1854) **2**.110–16
Chevalier, Michel
  Free Trade and the European Treaties of Commerce (1875) **2**.304–11
  free trade, in Dionysus Lardner, *The Great Exhibition and London* (1852) **2**.83–90
  The History of Political Economy (1869) **2**.143–7
  Political Economy Society of Paris, meeting (1875) **2**.304–11
child labour **4**.279–81
Citrine, Walter M., Ottawa Imperial Economic Conference (1931–2) **3**.360–1
'The City and Tariff Reform' (1910) **3**.142–3
'The City and the Tariff Question' (1903) **3**.106–14

Clarendon, Lord, letter to Lord Palmerston (1856) **2**.129–30
Clark, W. H.
  cotton trade **3**.353–5
  letter to Sir Edward Harding (1932) **3**.344–5
  letter to G. G. Whiskard (1932) **3**.353–5
  'Memorandum of a Conversation with the [Canadian] Prime Minister' (1931) **3**.340–3
  Ottawa Imperial Economic Conference (1931–2) **3**.340–3, 344–5, 353–5
Clinton, Bill
  Second NAFTA Presidential Debate (1992) **4**.173–6
  Third NAFTA Presidential Debate (1992) **4**.177–86
  WTO, President's remarks to Farmers, Students from the Seattle-Tacoma Area (1999) **4**.286–92
Coal and Steel Community, European
  1951 **4**.63
  1954 **4**.67–8
  1956 **4**.69–70
  meeting, Harold Wilson/Albert Coppé (1967) **4**.88–95
  tariff reduction proposal (1956) **4**.69–70
Coates, J. G.
  letter to Stanley Baldwin (1932) **3**.362–3
  New Zealand delegation **3**.362–3
  Ottawa Imperial Economic Conference (1931–2) **3**.362–3
Cobbett, William
  'Commons Debate on Lord North's Propositions for the Relief of the Trade of Ireland' (1779) **1**.14–22
  'House of Commons Debate' (1779) **1**.9–11
  'Motion respecting Trade in Ireland' (1779) **1**.7–8
Cobden, Richard **2**.4–5, 55–7, 138–40
  Account of a Dinner to Mr Cobden at Rome (1847) **2**.67–70
  Arbitration Instead of War (1848) **2**.41–3
  Corn Laws **1**.319–30, 333, 386, **2**.35–40
  free trade **2**.41–3, 61–2, 63–72, 82
  'Free Trade and Peace' (1847) **2**.44–6

letters
  to John Bright (1860) **2**.148–52
  to Michel Chevalier (1851) **2**.82
  to Arlés Dufour (1860) **2**.153
  to Marco Minghetti (1847) **2**.61–2
  to John Norton (1838) **1**.333
  to William Rathbone (1846) **1**.386
  to George Wilson (1841) **1**.369
'Modern History of the Corn Laws' (1839) **1**.319–30
Public Banquet to Mr Cobden at Florence (1847) **2**.70–2
Recollections of Richard Cobden and the Anti-Corn-Law League (1877) **2**.35–40
speeches
  at Genoa **2**.66–7
  at Free Trade Banquet at Cadiz (1846) **2**.64–6
  at Free Trade Banquet at Madrid (1846) **2**.63–4
  in Europe, in *Reminiscences of Richard Cobden* (1895) **2**.63–72
Cobden Club, *Free Trade and Imperial Preference* (1905) **3**.137
Cole, George Ward, *Protection as a National System Suited for Victoria* (1860) **2**.327–33
colonial policy
  Five Free Trade Essays (1875) **2**.338–47
  Free Trade and No Colonies (1848) **2**.312–22
'Colonial Preference and Imperial Reciprocity' (1908) **3**.138–41
colonies
  Henry Ashworth **2**.334–7
  'Colonial Preference and Imperial Reciprocity' (1908) **3**.138–41
  'Our Colonies: Their Commerce and their Cost' (1862) **2**.334–7
  'Commercial Union between the United Kingdom and its Colonies' (1891) **3**.64–6
  Commercial Union of the Empire (1891) **3**.67–71
  customs unions **3**.64–6
  fair trade **3**.56–8
  R. Giffen **3**.64–6

  'Imperial Federation in its Commercial Aspect' (1886) **3**.56–8
  Howard Vincent **3**.67–71
  see also Australia; Canada; Victoria (colony)
'Commercial Diplomacy 1860–1902' **3**.106–14
  France, commercial policy since 1870 **3**.106–14
  protectionism **3**.106–14
commercial policy
  American **1**.131–2
  British
    Cardwell Memorandum on Commercial Policy towards Russia (1854) **2**.131–6
    The Commercial Policy of England (1877) **2**.241–53
    W. Farrer Ecroyd **2**.262–9
    evolution of British commercial policy (1832–46) **1**.281–7
    John Harris **2**.241–53
    The Policy of Self Help (1879) **2**.262–9
  European (1879) **2**.175–8
  French, since 1870, France **3**.106–14
  reform, William Huskisson **1**.129–31
'The Commercial Restraints of Ireland' (1779) **1**.23–32
commercial treaties *see* treaties of commerce
'Commercial Treaty with Austria' (1866) **2**.196–206
'Commercial Union between the United Kingdom and its Colonies' (1891) **3**.64–6
Commercial Union of the Empire (1891) **3**.67–71
commodity arrangements, ITO proposals (1947) **4**.52–3
Commonwealth trade promotion **3**.374–6
conferences *see* Ottawa Imperial Economic Conference (1931–2); Paris Economic Conference (1916)
Continental System **1**.69–71, 75–128
  America **1**.111–20
  Anglo-American Treaty abstract (1795) **1**.75–8
  appeal against **1**.121–8

article following Berlin Decree (1806) 1.82–4
Berlin Decree 1.82–4, 106–13, 117
blockade 1.98–100
Madame de Stael Holstein 1.121–8
'Financial Situation of England and France' (1810) 1.102–3
A Key to the Orders in Council (1812) 1.106–20
legal issues 1.88–100
letters
  Mr Foster to Viscount Castlereagh (1812) 1.105
  George Sinclair to Henry Dundas (1796) 1.81
  James Stephen to Spencer Perceval (1808) 1.101
Milan Decree 1.109–13, 117
Non-Intercourse Law (1809–10) 1.113–17
Orders in Council 1.85–7, 88–100, 101, 104
Spencer Perceval 1.85–7
policy 1.93–100
Prince Regent (1812) 1.104
Southwark Petition (1795) 1.79–80
James Stephen 1.85–7, 101, 106–20
conventional tariff, France 3.84–7
Conway, General 1.11
copper trade (1825) 1.174–5
copyright protection, NAFTA (1993) 4.248–9
Corn Laws
  'Address of the Metropolitan Anti-Corn Law Association' (1840) 1.349–52
  'An Address to the People of England, on the Corn Laws' (1834) 1.289–96
  Agricultural Protection Society for Great Britain and Ireland (1844) 1.376
  'America and the British Corn Law' (1842) 1.370–2
  Anti Corn-Law Association (1834) 1.297–8
  and 'aristocracy' (1846) 1.383–5
  Henry Ashworth 2.35–40
  P. Bennet, speech to Central Suffolk Agricultural Society (1846) 1.381–2
  bread tax 1.353–4, 356–8, 359–60

'The Bread-Taxing Bishops and the Bible-Reading People' (1840) 1.356–8
Sir Francis Burdett 1.327
George Canning 1.322–5
Central Society for the Protection of British Agriculture and Industry 1.391–4
Central Suffolk Agricultural Society 1.381–2
Richard Cobden 1.319–30, 333, 386, 2.35–40
Corn Act, 1791 1.304–5
'Corn-Law Agitation Humbug' (1840) 1.355
'Corn Laws are Potato Laws' (1842) 1.373–4
'The Corn Laws' (1836) 1.299–318
'The Corn Laws as a Buttress for the Aristocracy' (1846) 1.383–5
costs of staples 1.335–9
John Curtis 1.370–2
debate in 1830s 1.289–394
'Dilemmas on the Corn Law Question' (1839) 1.334–43
Dundee Operatives 1.222–35
Editorial outlining 'nightmare scenario' (1841) 1.364–5
Ebenezer Elliot 1.289–96
evolution of British commercial policy (1832–46) 1.281–7
J. Gadsby 1.373–4
'The Ghost of a Dead Monopoly' (1846) 1.391–4
House of Lords protest against Corn Bill (1846) 1.388–90
William Huskisson 1.129–30, 321–2, 329–30
Alex Kay 1.297–8
land rent 1.337–43
A Letter Addressed to the Landowners and Tenantry of the County of Forfar (1826) 1.202–21
letter to William Rathbone (1846) 1.386
Manchester Chamber of Commerce 1.331–2, 344–5
Manchester inhabitants 1.375
'Manifestations of Public Feeling on the Bread Tax' (1840) 1.353–4

Metropolitan Anti-Corn Law Association, address (1840) **1**.349–52
'Modern History of the Corn Laws' (1839) **1**.319–30
'nightmare scenario', food prices **1**.364–5
Notice and Details of Anti Corn Law League Meeting (1852) **2**.33–4
'Our Weapons of War' (1840) **1**.344–5
Robert Peel **1**.283–5
Petition of Inhabitants of Manchester (1843) **1**.375
'Petition! Petition! Petition!' (1840) **1**.359–60
petitions **1**.331–2, 344–5, 359–60, 375
'Petitions' (1840) **1**.344–5
Recollections of Richard Cobden and the Anti-Corn-Law League (1877) **2**.35–40
rent, land **1**.337–43
repeal **1**.283–7, 331–2
Report of the Proceedings of the Agricultural Meetings (1835) **1**.299–318
Report of the Select Committee on Agriculture (1833) **1**.299–318
Duke of Richmond **1**.376, 383–5
staples, cost **1**.335–9
Henry Stephens **1**.202–21, 222–35
'Support of the Anti Corn-Law League by the Working Classes' (1840) **1**.346–8
tariff bill **1**.132
taxation **1**.307–13
wages issues (1841) **1**.364–5
wages issues, American view (1842) **1**.371–2
Mr Whitmore **1**.321–2
working classes, support of Anti Corn-Law League (1840) **1**.346–8
workmen's petition **1**.360
Cosmopolite, *Free Trade and No Colonies* (1848) **2**.312–22
cost of staples **1**.335–9
cotton trade
America **1**.152–3
W. H. Clark **3**.353–5
France **1**.252–3
Ottawa Imperial Economic Conference (1931–2) **3**.353–5, 379–80

speech on 'Foreign Commerce of the Country' (1825) **1**.169–71
Henry Stephens **1**.219
'Textile Industry Reserves Opinion' (1932) **3**.379–80
country statistics, exports (1904–16) **3**.201–5
Curtis, John, 'America and the British Corn Law' (1842) **1**.370–2
customs administration, Ottawa Imperial Economic Conference (1931–2) **3**.376–7
customs unions
colonies **3**.64–6
Prussian Commercial Union **1**.239–41
Zollverein **1**.239–41, 260–5, 268–80

Decker, Sir M. **1**.40
Denman, R. D., 'The City and the Tariff Question' (1903) **3**.106–14
dependence of British Empire on United States (1916) **3**.218–28
depression in trade
'Causes of Trade Depression' (1886) **3**.36–9
'Our Tariff and the Depression' (1931) **3**.300–10
Royal Commission on Depression in Trade and Industry, 'Minority "Fair Trade" Report' (1886) **3**.40–3
Dingley Tariff Act (1897) **3**.146
Arguments against the Dingley Bill (1897) **3**.157–9
Bradford **3**.178–9
The Fruits of American Protection (1907) **3**.160–4
wool trade **3**.178–9
diplomacy
'Commercial Diplomacy, 1860–1902' **3**.106–14
tariff wars in Europe (1880–1914) **3**.106–14
'double tariff', France **3**.112
Duchâtel, Count Tanneguy **1**.257–9
Duke of Richmond
Agricultural Protection Society for Great Britain and Ireland (1844) **1**.376

aristocracy and Corn Laws (1846) 1.383–5
Dunckley, Henry, *The Charter of the Nations* (1854) 2.110–16
Dundee Operatives, and Corn Laws 1.222–35

earthenware trade 1.172
ECJ *see* European Court of Justice
economic depression (1931) 3.300–10
economic development, ITO proposals (1947) 4.50–1
economic union
　'The Allies' Economic Combine' (1916) 3.215–17
　Paris Economic Conference, 10 February 1916 3.215–17
'The Economic War' (1916) 3.212–14
Ecroyd, W. Farrer
　fair trade 3.10–11
　The Policy of Self Help (1879) 2.262–9
Eden, William
　Anglo-French Commercial Treaty (1786) 1.52, 53–4, 56
　'Letter on the Representations of Ireland, respecting a Free Trade' (1779) 1.33–43
　letters
　　from William Pitt (1786) 1.53–4
　　to Lord Carmarthen (1786) 1.52
　　to Robert Liston (1786) 1.56
Edinburgh Petition for Free Trade (1820) 1.166–7
EEC *see* European Economic Community
Egerton, Sir Thomas 1.9
Elliot, E. J.
　FBI (1948) 4.57
　ITO 4.57
Elliot, Ebenezer, 'An Address to the People of England, on the Corn Laws' (1834) 1.289–96
Empire and tariffs (1880–1914) 3.45–8
employment, ITO proposals (1947) 4.48–50
'The End of the War and After' (1916) 3.197–200
energy policy, EEC (1967) 4.93
England
　evolution of British commercial policy (1832–46) 1.281–7
　'Financial Situation of England and France' (1810) 1.102–3
　see also Anglo-; British Empire
entertainment industry, NAFTA (1993) 4.248–9
Europe
　commercial policy 2.175–8
　imports/exports (1860s–70s) 2.202–4, 220–4
　C. M. Kennedy 2.212–28
　'Memorandum on the Commercial Policy of European States and British Trade' (1879) 2.175–8
　'Treaties of Commerce with, and between, European Powers' (1875) 2.212–28
　wool trade 1.40–2
European Coal and Steel Community *see* Coal and Steel Community, European
European Court of Justice (ECJ)
　'Cassis' Decision (1979) 4.104–9
　German Beer Purity Law Decision (1987) 4.110–24
European Economic Community (EEC) 4.63–124
　background 4.63–6
　Britain's entry (1967) 4.90–1
　Charles de Gaulle's comments 4.74–7, 78–80
　Coal and Steel Community 4.63, 67–8, 69–70, 88–95
　Cooperation Agreement with ASEAN (1980) 4.159–64
　ECJ 'Cassis' Decision (1979) 4.104–9
　ECJ German Beer Purity Law Decision (1987) 4.110–24
　energy policy (1967) 4.93
　French influence (1965) 4.81–7
　Charles de Gaulle, Press Conference (1963, 1967) 4.74–7, 78–80
　historical background 4.63–6
　Kennedy Round 4.90–1
　Selwyn Lloyd 4.71–3
　Memorandum on EEC/ASEAN Relations (1975) 4.147–8
　Sir Con O'Neill 4.81–7

Report on EEC Visit to Thailand (1973) 4.143–6
Sir Geoffrey Rippon and Dr Rui Patricio, conversation (1972) 4.98–103
tariff reduction proposal (1956) 4.69–70
'Ten Reasons Why Britain Should Join the Common Market' (1970) 4.96–7
Evans, Gower, *Free Trade and the European Treaties of Commerce* (1875) 2.348–51
exchange control, ITO proposals (1947) 4.44–7
exports, country statistics (1904–16) 3.201–5
exports/imports
  Europe (1860s) 2.202–4
  fair trade 3.19–20
  Memorandum on Terminating the Belgian and German Commercial Treaties (1897) 3.90–5
  Paris Economic Conference (1916) 3.256–8
  reciprocity 2.277–9
  tariff wars in Europe (1880–1914) 3.90–5

fair trade 3.1–75
  agriculture 3.23–4, 36–9
  Australian colonies 3.26–8, 40–3
  J. B. Barkworth 3.30–3
  Annie Besant 3.17–22
  S. Bourne 3.56–8
  Jacob Bright 3.34–5
  'Causes of Trade Depression' (1886) 3.36–9
  W. Farrer Ecroyd 3.10–11
  'England under Free Trade' (1881) 3.15–16
  exports 3.19–20
  'The Fair-Trade Party' (1886) 3.30–3
  'The Fair Trade Policy' (1882) 3.23–9
  'The Fair Trade Scheme of Commercial Federation' (1887) 3.62–3
  Free Trade and Imperial Preference (1905) 3.133–7
  Sir Alexander Galt 3.60
  grain trade 3.23–4, 36–9
  growth 3.88–9
  'Imperial Federation' (1886) 3.59–61
  'Imperial Federation in its Commercial Aspect' (1886) 3.56–8
  imports 3.19–20
  Sampson S. Lloyd 3.23–9
  Robert Andrew Macfie 3.13–14, 30–3, 44
  David MacIver 3.11
  Manchester Chamber of Commerce 3.34–5
  G. W. Medley 3.15–16
  New South Wales (colony) 3.26–8
  origins 3.2, 7–9
  'The Past and the Future' (1885) 3.7–9
  'Protection for Home Agriculture' (1886) 3.30–3
  'Protection for Manufacturing Industries' (1886) 3.30–3
  'The Relative Growth of Free Trade and Protection' (1892) 3.88–9
  rise and fall (1879–92) 3.1–5
  Royal Commission on Depression in Trade and Industry, 'Minority "Fair Trade" Report' (1886) 3.40–3
  Professor Seeley 3.60
  'The Story of the Movement' (1888) 3.10–12
  Victoria (colony) 3.26–8
  Queen Victoria 3.26–7
  wealth 3.17–22
  D. Wells 3.21
  'What is Really Free Trade' (1881) 3.17–22
  B. R. Wise 3.133–7
  wool trade 3.15–16
  see also free trade
'The Fair-Trade Party' (1886) 3.30–3
'The Fair-Trade Policy' (1888) 3.44
'The Fair Trade Scheme of Commercial Federation' (1887) 3.62–3
farm aid
  'Hoover Promises to Call Congress to Act on Farm Aid' (1928) 3.267–8
  Smoot-Hawley Tariff Act (1930) 3.267–8
Federation of British Industries (FBI) 4.18–22, 57
Ferguson, Jonathan, 'NAFTA: Canada's Concerns' (1993) 4.252–5

'Financial Situation of England and France' (1810) **1**.102–3
'Fiscal Reform' (1904) **3**.129–32
Foster, Mr, letter to Castlereagh (1812) **1**.105
Fox, Mr **1**.21–2
France
    Anglo-French commercial relations **1**.242–80
    Anglo-French Commercial Treaty (1786) **1**.1–6, 44–67
    Anglo-French Commercial Treaty (abortive; 1852) **2**.117–25
    Anglo-French Treaty (1860) **2**.137–73, **3**.7–9
    autotrade tariff (1930) **3**.282–9
    Chamber of Commerce, Boulogne-sur-Mer **1**.246–51
    Chamber of Commerce, Havre **1**.252–3
    Michel Chevalier
        in Lardner, *The Great Exhibition and London* (1852) **2**.83–90
        The History of Political Economy (1869) **2**.143–7
    commercial policy **2**.91–109, **3**.106–14
    'Commercial Situation of England and France' (1810) **1**.102–3
    conventional tariff **3**.84–7
    cotton trade **1**.252–3
    'double tariff' **3**.112
    EEC **4**.74–7, 78–80, 81–7
    'Financial Situation of England and France' (1810) **1**.102–3
    Franco-Italian tariff war (1888–99) **3**.96–9
    Franco-Swiss tariff war (1893–5) **3**.103–5
    Free Trade Meeting at Marseilles (1847) **2**.79–81
    The French and American Tariffs Compared (1861) **2**.179–86
    Charles de Gaulle **4**.74–7, 78–80
    general tariff **3**.84–7
    grain trade (1851) **2**.95–100
    Robert Andrew Macfie
        'Letter to the Shipping and Mercantile Gazette (1880) **3**.13–14
    'Notes on the French Treaty' (1860) **2**.164–8
    Marseilles Free Trade Society Meeting (1847) **2**.79–81
    'The Past and the Future' (1885) **3**.7–9
    phylloxera influence **3**.109
    prohibitions, removal demands **1**.246–51, 252–3
    protectionism **3**.106–14
    reduction of British duties (1846) **1**.387
    shipping bounties (1880) **3**.13–14
    silk trade **1**.387
    tariff of 1892 **3**.112
    tariff wars in Europe (1880–1914) **3**.84–7, 96–9, 103–5, 106–14
    tariffs **1**.237–9, 246–51, 252–3, **3**.84–7
    M. Thiers, speech on Commercial Policy of France (1851) **2**.91–109
    Trade and Treaties Committee (1891) **3**.84–7
    treaties *see* Anglo-French Commercial Treaty (1786)
    wool trade **1**.252–3
    see also Paris Economic Conference (1916)
Franco-Italian tariff war (1888–99) **3**.96–9
free trade
    Account of a Dinner to Mr Cobden at Rome (1847) **2**.67–70
    Arbitration Instead of War (1848) **2**.41–3
    Henry Ashworth **2**.35–40
    Australia **2**.323–6, 348–51
    Austria **2**.283–91
    Belgian Association, 'Congress of Political Economists at Brussels' (1847) **2**.73–8
    Michel Chevalier, in Lardner, *The Great Exhibition and London* (1852) **2**.83–90
    Richard Cobden
        Arbitration Instead of War (1848) **2**.41–3
        letter to Michel Chevalier (1851) **2**.82
        letter to Marco Minghetti (1847) **2**.61–2
        speeches in Europe **2**.63–72

Recollections of Richard Cobden and the Anti-Corn-Law League (1877) **2**.35–40
colonial policy, 1848 **2**.312–22
colonies **2**.338–47
'Commercial Treaties and Free Trade' (1860) **2**.161–3
'Congress of Political Economists at Brussels' (1847) **2**.73–8
diffusion abroad (1847–60) **2**.55–136
Five Free Trade Essays (1875) **2**.338–47
Free Thoughts on Free Trade (1852) **2**.25–32
Free Trade and Imperial Preference (1905) **3**.133–7
'Free Trade and Peace' (1847) **2**.44–6
Free Trade Meeting at Marseilles (1847) **2**.79–81
'Free Trade' (1890) **3**.149–51
Freedom and Independence for the Golden Lands of Australia (1852) **2**.323–6
Germany **2**.283–91
Sir James Graham, letters to W. E. Gladstone (1852) **2**.53, 54
influence on moral renovation of the world (1854) **2**.111–16
Italy **2**.291–8
John Dunmore Lang **2**.323–6
Marseilles Free Trade Society Meeting (1847) **2**.79–81
national independence **2**.28–32
navigation/shipping benefits **2**.10–13
'Peace on Earth – Good Will Towards Men' (1848) **2**.47
Public Banquet to Mr Cobden at Florence (1847) **2**.70–2
ramifications **2**.41–54
Lord Stanhope, letters to G. F. Young (1849) **2**.19–20, 21
and tariff reform **3**.115–18
taxation **2**.48–52
under threat (1870–9) **2**.229–351
treaties of commerce **2**.348–51
Universal Free Trade (1852) **2**.48–52
Victoria (colony) **2**.338–47
Max Wirth **2**.283–9
see also fair trade; protectionism
Free Trade and No Colonies (1848) **2**.312–22

Free Trade and the European Treaties of Commerce (1875) **2**.283–311
Austria **2**.283–91
George von Bunsen **2**.289–91
Michel Chevalier **2**.304–11
William Lloyd Garrison **2**.302–3
Germany **2**.283–91
Italy **2**.291–8
Political Economy Society of Paris (1875) **2**.304–11
James Montgomery Stuart **2**.291–8
United States **2**.299–303
David A. Wells **2**.299–301
Horace White **2**.301–2
Max Wirth **2**.283–9
Freedom and Independence for the Golden Lands of Australia (1852) **2**.323–6
Freedom of Transit (1916) **3**.253
Freville, Baron, Anglo-French commercial relations **1**.257–9
The Fruits of American Protection (1907) **3**.160–4

Gadsby, J., 'Corn Laws are Potato Laws' (1842) **1**.373–4
Galt, Sir Alexander **3**.60
Garrison, William Lloyd **2**.302–3
de Gaulle, President Charles
Press Conference (1963) **4**.74–7
Press Conference (1967) **4**.78–80
General Convention of Agriculturists and Manufacturers (1827) **1**.141–2
general tariff, France **3**.84–7
Germany
Belgian and German Commercial Treaties, terminating (1897) **3**.90–5
George von Bunsen **2**.289–91
ECJ Beer Purity Law Decision (1987) **4**.110–24
Free Trade and the European Treaties of Commerce (1875) **2**.283–91
'The New Protectionism' (1916) **3**.160–4
'The Paris Economic Conference and After' (1916) **3**.207–8
protectionism **3**.160–4
tariff war between Germany and Russia (1879–94) **3**.99–103

tariff wars in Europe (1879–1914) 3.78–80, 99–103
treaties of commerce 2.216
Max Wirth 2.283–9
Zollverein 1.239–41, 260–5, 268–80, 2.216
'The Ghost of a Dead Monopoly' (1846) 1.391–4
Giffen, R.
  colonies 3.64–6
  'The Relative Growth of Free Trade and Protection' (1892) 3.88–9
Gladstone, John, 'Remedy for the Distress of the Working Classes' (1841) 1.361–3
Gladstone, W. E., 'Free Trade' (1890) 3.149–51
glass trade (1825) 1.172
globalization (2006) 4.312–17
gloves trade(1825) 1.172
Gore, Al 4.203–43
Gorman-Wilson tariff 3.178
  Graham, Sir James 2.53, 54
grain trade
  'Causes of Trade Depression' (1886) 3.36–9
  fair trade 3.23–4, 36–9
  France, commercial policy (1851) 2.95–100
  A Letter Addressed to the Landowners and Tenantry of the County of Forfar (1826) 1.202–21
  'Protection Disinterred' (1849) 2.15–18
  Henry Stephens 1.202–21
  see also agricultural trade; Corn Laws
Greene, Conyngham
  Franco-Italian tariff war (1888–99) 3.96–9
  Franco-Swiss tariff war (1893–5) 3.103–5
  Japanese participation in Paris Economic Conference (1916) 3.229–31
  Paris Economic Conference (1916) 3.229–31
  tariff war between Germany and Russia (1879–1894) 3.99–103
Grey, Edward
  letters to Sir Francis Villiers (1916) 3.189–91, 209

Paris Economic Conference (1916) 3.187–91

Hailes, Daniel, letter to the Marquis of Carmarthen (1786) 1.58–63
Hamilton, Alexander
  commercial policy, American 1.131–2
  manufactures report 1.147–8
Hanbury, William Bateman, *Plea for Limited Protection* (1877) 2.257–61
Hannon, Sir Patrick, letter to Sir Stafford Cripps (1946) 4.8–9
Harris, John [Kuklos], *The Commercial Policy of England* (1877) 2.241–53
Havana Charter (1948) 4.59–62
Herries, John Charles
  letters to George Frederick Young (1849) 2.14, 24
  Navigation Laws, British 2.14
Hirst, F. W., 'The City and Tariff Reform' (1910) 3.142–3
Hobson, J. A.
  The Fruits of American Protection (1907) 3.160–4
  'The New Protectionism' (1916) 3.192–6
Hoover, Herbert
  '1028 Economists Ask Hoover to Veto Pending Tariff Bill' (1930) 3.272–4
  campaign speech (1932) 3.314–21
  farm aid 3.267–8
  Smoot-Hawley Tariff Act (1930) 3.267–8, 269–71, 272–4, 290–3, 314–21
  State of the Union Address (1929) 3.269–71
  Statement upon Signing the Tariff Bill into Law (1930) 3.290–3
Horie, Kilchi 3.234–6
House of Lords protest against Corn Bill (1846) 1.388–90
Hull, Cordell
  'Economic Policies of the Government' (1931) 3.296–9
  Smoot-Hawley Tariff Act (1930) 3.296–9, 322–3
  Statement on Tariffs and an International Tariff Congress (1916) 4.263–6
  'Trade Agreements or Free Trade?' (1934) 3.322–3

Huskisson, William
  commercial policy reform 1.129–31
  copper trade 1.174–5
  Corn Laws 1.129–30, 321–2, 329–30
  cotton trade 1.169–71
  earthenware trade 1.172
  glass trade 1.172
  gloves trade 1.172
  iron trade 1.172–4
  lead trade 1.175
  Levant trade 1.185–7
  linen trade 1.172
  Manchester Chamber of Commerce 1.188–9
  metals trade 1.172–5
  Navigation Laws, British 1.130
  navigation/shipping 1.182–5
  paper trade 1.172
  raw materials trade 1.181–2
  Reciprocity of Duties Act (1823) 1.130
  silk trade 1.168–9
  smuggling 1.176–8
  speech on the 'Foreign Commerce of the Country' (1825) 1.168–87
  Spitalfields Act 1.129–30
  Stamp Duty 1.183–4
  wool trade 1.170–1, 181, 182
  zinc trade 1.175
Hutchinson, John Hely, 'The Commercial Restraints of Ireland' (1779) 1.23–32

IMF *see* International Monetary Fund
'Imperial Federation' (1886) 3.59–61
'Imperial Federation in its Commercial Aspect' (1886) 3.56–8
import restrictions 4.32–6
imports/exports
  Belgian and German Commercial Treaties, terminating (1897) 3.90–5
  Europe (1860s, 1870s) 2. 202–4, 220–4
  fair trade 3.19–20
  Paris Economic Conference (1916) 3.256–8
  reciprocity 2.277–9
  tariff wars in Europe (1880–1914) 3.90–5
intellectual property 4.248–9, 300

International Monetary Fund (IMF) 4.312–17
international perspective (1830–42) 1.237–42
  customs unions 1.239–41
International Trade Organization (ITO) 4.1–62
  background 4.1–4
  Board of Trade 4.10–17, 23–6, 58
  British strength 4.6
  commodity arrangements 4.52–3
  'Conflicts of Principle in Drafting a Trade Charter' (1947) 4.27–41
  economic development 4.50–1
  E. J. Elliot 4.57
  Empire influence 4.6–7
  employment 4.48–50
  exchange control 4.44–7
  FBI 4.18–22, 57
  Havana Charter (1948) 4.59–62
  imperial preference (1947) 4.54–6
  import restrictions 4.32–6
  loans 4.54–6
  'The London Draft of a Charter' (1947) 4.42–53
  Roger Makins 4.54–6
  National Union of Manufacturers (1946) 4.8–9
  omissions 4.39–41
  preferences 4.47–8, 54–6
  problems 4.39–41
  quantitative restrictions 4.44–7
  restrictive business practices 4.52
  'Retaliation and Other Indirect Consequences' (1947) 4.10–17
  Russia 4.37–9
  R. J. Shackle 4.58
  tariffs 4.47–8, 54–6
  'Trade Agreements' (1946) 4.5–7
  United States possible retaliation 4.10–17
  Jacob Viner 4.27–41
Ireland
  Anglo-Irish commercial relationship 1.1–6
  Anglo-Irish relations (1779–85) 1.7–43
  'The Commercial Restraints of Ireland' (1779) 1.23–32

Sir M. Decker **1**.40
William Eden **1**.33–43
Mr Fox **1**.21–2
'House of Commons debate' (1779) **1**.9–11
John Hely Hutchinson **1**.23–32
'Letter on the Representations of Ireland, respecting a Free Trade' (1779) **1**.33–43
linen trade **1**.16–18
'Motion respecting trade in Ireland' (1779) **1**.7–8
Navigation Laws, British **1**.2, 37
'Lord North's Propositions for the Relief of the Trade of Ireland' (1779) **1**.14–22
'Speech of the Lord Lieutenant to the Irish Parliament' (1779) **1**.13
Mrs Stopford-Sackville **1**.12
sugar trade **1**.20–1
wool trade **1**.15–18, 24–5, 27–32, 36–7
Irish constitutional ambiguity **1**.1–6
Irish free trade agitation (1779–85) **1**.7–43
Irish trade constraints **1**.1–6
iron trade
  Anglo-French Commercial Treaty (1786) **1**.50–1
  speech on the 'Foreign Commerce of the Country' (1825) **1**.172–4
Italy
  Franco-Italian tariff war (1888–99) **3**.96–9
  Free Trade and the European Treaties of Commerce (1875) **2**.291–8
  James Montgomery Stuart **2**.291–8
  tariff wars in Europe (1880–1914) **3**.96–9
  treaties of commerce **2**.217–18
ITO *see* International Trade Organization

Japanese participation, Paris Economic Conference (1916) **3**.229–36
  extracts from Japanese press **3**.231–6
  Conyngham Greene **3**.229–31
  Kilchi Horie **3**.234–6
  suppression of newspapers **3**.234
Jefferson, Mr **1**.159–60

Kay, Alex **1**.297–8
Kennedy, C. M., 'Treaties of Commerce with, and between, European Powers' (1875) **2**.212–28
Kennedy Round, EEC **4**.90–1
A Key to the Orders in Council (1812) **1**.106–20
Keynes, John Maynard **3**.262–3, 326
Kuklos (John Harris), *The Commercial Policy of England* (1877) **2**.241–53

Labour representatives (1904) **3**.124–6
Lack, H. Reader, *The French Treaty and Tariff of 1860* (1861) **2**.154–60
land rent **1**.337–43
Lang, John Dunmore, *Freedom and Independence for the Golden Lands of Australia* (1852) **2**.323–6
Laurier, Sir W. **3**.165–7
LDCs *see* least-developed countries
lead trade (1825) **1**.175
League of Nations **3**.250–1
least-developed countries (LDCs) **4**.306–7
Lee Kwan Yew, Opening Session of the ASEAN Summit (1976) **4**.149–51
legal issues **1**.88–100
Levant trade (1825) **1**.185–7
linen trade **1**.172
  Anglo-French Commercial Treaty (1786) **1**.46–7
  Ireland **1**.16–18
  Henry Stephens **1**.219
Llewelyn Davies, Margaret, 'What Co-Operative Women Think' (1903) **3**.127–8
Lloyd, Sampson S., 'The Fair Trade Policy' (1882) **3**.23–9
Lloyd, Selwyn, conversation, Netherlands Ambassador (1960) **4**.71–3
Louis, Baron, Anglo-French commercial relations **1**.256–7
lumber industry **3**.381
Lyons, Lord, American-Canadian Reciprocity Treaty of 1854 (1862) **2**.126–8

McClure, A. K., *The McKinley Tariff Robbery and Fraud* (1892) **3**.154–6

Macfie, Robert Andrew
   fair trade 3.13–14, 30–3, 44
   'The Fair-Trade Policy' (1888) 3.44
   free trade 2.164–8
   'Letter to the Shipping and Mercantile Gazette' (1880) 3.13–14
   'Notes on the French Treaty' (1860) 2.164–8
   'Protection for Manufacturing Industries' (1886) 3.30–3
   shipping bounties, French 3.13–14
MacIver, David 3.11
McKinley tariff law 3.177–8
The McKinley Tariff Robbery and Fraud (1892) 3.154–6
Makins, Roger, Memorandum on Imperial Preference (1947) 4.54–6
Malik, Adam, ASEAN Conference (1967) 4.132–3
Mallet, Sir Louis
   'Commercial Treaty with Austria' (1866) 2.196–206
   'The Commercial Treaty with France' (1877) 2.254–5
   Memorandum on Modifications of the Anglo French Treaty (1871) 2.207–11
   Reciprocity (1879) 2.270–82
malt tax 2.16–18
Manchester, Petition of Inhabitants (1843) 1.375
'Manchester and the Manchesterians' (1886) 3.34–5
Manchester Chamber of Commerce
   Jacob Bright 3.34–5
   Corn Laws 1.331–2, 344–5
   fair trade 3.34–5
   'Manchester and the Manchesterians' (1886) 3.34–5
   petition on Corn Law repeal (1838) 1.331–2, 344–5
   vote of thanks to William Huskisson 1.188–9
Manchester Manufacturer, letter to Charles James Fox (1787) 1.65–7
manufacturing industries 1.195–6
The McKinley Tariff Robbery and Fraud (1892) 3.154–6

de la Mare, Arthur, Report on EEC Visit to Thailand (1973) 4.143–6
meat duty 3.364–9
Mecklenburg und der Zollverein (1841) 1.268–80
Medley, G. W., 'England under Free Trade' (1881) 3.15–16
Méline tariff 3.77–8
Merchants' Petition in favour of Free Trade (1820) 1.162–5
metals trade 1.50–1, 172–5
Mexico
   'Canada Prepared if NAFTA Fails' (1993) 4.244–5
   NAFTA (1993) 4.248–9
Milan Decree
   A Key to the Orders in Council, 1812 1.109–13, 117
   Napoleon 1.70
mining 1.307
Minutes of the Committee of Trade (1786) 1.50–1
Morier, R.
   Commercial Treaties (1870) 2.187–95
   reciprocity 2.192–5
motor trade
   meeting prior to Ottawa Imperial Economic Conference (1932) 3.346–8
   tariff, French, Smoot-Hawley Tariff Act (1930) 3.282–9
   'U.A.W. Wants Trade Payoff in Jobs' (1994) 4.256–8
Murakami, Kerry, 'Geneva Sounded WTO Warning That Went Unheeded in Seattle' (2000) 4.293–5

NAFTA *see* North American Free Trade Agreement
NAOT *see* National Association of Organized Trades for the Industrial, Social and Political Emancipation of Labour
Napoleon
   Continental System 1.69–71
   Madame de Stael Holstein's views of 1.123–5
   Milan Decree 1.70
   trade as an instrument of war (1793–1812) 1.69–74

National Association for the Protection of
  British Industry and Capital 2.3–4,
  22–3
National Association of Organized Trades
  for the Industrial, Social and Political
  Emancipation of Labour (NAOT)
  2.3–4
national independence 2.28–32
National Union of Manufacturers 4.5–7,
  8–9, 23–6
Navigation Laws, British 1.130, 2.9–13, 14
  Ireland 1.2, 37
navigation/shipping 1.182–5
  Solomon Atkinson 1.193–5
  competition (1847) 2.9–10
  free trade benefits 2.10–13
  French shipping bounties (1880)
    3.13–14
  Robert Andrew Macfie, 'Letter to the
    Shipping and Mercantile Gazette'
    (1880) 3.13–14
  protectionism 2.9–13
  John Lewis Ricardo 2.9–13
  Stamp Duty 1.183–4
  Henry Stephens 1.219–20
*The New American Tariff (Simmons-Under-
  wood) and the Wool Industry of Bradford*
  (1914) 3.175–82
Newhaven, Lord 1.9
'The New Protectionism' (1916) 3.192–6
New South Wales (colony)
  fair trade 3.26–8
  'Protection in Young Communities'
    (1882) 3.51–5
New Zealand 3.362–3, 364–9
'nightmare scenario', food prices 1.364–5
Non-Intercourse Law (1809–10) 1.113–17
North American Free Trade Agreement
  (NAFTA) 4.169–258
  background 4.169–72
  George H. W. Bush 4.173–6, 177–86
  Canada, House of Commons Debates
    (1993) 4.187–202
  'Canada Prepared if NAFTA Fails'
    (1993) 4.244–5
  Bill Clinton 4.173–6, 177–86
  copyright protection (1993) 4.248–9
  entertainment industry (1993) 4.248–9

Jonathan Ferguson 4.252–5
Al Gore 4.203–43
intellectual property (1993) 4.248–9
Mexico 4.248–9, 250–1
'NAFTA All Clear in Mexico' (1993)
  4.250–1
'NAFTA Backers Must Speak Now'
  (1993) 4.246
'NAFTA: Canada's Concerns' (1993)
  4.252–5
'NAFTA Debate: Gore vs. Perot' (1993)
  4.203–43
'The National Interest' (1993) 4.247
Ross Perot 4.173–6, 177–86, 203–43
Second Presidential Debate, Clinton-
  Bush-Perot (1992) 4.173–6
Third Presidential Debate, Clinton-Bush-
  Perot (1992) 4.177–86
'U.A.W. Wants Trade Payoff in Jobs'
  (1994) 4.256–8
Dennis Wharton 4.248–9
North, Lord 1.10, 14–22
Nugent, Lord 1.7–8, 10–11

O'Brien, Bronterre, 'Corn-Law Agitation
  Humbug' (1840) 1.355
O'Neill, Sir Con 4.81–7
Orders in Council
  blockade 1.98–100
  Continental System 1.85–7, 88–100,
    101, 104
  A Key to the Orders in Council (1812)
    1.106–20
  legal issues 1.88–100
  Spencer Perceval 1.85–7
  policy 1.93–100
  Prince Regent 1.104
  repealing 1.118–20
  James Stephen 1.85–7, 101, 106–20
Orloff, Count 2.129–30
Ottawa Imperial Economic Conference
  (1931–2) 3.325–92
  agenda, proposed 3.329–58
  Australia 3.364–9, 382–3, 384–5
  Richard Bennett 3.327
  John Bromley 3.360–1
  Walter M. Citrine 3.360–1
  W. H. Clark 3.340–3, 344–5, 353–5

J. G. Coates 3.362–3
commercial relations, foreign countries 3.377–8
cotton trade 3.353–5, 379–80
customs administration 3.376–7
'Dominion Industries' (1931) 3.337–9
'The Harvest of Ottawa' (1932) 3.386–8
'Imperial Preference' (1932) 3.349–52
lumber industry 3.381
meat duty 3.364–9
Memorandum by Industrial Advisors (1932) 3.360–1
'Memorandum of a Conversation with the [Canadian] Prime Minister' (1931) 3.340–3
motor trade meeting (1932) 3.346–8
New Zealand delegation 3.362–3, 364–9
'An Ottawa Impression' (1932) 3.389–92
'Ottawa Reactions' (1932) 3.382–3
political consequences 3.328
pre-conference report (1931) 3.329–36
promotion of trade 3.374–6
Report of the Committee on the Proposed Conference (1931) 3.329–36
resolutions 3.370–3
'The Riddle of Ottawa' (1932) 3.384–5
Selections from the Ottawa Agreement (1932) 3.370–8
Louis-Alexandre Taschereau 3.381
'Textile Industry Reserves Opinion' (1932) 3.379–80
trade promotion 3.374–6
Trades Union Congress 3.360–1
United Kingdom delegation 3.356–9
wool trade 3.379–80

Palmerston, Lord 1.266–7, 380
paper trade (1825) 1.172
Paris Economic Conference (1916) 3.183–242
'The Allies' Economic Combine' (1916) 3.215–17
Alsace-Lorraine 3.244–5
American press, response 3.210–11
Belgian issues 3.189–91, 209
Board of Trade memorandum (1918) 3.251
Control of Imperial Resources 3.248

countries' views 3.183–6
economic desiderata 3.243–6, 247–51
economic union 3.215–17
'The Economic War' (1916) 3.212–14
'The End of the War and After' (1916) 3.197–200
exports 3.256–8
Freedom of the Seas 3.251
Freedom of Transit 3.253
Germany 3.207–8
Conyngham Greene 3.229–31
Imperial War Cabinet 3.247–51
imports 3.256–8
indemnities 3.248–9
invitation to British government 3.187–8
Japanese participation 3.229–36
League of Nations 3.250–1
'The New Protectionism' (1916) 3.192–6
'The Paris Economic Conference and After' (1916) 3.206–8
permanent measures 3.241–2
Poland 3.246
Private Claims Settlement 3.250
'pro-Prussian peace talk' (1916) 3.212–14
recommendations 3.237–42
removal of treaties 3.248
resolutions 3.247–8
Russia 3.208, 212–14
Serbia, reconstitution 3.245–6
A. Stanley 3.243–6
territorial readjustments 3.244–6
transitory measures 3.239–40
Turkish Dominions 3.246
war period measures 3.238–9
'Who Were Our Best Customers?' (1916) 3.201–5
Parkes, Henry, *Free Trade and the European Treaties of Commerce* (1875) 2.348–51
Patricio, Dr Rui 4.98–103
Peel, Robert 1.283–5
Perceval, Spencer 1.85–7
Perot, Ross
  NAFTA Debate: Gore vs Perot (1993) 4.203–43
  Second NAFTA Presidential Debate (1992) 4.173–6

Third NAFTA Presidential Debate (1992) **4**.177–86
petitions
  bread tax **1**.359–60
  Continental System **1**.79–80
  Corn Laws **1**.331–2, 344–5, 359–60, 375
  Edinburgh Petition for Free Trade (1820) **1**.166–7
  Manchester Chamber of Commerce (1838) **1**.331–2, 344–5
  Manchester inhabitants **1**.375
  Merchants' Petition in Favour of Free Trade (1820) **1**.162–5
  Southwark Petition (1795) **1**.79–80
phylloxera influence, France **3**.109
Pitt, William
  Anglo-French Commercial Treaty (1786) **1**.3, 53–4, 55
  Corn Act (1791) **1**.304–5
  Irish constitutional ambiguity **1**.1–2
  letter to the Marquis of Stafford (1786) **1**.55
  letter to William Eden (1786) **1**.53–4
Poland **3**.246
policy, commercial *see* commercial policy
Political Economy Society of Paris, meeting (1875) **2**.304–11
preferential movement (1908) **3**.138–41
Prince Regent **1**.104
Protection as a National System Suited for Victoria (1860) **2**.327–33
'Protection in Germany' (1881) **3**.83
'Protection in Young Communities' (1882) **3**.51–5
protectionism **3**.30–3
  agricultural trade **3**.111–12
  America **3**.157–9, 160–4
  The Anatomy of the Navigation Laws (1847) **2**.9–13
  Anglo-French Commercial Treaty (1786) **1**.1–6
  Anglo-Irish commercial relationship **1**.1–6
  Arbitration Instead of War (1848) **2**.41–3
  'Commercial Diplomacy 1860–1902' **3**.106–14
  decline (1846–52) **2**.1–54

  defeat in Britain (1847) **2**.9–13
  Dingley Tariff Act (1897) **3**.157–9, 160–4
  France **3**.106–14
  Free Thoughts on Free Trade (1852) **2**.25–32
  'Free Trade and Peace' (1847) **2**.44–6
  The Fruits of American Protection (1907) **3**.160–4
  Germany **3**.160–4
  J. A. Hobson **3**.160–4, 192–6
  malt tax **2**.16–18
  National Association **2**.3–4
  National Association for the Protection of British Industry and Capital **2**.22–3
  navigation/shipping **2**.9–13
  'The New Protectionism' (1916) **3**.192–6
  post-war protection (1824) **1**.137–61
  'Protection Disinterred' (1849) **2**.15–18
  Recollections of Richard Cobden and the Anti-Corn-Law League (1877) **2**.35–40
  Universal Free Trade (1852) **2**.48–52
  see also free trade
Prussia
  Anglo-Prussian commercial relations **1**.260–5, 266–7, 268–80
  Mecklenburg und der Zollverein (1841) **1**.268–80
  Lord Palmerston **1**.266–7
  Paris Economic Conference (1916) **3**.212–14
  'pro-Prussian peace talk' (1916) **3**.212–14
  Prussian Commercial Union **1**.239–41

Rajaratnam, H. E. S., ASEAN Conference (1967) **4**.129–31
raw materials trade (1825) **1**.181–2
reciprocity
  Lord Bateman **2**.257–61
  exports/imports **2**.277–9
  William Bateman Hanbury **2**.257–61
  Sir Louis Mallet **2**.270–82
  R. Morier **2**.192–5
Reciprocity (1879) **2**.270–82
Reciprocity of Duties Act (1823) **1**.130

Reciprocity Pact, 'Canada's Answer' (1911) 3.170–2
Reciprocity Treaty of 1854 2.126–8
Reciprocity with the United States (1911) 3.168–9
Reid, George H.
  Five Free Trade Essays (1875) 2.338–47
  free trade, Australia 2.348–9
  Victoria (colony) 2.338–47
'The Relative Growth of Free Trade and Protection' (1892) 3.88–9
rent, land 1.337–43
restrictive business practices 4.52
'Revivers Association' (1869) 2.235–40
Ricardo, John Lewis, *The Anatomy of the Navigation Laws*, 1847 2.9–13
Richmond, Duke of
  Agricultural Protection Society for Great Britain and Ireland (1844) 1.376
  'aristocracy' and Corn Laws (1846) 1.383–5
Rippon, Sir Geoffrey 4.98–103
Roosevelt, Franklin D., 'Forgotten Man' (1932) 3.311–13
Russell, Lord John 2.117–20
Russia
  Cardwell Memorandum on Commercial Policy (1854) 2.131–6
  'Conflicts of Principle in Drafting a Trade Charter' (1947) 4.37–9
  'The End of the War and After' (1916) 3.198
  ITO (1947) 4.37–9
  Paris Economic Conference (1916) 3.212–14
  'The Paris Economic Conference and After' (1916) 3.208
  'pro-Prussian peace talk' (1916) 3.212–14
  Soviet Response to South-East Asian Regional Cooperation (1967) 4.136–7
  tariff war between Germany and Russia (1879–94) 3.99–103

Seeley, Professor 3.60
Serbia, reconstitution 3.245–6
Shackle, R. J. 4.58

Sheffield and the American Tariff (1890) 3.152–3
shipping/navigation *see* navigation/shipping
silk trade 1.387, 168–9, 218–19, 2.139
Simmons-Underwood Tariff (1914) 3.175–82
Sinclair, George 1.81
Slagg, J., 'The Commercial Treaty with France' (1877) 2.254–6
Slavery (1848) 2.314–15
Smith, Adam 1.1, 2.314–17, 320–1
Smith, G., 'The Canadian Tariff' (1881) 3.49–50
Smith, Swire, *The New American Tariff (Simmons-Underwood) and the Wool Industry of Bradford* (1914) 3.175–82
Smoot, Reed, 'Our Tariff and the Depression' (1931) 3.300–10
Smoot-Hawley Tariff Act (1930) 3.261–323
  '1028 Economists Ask Hoover to Veto Pending Tariff Bill' (1930) 3.272–4
  autotrade tariff, French 3.282–9
  'Economic Policies of the Government' (1931) 3.296–9
  farm aid 3.267–8
  foreign government protests 3.272–4
  Herbert Hoover 3.267–8, 269–71, 272–4, 290–3, 314–21
  'Hoover Promises to Call Congress to Act on Farm Aid' (1928) 3.267–8
  Hull, Cordell 3.296–9, 322–3
  'The New American Tariff' (1930) 3.294
  Official Protests about Tariff Bill (1930) 3.272–4
  'Our Tariff and the Depression' (1931) 3.300–10
  Republican Party Platform (1928) 3.265–6
  Roosevelt, Franklin D. 3.311–13
  Reed Smoot 3.300–10
  State of the Union Address (1929) 3.269–71
  Swiss trade 3.295
  'Trade Agreements or Free Trade?' (1934) 3.322–3
  'The United States Tariff and Swiss Trade' (1930) 3.295
smuggling (1825) 1.176–8

Snowden, Philip, *The Chamberlain Bubble* (1903) 3.121–3
Southwark Petition (1795) 1.79–80
Spitalfields Act 1.129–30
de Stael Holstein, Madame, *An Appeal to the Nations of Europe* (1813) 1.121–8
Stamp Duty 1.183–4
Stanhope, Lord 2.19–20, 21
Stanley, A., 'Economic Desiderata in the Terms of Peace' (1917) 3.243–6
Stanley, Mr 1.8, 10
staples, costs, Corn Laws 1.335–9
statistics, exports (1904–16) 3.201–5
steel industry (2002) 4.310–11
Stephen, James
 Continental System 1.85–7, 101, 106–20
 A Key to the Orders in Council (1812) 1.106–20
 letters to Spencer Perceval (1807–8) 1.85–7, 101
 Orders in Council 1.85–7, 101, 106–20
Stephens, Henry
 Corn Laws 1.202–21, 222–35
 cotton trade 1.219
 grain trade 1.202–21
 A Letter Addressed to the Landowners and Tenantry of the County of Forfar (1826) 1.202–21
 linen trade 1.219
 shipping/navigation 1.219–20
 silk trade 1.218–19
 wool trade 1.219
Stopford-Sackville, Mrs 1.12
Stuart, James Montgomery 2.291–8
sugar trade 1.20–1
Switzerland
 Franco-Swiss Tariff War (1893–5) 3.103–5
 'The United States Tariff and Swiss Trade' (1930) 3.295

tariff battles (1880–1914), America 3.145–82
tariff bill 1.132, 143, 157, 159–60
Tariff Commission 3.124–6, 138–41
Tariff of 1892, France 3.112
'Tariff of Abominations' (1828) 1.133

tariff policy, America 1.133
tariff reform 3.115–18, 142–3, 165–7
tariff wars in Europe (1879–1914) 3.77–81, 83–114
 Belgian and German Commercial Treaties, terminating (1897) 3.90–5
 'Commercial Diplomacy 1860–1902' 3.106–14
 diplomacy 3.106–14
 France 3.84–7, 96–9, 103–5, 106–14
 Franco-Italian tariff war (1888–99) 3.96–9
 Franco-Swiss tariff war (1893–5) 3.103–5
 Germany 3.78–80, 83, 99–103
 Italy 3.96–9
 Méline tariff 3.77–8
 'Protection in Germany' (1881) 3.83
 'The Relative Growth of Free Trade and Protection' (1892) 3.88–9
 Russia 3.99–103
 Switzerland 3.103–5
 tariff war between Germany and Russia (1879–94) 3.99–103
 Trade and Treaties Committee (1891) 3.84–7
tariffs
 H. U. Addington 1.137–9
 America 1.132, 133, 137–9, 140
 'The American Tariff' (1828) 1.144
 'The Canadian Tariff' (1881) 3.49–50
 Chamber of Commerce, Havre 1.252–3
 Committee on Commerce (1824) 1.140
 conventional tariff 3.84–7
 and Empire (1880–1914) 3.45–8
 France 1.237–9, 246–51, 252–3, 3.84–7
 general tariff 3.84–7
 Cordell Hull, Statement on Tariffs (1916) 4.263–6
 ITO 4.47–8, 54–6
Taschereau, Louis-Alexandre 3.381
taxation 1.307–13, 2.48–52
territorial readjustments 3.244–6
'Textile Industry Reserves Opinion' (1932) 3.379–80
textiles *see* cotton trade; wool trade
Thiers, M., speech on Commercial Policy of France (1851) 2.91–109

Thomas, J. H.
  'Dominion Industries' (1931) **3**.337–9
  Report of the Committee on the Proposed Imperial Economic Conference at Ottawa (1931) **3**.329–36
timber trade **1**.193
tobacco trade **1**.48–9
Townshend, T. **1**.8
Trade and Treaties Committee **3**.84–7
trade as an instrument of war (1793–1812) **1**.69–74
trade charters **4**.27–41
  see also International Trade Organization
trade depression
  'Causes of Trade Depression' (15 January 1886) **3**.36–9
  Royal Commission on Depression in Trade and Industry, 'Minority "Fair Trade" Report' (1886) **3**.40–3
trade promotion **3**.374–6
Trades Union Congress (1931–2) **3**.360–1
treaties of commerce
  Anglo-French Commercial Treaty (abortive; 1852) **2**.117–25
  ASEAN (1976) **4**.152–6
  Australia **2**.348–51
  Austria **2**.216–17
  Belgian and German Commercial Treaties, terminating (1897) **3**.90–5
  Belgium **2**.217
  'Commercial Treaties and Free Trade' (1860) **2**.161–3
  Commercial Treaties (1870) **2**.187–95
  'Commercial Treaty with Austria' (1866) **2**.196–206
  'The Commercial Treaty with France' (1877) **2**.254–6
  Commercial Union of the Empire (1891) **3**.67–71
  Free Trade and the European Treaties of Commerce (1875) **2**.348–51
  Germany **2**.216
  Italy **2**.217–18
  Sir Louis Mallet **2**.196–206
  R. Morier **2**.187–95
  and public opinion in Europe (1875) **2**.304–11
  J. Slagg **2**.254–6
  terminating **3**.90–5
  'Treaty of Amity and Cooperation in Southeast Asia' (1976) **4**.152–6
  Turkey **2**.218
  see also Anglo-American Treaty abstract (1795); Anglo-French Commercial Treaty (1786); Treaty of Commerce (1806)
'Treaties of Commerce with, and between, European Powers, with Especial Reference to the Trade of the United Kingdom' (1875) **2**.212–28
Treaty of Commerce (1806) **1**.112–20
treaty system and promotion of free trade **2**.174–228
  Richard Cobden, letter to E. A. Billeroche (1861) **2**.174
  'Commercial Policy of European States and British Trade' (1879) **2**.175–8
Turkey, treaties of commerce **2**.218
Turkish Dominions **3**.246

Underwood Tariff **3**.173–4, 175–82
United Automobile Workers Union **4**.256–8
United States *see* America

Vaughan, Charles Richard **1**.143
Victoria (colony)
  Henry Ashworth **2**.334–5
  George Ward Cole **2**.327–33
  'Our Colonies: Their Commerce and their Cost' (1862) **2**.334–5
  fair trade **3**.26–8
  Five Free Trade Essays (1875) **2**.338–47
  growth/prosperity **3**.51–5
  Protection as a National System Suited for Victoria (1860) **2**.327–33
  'Protection in Young Communities' (1882) **3**.51–5
  George H. Reid **2**.338–47
  see also Australia; colonies
Victoria, Queen **3**.26–7
Villiers, George **1**.254–9
Vincent, Howard, *Commercial Union of the Empire* (1891) **3**.67–71
Viner, Jacob, 'Conflicts of Principle in Drafting a Trade Charter' (1947) **4**.27–41

wages 1.364–5, 371–2
Walker tariff 1.133
war-period measures (1916) 3.238–9
war, trade as an instrument of (1793–1812) 1.69–74
wars, tariff *see* tariff wars in Europe
Watts, A. D., Memorandum on EEC/ASEAN Relations (1975) 4.147–8
wealth 3.17–22
Webster, Mr 1.157
Wells, D. 3.21
Wells, David A. 2.299–301
Wharton, Dennis 4.248–9
wheat trade *see* grain trade
White, Horace 2.301–2
Whitmore, Mr 1.321–2
'Who Were Our Best Customers?' (1916) 3.201–5
Wilcox, Clair, 'The London Draft of a Charter for an International Trade Organization' (1947) 4.42–53
Wilson, Woodrow 3.147
Wirth, Max 2.283–9
Wise, B. R., *Free Trade and Imperial Preference* (1905) 3.133–7
Wodehouse, Edmond, election address (1841) 1.366
Women's Co-Operative Guild 3.127–8
Woodford, Ralph 1.57, 64
wool trade
  Abbeville 1.40–1
  America 1.150–2
  Bradford 3.175–82
  Dingley Tariff Act (1897) 3.178–9
  Europe 1.40–2
  fair trade 3.15–16
  France 1.252–3
  Gorman-Wilson tariff 3.178
  history of wool tariffs 3.176–7
  Ireland 1.15–18, 24–5, 27–32, 36–7
  McKinley tariff law 3.177–8
  The New American Tariff (Simmons-Underwood) and the Wool Industry of Bradford (1914) 3.175–82
  Ottawa Imperial Economic Conference (1931–2) 3.379–80
  speech on the 'Foreign Commerce of the Country' (1825) 1.170–1, 181, 182
  Henry Stephens 1.219
  tariff influences 3.180–1
  'Textile Industry Reserves Opinion' (1932) 3.379–80
working classes 1.346–8
workmen's petition 1.360
World Trade Organization (WTO) 4.259–317
  agriculture 4.298–9
  background 4.259–62
  Gordon Brown, UK Statement to IMF (2006) 4.312–17
  George W. Bush, US steel industry temporary safeguards (2002) 4.310–11
  capacity building 4.305–6
  child labour 4.279–81
  Bill Clinton, 'Remarks to Farmers, Students from the Seattle-Tacoma Area' (1999) 4.286–92
  competition policy 4.301–2
  dispute settlement 4.303
  Doha Ministerial Declaration (2001) 4.296–309
  electronic commerce 4.304
  'Geneva Sounded WTO Warning That Went Unheeded in Seattle' (2000) 4.293–5
  government procurement transparency 4.302
  Cordell Hull, Statement on Tariffs and an International Tariff Congress (1916) 4.263–6
  intellectual property 4.300
  least-developed countries (LDCs) 4.306–7
  market access for non-agricultural products 4.300
  organization and management of work programme 4.308–9
  rules 4.302–3
  Seattle Demonstration (1999) 4.282–5
  Senate Debate (1994) 4.267–81
  services 4.299–300
  small economies 4.304–5
  special and differential treatment 4.307
  steel industry temporary safeguards (2002) 4.310–11
  technical cooperation 4.305–6

technology transfer **4**.305
trade and environment **4**.303–4
trade, debt and finance **4**.305
trade/investment relationship **4**.300–1
Uruguay Round Agreements Act (1994) **4**.267–81

Yonge, Sir George **1**.8, 10
Young, George Frederick
The French Treaty, a Mockery, a Delusion, and a Snare (1860) **2**.164–8
National Association **2**.3–4, 22–3

zinc trade **1**.175
Zollverein **1**.239–41, **2**.140
Anglo-Zollverein commercial relationship **1**.260–5, **3**.45–8
The Chamberlain Bubble (1903) **3**.121–3
imperial, Empire and tariffs (1880–1914) **3**.45–8
Mecklenburg und der Zollverein (1841) **1**.268–80
Minute of the Board of Trade (1826) **1**.260–5
tariff stipulations **2**.216

For Product Safety Concerns and Information please contact our EU representative GPSR@taylorandfrancis.com Taylor & Francis Verlag GmbH, Kaufingerstraße 24, 80331 München, Germany

Printed and bound by CPI Group (UK) Ltd, Croydon, CR0 4YY
08/05/2025
01864526-0002